Community Psychiatry

Community Psychiatry:

Epidemiologic and Social Themes

Mervyn Susser

Columbia University School of Public Health and Administrative Medicine

FIRST PRINTING

 Published in the United States by Random House, Inc., and simultaneously in Canada by Random House of Canada Limited, Ontario.

Library of Congress Catalog Card Number: 68-13167

This book was printed by the Halliday Lithograph Corporation, West Hanover, Mass. Bound by The Haddon Craftsmen, Inc., Scranton, Pa.

Design by Diana Hrisinko

Preface

In this book I sift and organize my thought, experiences, and research from a decade of engagement with the care of mental disorder outside mental hospitals. The need for rationale in community psychiatry seems pressing. In Britain purposeful work in community psychiatry began during World War II and was given legislative form in 1959. In the United States recent government policy has given impetus and concreteness to a similar movement. The British work has been pragmatic and supported by a meager theoretical literature. In the United States there has been more theory and literature but meager action. In neither country have advocates of care for mental patients outside conventional mental hospitals done much to rationalize the course they follow, to make explicit the assumptions by which they act, or to bring their thought into line with that of other disciplines. In the aphorism of a great physician (Sir William Osler), to practice without theory is to sail an uncharted sea; theory without practice is not to set sail at all.

This book seeks to give form and direction to what has been learned in practice and to bring into conjunction a mix of knowledge from relevant disciplines. In essence, it has applied epidemiology and the social sciences to a health problem (which in British terms is an exercise in social medicine). By means of epidemiology we study the distribution of health, sickness, and disease in social collectivities, and the factors that cause the distributions. By means of social science we interpret the significance of these distributions for society, study behavior related to health and sickness, and analyze the structure and function of health and medical organizations.

The work falls into four parts. The first part aims to clarify the objectives of community care of mental disorder by an examination of its historical development and to synthesize established fact, plausible interpretation, and promising hypotheses about the social forces that may influence prognosis in mental disorders. The second part continues in the same manner to examine the prospects for the prevention of those mental disorders that may have an origin in social causes. The third part deals with the operation of services, in particular with their common problems, their evaluation and measurement, and their coordination. The fourth part takes the subject of mental subnormality to develop a paradigm of rational health and medical care. Each part has its special problems.

In parts One and Two the method by which I proceed is to select findings from a large number of studies and weave them together to back the theme of adaptation to mental disorder. This method carries the risks of secondary analysis. The primary studies are made to appear continuous with each other when in fact they were discontinuous; they were variously conceived and had treated of widely separate environments in more than one region or country. Some of the studies are themselves secondary analyses of existing data, others are surveys. The complacent certitude that comes with the random allocation of control and experimental groups is seldom vouched to sociomedical research, as with human medicine in general. A high degree of plausibility is as much as can be hoped for.

Parts Three and Four present added scientific and literary problems. In contrast with the concern of the first half of the book with social forces as they act upon people, the chief concern of the latter half of the book is with the social dynamics and organization of services. The forms and organization of services are more particular and less universal than those of persons. Although general observations can be derived from their study, more particular and closer description is usually needed to demonstrate these observations. The descriptions are anchored to my own experience and research, and the reader will find more references to them than could be justified in a fair representation of the programs and the writing in this field. The reader is referred to the extensive appendixes for data supporting these references and the text generally. Where there were few landmarks and many options, it seemed wise to develop themes around work with whose flaws one was closely acquainted. As an indirect dividend, reader and writer are saved the boredom of repetitive description and the mere division of narrative.

The book should be viewed as an introduction and not as an all-encompassing, definitive text. To cover so large an area in the time available, even in introductory fashion, stretches thin any one person's resources of scholarship. By intent the book deals sketchily with the many studies focused on the milieu within psychiatric wards. Some readers will miss an extended treatment of community organization, particularly the place of voluntary agencies and local influentials that are so important in the United States. These choices are dictated partly by personal experience but also by what has been studied and written on the topic, whether too much or too little.

A considerable literature, chiefly English and American, is cited. These references are meant to give the reader access to primary sources, as well as to buttress the authority of the book. The great part of the references to research findings is based on examination of the primary sources. In a few cases, however, and particularly with historical material, the writer must admit apologetically to the use of secondary sources. In those instances both the secondary and the primary sources are given, usually with an attribution to the secondary source. The demands of accuracy had to be weighed against the seclusion of the cited work from the reader's attention.

The validity of the selection I have made must be taken on trust. It has its own overriding bias in the limitations of one person's viewpoint and critical apparatus. Violations and elisions of data are bound to occur. Yet because it is difficult to gain knowledge in the field of human behavior, a special effort must be made to assemble and order it. The cumulation of verified fact and tested hypotheses is fundamental to development through science. So too is generalization: In order to advance, we assume the lawfulness of nature and society.

Practitioners may gain from such generalizations a base for development. Many psychiatrists are gloomy about the outcome of psychiatric illness. Most other doctors have had little difficulty in maintaining the optimism and belief in themselves necessary to the effective performance of their roles as doctors. A comparison of the actual results of psychiatrists and of internists on medical wards leads one to think that greater optimism among internists may be related to successful short-term action combined with a lack of feedback in the long term. Many of their discharged patients die off and are silent. In Scotland, in a follow-up of patients discharged two years before from acute medical wards, only about 50 per cent had achieved lasting improvement, about 25 per cent had never worked again, and another 25 per cent were dead.[1] Results little different have been reported from Holland.[2] Schizophrenia has reputedly the worst prognosis of functional mental disorders, and for rough comparison one might take a follow-up study of schizophrenic patients in London, discharged from the hospital one year before. Of these patients, 25 per cent had a good work record, 25 per cent had a good work record but were readmitted, and about 50 per cent worked irregularly.[3] Five years after admission about 50 per cent of these patients were doing well and were independent, about 25 per cent were handicapped by symptoms to some degree, and the remaining 25 per cent were severely handicapped.

A significant difference here between psychiatry and internal medicine is that the majority of patients with chronic mental disorders survive for many years, and the survival rates continuously improve. As their number in the community grows, theory on which to found their care has increasing practical import. It can guide us in specifying what data are relevant to care and in discovering new situations that extend the social roles available to the patient.

New York, 1968 MERVYN SUSSER

1. Ferguson T. and McPhail A. N. 1954 *Hospital and Community* London, New York & Toronto, Oxford

2. Querido A. 1959 Forecast and follow-up: an investigation into the clinical, social and mental factors determining the results of hospital treatment *Brit J Prev Soc Med* 13:33–49

3. Monck E. M. 1963 Employment experiences of 127 discharged schizophrenic men in London *Brit J Prev Soc Med* 17:101–10

Acknowledgments

The time and the conditions in which I could write this book I owe to the Association for the Aid of Crippled Children, of which I was Belding Fellow. In later stages help from the Psychiatric Epidemiology Research Unit of Columbia University, directed by Dr. E. M. Gruenberg, enabled the book to be completed.

Research on mental disorders in Salford City is discussed in many places throughout the book. This research was variously supported by the Salford Health Department, the Medical Research Council of Great Britain, the Salford Mayoral Fund (Mellor), the National Society for Mentally Handicapped Children, and the Nuffield Provincial Hospitals Trust.

My onetime colleagues at the Salford Health Department and at the Manchester University Department of Social and Preventive Medicine have contributed to this book, although not by design, for many of our joint efforts have finally found expression in it. I thank them all and in particular Dr. A. M. Adelstein, Dr. J. L. Burn, Dr. Albert Kushlick, Mr. George Mountney, and Dr. Zena Stein.

Drs. Ernest Gruenberg, Albert Kushlick, and John Wing read

the manuscript and made valuable comments. Mrs. H. Lieb and Miss K. McCausland did much to collate and prepare the book for the press; Mrs. B. Levin and Ezra Susser helped with the references. I am grateful to them and to the others who typed the manuscript but whose names are too numerous to mention.

Dr. Zena Stein accepted much on behalf of this book in her conjugal roles as spouse, supporter, and whipping boy and added to it beyond accounting in her professional roles as critic, discussant, data gatherer, reference chaser, and source of ideas.

M. S.

Contents

PREFACE v

ACKNOWLEDGMENTS ix

PART ONE. **Community Care of Mental Disorder: Rationale and Social Factors in Prognosis 1**

1. Rationale for Community Care of Mental Disorder 3

Evolution of the Concept of Community Care 3
The Medical Model of Mental Disorder 10

2. Factors in Performance of Mental Patients: Chronic Sickness and the Family 29

3. Specific Factors in Prognosis 41

Primary Accommodation to Mental Disorder: Family Roles 41
Secondary Accommodation to Mental Disorder: After the Return of the Mental Patient 46
Accommodation and Expectations 48
Accommodation and Hostility 51
Accommodation to Specific Disorders 53

Kin Support 56
Employment and Occupation 57

PART TWO. **Antecedent Factors in Mental Disorder: Prospects for Prevention 69**

4. *Preventable Stressors and Stress Responses* 71
5. *Stressful Situations: Extremes of War and Social Transitions* 80
   The Extremes of War 80
   Social Transitions 84
6. *Stressful Situations: Anomie, Social Isolation, and Social Disintegration* 118
   Anomie and Social Isolation 121
   Social Isolation 123
   Social Isolation and Schizophrenia 125
   Anomie 129
   Status Inconsistency 134

PART THREE. **The Operation of Services 141**

7. *Facilities for Community Care: Problems of Operations* 143
   Day Centers, Social Clubs, and Residential Arrangements 143
   Group Relations in Community Care 148
   Social Work 152
8. *The Tools of Evaluation* 165
   Surveys 168
   Case Studies 182
   Social Experiments 186
9. *Measuring the Amount of Mental Illness in the Community* 204
   Prevalence 205
   Incidence 215
10. *Coordination of Community Care: A Case Study* 233
   Psychiatric Roles in Different Service Settings 236
   Coordination of Services 246
   Interpretations 260
   Remedies 265

PART FOUR. **Mental Subnormality in the Community: A Medical-Care Paradigm** 273

11. The Mentally Subnormal: Population and Natural History 275

Differentiation of the Subnormal Population 280
Mild Subnormality: Natural History 283
Severe Subnormality: Natural History 285

12. The Causes and the Care of Mild Subnormality 299

The Cultural Syndrome 312
Remedies for Retardation 313

13. The Care of Severe Subnormality 322

Alienation in Medical Care 324
The Social Structure of Traditional Institutions and Day Centers 329
The Impact of Care on Individual Development 338
Impact of Community Care on the Family 343

14. Epilogue 353

APPENDIXES 357

Appendix A. Episodes of Mental Illness in an English City 358
Appendix B. Movements in and out of Hostels 378
Appendix C. Registered Prevalence of Ascertained Subnormality 380
Appendix D. Location of the Subnormal 384
Appendix E. Marriage Between Social Classes 386
Appendix F. The Inception of Mental Illness Related to Widowhood 387
Appendix G. Secular Change in Backwardness in England 389

INDEX 391

part one

Community Care of Mental Disorder: *Rationale and Social Factors in Prognosis*

1

Rationale for Community Care of Mental Disorder

Evolution of the Concept of Community Care

In Europe and America the postwar expansion of economies and populations turned attention from the problems of poverty to the problems of plenty. Populations grew larger as a result of high survival rates from conception onward. They also grew older as a result chiefly of lower birth rates. Infections no longer presented a major threat, and the aberrant growth, degeneration, and aging of tissues were the underlying pathology of the newly important diseases. Public health and medical care adjusted their focus. With this change in the nature of diseases, people became aware of a miasma of mental sickness, emerging from behind a smoke screen laid by ignorance, indifference, avoidance, and preoccupation with day-to-day immediacies (1, 2).

This awareness of mental sickness now begins to penetrate the darker interstices of society. Poverty and its deprivations have been rediscovered even in the wealthy United States, if not yet in poorer countries. Fortunately, poverty is no longer tolerated on the grounds of a Social Darwinism that decrees it the inevitable and the proper condition of the "unfit." Nor does it have the same social and medical accompaniments as before. There has been a qualitative change in the nature of the problems of poverty, or at least in the priorities of concern. Mental health and mental disorder, we have slowly come to understand, are issues even more pressing for those excluded from affluence than for the large body of society.

Psychopathology has described the nature of mental disorder, and its scale has been made visible by the tallies of several decades. In these studies the problems of mental disorder have been seen to pervade daily life. This view has accompanied a radical change in the dominant concepts about mental disorder. The movement toward community care of mental disorder is founded on these new concepts. "Mental disorder" is the term used in this book to include all forms of disordered mental functioning. "Mental illness" is the term used to describe psychoses, neuroses, and personality disorders. "Mental subnormality" and "mental deficiency" are the terms used to describe deficits of intellect.

Community mental-health centers are coming into being throughout the United States under the aegis of the National Institute of Mental Health and through the provisions of an act of Congress.[1] New York State set the stage for this development in 1954 with its Community Mental Health Services Act. The revolutionary idea of providing care for all mental disorders in local communities first achieved official sanction in Britain in the provisions and the accompanying regulations of the Mental Health Act of 1959. It was a quiet revolution. The bill ran the parliamentary gauntlet with little of the expected clangor. Remarkably, the quiet seemed to be the result less of apathy than of a degree of consensus about the concepts of mental disorder embodied in the act.

On the recommendation of the Great Britain Royal Commission on the Law Relating to Mental Illness and Mental Deficiency of 1954–1957, the act set up legal machinery to facilitate care for mentally disordered persons in the community. The notion of care in the community drew on a few enlightened experiments that had shown that it was feasible

1. Mental Retardation Facilities and Community Mental Health Centers Construction Act of 1963, Public Law 88–164.

to abandon constraint and long-term custody in the care of mental patients (3). It drew equally on the negative aspects of the kind of care then in force. The report pointed to the anxiety inspired by the forbidding image of mental hospitals and to the frustration of the ideal of early treatment by elaborate juridical procedures of certification and admission. The argument also relied on a shrewd appraisal of the emerging trends in the statistics of mental hospitals; the trends were toward declining use of legal constraints and shorter hospital stays. In short, the Report's recommendation of community care had the appearance of a typical piece of British empiricism. The official adoption of the policy was made easier by the surface appearance of economy that it entailed. To this economy could be added the richer and more productive lives the policy was expected to bring to mental patients.

It is true that the idea of the "therapeutic community" was abroad and had begun to take theoretical form. Early in the twentieth century Sigmund Freud had insisted, in his famous interpretation of the published autobiography of a psychotic man, that psychotic symptoms had meaning rooted in experience. Further theoretical advance was made when E. Bleuler distinguished primary symptoms of psychosis from secondary symptoms. He held that the form and severity of secondary symptoms depend on past and present events, including the hospital situation, and not on the disease (4). Much that follows in this book is founded on the distinction noted by Bleuler, for its corollary is that the social environment may have beneficial as well as harmful effects on the course of mental disorders. Attempts to exploit the therapeutic content of the environment included the "total push" treatment and similar methods of the 1930s. These methods aimed at propelling patients into activity and guided interaction (5).

By the 1930s H. S. Sullivan in the United States was revising psychoanalytic theory in order to describe his work on an experimental ward for schizophrenic patients (6). Sullivan held that psychic structure evolved through relations with "significant others." It followed that psychiatry should be the study of interpersonal relations. Sullivan's ideas were reinforced by cultural anthropologists whose work pointed up the plasticity of personality (7). Later in the 1930s, H. Rowland published his sociological analysis of a state mental hospital, and R. E. L. Faris and H. W. Dunham published their ecological study of schizophrenic patients in Chicago (8). Psychiatry was thus primed for the juxtaposition of the patient and his milieu, on one side by psychological analysis looking outward from the individual to society, and on the other by parallel sociological analysis looking inward from society toward the mental patient.

World War II brought a reorientation of views about the potential of psychiatry. Psychiatrists gained new standing from their part in the medical assessment and care of troops. Rapid changes in the professional structure, the institutions, and the practices of psychiatry followed. (See pp. 236 ff.) Soon after the war, a number of writers described their work and enumerated principles upon which therapeutic communities should be founded (9). These workers tried to convert relationships in mental hospitals to therapeutic purposes, most often by engaging staff and patients together in special programs of occupational, productive, and recreational activity; by relaxing discipline and unlocking wards; and by exposing personal and administrative issues of therapy to group discussion. Here was a fresh beginning on the path opened in the eighteenth century. Vincenzo Chiarugi in Florence, Philippe Pinel in Paris, and William Tuke in York pioneered the "moral treatment" movement (10), which their followers sustained through the first half of the nineteenth century (11). In this treatment everything depended on creating a favorable environment that would facilitate, not obstruct, recovery. This environment is the essence of the therapeutic community one hundred years later.

Despite the semantic overlap between the terms "therapeutic community" and "community care," the ideas about the therapeutic community implied seclusion from open society during treatment, and those about community care implied exposure to society. The mental hospital was commonly taken for granted as the site on which to build the therapeutic community. No logical imperatives about care outside the hospital derived from the ideas on the therapeutic community, and therefore there was no adequate theoretical foundation for care outside the hospital. The new ideas on community care did lead to the accumulation of evidence about the negative effects of traditional mental hospitals and to appreciation of the possibilities of manipulating the milieu (12).

Some of the confusion arises from the repetition of the word "community," which is not easy to define. A community can be described as an aggregate of people who have collective social ties by virtue of their shared locale for residence, for services, and for work. The limits of the locale are conveniently marked by the jurisdiction of some form of local authority or administration. Such a locale may be shared for residence alone or for services, work, and all the purposes of daily life. The collective social ties vary in strength and complexity according to the coincidence and duration of these various purposes (13, 14).

The isolated mental hospitals of the first half of the twentieth century clearly qualified as communities. As a result, the principles of the therapeutic community could be circumscribed and plain. The object of those who wished to convert the hospitals from custodial to therapeutic purposes was to overcome the disturbance and the handicaps of the individual psyche by engaging patients in a special structure of relationships. Patients might thus explore modes of relating with others and discover alternates to their habitual behavior. As in all psychotherapy, the aim was to free the patient from his past. Implicit in this position was the assumption that on the discharge of the patient the newly learned behavior would be transferred from the special situation of the mental hospital to the more diffuse situation outside. The theories of the therapeutic community did not treat concretely the relations of the mental patient outside the walls of the hospital with family, neighbors, peers, colleagues, employers, and social institutions.

Social collectivities other than mental hospitals qualify less clearly as communities. Ambiguities are evident from the briefest comparison of a mining village, a market town, a commuters' suburb, and a metropolitan center. The term "community care" refers to care in such collectivities outside the hospital. Its principles have been similarly loose and vague. In 1957 the Royal Commission could draw only from a patchwork of practical examples of community care, excellent as some of them were (15). No developed theory or set of hypotheses was available to it.

The scope of community care, when defined merely as the obligation of local health authorities to supply services in a local area, is less difficult to comprehend than the idea of community itself. In common usage it connotes more than this, however, and implies the extension of responsibility beyond accredited agencies to others living in propinquity with patients. Families and others must perforce participate in care through their relations with patients. Yet by the nature of our social collectivities, responsibilities can often not be specified. Social ties are ill-defined and the communities too various.

The attempt to clarify the notion of community care thus leads us to recognize both the deficiencies of the theory when it was formally put into practice in Britain and the complexity of the central idea of community. Seen in this shadowed light, the recommendations of the Royal Commission of 1957 and the provisions of the act that followed in 1959 were bold and imaginative.

There were reasons to disquiet the cautious. Available evidence did not point to a happy reception by communities of the propositions of community care. Several studies in North America have revealed a persisting set of attitudes unfavorable to mental disorder. Many people fear violence from mental patients, wish to keep their social distance from them, and have their anxieties aroused by the connotations of mental illness (16, 17). There has been controversy among investigators about whether to interpret the trend of these surveys as optimistic or pessimistic for the prospects for community care. Some results point to more favorable public attitudes (2) and to improvement through time (14). In one questionnaire study a local population showed unexpected agreement with psychiatrists in their judgments of the kinds of behavior that pointed to mental illness (18). Whatever may be the view of interested researchers, the early results can be taken as sufficient to have intimidated any civil servant who conformed to stereotype. In the United States even some enlightened people concerned with the care of mental disorder contemplate uneasily the reaction of public opinion should an "open door" policy be attempted on a large scale. On the other hand, successful demonstrations of the open-door policy provide one more example of the discontinuity that can exist between opinions and attitudes and actual behavior (19).

A pragmatist can now point to a working system in Britain and in some pioneer areas of the United States that continue without furor or disaster. Yet a body of scientific data organized to provide a rationale for the procedures of community care is not at hand, although a good deal has been collected in symposia and similar collaborative publications (20). For practitioners of community psychiatry the absence of organized data constitutes a serious lack. In the absence of such data they must move step by step, first by intuition and then by experience. Not all proponents are cautious. Some writers fear that exaggerated hopes founded on inadequate premises about community psychiatry will be self-defeating (21).

I shall try to lay a base for a rational approach to community care by gathering and pooling relevant findings. On some topics, exposition takes the place of findings for want of suitable material. This is not an attempt to develop a rounded theory of community care. Such a theory goes outside the field of social medicine and beyond my competence, for it must integrate intrapsychic processes with social processes. From the point of view of the psychiatrist, therefore, this account may proceed as if suffering from a central scotoma in that it focuses a good deal on the peripheral field of the environment and hardly at all on the field of the psyche. From the point of view of social medicine, however, intrapsychic dynamics should be approached with the diffidence of naïveté, and the environment, far from being peripheral, is the larger setting that defines the limits for what occurs within it.

Syntheses of the two points of view have been attempted (14, 22). These syntheses contribute to the direction of further research, but they do not provide a sufficient basis for action in the care of patients. Firm knowledge of both psychic processes and social processes usually passes into the axioms of common lore. What remains and what is new do not yet allow us to make clear choices between competing theoretical constructions.

The Medical Model of Mental Disorder

In large-scale societies governed by powerful centralized authorities, central legislation and disposition of resources create the broad structure of the therapeutic setting. Prevailing concepts of mental disorder are crucial antecedents of central action, as well as intervening factors in subsequent operations. These concepts have a long history. Beginning at the latest with Hippocrates, medical thinkers have tried to apply to mental disorder the conceptual model of organic disease (10, 23). During the eighteenth and nineteenth centuries a more specific "disease model" gained great power in medicine. Physicians defined many separate diseases, each with its own etiology and its characteristic alterations in bodily structure and function (24).

Psychiatrists, too, have searched for hidden causes and described clinical entities, their outcome, and treatment. In trying to develop a deterministic view of mental disorder, they have had to compete with folk concepts of witchcraft, religious personifications of evil, and philosophies that take the world as given and human behavior as manifestly purposeful. Their struggle is won. Although the concreteness given to diagnostic entities varies much among schools of psychiatry, determinism is now common to all schools. A mentally disordered patient is generally regarded as having an illness for which a cause might be found. Even crime, amoral behavior, and marital discord are sometimes subsumed to medicine under the head of psychopathology.

Such extensions of the sphere of medical competence have

provoked some recent writers to put forward new grounds for questioning the medical concept of mental disorder (25). The law is confounded by uncertainties when clinical criteria are applied to judgments of individual responsibility for behavior. Medical authority is founded on such uncertainties, and it therefore comes under attack for the divergencies among its experts, as well as for expanding beyond the proper limits of its competence. These attacks have so far failed to detract from the power of the disease model of mental disorder. It remains for the medical profession to cope with mental disorder in its own terms.

The disease model of mental disorder can also be questioned from a theoretical point of view that interprets deviance as a phenomenon determined by society (26, 27). In this view, behavior is deviant only insofar as it is so defined by a particular society. This view contrasts with dominant medical concepts that consider deviance as individual abnormality. Physicians seek the source of deviance in the experiences, motivations, and psychophysiological processes encompassed in the individual. In accord with the "disease model," physicians have sought specific pharmacological and surgical treatments. At the same time, however, they have made use of the patient's interaction in his social setting. We shall see that a medical model in fact subsumes more than individual disease; it requires the synthesis of these contrasting individual and social concepts of mental disorder.

To conceive of mental disorder as illness carries wide social implications. Sickness is more than a matter of disease. Disease is a disturbance of normal function confined to the individual organism. Sickness is a disturbance of normal social relations. The sick person has a special status or social position in relation to others and an implicit role, a "sick role" (28). This status absolves him of most social responsibilities, except that of seeking his recovery, and entitles him to the help of his fellows. The grounds on which an individual is given these privileges do not depend only on the presence of disease; some diseases, for instance malnutrition or bronchitis, entitle sufferers to sick privileges in one society and not in another.

Plato, in Book III of *The Republic,* describes how the sick role varies with social position within a single society:

> . . . Asclepius was aware that in all well-regulated communities, each has work assigned to him in the state which he must needs do, and that no-one has leisure to spend his life as an invalid in the doctor's hands: a fact which we perceive in the case of the laboring populations, but which with ludicrous inconsistency we fail to detect in the case of those who are rich and happy.
>
> When a carpenter is ill, he expects to receive a draught from his doctor, that will expel the disease by vomiting or purging, or else to get rid of it by cauterising, or a surgical operation; but if any one were to prescribe to him a long course of diet, and to order bandages for his head, with other treatment to correspond, he would soon tell such a medical adviser that he had no time to be ill, and hint that it was not worth his while to live in this way, devoting his mind to his malady, and neglecting his proper occupation: and then, wishing his physician a good morning, he would enter upon his usual course of life, and either regain his health and live in the performance of his business; or, should his constitution prove unable to bear up, death puts an end to his troubles.
>
> "Yes, and for a man in that station of life, this is thought the proper use to make of medical assistance. . . ."(29)

This passage makes it clear that the behavior of a person with a disease is prescribed by society. Sickness and disease can be dissociated as categories for theoretical analysis, although sometimes with difficulty as categories in practice. The rules for according the sick role are implicit in the values and attitudes of each society. Accordingly, they influence both the apparent prevalence of mental disorder and the mode of dealing with it (30). In conformity with each society's values, mental disorder may be accepted as supernatural or rejected as an aberration. In Ghana spontaneous confessions of witchcraft by people suffering from depression are taken at face value (31). In seventeenth-century Europe and America such confessions were followed by horrendous persecution of the insane (10).

The current dominance in Britain of the medical interpretation of mental disorder has much to do with the transformation in the care of mental patients. In a society that interprets mental disorder as illness, the mentally disordered person can be accorded the socially privileged position of the sick. The Mental Health Act of 1959 framed the laws relating to the management of mental disorder on the medical model. No reader of the report of the Royal Commission that preceded the Act could be left in any doubt on this score. The mental hospital, it held, should approximate to the general hospital in the rights and the status accorded its patients and in modes of admission and discharge; the professional responsibility of psychiatrists should be of the same independent kind as that of other medical consultants. The effect of the subsequent Act is thus that patients are referred to psychiatric agencies as sick people, with the expectation that they will receive medical treatment and improve. The function of the agency is primarily to bring about recovery or improvement, and only incidentally is it custodial. The patient may not always voluntarily seek aid as in the "ideal type" of the sick role, but the convenient assumption is made that he would if his disease did not prevent him from recognizing his need. So far has this concept permeated medical thought that some see no need to distinguish the custodial and disciplinary work of mental institutions from therapy.

The legal adoption of the medical model of psychopathology has in itself affected the careers of mentally sick persons. Many patients who formerly might have been confined for long periods are allowed to live free from constraint in the community. This alteration can be deduced from the great reduction in the average duration of stay in mental hospitals and the decline in the occupation of beds, whereas there is no sign of a reduction in the number of people affected (32). The needs of the many patients and ex-patients now living in the community have in turn underlined the need for care in the community.

The change in the careers of mentally sick persons cannot be ascribed to tranquilizing drugs alone, for it began before their introduction (33). Drugs came into general use in the mid-1950s.

In 1930, 60 per cent of patients with schizophrenia admitted to mental hospitals in an English county remained for at least two years, and in 1955 only 10 to 15 per cent remained as long. In some countries where drugs are much used comparable changes have not been reported. One study confirmed that patients admitted to a mental hospital for the first time in 1955–1956 had a better chance of discharge than those admitted around 1953, before the drugs came into general use. They enjoyed this better chance, however, whether or not they had been treated with drugs (34).

A gradual trend toward improved prognosis has been traced in sporadic samples provided by follow-up studies of schizophrenia through half a century (35). In the 1920s, 35 per cent of the patients admitted to the Heidelberg Clinic were reported independent in the community sixteen years after their admission in 1912–1913 (36); in the 1930s, 43 per cent of a series of Maudsley Hospital patients in London were reported independent at a three-year follow-up (37); in the decade after World War II, 50 per cent of a Maudsley series were independent at a five-year follow-up (38); and in the 1960s, between 50 and 67 per cent of Maudsley and other British series were reported independent at a follow-up ranging from one to five years (39).

The studies are not comparable in several respects: There are variations in severity at admission, in duration of hospital stay, in the follow-up period, and in criteria of diagnosis and of social independence. Nonetheless, the gradual trend looks consistent over time. Functional psychosis now often takes the form of a series of acute episodes with quiescent intermissions, rather than of a chronic deteriorating condition. In the city of Salford in the North of England, six recurrent episodes of schizophrenia occur for each new episode, and two to three for each new episode of depressive psychosis (40).

The influence of the medical model in British law relating to mental disorder can be detected as early as the Mental Treat ment Act of 1930. Law evidently legitimized emerging practice and in turn accelerated it.

It may be supposed that the altered career of mental pa

tients in society has had an influence on their behavior independent of any underlying pathological process. That underlying pathological processes exist in mental disorders is an assumption that carries authoritative sanction in European psychiatry, if not in all schools. Pathological processes are conceived as discontinuous with the range of "normal" psychic function. Although this assumption is implied here, it is not essential to the proposition that the altered careers of mental patients have influenced their behavior. Nor does it exclude the additional proposition that social experience can influence intrapsychic processes at all levels. My aim is to resort to as few unproven assumptions as possible.

The relationship between pathological processes and social influences can be restated in the more general terms of E. M. Lemert's theory of social deviance (26, 41). In this theory the sickness of mental disorder would be but one form of deviance. Lemert distinguishes between two stages of deviance. Primary deviation is the initial act of the individual, which can be the result of a wide variety of social, psychological, and physiological contexts. The primary act itself has few implications for the individual's attitude of self-regard or for his performance of social roles. Secondary deviation has greater social implications. It is deviant behavior that follows on society's reaction to the primary act, and it may take on the continuing character of a social role. In effect, the original causes of deviation give way to the play among the social forces of disapproval, degradation, or isolation and the individual's defensive, aggressive, or adaptive responses to these forces.

To summarize in terms of Lemert's formulation, mental disorders are primary deviations; the careers of mental patients are secondary deviations, which express the influence of social forces. The considerable changes in the sequence of the careers of mental patients are thus an outcome of an active process of social control. These changes are organized innovations given official form in legislation, and they have redefined the appropriate social responses to deviance. They will further shape the passive social controls to be found in existing attitudes and norms about mental disorder. Some acts once acceptable for the control of deviance are themselves made deviant by the new rules.

The change in the careers of mental patients impinges on many relationships that we know to be influential in determining the nature of patient responses. We do not know to what extent external circumstances precipitate acute spells of mental illness, but they are certainly important in phases of remission and in less severe forms of mental illness. The status and roles of the patient in the family, at work, and elsewhere influence the level of his performance in the community. In mental hospitals as well, characteristic reactions to the social situation have been described: "Institutional neurosis" is an example of adaptation in the old-time hospital to the system of authority, the administrative structure, and the allocation of roles in the structure (42).

Separating reactions to social situations from the symptoms of disease is especially difficult with mental disorder because the diagnosis both of reaction and of disease must usually rest on their manifestations in observed behavior, without the anchor of organic pathology. The therapeutic rationale of treating mental disorder outside the hospital, however, depends on the distinction between social behavior and the symptoms of disease, that is, on the segregation of the social from the intrapsychic components of individual responses.[2]

Situations outside the hospital, no less than those within it, elicit characteristic responses, although these responses are likely to conform more closely to the norms of behavior in the community. Community care extends the number of situations in which relatively normal social roles can be learned or resumed by the patient. Multiple situations offer multiple roles. In the demarcated community of the hospital, the set of roles offered the encapsulated patient is relatively simple, and the range of interaction narrow. The object of community care is to expand the activities and obligations of the patient

2. In the past, psychiatrists have failed to give due weight to the social component of mental disorders. In the present, sociologists sometimes fail to give due weight to the intrapsychic components. The authors of one large-scale follow-up study of ex-patients recognize that they encountered difficulties because of a hypothesis that was entirely social (43).

to a level at which they approximate the complex set of roles that fully functioning individuals assume in everyday life.

Admission to a hospital, considered in these terms, can be one form of situational change and is properly a part of consideration of community facilities. It administers a situational shock, which forces the patient to recast, or at least to review, his perceptions of himself and the order of his relations with others. These others too must review their perceptions of the patient and their relations with him (44, 45). Responses to the shock are various, but in assessing the effect of hospital admission they must be weighed together with the influence of psychotherapy, drugs, and electroconvulsive therapy given in the hospitals. The relatives of patients report measurable relief within a short time of a patient's referral to a psychiatric agency whether or not he is admitted to hospital and before treatment can have had much effect (46). The confrontation and the summoning of external arbiters seem to be significant in themselves.

A community service for mental disorder does not rely only on the automatic transfer of learning from the hospital to the society outside. It aims to devise institutions and groups that can supply controlled experience, tolerance, and approbation throughout a continuous process of graded learning. The functions of these institutions and the extensions of the therapeutic situation that they provide can be summed up under two headings:

1. To "socialize" mentally disordered individuals, whether they are retarded in development or have lost the ability to fulfill everyday social functions because of mental illness. (This process ends only with rehabilitation and the assumption of normal social roles.)
2. To provide social support for people dependent because of mental disorder, particularly when they lack effective kin. (This support includes residential care, and "minding" to relieve family tension and strain.)

Organic capacities and incapacities set limits on what can be done. Within these limits socialization offers room for maneuver. Social behavior is learned by individuals from others and together with others. The content of what can be learned resides in a common culture; access to it depends on participation in the culture. Through participation a person comes to recognize the values of the culture as they are expressed in the norms and sanctions attached to its multiple social roles. The aim of therapy is to stimulate awareness of these norms and responsiveness to them and to nurture aspirations to assume roles functional in the community and attainable by the patient.

A risk of such therapy is that it may be perverted toward inculcating conformity with the personal moralities of the therapist and those of his social class. The therapist may, in good faith while correcting psychological deviance, iron out dissidence and eschew social conflict. If social therapies are not to be repressive, or even oppressive, psychotherapy must nurture individuation and sensitivity to idiosyncrasy. Thoreau wrote, "If a man does not keep pace with his companions, perhaps it is because he hears a different drummer."

Perhaps more than any school, psychoanalysis taught therapists to pay heed to each man's drummer. Some protection against oppression is to be had from a therapeutic ideology that gives unquestioning priority to the needs of the individual patient and regards him as an active collaborator in treatment. As has been well said, the patient is both object and agent of change (47).

The same dilemma appears more frankly in those judgments of "irresponsibility" by which compulsion must be justified, for the judgments must draw on dominant social values. E. Goffman described the subtle collusions by which compulsion can be accomplished (45). The issues cannot be avoided in day-to-day practice. Community care is controlled experience; although voluntary by preference, it is sometimes compulsory. Later we shall examine which types of situations hinder individuation and which are conducive to it. From them we may learn how better to construct safeguards for individuality.

It must be allowed that there are as yet meager grounds, in the few and somewhat inadequate tests to which particular treatments have been put, for attributing long-term effects to any. Even intensive psychotherapy has yielded little in measurable personality change or social performance, effects usually looked for by psychiatrists in evaluating treatment. Methods for examining large bodies of detailed psychoanalytic records are only now being devised (48). One unequivocal effect of psychoanalysis has been demonstrated: The patient who continues in treatment gradually learns to conform to his new role and adopts the forms of response appropriate to the analytic interview (49). Such changes, not specifically sought by the therapist, are salient for community care; they show the capacity of patients to learn social roles afresh.

Treatment by drugs too has its place in the socialization of patients. Deceptively specific, the prescription of drugs is in fact a complex exchange between therapist and patient. The types of treatment offered and the results expected are influenced by the psychiatrist's ideology, although not entirely governed by it; the patient's expectation of effects in turn is influenced by the instruction he is given and by the state of mind created by the social environment. These expectations on the part of therapists and patients modify both subjective and physiological responses to drugs (50). The milieu thus influences the patient's receptivity to drugs, and drugs influence his receptivity to learning from the milieu.

Learning in the patient role can be of several kinds. It can be direct, by conscious effort to acquire new knowledge; it can be more a matter of acquiring a cast of mind that facilitates new learning, in Gregory Bateson's phrase "deutero-learning," or learning to learn; it can be conditioned learning, as in operant conditioning or the varied techniques of behavior therapy; or it can be introceptive learning, meaning to acquire empathy, insight into the self, and a psychological orientation (51).

The degree to which therapeutic learning can be stable, so that new norms are internalized and old ones inhibited, is still to be explored. Much of what is done in community care must be empirical, just as with other treatment. Nevertheless it is probably fair to say that recent studies have given as many leads about community care as about other kinds of therapy, including drugs, and I shall discuss some of these leads in what follows. Psychiatrists can add to their range of treatments by devising social situations to exploit this knowledge on behalf of their patients. The work of a psychiatric agency seldom needs to be viewed solely as a caretaking operation except in the case of rapidly progressive organic diseases.

References

(1) Ramsey G. V. and Seipp M. 1948 Public opinion and information concerning mental health *J Clin Psychol* 4: 397–406

Redlich F. C. 1950 What the citizen knows about psychiatry *Ment Hyg* 34:64–79

Woodward J. L. 1951 Changing ideas on mental illness and its treatment *Amer Sociol Rev* 16:443–454

Rose A. M. 1957 Attitudes of youth toward mental health problems *Sociol Soc Res* 41:343–348

Rosen E. J. 1960 The changing attitude of the community towards mental health *Canad J Pub Health* 51:361–363

Gerbner G. 1961 Psychology, psychiatry and mental illness in the mass media: a study of trends, 1900–1959 *Ment Hyg* 45:89–93

(2) Lemkau P. V. and Crocetti G. M. 1962 An urban population's opinion and knowledge about mental illness *Amer J Psychiat* 118:692–700

(3) Bell G. M. 1955 A mental hospital with open doors *Int J Soc Psychiat* 1:42–48

Rees T. P. and Glatt M. M. 1955 The organization of a mental hospital on the basis of group participation *Int J Group Psychother* 5:157–161

(4) Bleuler E. Zinkin J. trans. 1950 *Dementia Praecox or the Groups of Schizophrenias* New York, International Universities Press

For a review see Zusman J. 1966 Some explanation of the changing appearance of psychotic patients: antecedents of the social breakdown syndrome concept *Milbank Mem Fund Quart* 44:Part 2, 363–394

(5) Simmel E. 1929 Psychoanalytic treatment in a sanatorium *Int J Psychoanal* 10:70–89

Simon H. 1929 *Aktivere Krankenbehandlung in der Irrenanstalt* Berlin, DeGroyter

Menninger, W. C. 1936 Psychiatric hospital therapy designed to meet unconscious needs *Amer J Psychiat* 93:347–360

Meyerson A. 1939 Theory and principles of the "total push" method in the treatment of chronic schizophrenia *Amer J Psychiat* 95:1197–1204

(6) Sullivan H. S. 1931 The modified psychoanalytic treatment of schizophrenia *Amer J Psychiat* 11:519–540

Sullivan H. S. 1931 Socio-psychiatric research: its implications for the schizophrenia problem and for mental hygiene *Amer J Psychiat* 10:977–991

(7) Du Bois C. A. with analyses by Kardiner A. and Oberholzer E. 1944 *The People of Alor* Minneapolis, University of Minnesota Press

Benedict R. F. 1947 *The Chrysanthemum and the Sword: Patterns of Japanese Culture* London, Secker & Warburg

Kluckhohn C. and Murray H. A. eds. 1953 *Personality in Nature, Society and Culture* New York, Knopf

Mead M. 1960 *Growing Up in New Guinea* New York, New American Library

(8) Rowland H. 1938 Interaction processes in a state mental hospital *Psychiat* 1:323–327

Faris R. E. L. and Dunham H. W. 1939 *Mental Disorder in Urban Areas* Chicago, University of Chicago Press

Rowland H. 1939 Friendship patterns in a state mental hospital *Psychiat* 2:363–373

(9) Bierer J. 1944 New form of group psychotherapy *Mental Health* 5:23–26

Main T. F. 1946 The hospital as a therapeutic institution *Bull Menninger Clin* 10:66–70

Fromm-Reichmann F. 1947 Problems of therapeutic management in a psycho-analytic hospital *Psychoanal Quart* 16:325–356

Hyde R. W. and Solomon H. C. 1951 Clinical management of psychiatric hospitals *Conn State Med J* 15:391–399

Jones M. 1953 *The Therapeutic Community* New York, Basic Books

Martin D. V., Glatt M. M. and Weeks K. F. 1954 An experimental unit for the community treatment of neurosis *J Ment Sci* 100:983–989

Dax E. C. 1955 Social activities in mental hospital treatment *Med J Aust* 1:25–31

Greenblatt M., York R. and Brown E. L. 1955 *From Custodial to Therapeutic Patient Care in Mental Hospitals: Explorations in Social Treatment* New York, Russell Sage Foundation

(10) Deutsch A. 1949 *The Mentally Ill in America* New York, Columbia University Press

(11) Conolly J. 1856 *The Treatment of the Insane without Mechanical Restraints* London, Smith & Elder

(12) Greenblatt M., Levinson D. J. and Williams R. H. eds. 1957 *The Patient and the Mental Hospital* New York, Free Press

(13) Murdock G. P. 1949 *Social Structure* New York, Macmillan

Hawley A. H. 1950 *Human Ecology* New York, Ronald

Firth R. 1951 *Elements of Social Organization* London, Watts pp. 41–79

Arensberg C. M. 1954 The community-study method *Amer J Sociol* 60:109–124

Redfield R. 1955 *The Little Community* Chicago, University of Chicago Press

Sanders J. T. 1958 *The Community* New York, Ronald

Susser M. W. and Watson W. 1962 *Sociology in Medicine* London, Oxford

Watson W. 1964 Social mobility and social class in industrial communities in Gluckman M. ed. *Closed Systems and Open Minds* London, Oliver & Boyd

Frankenberg R. 1966 *Communities in Britain* Harmondsworth, Eng., Penguin

(14) Leighton A. H. 1959 *My Name Is Legion* New York, Basic Books

(15) Macmillan D. 1956 An integrated mental-health service *Lancet* 2:1094–1095

Querido A. 1956 Early diagnosis and treatment services in *Elements of a Community Mental Health Program* New York, Milbank Memorial Fund pp. 158–169

Macmillan D. 1958 Hospital-community relationships in *An Approach to the Prevention of Disability from Chronic Psychoses* New York, Milbank Memorial Fund pp. 29–39

(16) Cumming J. and Cumming E. 1955 Mental health education in a Canadian community in Paul B. *Health, Culture and Community* New York, Russell Sage Foundation pp. 43–70

Phillips D. L. 1963 Rejection: a possible consequence of seeking help for mental disorders *Amer Sociol Rev* 28:963–972

Padilla E., Elinson J. and Perkins M. E. 1966 The public image of mental health professionals and acceptance of community mental health services *Amer J Pub Health* 56:1524–1529

(17) Halpert H. P. 1963 *Public Opinions and Attitudes About Mental Health* Research Utilization Series Publ 1045 Washington, D. C., U. S. Dept Health, Education & Welfare

(18) Manis J. G., Hunt C. L., Brawer M. J. and Kercher L. C. 1965 Public and psychiatric conceptions of mental illness *J Health Hum Behav* 6:48–55

(19) Festinger L. 1964 Behavioral support for opinion change *Pub Opin Quart* 28:404–417

(20) Brockington F. ed. 1954 *Mental Health and the World Community* London, World Federation of Mental Health

Kotinsky R. and Witmer H. L. 1955 *Community Programs for Mental Health: Theory, Practice, Evaluation* Cambridge, Mass., Harvard University Press

Lemkau P. V. 1955 *Mental Hygiene in .Public Health* 2d ed. New York, McGraw-Hill

Milbank Memorial Fund 1956 *Elements of a Community Mental Health Program* New York, Milbank Memorial Fund

Milbank Memorial Fund 1957 *Programs for Community Mental Health* New York, Milbank Memorial Fund

Hargreaves G. R. 1958 *Psychiatry and the Public Health* London, Oxford

Greenblatt M. and Simon B. eds. 1959 *Rehabilitation of the Mentally Ill* Washington, D. C., American Association for the Advancement of Science No. 58

Milbank Memorial Fund 1959 *Progress and Problems of Mental Health Programs* New York, Milbank Memorial Fund

Milbank Memorial Fund 1960 *Steps in the Development of Integrated Psychiatric Services* New York, Milbank Memorial Fund

Freeman H. L. and Farndale W. A. J. eds. 1962 *Trends in the Mental Health Services* Oxford, Pergamon

Harvard Medical School and Psychiatric Service Massachusetts General Hospital 1962 *Community Mental Health and Social Psychiatry: A Reference Guide* Cambridge, Mass., Harvard University Press

Milbank Memorial Fund 1962 *Decentralization of Psychiatric Services and Continuity of Care* New York, Milbank Memorial Fund

Bellak L. ed. 1964 *Handbook of Community Psychiatry and Community Mental Health* New York, Grune & Stratton

Group for the Advancement of Psychiatry 1964 *Urban America and the Planning of Mental Health Services* New York, Group for the Advancement of Psychiatry

Milbank Memorial Fund 1964 Mental hospitals join the community *Milbank Mem Fund Quart* 42: Part 2

Reissman F., Cohen J. and Pearl A. 1964 *Mental Health of the Poor* New York, Free Press

Schwartz M. S. and Schwartz C. G. 1964 *Social Approaches to Mental Patient Care* New York, Columbia University Press

Driver E. D. 1965 *Sociology and Anthropology of Mental Illness: A Reference Guide* Amherst, University of Massachusetts Press

Goldston S. E. ed. 1965 *Concepts of Community Psychiatry* Washington, D. C., U. S. Dept. Health, Education & Welfare

Freeman H. L. and Farndale W. A. J. eds. 1967 *New Aspects of the Mental Health Services* Oxford, Pergamon

(21) Dunham H. W. 1965 Community psychiatry: the newest therapeutic bandwagon *Int J Psychiat* 1:553–584

(22) Caplan G. 1961 *An Approach to Community Mental Health* New York, Grune & Stratton

Cumming J. and Cumming E. 1962 *Ego and Milieu* New York, Atherton

Parsons T. 1964 *Social Structure and Personality* New York, Free Press

(23) Ackernecht E. H. 1955 *A Short History of Psychiatry* New York, Ronald

Hunter R. and MacAlpine I. 1963 *Three Hundred Years of Psychiatry, 1535–1860* London, Oxford

(24) Shryock R. H. 1936 *The Development of Modern Medicine* Philadelphia, University of Pennsylvania Press

(25) Wootton B., Seal V. G. and Chambers R. 1959 *Social Science and Social Pathology* London, Allen & Unwin

Szasz T. S. 1962 *The Myth of Mental Illness* London, Secker & Warburg

(26) Lemert E. M. 1951 *Social Pathology* New York, McGraw-Hill

(27) Scheff T. 1964 The societal reaction to deviance: ascriptive elements in the psychiatric screening of mental patients in a midwestern state *Soc Prob* 11:401–413

(28) Parsons T. 1951 *The Social System* New York, Free Press

Sigerist H. E. 1960 The special position of the sick in Roemer M. I. ed. *The Sociology of Medicine* New York, M.D. Publications

(29) Plato Davies J. L. and Vaughan D. J. trans. 1950 *The Republic Book III* New York, Macmillan p. 103

(30) Eaton J. W. and Weill R. J. 1955 *Culture and Mental Disorders* New York, Free Press

Opler M. K. 1956 *Culture, Psychiatry and Human Values* Springfield, Ill., Thomas

(31) Field M. J. 1960 *Search for Security* London, Faber & Faber

(32) Kramer M., Goldstein H., Israel R. H. and Johnson N.A. 1954 *A Historical Study of the Disposition of First Admissions to*

a State Mental Hospital Pub Health Monogr 32 Washington, D. C., U. S. Dept. Health, Education & Welfare

Brooke E. M. 1959 National statistics in the epidemiology of mental illness *J Ment Sci* 105:893–908

Tooth G. A. and Brooke E. M. 1961 Trends in the mental hospital population and their effect on future planning *Lancet* 1:710–713

General Register Office 1962 *The Registrar-General's Statistical Review of England and Wales 1959—Supplement on Mental Health* London, H. M. Stationery Office

Susser M. W. 1963 *A Report on the Mental Health Services for the City of Salford for the Year 1962* City of Salford, Eng., Health Department

Moon, L. E. and Patton R. E. 1965 First admissions and readmissions to New York State mental hospitals: a statistical evaluation *Psychiat Quart* 39:476–486

(33) Shepherd M. 1957 *A Study of the Major Psychoses in an English County* Maudsley Monogr 3 London, Chapman & Hall

Brown G. W. 1959 Social factors influencing length of hospital stay of schizophrenic patients *Brit Med J* 2:1300–1302

(34) Linn E. L. 1959 Drug therapy, milieu change and release from a mental hospital *Arch Neurol Psychiat* 81:785–794

(35) Wing J. K. 1966 Five-year outcome in early schizophrenia *Proc Roy Soc Med* 59:17–18

(36) Mayer-Gross W. 1930 in Bumke O. *Handbuch der Geisteskrankheiten* Berlin, Springer 9:534–536

(37) Guttman E., Mayer-Gross W. and Slater E. T. O. 1939 Short distance prognosis of schizophrenia *J Neurol Neurosurg Psychiat* 2:25–34

(38) Harris A., Linker I., Norris V. and Shepherd M. 1956 Schizophrenia, a prognostic and social study *Brit J Prev Soc Med* 10:107–114

(39) Renton C. A., Affleck J. W., Carstairs G. M. and Forrest A. D. 1963 A follow-up of schizophrenic patients in Edinburgh *Acta Psychiat Scand* 39:548–600

Kelly D. H. W. and Sargant W. 1965 Present treatment

of schizophrenia: a controlled follow-up study *Brit Med J* 1:147–150

(40) Stein Z. A. 1964 Some preliminary results of the survey of mental sickness in Salford in Susser M. W. *Report on the Salford Mental Health Services for 1963* City of Salford, Eng., Health Department

(41) Lemert E. M. 1964 Social structure, social control and deviation in Clinard M. B. ed. *Anomie and Deviant Behavior* New York, Free Press

(42) Stanton A. H. and Schwartz M. S. 1954 *The Mental Hospital* New York, Basic Books

Martin D. V. 1955 Institutionalism *Lancet* 2:1188–1190

Goffman E. 1957 Characteristics of total institutions in *Symposium on Preventive and Social Psychiatry* Washington, D. C., U. S. Government Printing Office

Barton R. W. A. G. 1959 *Institutional Neurosis* Bristol, Wright

Wing J. K. and Brown G. W. 1961 Social treatment of chronic schizophrenia: a comparative survey of three mental hospitals *J Ment Sci* 107:847–861

Gruenberg E. M. and Zusman J. 1964 The natural history of schizophrenia *Int Psychiat Clin* 1:699–710

(43) Freeman H. E. and Simmons O. G. 1963 *The Mental Patient Comes Home* New York, Wiley

(44) Sampson H., Messinger S. L. and Towne R. D. 1964 *Schizophrenic Women: Studies in Marital Crisis* New York, Atherton

(45) Goffman E. 1961 The moral career of the mental patient in Goffman E. *Asylums* Chicago, Aldine

(46) Sainsbury P. and Grad J. 1966 Evaluating the Graylingwell Hospital psychiatric service in Chichester: aims and methods of research (A preliminary report on the Chichester study) *Milbank Mem Fund Quart* 54: Part 2, 231–242

(47) Levinson D. J. and Gallagher E. B. 1964 *Patienthood in the Mental Hospital* Boston, Houghton Mifflin

(48) Moss L. M., Weber J. J. and Elinson J. eds. in press *The Application of Electronic Machine Techniques to Psychoanalytic Clinic Records* Amsterdam, Excerpta Medica Foundation

(49) Lennard H., Bernstein A., Henden H. C. and Palmore E. B. 1960 *The Anatomy of Psychotherapy* New York, Columbia University Press

(50) Fisher S. 1961 NIMH-PSC outpatient study of drug-set interaction *Psycho-pharmacol Ser Cen Bull* Bethesda, National Institute of Mental Health pp. 4–7

Liberman R. 1962 An analysis of the placebo phenomenon *J Chron Dis* 15:761–783

Ross S., Krugman A. D., Lyerly S. B. and Clyde D. J. 1962 Drugs and placebos: a model design *Psychol Rep* 10:383–392

Lyerly S. B., Ross S., Krugman A. D. and Clyde D. J. 1964 Drugs and placebos: the effects of instructions upon performance and mood under amphetamine sulphate and chloral hydrate *J Abnorm Soc Psychol* 68:321–327

Klerman G. L. 1966 *The Social Milieu and Drug-Response in Psychiatric Patients* Paper read at Annual Meeting of American Sociological Association, Miami Beach

(51) Murray H. A., Barrell W. G. and Homburger E. 1938 *Explorations in Personality* London, Oxford

Wolpe J. 1958 *Psychotherapy by Reciprocal Inhibition* Stanford, Stanford University Press

Eysenck H. J. ed. 1960 *Behaviour Therapy and the Neuroses* London, Pergamon

Watson, L. S. 1967 Application of operant conditioning techniques to institutionalized severely and profoundly retarded children *Mental Retardation Abstracts* 4:1–18

2

Factors in Performance of Mental Patients: Chronic Sickness and the Family

The social factors that influence the performance of mental patients can be grouped for discussion in three categories. The first category relates to the effects on prognosis of the general manifestations of long-standing sickness; many of these factors are hypothetical or derived from observations and impressions that await testing. The second category relates to the effects on prognosis of specific manifestations of mental disorder; these factors derive from the measured observations of special studies that afford highly plausible hypotheses. The third, a mixed category, relates to those environmental antecedents of mental disorder that might be anticipated; some of these factors rest on measured observations and plausible hypotheses, but in the main they await the practical test of preventive programs.

We shall consider each of these three classes of factors in turn in the succeeding chapters of Parts One and Two.

The first category of factors to be discussed relates to the consequences of chronic mental sickness. The characteristic strain that chronic sicknesses have in common is on resources that must be mobilized to support dependence. The execution of a policy of community care of mental disorders places a heavy burden on the resources of social agencies outside the hospital and the families of the sick. The policy of community care runs counter to the marked trend of the last century, which was toward greater use of hospitals by the sick population; as a result hospitals have become the dominant institutions for medical care in all industrial societies, and in Britain of the 1960s account for more than half the expenditure on the National Health Service. Even the U.S.S.R. plans to build many more mental hospitals, notwithstanding its reliance on a well-developed system of out-patient services (1). But in Britain and the United States mental hospitals, together with fever hospitals and tuberculosis sanatoriums, are among the few hospitals that have experienced a decline in usage in the period following World War II (2).

Hospitals undertake to meet all the physical and social needs of a dependent individual, whereas medical and social services outside the hospital have been less comprehensive. In order to substitute fully for the mental hospital in the appropriate cases, therefore, outside agencies of social support must undertake new functions and new services and must devise new methods of care. To provide an adequate substitute for the mental hospital is especially difficult because of the long duration of episodes and the strains imposed by the disordered behavior of mental patients.

Further difficulties reside in the social adaptations of the family created by developing class societies. There has been a rapid reduction in the formal structure of the family to its nucleus of parents and dependent children (3). The class system of an industrial society requires that employers and employees be free to enter into contracts and that individuals be free to move to new places or into new social classes without regard for obligations to kinsmen. Formal and legal obligations between kinsmen hinder the operation of the class system, and apart from obligations between spouses and minors within the nuclear family (and some vestiges related to titles and land) they no longer exist in Britain and other industrialized countries, and only informal obligations remain. The force of these informal obligations varies with the circumstances of social class, social mobility, and property, but even where they appear to be strongest they are insufficient to support all dependent family members (4, 5, 6).

The reduction in the structure of the family has been accompanied by a reduction in functions. The family retains fewer essential functions than formerly in the processes of orderly replacement of social positions and of cultural transmission between generations. Each generation more than reproduces itself, and many offspring therefore cannot be prepared for occupying the same social positions as their parents. At the same time schools have replaced families as the chief educators of children. Together with this consequent narrowing of family functions, the emancipation of women from legal discrimination, economic dependence, and the constant bearing and rearing of children has made adults almost permanently available for marriage and remarriage (7). Rising rates of divorce and rapid remarriage reflect not only the longevity of spouses, with the ensuing protracted period of risk, but also the decline in familial cohesion and supporting capacity that has followed on these social changes.

Demographic trends have abetted the changes in the functions of the family and in social structure. The sharp reduction in family size during the last half-century has also reduced the number of potential surrogates within the family. The popularity of marriage has added to this effect; age at marriage has fallen progressively so that daughters leave home sooner, and fewer remain single and available to kin. The necessity thus arises for social supports from outside the kin group.

The decline in the ability of families in our society to provide substitutes for the adults who maintain the home, earn money, and take care of its members has been accompanied by an absolute increase in the need to provide such substitutes. This results from the increase in the numbers of adult dependents and the chronic sick. The population as a whole has aged, and modern medicine maintains many sick individuals outside the hospital in an ambulant or semiambulant state.

In the face of all these forces the nuclear family is not well adapted to meet the needs of dependent adult members, whether the cause of their dependence is physical, mental, or social (8). Each spouse has a cluster of social roles in earning money, in establishing the connections of the family with the surrounding society, and in rearing and socializing children. In our society, substitutes for these roles are not easily found outside the nuclear family, nor can one spouse substitute for the other without imposing severe social and psychological strains within the family. The effect of the changes in the family can be seen in several countries in the trends toward hospital admission in the nonpathological episode of normal childbirth. When British health authorities have tried to reduce the duration of stay in maternity hospitals in order to cope with these greater numbers of admissions, they have faced many difficulties in providing enough nursing and family support.

The aged have been the segment of the population most affected by the change in family structure and function. In Massachusetts among people aged twenty to fifty years, the age-specific rates for first admissions to institutions for the care of mental illness showed remarkable stability through the 100 years since the mid-nineteenth century. Only among the aged did the first admission rates show a notable rise. There is nothing to suggest that the rise was caused by an increase in rates of mental disorder among old people. In the nineteenth century the risk of admission among mentally disordered people was much higher among the young than among the old. In the mid-twentieth century the reverse is true: The mentally ill among the old are less prone to be retained and supported in the community (9).

Sick-Role Threshold. Although in industrial societies the bedridden patient has long existed, the emergence of the chronic ambulant patient in any numbers is a recent phenomenon. The ambulant sick role, because it does not fit the stereotype of the past, presents society with a problem of adaptation (10). "Galen says that medicine is the science of the healthy, the sick, and the chronic who are neither." So wrote Dr. Christobel

Mendez in 1553, in the first printed book on the merits of exercise (11). It was the "chronic" who most taxed Dr. Mendez. The patient is neither obviously ill nor obviously well, and his condition is not temporary but permanent. This permanent state of semidependence makes possible a prolonged escape from many everyday responsibilities. Any chronic ambulant patient may therefore meet with suspicion from relatives and others who resent his exemption or suffer by it. "If he is sick, why doesn't he improve with treatment?" Doctors too (when no fee is proffered for a service) may be quick to suspect valetudinarianism.

Treatment agencies face a further dilemma, not peculiar to psychiatry, in accommodating families and the wider society to the chronic ambulant sick role. In many disorders, including schizophrenia, the best treatment is often to keep the patient active rather than inactive and resting. Therapists present families with conflict when families are asked to regard mental disorder as disease yet to deny patients the usual exemptions from social obligations conferred by the sick role.

The precise threshold at which chronic disease leads to the outright assumption of the sick role depends not only on the patient's physiological and psychological condition but also on the supportive capacity of his social and family relations (12). The nuclear family, we noted above, draws on relatively meager human resources and is not well suited to cope with sickness. Should a parent fall sick, the family is deprived of important adult roles and services. The loss of the paternal breadwinner may cripple the family economically, and the loss of a mother threatens it with breakup. A study of poliomyelitis victims utterly disabled and kept alive by respirators confirms that the effects of crippling are specific to each role. Fathers tended to be kept in hospital and sometimes to be deserted by their families, useless like worker bees after the death sting. Mothers tended to be brought home in order to become, like queen bees, the focal point of family continuity (13). Specific consequences for each role have also been documented in family studies of schizophrenia (14). At the emotional level, the demands set up by the dependence of a sick parent conflict with the similar demands of dependent children, so that there is overlap and competition in the performance of the sick role and the child's role.

These outcomes reflect the *internal structure* of the family. The term is used here in the sense of the statuses that the family comprises, the allocation of roles to each status, and the ordered relationships among them (15). Structure is not constant but varies with the stage of the family cycle. The capacity of the family to support a dependent member fluctuates with the progress of its cycle of development. During the phase of expansion and child rearing, its capacity to support others than offspring is diminished.

Supportive capacity also varies with the *external relations* of the family. These relations include the type of social network of which the nuclear family is a component part. Networks are founded on the formal obligations among kin and on the material resources of the society (5, 6, 10). They may be close-knit and contained in small areas or loose-knit and dispersed, according to the migration and mobility engendered by occupation and marriage. A close-knit network may compensate in supportive strength for poor material resources.

The family's external relations within any one society are mediated by its social position and the culture attendant on that position (3, 4). Position governs access to social relations and the use to which resources available for support may be put. In the first half of the twentieth century, at least, English working-class cultures enjoined support for dependent relatives rather than the alternative of care in institutions, especially those institutions stigmatized by their past associations with the Poor Law (6, 16). Families who have shared this culture have been loath to give up the home care of subnormal children even in the most difficult circumstances (17). These attitudes were viable and the strains of dependency tolerated as long as mutual aid could be exchanged through local close-knit social networks.

Social class and the attendant culture also have profound influence on family concepts of mental disorder. In turn these concepts influence the stage at which mentally ill individuals are recognized as sick and the manner in which recognition comes about (18). In New Haven, Connecticut, upper-class people, upon exhibiting even mild intrapsychic symptoms, tended to be classed as mentally ill and to be handled by psychiatrists. Lower-class people tended to be classed as normal; their aberrations were ascribed to personality, until severe behavior disturbance brought them into the hands of the police and disciplinary agencies.

Family capacity to absorb and support the chronic sick role is founded on the concrete features of internal structure and external relations. These are structural sources of support. There is also a functional source in the current of *interaction* within the family. Regularities in interaction flow from the playing out of the roles allocated to each family member. Each role, even that of the Hindu Saddhu who withdraws from society, is complementary to others and involves reciprocal two-way relationships. The pattern and predictability of interaction are sustained by the expectations of others. These expectations are enforced by sanctions as diverse as the exercise of law and the manipulation of affection. The way in which a person plays his role depends on what he learns of the expectations of others and on how he learns them, that is, on how he incorporates them into his concepts and into his personality. Conformity and idiosyncrasy have social as well as psychological sources.

Interaction has been studied intensively in familes one of whose members suffered from schizophrenia. Following on initial reports that disordered family relations centered on dominant mothers, and in some cases also on inadequate fathers (19, 20), a number of research teams have formulated hypotheses about the types of interaction between parents and child that might derange socialization and generate schizophrenia. T. Lidz's theories of the distorted transmission of culture that arises where family roles are "skewed" or "schismatic" (21), G. Bateson's theories about the "double-bind," a communication whose explicit and implicit meanings are contradictory (22), and L. C. Wynne's theories about the "pseudomutuality" of roles causing fragmentation of communication (23) all point to modes of interaction that are being investigated for causal connections with schizophrenia (24). These investigators have attempted to study interaction within family units and have devised a number of methods for doing so. The insights from these studies, which deal with overlapping concepts from different sociological and psychological viewpoints, have yet to be integrated. Furthermore, although the hypotheses are framed in causal terms, the question of whether the illness or the interaction is prior must be left aside. For it is not clear whether these patterns of interaction are specific to schizophrenia; or whether they are general to the chronic sick role in mental illness; or whether they are even more general in families and are elicited and exaggerated by schizophrenia or chronic mental sickness.

Some of the work on family interaction in mental illness is framed in more general terms. Thus J. P. Spiegel has described family interaction in terms of a web of complementary roles that are maintained in equilibrium. The adoption of a particular style of playing a role imposes complementary styles on others in the family. These styles may induce pathological behavior, but a number of mechanisms can be brought into play to shift the status quo (25). A few efforts have been made to apply some of these interpretations of family behavior to the support of mental patients (26). This supportive aspect, and not the pathogenic qualities of patterns of interaction, is our concern in the present context.

Patterns of family interaction can be conceived of as family *microculture*. Small intensive studies suggest that families tend to share a theme around which interaction is oriented (27). Microcultures have practical effects on the supportive capacity of families. Thus families with an orientation shared by both parents maintain their integration better in the face of the challenge of a severely subnormal child than those without a shared parental orientation (28). The inference that a shared orientation is supportive gains strength from a study of low-income families in New York tenements. All the families in the study were exposed to much the same buffeting from an unfriendly environment, but the trials and interpersonal tribulations generated within families were less frequent and severe in those few that had a discernible sense of solidarity, congruent goals, and a feeling for the common good (29). Concordant values about family life, and the stability of family ties, are aspects of family microculture that to some extent can be predicted. Factors that increase the risks of divorce also predict discordant values: These factors include early age at marriage, marriages across faith and ethnic groups, and previous marriages (30).

Family microculture is the expression of the complex of interaction, internal structure, and external relations. It is the resultant of these forces and sums them up. In a sense microculture is interaction, or at least its repetitive and persistent content. But the microculture has intimate connections with the internal structure of the family, for this structure determines the number and the relative position of the interacting parties—and thus the objective conditions for interaction. In this complex, historical factors such as the origins of each spouse must also be taken into account. To the family of marriage, spouses bring contributions, in the form of values, beliefs, and aspirations, from their families of origin. Whether or not marriages are circumscribed by one geographic area, one faith, one ethnic group, or one age group gives an index of concordance; this index describes at once the probabilities of the congruence of culture, of the density of family networks, and of the appropriate allocation of conjugal roles (10).

The more diffuse forces that create the microculture are its connections with the enveloping field of external relations. Family microculture can be more or less consonant with the macroculture of the society as a whole and with any subculture of which it is a part. The impact of the macroculture on family culture depends on the ability of the parental figures to transmit the macroculture without distortion and to serve as models with whom children can identify, and of family members to select from it. The content of the macroculture thus conveyed depends on the social position of the family in terms of occupation, education, and other determinants of social class, for these determine access to its many facets.

The paradigm of microculture, internal structure, and external relations provides a frame for the analysis of family processes as they affect sick-role thresholds. Variations in types of family response to chronic sickness can be taken to reflect the interplay of the pre-existing microculture and the phenomenon of dependency within particular family roles.

It should be borne in mind that the family is but one milieu of interaction. The individual's statuses and roles and interactions outside the family can have an equally potent influence on the threshold for taking up the sick role. Their actual force at any point in time is decreed by the stage of the life cycle and the balance of roles at that stage.

References

(1) Kline N. S. 1960 The organization of psychiatric care and psychiatric research in the Union of Soviet Socialist Republics *Ann N Y Acad Sci* 84:147–223

Robinson K. 1961 *Patterns of Care* London, National Association for Mental Health

(2) Kramer M., Pollack E. S., Locke B. and Bahn A. K. 1958 Problems in the interpretation of trends in the population movement of the public mental hospitals *Amer J Pub Health* 88:1003–1019

Tooth G. C. and Brooke E. M. 1961 Trends in the mental hospital population and their effect on future planning *Lancet* 1:710–713

Rehin G. F. and Martin F. M. 1963 Psychiatric services in 1975 *PEP* 29

Moon L. E. and Patton R. E. 1965 First admissions and readmissions to New York State mental hospitals: a statistical evaluation *Psychiat Quart* 39:476–486

(3) Parsons T. 1949 *Essays in Sociological Theory* New York, Free Press

(4) Firth R. ed. 1956 *Two Studies of Kinship in London* London, Athlone

Young M. and Willmott P. 1957 *Family and Kinship in East London* London, Routledge

(5) Bott E. 1957 *Family and Social Network* London, Tavistock

(6) Townsend P. 1957 *The Family Life of Old People* London, Routledge

(7) Farber B. 1964 *Family: Organization and Interaction* San Francisco, Chandler

(8) Parsons T. and Fox R. C. 1952 Illness, therapy and the modern urban American family *J Soc Issues* 8:Part 4, 31–44

(9) Goldhamer H. and Marshall A. 1953 *Psychosis and Civilization* New York, Free Press

(10) Susser M. W. and Watson W. 1962 *Sociology in Medicine* London, Oxford

(11) Mendez C. 16th century Guerra F. trans. Kilgour F. G. ed. 1960 *The Book of Bodily Exercise* New Haven, Licht

(12) Mechanic D. 1962 The concept of illness behavior *J Chron Dis* 15:189–194

Stoeckle J. D., Zola I. K. and Davidson G. E. 1963 On going to see the doctor: the contributions of the patient to the decision to seek medical aid *J Chron Dis* 16:975–989

Susser M. W. 1965 Rationale for the community care of mental disorder *Medical Care* 3:52–59

(13) Deutsch C. P. and Goldston J. A. 1960 Family factors in home adjustment of the severely disabled *Marriage Fam Liv* 22:312–316

(14) Rogler L. and Hollingshead A. B. 1965 *Trapped: Families and Schizophrenia* New York, Wiley

(15) Parsons T., Bales R. F. and Olds J. 1955 *Family Socialization and Interaction Process* New York, Free Press

Radcliffe-Brown A. R. Srinivas M. N. ed. 1958 *Method in Social Anthropology: Selected Essays* Chicago, University of Chicago Press

(16) Hoggart R. 1957 *The Uses of Literacy* Fairlawn, N. J., Essential Books

(17) Tizard J. and Grad J. 1961 *The Mentally Handicapped and Their Families* Maudsley Monogr 7 London, Oxford

(18) Hollingshead A. B. and Redlich F. C. 1958 *Social Class and Mental Illness* New York, Wiley

(19) Lidz R. W. and Lidz T. 1949 The family environment of schizophrenic patients *Amer J Psychiat* 106:332–345

(20) Gerard D. L. and Houston L. G. 1953 Family setting and the social ecology of schizophrenia *Psychiat Quart* 27:90–101

Alanen Y. O. 1958 *The Mothers of Schizophrenic Patients* Copenhagen, Munksgaard

Myers J. K. and Roberts B. H. 1959 *Family and Class Dynamics in Mental Illness* New York, Wiley

(21) Lidz T. 1963 *The Family and Human Adaptation* New York, International Universities Press

(22) Bateson G., Jackson D., Haley J. and Weakland J. H. 1963 A note on the double-bind 1962 *Family Process* 2:154–161

(23) Wynne L. C., Ryckoff I., Day J. and Hirsch S. 1958 Pseudo-mutuality in the family relations of schizophrenics *Psychiat* 21:205–220

Wynne L. C. and Singer M. T. 1963 Thought disorder and the family relations of schizophrenics: 1. A research strategy *Arch Gen Psychiat* 9:191–198

(24) Jackson D. D. ed. 1960 *The Etiology of Schizophrenia* New York, Basic Books

Mishler E. G. and Waxler N. E. 1965 Family interaction processes and schizophrenia: a review of current theories *Merrill-Palmer Quart* 11:269–315

(25) Spiegel J. P. 1957 The resolution of role conflict within the family *Psychiat* 20:1–16

(26) Jacobson S. and Klerman G. L. 1966 Interpersonal dynamics of hospitalized depressed patients' home visits *J Marriage Family* 28:95–102

(27) Hess R. D. and Handel G. 1959 *Family Worlds* Chicago, University of Chicago Press

(28) Farber B. 1959 *Effects of a Severely Mentally Retarded Child on Family Integration* Monogr Soc Res Child Develop Vol. 24 No. 2 Chicago, University of Chicago Press

Farber B. 1960 *Family Organization and Crisis: Maintenance of Integration in Families with a Severely Mentally Retarded Child* Monogr Soc Res Child Develop Vol. 25 No. 1 Chicago, University of Chicago Press

(29) Koos E. L. 1946 *Families in Trouble* New York, King's Crown

(30) Farber B. and Blackman L. S. 1956 Marital role tensions in number and sex of children *Amer Sociol Rev* 21:596–601

3

Specific Factors in Prognosis

Within the general setting of chronic sickness a number of factors special to mental disorder have been found to influence prognosis. They describe unique strains superimposed by mental disorders on the common strains imposed by chronic sickness.

Primary Accommodation to Mental Disorder: Family Roles

In each family the accustomed organization of roles, continually adjusted as children grow and achieve new statuses, creates a balanced system of relationships. The adaptation of the ensuing family microculture to the gradual reordering of structure occasioned by growth, and to the drastic reordering occasioned by bereavement or sickness, may be more or less successful.

When one of the family members suffers from mental disorder, special problems of adaptation arise. In the case of mental illness in a husband or wife, the spouse must find a means of accommodating to disordered behavior. Sometimes accommodation occurs only at the cost of inducing neurosis in the healthy spouse (1). *Folie à deux* can be seen as the extreme of such accommodation. In this condition couples achieve a bizarre congruence through sharing delusions and psychotic disorders of thought (2). When husband or wife has come to terms with psychosis in the spouse by an adjustment of conjugal roles, any added strain may tilt accommodation into declared sickness, to end perhaps with extrusion of the sick member from the family (3).

A study of schizophrenic wives showed how accommodation insulated them from psychiatric services for a considerable period although they were grossly disturbed. In one pattern of accommodation husband and wife moved away from each other emotionally, and withdrawal was reciprocated by further withdrawal. In this way the patient was excluded from interpersonal family ties. The situation allowed a high tolerance of aberrations, which were ignored by the husband and invisible to others. A second pattern was triadic and included a mother on whom the wife was extremely dependent, a dependence encouraged by her husband. In this form of accommodation outside help was avoided since it threatened the interdependence of mother and daughter (4).

Complementary studies of schizophrenic husbands, and others of alcoholic husbands, suggest that when the cycle of interaction is not disturbed by professional intervention, families likewise react in typical patterns (5). The husband's behavior is at first accounted for by explanations within the range of normality, which deny the existence of mental disorder. Denial is followed by recognition with concealment; concealment may be followed by isolation of the deviant spouse within the family and finally by "freezing out" and extrusion. A study in New York of hospital patients and their families found that although early admission consistently followed violent and bizarre behavior, social situations seemed influential in determining the duration of other symptoms at the time of admission. Patients in critical family roles were brought to the hospital sooner than others (6).

The patient's removal from everyday relationships, to the hospital if necessary, can relieve acute domestic tension built up in the preceding phase of illness. It allows time on all sides for cooling off and for reorientation of attitudes and creates a malleable situation in which behavior changes can sometimes be brought about. Admission to the hospital establishes new conditions of interaction between patient and family members. In some cases these new conditions bring pressures for the restoration of ties; many American procedures of commitment, for instance, call on kin to assume legal responsibilities (4). In other cases the new conditions after admission support the permanent exclusion of the patient from former ties. Treatment needs to recognize and exploit such crosscurrents in the interests of the patient rather than blindly to suffer them.

A more general prescription is called for by the late stage at which progressive deterioration of family relations often comes to notice. A preventive approach would seek to bring help at an earlier and perhaps more reversible stage. There is no direct evidence that these illnesses can be diagnosed early, however, nor that if they are diagnosed early that they can be brought into treatment, nor that if they are brought into treatment that it will be effective. This unproven string of assumptions does not mean that secondary prevention to arrest the progress of established disorder is not to be attempted. It does mean that the attempt should include tests of its effectiveness (7).

An obvious preventive step is education about the nature of mental illness and about the services that deal with it, together with the provision of services. Education would aim to alter the way in which people perceive their problems. People who interpret their difficulties in introspective and psychological terms are more likely to look for help than those who attribute such difficulties to external agents (8). Education is surely the most potent known means of altering interpretations of reality.

It can do this sometimes by conveying simple but much needed information. Many families that must deal with mental disorder are in a state of "pluralistic ignorance" (9). This is a state in which people, like white liberals in the southern United States and like many parents of handicapped children, perceive their own situations as exceptional and the attitudes of the world about them to their problems as negative, whereas in reality others share their plight in mutual unawareness. Social clubs for patients and their families, and other institutions that bring the users of mental-health services together, help to dispel this ignorance and its accompanying sense of alienation. More than 20 per cent of the patients who attended a "therapeutic" club in Salford, England, came together with relatives. Participant observers found that one use that these relatives made of the club was to commune about the problems arising from the patient's illness (10).

Research has indicated some safeguards that protect the persuasiveness of educational messages (11). Two experimental conditions make messages more effective: They should avoid stirring latent pools of anxiety about mental illness, and they should point with a minimum of uncertainty to possible action, if not to solutions (12, 13). The second of these experimental conditions is consistent with the idea that, once the desire to act has been aroused, a "cognitive map" of the pathways by which the desire can be satisfied facilitates action (14).

Some confirmation of the effectiveness of the cognitive map can be had from a national survey of mental health in the United States. Among people who recognized that they had personal problems, it was more the facilitating factors of knowledge about services and their accessibility that influenced their use of these services than the psychological factors of perception and interpretation of the problems. Among those who sought help for personal problems, for example, churchgoers turned to the readily accessible clergy. Others turned to the medical profession, and among the latter it was the better off who gained access to psychiatrists (8).

The conclusion is elementary but often ignored: For mental-health education to be successful, not only must it make known possible solutions to individual problems, but facilities must also exist to fulfill the solution if frustration and self-defeat are to be avoided (15).

Education about mental-health services should foster discriminating use, and to achieve this end it should not neglect the purveyors of service. The response of agencies in New York to patients ill enough to be taken to mental hospitals was often to exert their full institutional power: The patients were arrested by the police, landlords evicted them, and employers dismissed them (6). In one American study negative views of mental illness were found to be as prevalent among general practitioners as among the public (12). A main factor in the negative attitudes of physicians toward their psychiatric patients seems to be lack of confidence in their own training and capacity to treat such patients (16). This problem is one that can be remedied by education.

It is important to do so. General practitioners are among the chief keepers of the gates to service. In Britain they make by far the most referrals to psychiatric services (17). In the United States, of the available agencies, they are, next to the clergy, most often called on for aid for personal and emotional problems (8, 12). Public-health nurses too are in a unique position to assist in finding cases at an early stage through unsolicited but legitimate visiting. Many fail to fulfill this potential because they do not recognize problems or lack knowledge about handling them (18). Health workers, including doctors, are aware that they have been ill-equipped by their training to deal with such problems (16). The demand for more training in psychiatry and the response of practitioners when it is offered testify that many are anxious to correct this educational lack.

Reorientation is needed in the psychiatric and hospital services as well as among nonspecialists. At the Massachusetts General Hospital less than 1 per cent of alcoholics admitted to the emergency service followed recommendations for further outpatient treatment, seeming confirmation of the belief that they were untreatable because they did not want to be helped. This belief proved to be one more example of a self-fulfilling prophecy. A system of treatment was designed to encourage the participation of patients and to remove the disincentives. About half the cases persisted in treatment through five or more visits compared with one in a hundred or less in controls (19). The treatment was based on meeting as many of the patient's needs as possible, on reducing frustrations met by patients in the service organization, and on continuity of relationships with a team of workers. Subsequent work in an acute psychiatric service suggested that the results with alcoholics could be generalized to many forms of mental disorder.

The disparities in the treatment afforded to patients with different diagnoses have a parallel in the treatment afforded to patients of different social classes. In a study of psychiatric illness in New Haven, the treatment given in each of the psychiatric agencies was related to the social class of the patient in its type, frequency, and duration. Among private psychiatrists, for instance, the average time for the therapeutic session declined regularly from the higher social classes to the lower (20). Similar results have been obtained more than once in the United States (21), although not in Britain. The gulf of class and culture affected the ability of professionals to give treatment and of patients to accept it (22). The American experiments with alcoholics suggest that there are ways of crossing the gulf.

Secondary Accommodation to Mental Disorder: After the Return of the Mental Patient

Accommodation is a process of continuous adjustments through which the system of family relationships is kept in some kind of balance as family members strive toward reciprocity in their roles. So far we have considered some patterns that arise within families with the unfolding of mental illness. After the extrusion of a mentally ill member a new balance is established, and his return after prolonged absence may then lead to difficulties in reallocation of family roles.

The analogy of returning prisoners of war illustrates these difficulties (23). In the absence of fathers taken prisoner during World War II, families had of necessity rearranged the roles of mother and children. The father's return disturbed existing relations. Wives and children were older and had grown unaccustomed to authoritative males, and the resumption of family roles by the fathers often proved a painful process. The necessity to adjust to new roles sometimes led to the break-up of families, but the husbands and wives who had spent time in special rehabilitation centers made the transition more successfully.

In follow-up studies of mental hospital patients a recurrent finding is that patients discharged after a long stay in the hospital are more likely than others to be readmitted within a defined period (24, 25, 26). Among such possible causes of this pattern as the nature of the illness and the dissolution of supportive networks, the history of rearrangements of family roles must also be considered. With time the reallocated family roles take on increasing stability. Where this is a discernible factor upon the return of the long-separated patient, community services should be able to give help to families equivalent to that provided for the returned prisoner of war. Help is needed all the more because of the equivocal position of the ex-mental patient in many relationships. No dispensations for heroism are given the displaced deviant; he has the "spoiled identity" of stigma (27).

The ability of the ex-patient to sustain life outside the hospital is connected with the particular position in the domestic setting that he resumes as well as with the history of rearrangements within that setting. A study in Britain of young men discharged after a stay in the hospital for schizophrenia of at least two years discovered that the stability of accommodation, as judged by return to the hospital within one year, was more closely related to the domestic setting than to the severity of their symptoms. Most successful were those who lived in lodgings or with sibs, less so were those who returned to parents, and least those who returned to wives (28, 29). The results stand confirmed by some attempts to repeat them if not by all (26, 30, 31, 32).

These findings could reflect the latitude within each domestic setting in the standards of performance expected of the patient. The latitude in performance permitted to the patient, in other words the tolerance of deviant behavior, is one dimension of expectations. In these terms the expectation of "significant others" is the crucial link between domestic setting and social performance.

Expectations did not seem to explain the outcome in another study of patients discharged from the hospital after being treated for functional psychoses. What relatives said they expected of the patients could not be related to the patients' success in staying out of the hospital (26). Readmission to a mental hospital, however, is a doubtful criterion for judging the effect of expectations about role performance; it is only one secondary effect among many.

Expectations provide a more powerful explanatory tool (as we shall see later) when the primary effect, namely the actual performance of roles to which the expectations attach, is taken as the criterion. Moreover, latitude for deviant behavior is related to other factors in the domestic setting, and these may determine the potency of expectations. For instance, the visibility of the patient's behavior to those who hold expectations of him, and the sanctions these others can exercise, are intervening variables between expectations and their effect. On the patient's side, his psychic state may similarly intervene. Thus a degree of social isolation and disengagement may best suit the psychological withdrawal and the incapacity of affect that often characterize schizophrenia.

In any event, accommodation in families to which patients return can be related to two factors: the duration of the patient's absence (probably in all types of illness) and the composition of the household (in the case of schizophrenia at least).

Accommodation and Expectations

One measure of accommodation is the consistency of expectations and performance between persons in reciprocal roles. The level of accommodation in a social situation can be described as the degree to which a person's performance matches what others expect and demand of him.

We have seen that parental families offer schizophrenic patients discharged from the hospital a better chance of survival in the community than do conjugal families (28, 29). Accommodation may permit the patient to remain in the family, however, without requiring of him a high level of social performance. Thus, in one study patients who returned to parental families and survived in the community were found to maintain a poorer level of social performance than those who survived in conjugal families. The variation in social performance can be attributed to different expectations (33).

Attempts have been made to devise measures of the expectations of family members about the performance of particular domestic roles to test this hypothesis. The social performance of mental hospital patients discharged to their families was found to vary directly with the expectations of others (26, 34). Expectations and performance were themselves connected with the formal status and roles of the patient in the family. Wives expected more of husbands (who must fulfill demands as spouses, breadwinners, and fathers) than did mothers of sons (who can remain socially dependent). Status and role are thus antecedent conditions that influence expectations and performance.

It proved difficult to go further and establish the time sequence between expectations and performance because the level of expectations is likely to be modified by the feedback from actual performance. When roles are demanding, expectations are high; when performance is poor, expectations are likely to be lowered. Such adjustment of expectations in relation to performance could explain the high expectations found in good performance, since on retesting after an interval a fall in expectations was associated with a decline in performance.

Experience in such therapeutic groups as day centers and hostels indicates that skilled leadership can influence behavior through appropriate expectations. The disciplined behavior necessary to maintain high levels of performance need not be won at the cost of initiative and individual effort. It can coexist with the growth of individual responsibility.

Experiments in a Californian Veteran's Hospital also showed that self-regulated groups of long-resident schizophrenic patients were able to respond to expectations clearly conveyed. Thus the patients allocated regular tasks to each individual within the group and performed group tasks over several weeks with a minimum of supervision (35). The patients proved responsive to others in reciprocal roles. In an experimental two-person situation, the performance of patients converged toward norms built in by the relationship of leader and follower (36). With virtually no verbal communication, those designated as followers carried out their tasks in the style set by those designated as leaders. The description of the subjects of these experiments indicates that they belonged in the category of the "social-breakdown syndrome." (These "distortions of personality functions associated with more or less severe destruction of the affected person's social relationships" usually accompany psychoses [37]. The pattern of reaction is withdrawal, anger and hostility, or both.) Such experiments only simulate over brief periods the more complex and continuous relationships of the world outside, but they indicate that even among deteriorated patients a foundation exists on which to build and develop.

Experiments in the same California Veteran's Mental Hospital have shown how the social performance of patients may be influenced (38). Controlled studies were made over a six-month period, and the experimental design was vulnerable to obvious bias only on the score that the initiators of the therapeutic program were also the researchers. Patients with chronic mental illness who were ready to enter an open ward were allocated to two settings. One comprised the routine procedure with close staff supervision, ward meetings, and workshop activity. The other comprised the experimental procedure. Small groups were formed. Staff supervision was substituted by consultations at fixed intervals, with only written communications in the interim. The small groups were made responsible for certain ward tasks and for recommending for each group member the appropriate clinical rating and its attached privileges.

The experimental group performed better on all measures leading up to discharge and employment, but not thereafter. Within the hospital they had developed group leaders and a degree of cohesiveness, communication, and adherence to group norms that were clearly supportive. Group support was lost after discharge, and then the same norms of performance were not maintained.

This study teaches that with appropriate incentive small task groups can cohere and generate norms and expectations to which members try to conform. For their own intragroup purposes they can be effective agents of socialization. But the context of such socialization may be highly specific. The groups were not successful vehicles for conveying to the patients the norms of the world outside the hospital, nor for promoting behavior that could be transferred out of the hospital, or even out of the groups, and maintained there. Hence the need to extend the range of therapeutic situations beyond the hospital and to devise supportive techniques to assist patients who assume the spoiled identity of ex-patient in the community.

Accommodation and Hostility

Accommodation depends on the mutuality of expectations and performance in social situations. Obvious discrepancy between what one person does and what others expect of him is likely to cause both social strain and bad feeling between them. An affective component of strained accommodation can therefore be inferred. A measure of this strain is the hostility expressed toward patients by their families. In a preliminary study of patients followed up from a community register of mental patients in Salford, we found that the relationship between accommodation measured in this way and social performance was as close as that between the intrapsychic state and social performance. A much more extensive study showed that on the schizophrenic patient's return from the mental hospital, pre-existing hostility among household members reduces his chances of survival in the community (39). A later study obtained a similar result. Although numbers were small, the sample had the advantage of having been selected on admission and not from the less representative group that gains release from the mental hospital. In this sample, disturbed family relationships were also associated with longer stays in the hospital (32).

To use hostility as a measure of accommodation requires care. The quality of feeling in a family is in part created by past experience; it cannot be taken as a consequence of the present situation alone. The sorting out of the time sequence and the interaction among events is a central problem of many studies that involve process through time, and we shall have occasion to return to it. The relevant variables can be treated, on the one hand, as independent, causal, and antecedent to the effects under study and, on the other, as dependent, consequent, and part of the effects. Such variables are "reciprocal" (40), and the result is an interaction of variables in which the whole is sometimes greater than the sum of the parts. A factor like sickness behavior can be simultaneously a cause of family tension and its result. Pre-existing hostility between family members and patient thus acts to upset accommodation and to reduce a patient's chance of survival in the community; the existing family situation, with its lack of accommodation, exacerbates the hostility and sets up continuing repercussions.

In this cycle, however, duration of daily face-to-face contacts between discharged schizophrenic patients and household members is a significant intervening element in the tensions of the current situation. The shorter the contact is, the better the result (39). When the highest level of tension preceded the patient's return and the greatest contact followed it, 60 per cent were readmitted to the hospital within one year. When tension was lowest and contact shortest, only 8 per cent were readmitted.[1]

Tension and hostility are thus factors in the equation of accommodation with prognosis. In this equation the patient's social performance is the outcome (or dependent variable), and his roles in the home and their attached expectations are antecedent determining factors (or independent variables). But fully stated the equation must include as intervening variables the other factors we have isolated, namely the visibility of the patient's role to others as measured by interpersonal contact,

1. Dr. Douglas Bennett of the Maudsley Hospital made this secondary analysis.

his accountability for his role in terms of sanctions, emotional tension in the members of the household, and the patient's mental state as it influences his desire to withdraw from or impinge on others.

The relationships among these variables can be conceived as a process with a sequence: role > expectations > visibility > accountability > emotional tone > psyche > performance.

The intervening variables may not all be influential, and the sequence could be short-circuited in several ways. There are many alternative structures of these variables. They need not form part of a sequence in a process. Some could equally well act simultaneously. Hostility in relatives and withdrawal in the patient can arise independently of role and expectations. They then form part of a configuration of factors determining outcome rather than part of a sequence.

Social workers and family doctors can possibly mitigate hostility by shortening contacts between the patient and household. Some of the benefit of limited contact may inhere in the conditions that bring it about. Contact is thus shortened by ensuring employment or attendance at day centers and by providing alternative residence, and in turn these arrangements in themselves reduce hostility because they lessen burdens on household resources of time, energy, and money.

Results of placements in hostels, shelters, and lodgings have been better than in hostile homes or in "common lodging houses," flophouses, and other refuges for the "down and out" (28, 29). Some workers have attempted to influence domestic interaction by social treatment aimed at clarifying and undoing the pattern of communication in which the patient and family are enmeshed (41). Controlled evaluation of such treatment is still to be carried out.

Accommodation to Specific Disorders

Although social roles in all types of mental disorder have much in common, each type has special problems. For instance, the anguish of periodic depression, explicable to the patient's relatives only in terms of a world of private values, seems to confuse communication in a less provocative way than does the private but seemingly painless incongruity of thought and affect in schizophrenia. In both these functional psychoses, however, interpretations of the illness probably help families to accommodate to the personal difficulties of relating and to the social difficulties of aberrant conduct. The social and interpersonal difficulties of the functional psychoses contrast with those of personality disorders. In these personality disorders unpredictable deviant conduct strains accommodation because the behavior appears to be willfully amoral.

The common configuration of relationships in families affected by mental disorder is related to the distinctive distribution of each type of illness in the population. (See Figure 4, p. 178.) For instance, psychotic depression affects women more often than men. Its onset most commonly occurs in their ripe years, when nearly all are married and have borne children, and it occurs evenly through the social classes. It thus most often arises as a condition of the mother in the family of procreation during its phase of expansion, when her children are being raised through infancy and the school years. Problems of accommodation are likely to center on child rearing and on the father's roles in relation to his children. Schizophrenia at onset particularly affects young men who are unmarried, who have acquired no special occupational skills, and who have low positions in the social class scale. It thus most often arises as the condition of a son in his family of origin during its phase of dispersion. Strains in accommodation are likely to center around efforts to establish for him the norm of independence from his family of origin and to maintain whatever unstable independence he may have gained.

Accommodation seems particularly difficult to achieve in deteriorative organic disorders. Senile dementia makes heavy physical and psychological demands on relatives (42), and the asymmetry of the felt obligations of husband, wife, and children to the dependent old person can create a growing focus of familial conflict. In one community study the emotional significance of the kin network for the elderly person seemed to alter with the onset of functional mental illness. Among those who were well, feelings of loneliness related to the reported frequency of the whole range of their social contacts. Among those who were mentally ill, feelings of loneliness and concomitant feelings of neglect related only to the reported frequency of visiting by relatives (43). In this and in many other disorders of mind, symptoms crystallize around intimate personal relations, and therefore stable accommodation within families is doubly difficult to maintain.

Fortunately, a number of physical factors that contribute to mental disorders of old age are remediable (44). These include the imbalance of brain metabolism and brain nutrients that arise with anemias, chronic respiratory and circulatory disorders, and malnutrition. Practical demonstration encourages the view that psychiatry and social work can also alleviate the household strain that so often precedes permanent hospital placement (45).

Severe subnormality in the child simulates the deterioration of organic disorders because the gap between the timetable for normal development and the child's progress steadily widens. It differs from organic disorders at older ages in that it places equal formal obligations on both parents. But clinical observations suggest that subnormality too may be a focus of marital conflicts, which disturb the child's behavior (46). (See pp. 343 ff.) A folklore of hereditary stigma is attached to subnormality. Shame, guilt, and anxiety may color the attitudes of parents. Moreover, parents may not accept equally the prospect of permanent dependence in a child who cannot fulfill normal parental hopes. For the father, whose role it is to abide by and to exact the external standards of society, tension in relation to a handicapped child tends to be greater than for the mother, whose role is a nurturant one (47). In the organic disorders of young and old, when kin are no longer effective because of strain or loss, the patient usually needs supervised care in a substitute home more than technical medical treatment.

High-grade subnormality without brain disorder also causes special problems (48). This condition appears as educational retardation and social deviance during pubescence and adolescence. When educational retardation is its main expression family strain is minimal, for the retardation is in part a product of the family culture and congruent with it. When social deviance is superadded, the patient has usually suffered personality damage from derangement of family function and structure. The problems of severe and mild subnormality are discussed at length in later chapters.

Kin Support

The social support available to patients influences both the likelihood of their admission to a hospital and the duration of their stay. Kin may be dispersed or altogether lacking, or they may be available but ineffective, or they may be both available and effective. These conditions vary according to the stage of the family cycle, the type of social network, social mobility, and material resources (49, 50). Lack of support from kin is a major factor in admission among the subnormal (51, 52). Among other mental patients, marital status gives some measure of *available* support. In mental hospitals those who are single, separated or divorced, and widowed are overrepresented (24, 53, 54). The divorced are overrepresented because of a high rate of mental disorder among them, which probably precedes divorce. The single and the widowed, and widowed men in particular, are overrepresented at least in part because they have higher admission rates than other patients (53, 54). Single patients have also been found to be overrepresented because the likelihood of their release from a mental hospital was less, and the likelihood of their readmission was greater, than that of married patients (55). In this study the number of living children did not aid in predicting outcome, but nothing was known of their connection with the domestic arrangements of the patients. One study of long-stay patients in mental hospitals estimated that as many as 17 per cent might have been discharged if a home had been available to them (56). In Salford in 1963 there were in mental hospitals nineteen residents between the ages of sixteen and sixty years, drawn from the city in the five-year period 1956 to 1960, who had been inmates for a minimum of three years. (They constituted one in 25,000 of the age group per year.) Only one of the nineteen was married.

The less kin support, the higher the risk of admission, and the higher the risk of long stay after admission. It follows that mental hospitals are in part the inadvertent substitutes for kin. Less specialized surrogates seem called for in order to relieve mental hospitals of an inappropriate burden and at the same time to give several unwitting actors of the mental patient role access to roles in the community.

In the value systems of nearly all societies available kin are likely to be looked to as the first and nearest source of help. The visiting of patients in the hospital by relatives can be taken as an indication of *effective* kin support. Thus in Britain the visiting of schizophrenic patients has been correlated with their chances of discharge from the hospital (25).[2] The goodwill of relatives cannot be translated directly into the capacity to give support to patients. In communities where the interest in patients shown by relatives was much the same, the willingness of kin to offer a place in the home was not (56). The variability in the responses of relatives of common culture can possibly be ascribed to the better resources of some communities than others in housing, finance, and the supportive strength of the family network (49, 57). Residence in hostels and shelters, foster homes, supervised lodgings, and self-governing households of patients can overcome such difficulties and prevent the needless immuring of homeless people away from their home communities. Social work can help to restore effective ties, even when these have lapsed between long-stay hospital patients and their families (58).

Employment and Occupation

Mental patients who obtain regular work on leaving the hospital tend to settle successfully in the community. For both

2. Now that discharge rates in Britain are so high, this correlation has disappeared.

psychotic and high-grade subnormal patients who are out of the hospital this correlation holds seemingly independent of their clinical condition (51, 59, 60, 61) and accords with the importance attached to occupational roles in industrial societies.

The chances of achieving regular employment can be improved when jobs are kept open during admission (30, 32, 59, 61). Jobs are more likely to be kept open for salaried workers than for wage earners, and this practice has probably contributed to the marked disparity in employment success between higher social classes and lower and between white-collar and manual workers (59, 62). Similar disparities between the social classes have been shown to exist among patients discharged from general hospitals (63). These results seem paradoxical, for most jobs rated high on the social scale make greater intellectual demands than manual jobs do. Possibly, higher-class jobs offer more scope for deviations from work routine. Alternatively, higher standards may exact better performance, as the association between high expectations and good performance suggests. Or patients entering mental hospitals from lower-class jobs may include higher proportions of people with deteriorated personalities who have drifted down the occupational scale.

Our ignorance underlines the need for research. These speculations derive from studies made after patients' release from psychiatric care, whereas the process of social selection of such patient populations had begun long before the research was undertaken. Studies of performance in patients observed at first admission or at the onset of illness might reshape our hypotheses. For instance, the duration of symptoms is known to affect outcome, and duration of symptoms in turn may be influenced by the type of work done. Responsible occupations that require contact with others might thus facilitate early recognition and entry into care, whereas secluded occupations or self-employment might delay them. Occupation influenced the chances of a patient's release from a Pennsylvania state mental hospital (55), but further study must establish the effects of such special features of occupations as social standing, relations with the public, intellectual demands, and special skills. Study from within the work organization itself is necessary in order to expand the opportunities available to mental patients.

Such studies could define the conditions most favorable to the integration of mental patients, including those related to foremen and men on the shop floor, as well as to the patient's functional capacity. The effects of the patient's dysfunction on production lines and incentive bonuses and the effects on workmates of his aberrant behavior or merely of his reputation for it are factors that must be taken into account in the recruiting and assimilation of mental patients to work groups. Special roles may be assumed by the individual on the shop floor according to his disability. The young mentally subnormal person may be accorded informal roles by the group with whom he works (64), as, for instance, pet, scapegoat, or intergroup messenger.

Probably much the same generalizations about employment and occupation apply to women workers as to men, and in the case of housewives the equivalent correlation for success after discharge must be with the performance of household tasks. Women who on their return from the hospital have to perform household tasks do better than those who do not. Their performance, like that of men, is related to expectations (65).

Employment chances are improved in the case of schizophrenic men who have had a lengthy stay in the hospital, and in the case of subnormal patients, by a period in a rehabilitation or industrial training center (66). Psychological studies give some leads about the kind of stimuli to which mental patients in training respond, with the caution that most results have been gathered from experiments that only simulate conditions of persisting groups and of real employment. Although schizophrenic patients function well in an aura of approval, experiments show that checks and admonitions seem to break through their retarded performance better than do competitive incentives and rewards (67). In effect, in these experiments patients with chronic schizophrenia did not act as though what they did were connected with rewards.

Unresponsiveness to experimental rewards in schizophrenic

patients could be characteristic of certain social relationships, as when the reward is offered by figures of authority or their representatives. G. Fairweather's experiment among chronic mentally ill patients, which studied patterns of response in the real-life setting of a rehabilitation program in a mental hospital, elaborates these results (38). The social structure of task-oriented work groups was found to be a critical variable in stimulating socially effective behavor. Autonomous groups working with a minimum of supervision were much superior to groups working in directed programs. In the undirected groups the underlying principles seemed to be the same as those that have been found by experiment in groups other than those of mental patients. Cooperation and identification between members can be induced by hinging individual rewards to group performance (68).

These results with schizophrenic patients are contrary to those obtained with severely subnormal patients. In workshop conditions subnormal patients respond well to incentives and rewards offered by figures of authority. Imbeciles can learn to carry out some simple tasks at the same speed as normal workers, although it takes them longer to learn. In Britain a surprising proportion, perhaps up to 10 per cent, of severely subnormal patients have been placed in open industry. In experiment, they have been found capable of retaining information and thus of transferring their learned abilities from one task to another, so that the period of training for subsequent tasks was reduced (69).

In their thinking and performance imbeciles lack the directional function of language. Their deficits in thinking arise chiefly from a failure to acquire information and to code it into words that relate accurately to appropriate objects. Consequently the normal links between the verbal system and motor behavior are weak. Some of their disability, however, resides in reluctance to handle symbols as well as in incapacity to do so. When forced into the use of symbols, they do better. There may thus be some hope of bringing about the association that is lacking between the verbal system and the system governing motor behavior (70).

The evidence on occupation and employment shows that much is to be gained for mental patients through training centers, through placement in appropriate work settings, and simply through the fact of employment. Coordinated use of facilities between psychiatrists and social workers, in the hospital and out, is wanted so that patients can make the best use of these opportunities.

References

(1) Pond D. A., Ryle A. and Hamilton M. 1963 Marriage and neurosis in a working class population *Brit J Psychiat* 109:592–598

Kreitman N. 1964 The patient's spouse *Brit J Psychiat* 110:159–173

Nielsen J. 1964 Mental disorders in married couples (assortative mating) *Brit J Psychiat* 110:683–697

Buck C. W. and Ladd K. L. 1965 Psychoneurosis in marital partners *Brit J Psychiat* 3:587–590

(2) Gruenberg E. M. 1957 Socially shared psychopathology in Leighton A., Clausen J. A. and Wilson R. *Explorations in Social Psychiatry* New York, Basic Books pp. 201–229

(3) Clausen J. A. and Yarrow M. R. 1955 Paths to the mental hospital *J Soc Issues* 11:25–32

Schwartz C. G. 1957 Perspectives on deviance: wives' definitions of their husbands' mental illness *Psychiat* 20:275–291

Sampson H., Messinger S. L. and Towne R. D. 1962 Family processes and becoming a mental patient *Amer J Sociol* 68:88–96

(4) Sampson H., Messinger S. L. and Towne R. D. 1964 *Schizophrenic Women: Studies in Marital Crisis* New York, Atherton

(5) Jackson J. K. 1954 The adjustment of the family to the crisis of alcoholism *Quart J Stud Alcohol* 15:562–586

Yarrow M. R., Schwartz C. G., Murphy H. S. and Deasy L. C. 1955 The psychological meaning of mental illness in the family *J Soc Issues* 11:12–24

(6) Hammer M. 1963–1964 Influence of small social networks as factors on mental hospital admission *Hum Org* 22:243–251

(7) Hutchinson G. B. 1960 Evaluation of preventive services *J Chron Dis* 2:497–508

(8) Gurin G., Veroff J. and Feld S. 1960 *Americans View Their Mental Health* Joint Commission on Mental Illness and Health Monogr Ser 4 New York, Basic Books

(9) Katz D. and Schanck R. L. 1938 *Social Psychology* New York, Wiley

(10) Kushlick A. 1962 Problems of co-ordination in centres for the subnormal in Susser M. W. and Kushlick A. *A Report on the Mental Health Services of Salford for 1961* City of Salford, Eng., Health Department pp. 7–11

(11) Berelson B. and Janowitz M. eds. 1950 *Reader in Public Opinion and Communication* New York, Free Press

Festinger L., Back K. W., Schachter S., Kelley H. and Thibaut J. 1950 *Theory and Experiment in Social Communication* Research Center for Group Dynamics Ann Arbor, University of Michigan Press

Hovland C. I., Janis I. L. and Kelley H. H. 1953 *Communication and Persuasion* New Haven, Yale University Press

Pennsylvania Mental Health Inc. 1960 *Mental Health Education: A Critique* Philadelphia, Pennsylvania Mental Health

(12) Nunnally J. C. 1961 *Popular Conceptions of Mental Health* New York, Holt, Rinehart & Winston

(13) Janis I. L. and Feshbach S. 1953 Effects of fear-arousing communications *J Abnorm Soc Psychol* 48:78–92

(14) Merton R. K., Fiske M. and Curtis A. 1946 *Mass Persuasion: The Social Psychology of a War Bond Drive* New York, Harper pp. 152–155

(15) Padilla E., Elinson J. and Perkins M. E. 1966 The public image of mental health professionals and acceptance of community mental health services *Amer J Pub Health* 56:1524–1529

(16) Taylor J. B. 1965 The organization of physician attitudes towards the emotionally disturbed patient *J Health Hum Behav* 6:99–104

(17) Susser M. W. 1962 Changing roles and co-ordination in mental health services in Halmos P. ed. *Sociology and Medicine: Studies within the Framework of the British National Health Service* Sociol Rev Monogr 5 pp. 61–90

Taylor Lord and Chave S. 1964 *Mental Health and Environment* London, Longmans

(18) Blane H. T. and Hill M. J. 1964 Public health nurses speak up about alcoholism *Nurs Outlook* 12:34–37

(19) Mendelson J. H. and Chafetz M. E. 1959 Alcoholism as an emergency ward problem *Quart J Stud Alcohol* 20:270–275

Chafetz M. E., Blane H. T., Abram H. S., Golner J., Lacy E., McCourt W. F., Clark E. and Meyers W. 1962 Establishing treatment relations with alcoholics *J Nerv Ment Dis* 134:395–409

Chafetz M. E., Blane H. T., Abram H. S., Clark E., Golner J., Hastie E. L. and McCourt W. F. 1964 Establishing treatment relations with alcoholics: a supplementary report *J Nerv Ment Dis* 138:390–393

(20) Hollingshead A. B. and Redlich F. C. 1958 *Social Class and Mental Illness* New York, Wiley

(21) Moore R. A., Benedek E. P. and Wallace J. G. 1963 Social class, schizophrenia and the psychiatrist *Amer J Psychiat* 120:149–154

(22) Gallagher E. B. and Levinson D. J. 1964 *Patienthood in the Mental Hospital* Boston, Houghton Mifflin

Riessman F., Cohen J. and Pearl A. eds. 1964 *Mental Health of the Poor* New York, Free Press

(23) Curle A. and Trist E. L. 1947 Transitional communities and social reconnection *Hum Rel* 1:42–69, 240–288

(24) Norris V. 1959 *Mental Illness in London* Maudsley Monogr 6 London, Oxford

(25) Brown G. W. 1959 Social factors influencing length of hospital stay of schizophrenic patients *Brit Med J* 2:1300–1302

(26) Freeman H. E. and Simmons O. G. 1963 *The Mental Patient Comes Home* New York, Wiley

(27) Goffman E. 1963 *Stigma* Englewood Cliffs, N. J., Prentice-Hall

(28) Brown G. W., Carstairs G. M. and Topping G. 1958 Post-hospital adjustment of chronic mental patients *Lancet* 2:685–689

(29) Brown G. W. 1959 Experiences of discharged chronic schizophrenic patients in various types of living groups *Milbank Mem Fund Quart* 37:105–131

(30) Renton C. A., Affleck J. W., Carstairs G. M. and Forrest A. D. 1963 A follow-up of schizophrenic patients in Edinburgh *Acta Psychiat Scand* 39:548–600

(31) Fischer G. J. 1965 Socio-economic factors and outcome of released mental patients: Influence of type of placement, occupational adjustment, compensation and type of hospital *J Health Hum Behav* 6:105–110

(32) Goldberg E. M. 1966 Hospital work and family: a four year study of young mental hospital patients *Brit J Psychiat* 112:177–196

(33) Davis J. A., Freeman H. E. and Simmons O. G. 1957 Re-hospitalization and performance level among former mental patients *Soc Prob* 5:37–44

(34) Angrist S., Dinitz S., Lefton M. and Pasamanick B. 1961 Social and psychological factors in the rehospitalization of female patients *Arch Gen Psychiat* 4:363–370

Dinitz S., Lefton M., Angrist S. and Pasamanick B. 1961 Psychiatric and social attributes as predictors of case outcome in mental hospitalization *Soc Prob* 8:322–328

(35) Lerner M. J. and Fairweather G. W. 1963 Social behavior of chronic schizophrenics in supervised and unsupervised work groups *J Abnorm Soc Psychol* 67:219–255

(36) Lerner M. J. 1963 Responsiveness of chronic schizophrenics to the social behavior of others in a meaningful task situation *J Abnorm Soc Psychol* 67:295–299

(37) Program Area Committee on Mental Health 1962 *Mental Disorders: A Guide to Control Methods* New York, American Public Health Association

(38) Fairweather G. ed. 1964 *Social Psychology in Treating Mental Illness: An Experimental Approach* New York, Wiley

(39) Brown G. W., Monck E. M., Carstairs G. M. and Wing J. K. 1962 The influence of family life on the course of schizophrenic illness *Brit J Prev Soc Med* 16:55–68

(40) Srole L., Langner T. S., Michael S. T., Opler M. K. and Rennie T. A. C. 1962 *Mental Health in the Metropolis: The Midtown Manhattan Study* New York, McGraw-Hill

(41) Esterson A., Cooper D. G. and Laing R. D. 1965 Results of family-oriented therapy with hospitalized schizophrenics *Brit Med J* 2:1462–1465

(42) Grad J. and Sainsbury P. 1963 Mental illness and the family *Lancet* 1:544–547

(43) Kay D. W. K., Beamish P. and Roth M. 1964 Old age mental disorders in Newcastle Upon Tyne: Part 1 A study of prevalence *Brit J. Psychiat* 110:146–158 Part 2 A Study of possible social and medical causes *Brit J Psychiat* 110:668–682

(44) Roth M. and Kay D. W. K. 1956 Affective disorder arising in the senium: II Physical disability as an aetiological factor *J Ment Sci* 102:141–150

(45) Macmillan D. 1958 Hospital-community relationships in *An Approach to the Prevention of Disability from Chronic Psychoses* New York, Milbank Memorial Fund pp. 29–39

(46) Adams M. 1956 Social work with mental defectives: Part I *Case Conf* 3:100–107

Adams M. 1957 Social work with mental defectives: Part II *Case Conf* 4:2–9

Tizard J. and Grad J. 1961 *The Mentally Handicapped and Their Families* Maudsley Monogr 7 London, Oxford

(47) Boles G. 1959 Personality factors in mothers of cerebral palsied children *Genet Psychol Monogr* 59:159–218

(48) Stein Z. A. and Susser M. W. 1963 The social distribution of mental retardation *Amer J Ment Defic* 67:811–821

(49) Susser M. W. and Watson W. 1962 *Sociology in Medicine* London, Oxford

(50) Stein Z. A. and Susser M. W. 1960 Estimating hostel needs for backward citizens *Lancet* 2:486–488

(51) Stein Z. A. and Susser M. W. 1960 The families of dull children: a classification for predicting careers *Brit J Prev Soc Med* 14:83–88

(52) Saenger G. 1960 *Factors Influencing the Institutionalization of Mentally Retarded Individuals in New York City* (report to the New York State Interdepartmental Health Resources Board)

Leeson J. E. 1963 The place of the hospital in the care of the mentally subnormal *Brit Med J* 1:713–717

(53) Stein Z. A. 1964 Some preliminary results of the survey of mental sickness in Salford in Susser M. W. *Report on the Salford Mental Health Services for 1963* City of Salford, Eng., Health Department

(54) Kramer M. 1965 *Some Implications of Trends in the Usage of Psychiatric Facilities for Community Mental Health Programs and Related Research* Paper read at annual meeting American College of Neuropsychopharmacology, San Juan

(55) Person P. H. 1964 *The Relationship Between Selected Social and Demographic Characteristics of Hospitalized Mental Patients and the Outcome of Hospitalization* Washington, D.C., American University

(56) Rawnsley K., Loudon J. B. and Miles H. L. 1962 Attitudes of relatives to patients in mental hospitals *Brit J Prev Soc Med* 16:1–15

(57) Eaton J. W. and Weil R. J. 1955 *Culture and Mental Disorders* New York, Free Press

Bott E. 1957 *Family and Social Network: Roles, Norms and External Relationships in Ordinary Urban Families* London, Tavistock

Townsend P. 1957 *The Family Life of Old People* London, Routledge

Willmott P. and Young M. 1960 *Family and Class in a London Suburb* London, Routledge

(58) Deykin E. 1965 The reintegration of the chronic schizophrenic patient discharged to his family and community in Greenblatt M., Solomon M. H., Evans A. S. and Brooks G. W. eds. *Drug and Social Therapy in Chronic Schizophrenia* Springfield, Ill., Thomas pp. 111–121

(59) Monck E. M. 1963 Employment experiences of 127 discharged schizophrenic men in London *Brit J Prev Soc Med* 17:101–110

(60) Charles D. C. 1953 Ability and accomplishment of persons earlier judged mentally deficient *Genet Psychol Monogr* 47:3–71

(61) Cohen L. 1955 Vocational planning and mental illness *Person Guid J* 34:28–32

(62) Cooper B. 1961 Social class and prognosis in schizophrenia: Parts 1 and 2 *Brit J Prev Soc Med* 15:17–41

(63) Ferguson T. and McPhail A. N. 1954 *Hospital and Community* London, Oxford

(64) Morgan D. 1965 Personal communication

(65) Dinitz S., Angrist S., Lefton M. and Pasamanick B. 1962 Instrumental role expectations and post-hospital performance of female mental patients *Social Forces* 40:248–254

(66) O'Connor N. and Tizard J. 1956 *The Social Problem of Mental Deficiency* London, Pergamon

Wing J. K. and Giddens R. G. T. 1959 Industrial rehabilitation of male chronic schizophrenic patients *Lancet* 2:505–507

(67) Winder C. L. 1960 Some psychological studies of schizophrenics in Jackson D. D. ed *The Etiology of Schizophrenia* New York, Basic Books

(68) Deutsch M. 1949 An experimental study of the effects of co-operation and competition upon group process *Hum Rel* 2:199–231

Deutsch M. 1949 A theory of co-operation and competition *Hum Rel* 2:129–152

(69) Clarke A. D. B. 1960 Laboratory and workshop studies of imbecile learning processes *Proceedings of the London Conference on the Scientific Study of Mental Deficiency* 1:90–96

(70) O'Connor N. and Hermlein B. 1963 *Speech and Thought in Severe Subnormality* Oxford, Pergamon

part two

Antecedent Factors in Mental Disorder: *Prospects for Prevention*

4

Preventable Stressors and Stress Responses

In the continuum of illness established mental disorder is a late stage at which to take action; no more can be accomplished than the lessening of the risks of chronicity through rehabilitation and through the stalling of recurrence. In the tradition of public health economical action demands primacy for preventing the onset of disorder.

This is not a demand that can now be satisfied by specific measures. To prevent a condition entirely we must be able to identify some crucial link in the sequences of environmental circumstances, agents, and personal make-up that give rise to it in the host organism. If we cannot identify causes, the clinical condition may yet be prevented or deflected if we can diagnose with reasonable certainty its precursors. Serological tests single out individuals susceptible to the chronic brain syndromes of syphilis. Lately hopes have been raised that biochemical tests might signal incipient schizophrenia or predisposition to it (1), although the precision of the tests and their validity as signs of schizophrenia remain in doubt (2). In the psychological field the symptoms attributed to stress responses are commonly conceived of as precursors of both psychic and somatic illnesses. The degree of certainty wanted in early diagnosis depends on an economic balance between the sensitivity and specificity of the diagnostic tests and the prevalence of the condition. Sensitive detectors may overdiagnose the risk and wastefully process false positives; specific detectors may underdiagnose the risk and dismiss potential cases as false negatives. In terms of effect related to cost, the predictive value of sensitive detectors is least in disorders of low frequency and improves with rising prevalence (3).

Identification of the causes or of the early stages of disease is a first requisite. Once we know what the precursors are, we must have the means to detect them, we must have treatment able to block their progress into overt clinical form, and we must be able to deliver the treatment and get it accepted by those in need of it. The present state of knowledge about functional mental disorder brings little of this program within immediate reach.

In a few conditions we know specific causes and appropriate remedies. The frequency and the possibilities of prevention of these conditions differ among societies. We can prevent the chronic brain syndromes of neurological syphilis by well-tried means of health education, case finding, treatment of early stages, and contact tracing. In industrial societies this condition in all its forms has become a rare one (although it has lately shown a rise in incidence). In preindustrial societies its distribution is patchy (for instance in black South Africans florid syphilis is common, but the tabetic form is exceedingly rare).

We can also hope to prevent those nutritional deficiencies that affect mental functioning. In industrial societies we can hope to prevent such nutritional deficiencies among the aged. Mass methods could possibly detect those in need of vitamins of the B complex. Chronic respiratory disorders give rise to an imbalance of nutrient oxygen and carbon dioxide in the brain. In countries like Britain where these disorders are common, screening could possibly be applied to detecting those who verge on hypercapnia. In preindustrial societies kwashiorkor in children and pellagra in adults can be averted by education in dietary matters and by the use of dietary supplements, although considerable barriers of poverty, contrary cultural values, and entrenched food habits may have to be overcome (4).

In a later chapter we shall consider the prevention of mental subnormality. Those forms that occur with chronic brain syndromes are in some degree amenable to methods of preventive medicine; the forms of cultural retardation without brain syndromes are more amenable to educational and social approaches. Alcoholism and other addictions give rise to clear-cut syndromes. The measures that can ward off the acute disorders from the toxicity of the addictions or from secondary nutritional deficiencies are known.

Epidemiologic study is beginning to describe the natural history of such disorders and to identify vulnerable groups. For instance, higher risks of suicide attend some attributes and some social circumstances: Risks are higher among men, among older people, and among those who live alone; the risks are much higher when there has been a previous attempt at suicide, a diagnosis of depression, or chronic sickness (5). Overt opiate addiction is being similarly defined. It appears to have a modal age and to be of limited duration (6). In this respect, and as an overt phenomenon that elicits the social reactions of secondary deviance, addiction resembles juvenile delinquency (7), psychopathic behavior, psychoneurosis (8), and possibly schizophrenia. (See Figure 4; see also Appendix A.) In the United States opiate users are found chiefly in younger age groups (with onset under 30 in about two thirds of cases and under 35 in about five sixths), in males, in large cities with minority populations, and in such specialized occupations as medicine and jazz music (6). This contrasts with other times and places. The chief users of the previous century were, it seems, older white women of the middle classes; chief users in England have been physicians, who until recently comprised 17 per cent of known addicts (9). These shifts in the distribution of the practice point to social processes and to its changing social functions. As yet, focused social action directed at vulnerable groups, either to prevent addiction or to bring those at risk of acute toxic disorders into timely treatment, remains largely untried.

Medicine and society are equipped to attack a number of mental disorders with specific causes (10). The ground of prevention is less sure with functional mental disorders in which the presumed causes are constitutional, psychological, or social. The main burden of this section will be to identify environmental circumstances and agents that give rise to functional mental illness or its precursors.

In theory they provide the leverage for prevention. This is not to gainsay the likelihood of benefit from sweeping social measures, as will emerge in our review. Edwin Chadwick fought for the independent circulation of water and sewage on the mistaken assumptions of the miasma theory. Although he opposed the germ theory to the end of his life and long after it had gained acceptance, his sanitary innovations prevented more disease than any single measure before and probably after.

The concept of *stress* is germane to this question. The word has been used to describe both stimuli in the environment and responses in the organism to those stimuli. Hans Selye named the stimuli stressors (11). Responses can be considered in four classes: immediate psychological reactions, immediate somatic reactions, chronic psychological reactions, and chronic somatic reactions. In this text "stressor" or "strain" will refer to stimulus, "stress" to the response.

Common observation is enough to tell us that stressors can provoke immediate psychological reactions. Research confirms these observations (12), and also that they can provoke immediate somatic reactions (13). In animals too, stressors provoke chronic somatic reactions and simulate natural disease process (11, 14). When we turn to chronic or recurrent somatic stress reactions *in man,* theory tends to outrun the data that can be garnered from experimental clinical medicine. Observations are taken from the course and treatment of such somatic disorders as asthma, urticaria and other skin reactions, colitis, and premenstrual syndromes; from the psychological states that coexist with these somatic states; and from histories of strain that preceded their onset (15). In a prospective study, family strain has been found to relate to upper respiratory infection (16). Peptic ulcer, ischemic heart disease, and hypertension have been subject to more extensive exploration. Because they give rise to serious and often fatal episodes, they come into the reach of hospital and death statistics and of investigators. In the case of duodenal ulcer the data suggest that stressors have a role. Anxiety induced by situation or by personality coexists with the lesion and precedes some of its complications like perforation (17). In ischemic heart disease (18) and in hypertension (19), a body of work points in the same direction. In all these conditions, however, the results have not always been confirmed by other approaches (20). The evidence is marred by weak methods or by its very nature: Unknowable antecedents cloud all retrospective studies of disorders that appear fully developed, like Athena when she sprang from Zeus' head, despite a slow but invisible unfolding.

The study of stressors in chronic psychological disorders is beset by the same problems. In addition, diagnosis is less certain. The definition of the case is a central problem of the epidemiology of mental illness. If we acknowledge that a case of mental illness is defined with difficulty, we also acknowledge that it is difficult to be precise about the effects of exposure to strain. For other reasons it is equally difficult to be precise about stressors. Classification aids precision, and the following discussion aims to classify stressors in social terms. First the extreme situations of war and combat will be considered, second the social transitions of civilian life, and third the deprivations of anomie, isolation, and social disintegration.

References

(1) Friedhoff A. J. and Van Winkel E. 1962 Isolation and characterization of a compound from the urine of schizophrenics *Nature* 194:897–898

Bourdillon R. E., Clarke C. A., Ridges A. P., Sheppard P. M., Harper P. and Leslie S. A. 1965 "Pink spot" in the urine of schizophrenics *Nature* 208:453–455

(2) Takesada M., Kakimoto Y., Sano I. and Kaneko Z. 1963 3, 4-dimethoxyphenylethylamine and other amines in the urine of schizophrenic patients *Nature* 199:203–204

Perry T. L., Hansen S. and MacIntyre L. 1964 Failure to detect 3, 4-dimethoxyphenylethylamine in urine of schizophrenics *Nature* 202:519–520

(3) Vecchio T. J. 1966 Predictive value of a single diagnostic test in unselected populations *New Eng J Med* 274:1171–1173

(4) Wiener J. S. and Hope J. M. 1959 Cerebral manifestations of vitamin B 12 deficiency *JAMA* 170:1038–1041

Cravioto J. 1964 Malnutrition and behavioral development in the pre-school child *Conference on the Prevention of Malnutrition in the Pre-School Child* Washington, D.C., Pan American Health Organization

Exton-Smith A. M. and Stanton B. 1965 *Report of an Investigation into the Dietary Habits of Elderly Women Living at Home* London, King Edward's Hospital Fund

Read A. E., Gough K. R., Pardoe J. L. and Nicholas A. 1965 Nutritional studies on the entrants to an old peoples' home with particular reference to folic acid deficiency *Brit Med J* 2:843–848

Brockington C. F. and Lempert S. 1966 *Social Needs of the Over-80's* Manchester, Manchester University Press

(5) Sainsbury P. 1955 *Suicide in London* Maudsley Monogr 1 London, Chapman & Hall

MacMahon B., Johnson S. and Pugh T. F. 1963 Relation of suicide rates to social conditions *Public Health Rep* 78:285–293

Gardner E. A., Bahn A. K. and Mack M. 1964 Suicide and psychiatric care in the aging *Arch Gen Psychiat* 10:547–553

(6) Winick C. 1965 Epidemiology of narcotics use in Wilner D. M. and Kassebaum G. G. eds. *Narcotics* New York, McGraw-Hill

(7) Glueck S. and Glueck E. T. 1945 *After-Conduct of Discharged Offenders* London, Macmillan

(8) Shepherd M. and Gruenberg E. M. 1957 The age for neuroses *Milbank Mem Fund Quart* 35:258–265

(9) Her Majesty's Government 1955 *Report to the United Nations on the Working of the International Treaties on Narcotics and Drugs for 1965* London, Home Office

(10) Carstairs G. M. 1958 Preventive psychiatry, is there such a thing? *J Ment Sci* 104:63–71

Gruenberg E. M. 1959 Prevention of mental disorders *J Chron Dis* 9:187–198

Program Area Committee on Mental Health 1962 *Mental Disorders: A Guide to Control Methods* New York, American Public Health Association

(11) Selye H. 1950 *The Physiology and Pathology of Exposure to Stress* Montreal, Acta

(12) Lindemann E. 1944 Symptomatology and management of acute grief *Amer J Psychiat* 101:141–148

Janis I. L. 1958 *Psychological Stress* New York, Wiley

(13) Wolf S. and Wolff H. G. 1947 *Human Gastric Function* London, Oxford

Grinker R. 1953 *Psychosomatic Research* New York, Norton

Hill S. R. Jr. 1956 Studies on adreno-cortical and psychological response to stress in man *Arch Intern Med* 97:269–298

Engel G. L. 1962 *Psychological Development in Health and Disease* Philadelphia, Saunders

(14) Wolff H. G. 1956 *The Stress of Life* New York, McGraw-Hill

(15) Funkenstein D. H. 1953 The relationship of experimentally produced asthmatic attacks to certain acute life stresses *J Allergy* 24:11–17

Prugh D. G., Staub E. M., Sands H. H., Kirschbaum R. M. and Lenihan E. A. 1953 A study of the emotional reactions of children and families to hospitalization and illness *Amer J Orthopsychiat* 23:70–106

Coleman R., Greenblatt M. and Solomon H. C. 1956 Physiological evidence of rapport during psychotherapeutic interviews *Dis Nerv Syst* 17:71–77

Rees L. 1956 Psychosomatic aspects of asthma in elderly patients *J Psychosom Res* 1:212–218

Dalton K. 1960 Effect of menstruation on schoolgirls' weekly work *Brit Med J* 1:326–328

Sainsbury P. 1960 Psychosomatic disorders and neurosis in out-patients attending a general hospital *J Psychosom Res* 4:261–273

Coppen A. and Kessel N. 1963 Menstruation and Personality *Brit J Psychiat* 109:711–721

Friedman S. B., Chodoff P., Mason J. W. and Hamburg D. A. 1963 Behavioral observations on parents anticipating the death of a child *Pediatrics* 32:Part I, 610–625

Pond D. A., Ryle A. and Hamilton M. 1963 Marriage and neurosis in a working class population *Brit J Psychiat* 109:592–598

(16) Meyer R. and Haggerty R. J. 1962 Streptococcal infections in families *Pediatrics* 29:539–549

(17) For reviews see:

Doll R., Jones F. A. and Buckatzsch M. M. 1951 *Occupational Factors in the Aetiology of Gastric and Duodenal Ulcers* Spec Rep Ser Med Res Counc No. 276, London, H. M. Stationery Office

Mirsky I. A. 1958 Physiologic, psychologic and social determinants in the etiology of duodenal ulcer *Amer J Dig Dis* 3:285–314

Susser M. W. 1967 Causes of peptic ulcer: a selective epidemiological review *J Chron Dis* 20:435–456

(18) Friedman M., Rosenman R. H. and Carrol V. 1958 Changes in the serum cholesterol and blood clotting time in men subjected to cyclic variation of occupational stress *Circulation* 17:852–861

Friedman M. and Rosenman R. H. 1959 Association of specific overt behavior pattern with blood and cardiovascular findings *JAMA* 169:1286–1296

Paffenbarger R. S., Notkin J., Krueger D. E., Wolf P. A., Thorne M. C., LeBauer E. J. and Williams F. L. 1966 Chronic disease in former college students: II Methods of study and observation on mortality from coronary heart disease *Amer J Pub Health* 56:962–971

(19) Cort J. H., Fencl V., Hejl Z. and Jirka J. eds. 1961 *Symposium on the Pathogenesis of Essential Hypertension* Prague, State Medical Publishing Co.

Geiger H. J. and Scotch N. A. 1963 The epidemiology of essential hypertension: I Biologic mechanisms and descriptive epidemiology *J Chron Dis* 16:1151–1182

Scotch N. A. and Geiger H. J. 1963 The epidemiology of essential hypertension: II Psychologic and socio-cultural factors in etiology *J Chron Dis* 16:1183–1213

(20) For example see:

Storment C. T. 1951 Personality and heart disease *Psychosom Med* 13:304–313

Franks C. M. and Leigh D. 1959 The theoretical and experimental application of a conditioning model to a consideration of bronchial asthma in man *J Psychosom Res* 4:88–98

Bainton C. R. and Peterson D. R. 1963 Deaths from coronary heart disease in persons 50 years of age and younger: a community-wide study *New Eng J Med* 268:569–575

5

Stressful Situations: Extremes of War and Social Transitions

The best hope of getting answers in the study of stress lies with research that can be sure of the existence of the stressor, that can define the population at risk of exposure to it, and that can sort out with certainty the fact of exposure and the dose. Such stressors have been sought among armed forces in wartime (1).

The Extremes of War

Troops are exposed to measurable and clearly perceived risks of bodily injury and death or to prolonged fatigue. They are populations always under observation and their movements are known.

The results obtained in research of this kind have been more equivocal than might have been expected. To define cases in a standard way throughout the observed population of the wartime forces was as slippery a matter as in peacetime. Standards varied with the practice of physicians in different areas and with fluctuating demands for manpower. To obtain data investigators had to rely on records maintained to satisfy administrative and clinical needs and not those of research (2, 3). In comparing groups it was difficult to rule out the effects of selection for occupations and tasks by special social and personal characteristics. For instance in the Royal Air Force in Britain the rate of psychiatric breakdown of airgunners was greater than that of other aircrew. The greater rate could have been due to their occupation. It could also have been due to their selection from certain social classes and from those who in training had failed to qualify as pilots (4).

The relationship to be expected between heavy casualties and high rates of reported sickness was found. Mental breakdown, however, was not proportional to amount of strain. Among bomber crews of the Royal Air Force the highest rate of breakdown occurred early in the standard operational tour of thirty sorties. It seems that some men were predisposed to stress reactions, and their vulnerability was made evident soon after exposure (5). These epidemiologic results reinforced clinical observations (3, 6).

Civilians were also studied. Investigations of absenteeism among factory workers found high rates of neurotic illness. Ten per cent of workers were thought to show definite neurotic illness and another 20 per cent nondisabling neurotic symptoms. The symptoms were greater where hours were longest and the physical conditions of lighting and noise were worst (7).

Indexes for whole civilian populations in World War II, however, revealed patterns at first sight contrary to the predictions of a stress hypothesis. Rates for mental hospital admissions and for suicide declined during the war. Interpretation must be guarded because of the abnormal times, yet these results were repeated in several countries (8, 9).

Each level of biosocial organization must be studied and interpreted in its own terms. Results obtained at the individual level of the psyche cannot be transposed directly to the social level of population groups, nor vice versa. Generalizations that hold at one level must be stated as hypotheses to be tested at another level. The results for the civilian populations as a whole are explicable in terms of Émile Durkheim's hypothesis that war rouses collective sentiment, integrates individuals into groups, and strengthens morale. Durkheim advanced this hypothesis to explain his finding that suicide rates dropped with remarkable consistency through the wars waged by many nations at different times in the nineteenth century (10).

The nature of society permits few generalizations that will hold at all extremes of time, place, and population. Thus in World War II no consistent drop in suicide rates was found in German cities exposed to the disruptive effects of strategic bombing (11). Bombing of cities was a new strategy of war. It depressed the morale of civilians and might have been expected to affect suicide rates in ways different from previous wars. The relation between strain and reaction, in this case as in that of bomber crews, was curvilinear. Thus the effects on civilian morale showed on light exposure to bombing; morale was little influenced by greater exposure (12).

Stressors cannot be isolated in pure culture, separate from the factors making for resistance to them. Resistance depends in part on the situations in which they occur. Like morale, rates of psychiatric breakdown in the armies of World War II were influenced by the sets of social relations that enmeshed soldiers (13). Societies prescribe styles of behavior, and these affected rates of breakdown among troops exposed to the same conditions. Indian soldiers had lower rates than their British officers in the jungles of Arakan, and they were distressed by different things (14). The Indians were reported less troubled than the British by hand-to-hand fighting, killing, and capture and more troubled by loss of face, physical ailments, and hospital care.

Culture regulates behavior partly through controls built into the personality by socialization and partly through expectations with which it unendingly confronts the individual in his social life. Small primary groups were the chief media of social life and expectations for fighting troops, and they had a powerful effect on behavior. Soldiers fought on against hopeless odds because the excessive dangers of death and injury were distant compared with the lesser but immediate dangers of losing the affection and approval of comrades. The power of group relations, recognized and exploited by army psychiatrists in World War I, was relearned in later wars. The psychiatrists found that the prognosis for return to duty was much better when psychiatric treatment was given in the forward lines than when the soldiers were withdrawn to the rear and treated there (13, 15).

The psychiatrists themselves were an important influence in prognosis. The psychiatrist at the rear referred for his criteria to his professional colleagues and traditional training; he saw patients as isolated individuals and their primary need as relief from strain. He faced conflict in returning a soldier to the front line that was the source of his strain. The psychiatrist at the front, on the other hand, referred for his criteria to fellow soldiers who were combat troops; he saw patients as members of a group and restoration to their function in the group as their primary need (15). These were accurate perceptions of the realities for fighting men placed in the two situations. A civilian analogy can be found in the success of psychiatric patients rehabilitated through task-oriented groups and their failure after discharge to a civilian life independent of the groups (16). (See pp. 50 ff.)

We may reasonably conclude that in war threats of death and injury and the fatigue and harsh working conditions affected the mental health of some participants in the short term. Little knowledge is available on their effects in the long term. Among United States veterans poor postwar adjustment was more frequent with older men who were unschooled and unskilled, with the single state or broken marriages, with ineffective wartime performance, and with overseas service of long duration (17). Studies of survivors of Nazi concentration camps suggest that in the aftermath the victims suffered an excess of mental illness, especially depressive, paranoid, and hysterical reactions described in Scandinavia as "reactive psychosis" (18). Their experiences were so diverse and manifold that the studies cannot isolate particular stressors or particular situations that gave rise to them. Inmates of concentration camps were beaten and starved at the same time as they were terrorized by threats and murder. Thus 90 per cent of some survivors with severe psychosocial problems are reported to have shown signs of permanent cerebral damage (19). Other ill-treated prisoners of war and survivors of disasters seem to have experienced similar psychological problems in the aftermath (20).

Taken together these studies of war and disaster suggest that extreme strain can have, in both the long and the short term, effects on mental state that are pathological by any clinical criterion. They demonstrate the power of external stressors in mental disorder if not the means for their prevention in normal circumstances.

Most wartime strains are atypical in intensity and in nature. Attention turned to the common round of civilian life might give a better foundation for prevention. Physiological responses to social situations have been well described (21). The next step is to seek out within the contemporary environment the patterns of social situations that can produce such responses.

Social Transitions

Social transitions that impose a readjustment of status and roles on an individual, some authors suggest, can lead to continuing emotional disturbance. These transitions are seen as crises (22). The individual in crisis suffers inner tension, unpleasant feelings, and disorganized behavior. He therefore strives to regain his equilibrium. Some solutions for disequilibrium are adaptive; emotional demands may thus be gratified or forgone. Other solutions are nonadaptive; in such cases the emotional disturbance may become chronic and irreversible (23). Given the validity of this concept, the transitional crisis could become a target for preventive work. Social transitions could be used as markers of vulnerable segments of the population. It is therefore a concept worth exploring.

Transitional crises include entry into school, transfer from one school to another and leaving school, the separation of children from families, migration, marriage, pregnancy and childbirth, bereavement, and retirement. These transitions have in common abrupt abdication from past statuses and the assumption of new statuses. Transitions must always be bound up with the values and feelings attached to the old statuses, as well as to the new statuses and their surrounding circumstances. The social and emotional significance of various transitions can be differentiated accordingly. Some transitions enlarge the individual's standing and competence; others diminish them. Some convert him to membership of a minority that may be more or less valued than the majority. Some transitions are desired, socially approved, and consonant with the individual's lines of development, and others are involuntary, rejected, and dissonant.

Transitions can be treated in three classes. They can be normal steps on the upward curve of the life arc. They can be normal steps in the downward curve of the life arc. Finally, they can be abnormal steps, accidents of life that affect minorities.

Normal Upward Steps. Entering and leaving school, marriage, and maternity, are stepping stones to enhanced statuses and new roles and obligations in the continuous process of growth and development. For the majority, strain is attached to negotiating the transitions, to assuming the responsibilities of the new status, and to learning its appropriate behavior. For a minority, strain is attached to failure to negotiate the transition. Those who fail to take a normal upward step remain in inferior or deviant social positions. In social terms they may appear to be in a state of arrested development or to combine a set of inconsistent statuses. This minority among the candidates for normal transitions probably has more psychiatric significance than the majority, although the original hypothesis was focused on those who change their status successfully. Examples are school children who are retarded, children who leave school and who fail to obtain employment, men and women who never marry, and married couples who are sterile.

School experience is clearly demarcated. It is a ready marker for research and prevention, and the captive school population is easily reached (24). Referral to child guidance clinics on all counts, and in particular for school phobia, is most common at ages usual for school entry and for transfer from one school to another (25). The high rate of referral at these ages may be due to the transition. Some thus ascribe school phobia to the child's anxiety about his separation from the mother and home (26). The referrals may also be due, however, to pre-existing behavior made apparent by the child's new role rather than to a stress response. Even so, in social terms the high referral rates must reflect strain in the social system of the school as well as failure of the individual child to accommodate to the new roles required of him.

Prompt intervention, it is claimed, helps children with school phobia to resume normal school careers and prevents chronicity (27, 28). Young children seem to respond to treatment; older ones are stubborn. The same symptoms seen in children of different ages, however, may not have the same clinical meaning (29). The children whose symptom of school refusal persists into adolescence could be suffering from a more severe condition than those in elementary school whose symptom remits under treatment. The remission among younger children may be spontaneous. Although nail biting, tics, tantrums, bed wetting, nervousness, and nightmares are often taken to signify mental disturbance, the interpretation of these symptoms must be qualified in the light of their frequent occurrence among all children (30, 31). They are so common at some ages and in some social groups that they can be regarded as falling within norms of development. Few efforts have been made to test directly the relationship of any of these symptoms to situations that might cause them. Relationships with situations have been demonstrated for nocturnal enuresis (32) but not in studies concerned with transition.

For a child, emotional disturbance is significant in itself. But its significance for his adult mental state has still to be clarified. Children who have attended child guidance clinics, according to some follow-up studies, experience large amounts of mental and social disturbance as adults (33). In another study little disturbance was found in later years (34). The source of the conflicting results is likely to reside in research method, for instance in the differing selection of children for clinics by local referral systems. No evidence is to hand to show that clinic treatment alters outcome (35).

Later at adolescence, the typical manifestations of disturbance have been described as a "crisis of identity" (36). The crisis reflects the child's problems in relinquishing his statuses in family and school, and his searchings about the nature and availability of adult statuses. Such crises are characteristic of societies in which much depends on individual choice and achievement and in which few adult statuses are ascribed by birth. Thus the psychological expression of the structural conflict between generations does not appear in the same forms in all societies and in all social classes (37). No epidemiologic studies seem to be available to confirm clinical impressions and to relate stress responses to the strains of adolescence.

Deviant behavior at the time of adolescence is better documented. A survey of European countries showed that all had registered an increase in adolescent crime and delinquency in the 1950s (38). In Britain (as elsewhere) rates of suicide, drinking offenses, crimes of violence, sex offenses, and road accidents have all risen (39). Many delinquents emerge from the lower social classes, their families tend to be large, and they often lack a father as breadwinner and figure of authority (40). The cause is not poverty alone, since rising living standards have accompanied rising rates of registered deviance.

Plausible theories point to the discordance between the roles prescribed and approved by the culture and the possibilities it affords of attaining them (41). Hence the association of delinquency with juvenile unemployment in the slums and ghettos of many large cities. In this view deviant behavior at adolescence is more an example of failure to negotiate transition than of the strains of transition itself. This failure results in an inappropriate combination of statuses, for instance of adulthood and economic dependence.

Strain produced by similar discordant combinations of statuses can be the lot of a minority at each stage of the life cycle. Adolescent girls who become pregnant or even marry while at school, or university students who start families before they can support them, have embarked on careers with a narrower set of choices than is available to the majority of their peers (42).

In the transition of *marriage,* epidemiological data show that those individuals affected to the degree that it produces mental disorder can be only a small minority of the large population exposed. In the achieved state of marriage, the risk of admission to mental hospitals is lowest. The risk rises in a gradient through the single, the widowed, and the divorced (43, 44).

Because single patients lack social support and mental hospitals provide social support, these rates could be more an index of response to a social than to a psychological strain, but the results hold outside the hospital. The incidence of new cases from a defined community coming into all kinds of special psychiatric service, when care is taken to control the factor of age, has been found to be distinctly lower among the married than the single, especially for men (45).

The married state thus seems more likely to cushion strain than to cause it. The highest rates of mental illness occur among divorced persons of both sexes and among single men. These relationships between rates by marital state appear reliable. Rates reported from prevalence surveys in Midtown Manhattan and from a study of old people in a city in New York resemble others from incidence studies reported from Norway; from Aberdeen, Scotland; from Salford, England; and from Monroe County, New York (45, 46, 47, 48, 49). The relationships of rates with marital state remain much the same when reports of subjective states of "happiness" are taken as the index (50).

Two mechanisms, which can be described as reactive and selective, may underlie these distributions. The predominant incidence of schizophrenia and of the psychopathies (including character disorders and sociopathic personalities) is among young single men and divorced persons. These disorders could represent reaction to the strains of the single state. Prolonged bachelorhood is deviant in that it marks either failure to take up a prescribed role or withdrawal from it. It also carries social and psychological penalties. With schizophrenia and the psychopathies, however, a selective mechanism is likely to be at work. Thus in a ten-year follow-up of a prevalence survey in one Swedish community, men with "abnormal personalities" were reported to have married less often than expected (51).

These results support a clinical impression of incompatibility between the demands of marriage and the schizophrenic personality. Marriage may be a crucial proving ground for that group of people vulnerable to schizophrenia who do marry. An intensive family study in California puts it further that in some young married women the difficulties of the marriage role itself can precipitate overt schizophrenia (52). In Puerto Rico too a family study (of a sample of marriages in which either spouse was schizophrenic) emphasized the strains for women among the poor of a male-dominated urban culture (53). In both these studies the schizophrenic break coincided with the early stages of marriage, but the surveys were not designed in a manner to test the imputation that marrying was the cause.

In the case of depression and psychoneurosis, the age distributions of inception suggest that predominant strains that can induce these reactions must be sought later in marriage and not at the point of transition to the married state. Peaks occur in the thirty-to-forty-year age group, a decade later than the most nubile age. These peak rates are higher among the single than the married, however, and the lower rates in middle age are low particularly among the married. (See Appendix A.)

The interpretation of these rates for marital state with age is complicated. Thus emotional disturbances mutual to married couples rise in frequency with the duration of the conjugal relationship (54). Mental illness among hospital patients has been recognized more frequently in both spouses, and the diagnosis is more often concordant, than would be expected by chance (55).

The possible explanations are several. Individuals of like constitution may marry (assortative mating) (56); partners may react in accord to shared environmental strain, to illness in the other, or to mutual interaction between them; finally the recognition and treatment of mental illness in one spouse may facilitate the recognition and entry into treatment of the other. The increasing concordance with duration of marriage found in couples not in psychiatric care (54) suggests that reaction is one of the mechanisms at work. The time of danger, however, does not coincide with the nuptial transition.

In the Salford data on the distributions of each diagnostic category by age, marital state emerges as a powerful factor that can outweigh even so basic an attribute as sex. The curves for the two sexes in each marital state resemble each other, while the curves for different marital states diverge a good deal from each other. (See Figure 1; see also Appendix A.) Neither selection nor reaction taken alone provide satisfying explanations for these patterns. Both are likely to be active, although in different proportion for different illnesses. One selective force can be discounted in the Salford data and in those of other registers, in contrast with mental hospital data. Although the unmarried may enter mental hospitals because they obtain the domestic support they lack at home, this factor cannot explain the similar findings in outpatient services.

The high rates of mental illness among the divorced could be taken also to support a reactive hypothesis. Their rates so far exceed those of the single, in whom the selective mechanism operates at high level, that added causes must be at work. These causes, however, may lie in an artifact of enumeration. The remarriage rate of divorcees is high, the population at risk is a fluid one, and the remainder of unmarried divorcees are the subject of considerable selection.

Maternity, with its increment of socially valued statuses, brings roles that are more demanding. Maternity is associated with mental disorder in the form of the common and transient puerperal depressions and in the form of the much rarer puer-

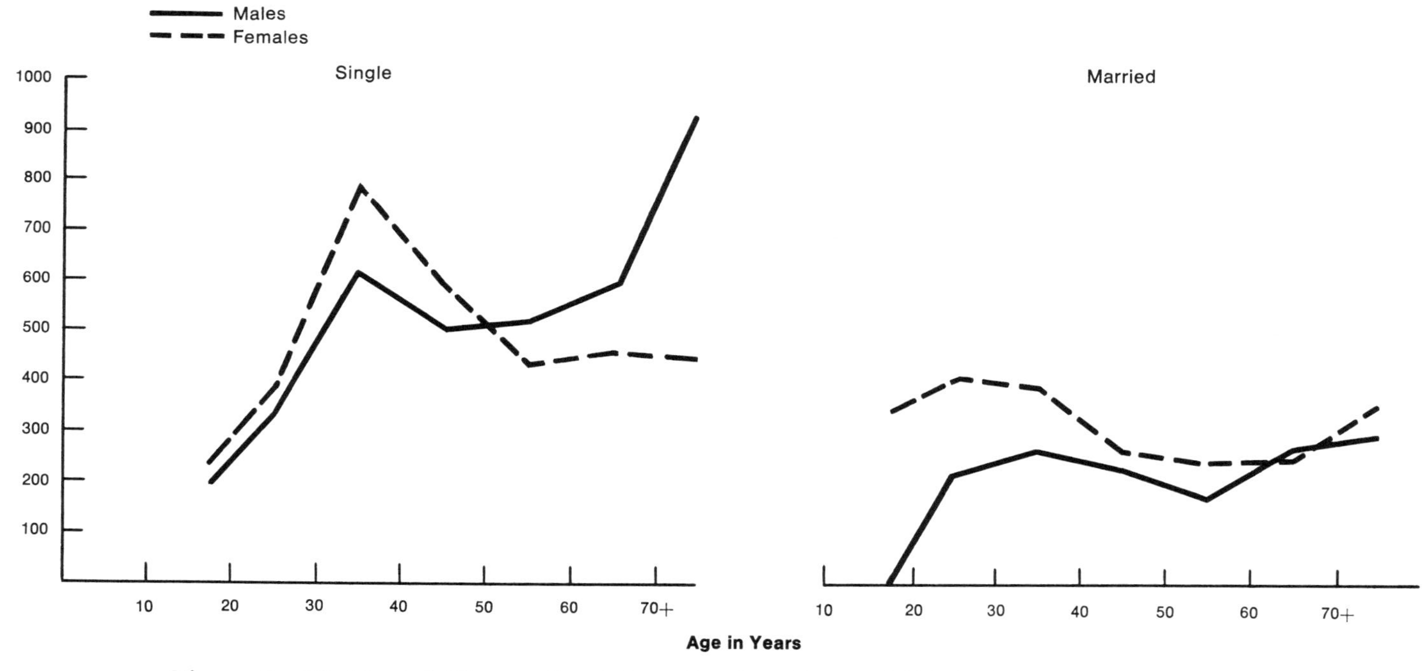

Figure 1. All Mental Illness—Inceptions by Age, Sex, and Marital State, Salford (1959–1963), Average Annual Rates Per 100,000

peral psychoses. The recurrence, in some cases, of psychosis with the puerperium suggests that the association is a result of more than coincidence. In the century since the first comprehensive work on the subject (57), studies in support have gradually accumulated (58), although some are in contention (59). The association of psychosis with the time of parturition can be accepted (60).

More study is needed to separate the factors of exogenous strain from predisposition to psychosis. Among exogenous strains social, physiological and psychological factors must also be separated. Physiological disturbance is well established at and after parturition (61), even to the extent of precipitating heart failure (62). Thus peripartum heart failure, like puerperal psychosis, tends not to occur in the first forty-eight hours after parturition (63). A controlled study, however, found no link between the physical and psychic aspects of puerperium (64). In line with this finding, multiple births are not associated with puerperal psychosis, although they add to the physiological strain of parturition and predispose to peripartum heart failure.

In the class of normal upward transitions, each is a break in continuous development that enhances status. Only a few individuals in the large exposed population exhibit prolonged stress responses in association with them. Good evidence is lacking to show that these transitions themselves cause or precipitate mental disorder, except after childbirth in the puerperium. Indeed, in the case of marriage for men at all ages and for women after their early twenties in the Anglo-American culture, the transition is more likely to cushion than to provoke strain.

Normal Downward Steps. Bereavement, and retirement for men and working women, are normal breaks each of which brings a decrement in statuses and roles, a diminution of obligations and a loss of standing.

The elaboration of the study of grief in the context of disaster and *bereavement* provided the initial impetus for research into the psychic effects of transition states in general (65). Clinical and field studies have described a characteristic unfolding of emotional disturbance with downward transitions among recent widows (66) and among retired men (67). In the field study of the families of young married lower-class schizophrenic men and women and their controls in Puerto Rico, intense grief following the loss of a child was a significant event that preceded the onset of schizophrenia in women (53).

There are few rigorous studies to confirm the reality and the strength of these various associations. In the case of bereavement a secondary analysis of hospital and census data does point to a higher incidence than expected of mental disorder, particularly of depression among middle-aged people (68). In particular, the number whose illness followed loss of a spouse was six times greater than an expected number calculated from death rates of the general population. This result is supported by the high inception rates of mental illness found in widows and widowers in the Salford survey.

Close standardization of age is needed in comparisons of married and widowed among old people, just as in comparisons of married and single (see Chapter 8, p. 195), because the frequencies of both widowhood and inceptions of mental illness rise rapidly at these ages (69). (See Appendix A.) Although some of the difference between the married and the widowed is erased by age standardization, it holds for depression among men and for senile dementia. (See Appendix A.) Among the widowed suicide rates also are high (70, 71). Good evidence of the causal effects of widowhood comes from the clustering of suicides, as compared with other deaths among widows, in the first years of bereavement (71). The high rate of mental disorders among the widowed in Salford also has the appearance of a true transition phenomenon, as the effect was greatest early in the widowed state. (See Appendix F.)

Much attention has been given to bereavement in childhood as a cause of mental disorder in later life (72). Loss of a parent by death as a cause of mental disorder has been the subject of many studies. We have noted the association of juvenile delinquency with the loss of fathers, but delinquent behavior cannot without qualification be attributed to mental disorder. The results of studies relating the mother's death to mental disorders are conflicting and often negative (73); the associations with other forms of maternal loss are usually more striking. For instance, the mother's active departure because of separation, divorce, or desertion, but not her death, could be related to attempted suicide in one study, and to enuresis in boys in another (32, 74).

The transition with bereavement is not uncommonly a passage into social isolation, especially among the aged. The possible contributions of the subsequent isolated state must therefore be taken into account in weighing cause and effect in bereavement reactions. (See pp. 123 ff.) In the case of *retirement* one can infer from the available data a sharp increase at least in declared morbidity and the consequent assumption of the sick role (37) if not in actual disease (49).

Accidental Transitions. A third group of transitions are not normal discontinuities either in phases of development or of replacement. Such discontinuities as the premature separation of a child from his home or migration between countries are accidents of experience, abnormal events that affect minorities in the population. No transition can be isolated from the configuration of circumstances in which it occurs. In normal transitions circumstances tend toward homogeneity; variation is limited by social norms that apply to the whole population. In the transitions that are accidental or special, circumstances are much more heterogeneous; in these cases circumstances must be more closely defined in order to specify possible effects.

The effects of *premature separations* on young children cannot be discussed without considering the cause of the separation, the age of the child, the duration of the separation, the circumstances under which the child leaves and those under which he enters, and the norm for separations in the population. For a child separation is always associated with a loss of statuses that are both socially and emotionally valued. The immediate distress of a young child separated from his home, for example by admission to a hospital, is often obvious and unlikely to be disputed (75).

The child's reactive behavior in response to the separation

may continue for some time after his return home, Persisting distress and other "sleeper" effects, which only become apparent after a latent period, have proved more difficult to demonstrate, even with long separations. There were hardly any discernible effects in children who spent long periods in tuberculosis sanatoriums as compared with controls who had stayed with their families (76).

Long separations that follow on the disruption of the families of young children have been more securely linked with emotional and behavior disorders. Much of the evidence is open to criticism and has indeed been criticized, but its sum is impressive (72, 77). The situations that precede the separation and those that follow it are probably of more importance than the transition itself. Many of the affected children have experienced severe deprivations in their own homes before separation (78). Their experiences after separation may bring further sensory, emotional, and social deprivations (79, 80). The power of selective factors was not always appreciated in the early studies (81). Selection can be entirely unbiased only with random allocation in experimental studies, but separations of children from mothers have been simulated in animal experiments. In the socialization of these animals, experiences subsequent to separation with a variety of mechanical substitutes for mothers and with a variety of social relations exert profound influences on behavior (82, 83).

Among separated children substitute homes can be reparative or noxious or both at once. Furthermore, they can influence nutrition and growth as well as the psyche. This information resulted from serendipitous discovery in a nutritional experiment in postwar Germany (84). The children of two orphanages were observed with most of the obvious variables that affect growth under control. Disparate rates of growth nonetheless emerged. The plausible hidden variable was the personality and behavior of the matrons and their emotional relations with the children in their charge. Widdowson takes a biblical text to illustrate her discovery: Better a dinner of herbs where love is, than a stalled ox and hatred withal.

Another study used nocturnal enuresis as an index of behavior that was likely to be sensitive to circumstances in substitute homes and that could yet be measured with fair accuracy (85). The symptom was found to persist longest in those children who had experienced the earliest and the most severe disruption of their homes. Among children all of whom had experienced prolonged separation, however, the symptom persisted longer in those placed in residential homes than in foster homes. It appeared that socialization through an exclusive and intimate relation with a mother, or even a foster mother, was more conducive to the norm of acquiring sphincter control than socialization through less diffuse and less exclusive relations with the adults and children in a children's home.

The stage of development at which experiences take place is also significant. Disturbances have often been shown to follow on early separations, seldom on late ones. But some stages may be critical for a particular aspect of development (83, 86). Thus children acquired sphincter control of the bladder at night later than their peers if their mothers had taken up work outside the home in the phase of "primary socialization" (or to be precise, when the children were aged six to twelve months) (87).

The knowledge that different long-term effects are elicited from children by dissimilar experiences of substitute homes can be put to use in remedial work and prevention. Clinical observation of treatment supports this deduction (88).

The problems of assessing the stress of the transitions of *migration* resemble those of assessing premature separations. Transitions of migration are of increasing import, for upward social mobility accompanied by geographical mobility is the common condition of large classes in both preindustrial and industrial societies. Furthermore, the pre-existing conditions of the migrant population and the conditions to which it is subsequently exposed can have as much significance for mental health as the transitions of status themselves (9, 37, 89).

For example, the transition from impoverished peasant in the countryside to proletarian in a fast-growing city bears little comparison with the transition from metropolitan scientist to scientist in another metropolis, even should they have in common migration to a foreign country. The peasant exchanges socially valued statuses, close social ties, and a familiar culture for statuses less valued in his new locale, few and tenuous social ties, and alienation. The scientist usually acquires valued statuses and enhanced standing within a short time. He possesses resources to manipulate dispersed social ties and is familiar with the culture of the professional classes, which is generic, national, and international.

On the other hand, the transitions of the wives and children of professionals may be less smooth. Each individual occupies a set of statuses; the significance for him of each status within the set differs according to his attributes of age, sex, occupation, and personality. The ties with kin of wives and children, and the informal and peer relationships from which wives and children are displaced, are likely to be of greater salience within their personal sets of relationships than within those of the professional himself (90).

Survey findings from the population of Midtown Manhattan substantiate the postulate about migration and social position: the differences between peasant and professional become manifest in their states of mind. At first, analysis seemed to give a negative result. The prevalence of mental impairment, when standardized for age and parental social class, varied hardly at all among people classified according to the length of their line of descent from American-born forebears. Variation emerged only when the foreign born were segregated by their social attributes. Mental impairment was almost twice as prevalent among people who had come to the United States from poor homes in Europe's farms, villages, and small towns as it was among those who came from well-off homes in the great European cities (47). Similar results have been obtained by a symptom inventory in an Israeli population (91). Variable first-admission rates to mental hospitals have also been shown to exist for different types of migrants within Norway. Those who moved into the capital city of Oslo had high rates; those who moved elsewhere had low rates (92).

With these qualifications about context in mind, we can turn to consider the main body of evidence on migration and mental disorders. Hippocrates noted that when people were sent to another country "a terrible perturbation always followed," and in 1685 Hofer coined the term *nostalgia* for a condition among migrants characterized by melancholia and anxiety (93). Although we noted above that in the Midtown study the prevalence of mental impairment in the population seemed no different between first-generation Americans and those of older stock, previous studies of immigrants had found differences.

In a seminal work Ø. Ødegaard thus compared Norwegians in the United States with both their parent population in Norway and their host population in the United States (94). He found high incidences of mental hospital admissions, particularly for schizophrenia and chronic brain syndrome of the aged. He attributed the high incidence of schizophrenia chiefly to the selection of predisposed persons and that of chronic brain syndromes to the hardships of emigration.

Later work most often compared immigrants with host populations alone. The statistical control of such factors extraneous to migration as age, sex, and social class lowered but did not dispel the impression of the immigrants' higher susceptibility to mental disorders (95).

In nailing down causes of this association we are at once faced with the same problems of interpretation as in all transitions. Selection must be sorted out from reaction. Social selection acts in complex fashion (96). In the United States the immigration laws of 1921 and 1924 stemmed the flow of the poor and the peasantry of Europe, and subsequent immigration drew more on social classes of higher rank and greater education and wealth (47). In the parent countries the forces that induce immigration are not the same from time to time among people of different age, sex, and social class. These many factors must be allowed for, because social groups have unequal risks of mental illness. In recent years in the United States, for instance, the excess of admissions to mental hospitals among the foreign born has been much reduced (97), and this change is consistent with the changed social composition of immigrant groups. Reaction too is complex. In assessing reaction, the host society may have a powerful influence. Wealth and facilities, hospitality to strangers, and ease of acculturation differ from one society to another.

Self-selection of those predisposed to psychosis may contribute to high rates of psychosis in immigrants, as it appears to do in certain occupations (98). The strain of adaptation is probably also important. Among migrants between the states of the United States, the risks of admission to mental hospitals are thus higher for those recently arrived (95). The most affected age group among immigrants has been the young, who could have had small part in electing to migrate (99). Selection would not account for rates greater among them than among their parents, nor for the finding that in the second generation the rates of mental illness are much lower. Indeed, the conditions imposed by emigration from Europe and by entry into the United States point rather to a selection of the healthy.

These interpretations of migration and mental illness are made difficult because in the main the sources are mental hospital statistics. To illustrate, we can turn to one of the earliest surveys of mental illness in immigrants. In 1865 in Massachusetts the ratio of foreign born to native born among first admissions was 1.5. Contemporary testimony leaves little doubt, however, that a main cause of the high rate among the foreign born was their higher chance of hospital admission. An extensive prevalence survey of insanity carried out at about the same time by Dr. Edward Jarvis revealed a ratio of foreign born to native born in institutions of 1.65 and a ratio in the total population of 0.87. In other words, the foreign born were twice as many in institutions for the insane as would have been expected from the prevalence of insanity among them (100).

A similar instance is the consistent high rate for admission to mental hospitals of the city as compared with the country. This rate can be the partial result, it has been shown, of a low threshold for admission in cities, so that mild cases are taken into the hospitals (101). The solution to this problem of the social selection of mental patients evidently requires data from beyond the mental hospitals. The available population studies that provide such data, however, have not surmounted all the obstacles of method (102, 103).

Migration between urban and rural areas in the same country is easier to study than that between countries. Although contrasts may be less, both parent and host populations are accessible to study, they are registered by the same statistical systems, and they can be tested for selective bias. A study of factory workers in a town in North Carolina compared first-generation migrants from a rural area with the urban-born second generation and was able to show higher rates among the recent immigrants both of absenteeism for sickness and of symptoms reported in a questionnaire (104). Among the Zulus of Natal, high blood pressure has been related to migration from country to city. The result can probably be attributed more to the urban-rural transition than to urban life *per se.* Blood-pressure levels were higher among urban than among rural dwellers, but among urban dwellers pressure levels were highest among recent arrivals (105). Several studies have also shown higher pressures in tribal populations adapting to the impact of money economies (106). Nevertheless, blood pressure is a very indirect measure of mental stress if it is one at all. It is cited for its association with migration; mental stress is only one of a number of features in the context of this transition that could cause a persisting rise in blood pressure.

Against these findings on migration there must be set the negative evidence, relating to both international and internal movement, of some American studies (47, 107) and of two British studies. The British studies looked for stress in people removed from their settled urban places in London to places strange to them. One was a study of removal to a new town (108), the other of removal to new housing estates (109). Instruments of measurement too insensitive to register change in tenor of mind could have produced false negative results, but the measures were different in the two studies. Neither symptom inventories, nor referrals for psychiatric treatment, nor the observations of family doctors, nor the reports of interviewers revealed any undue disturbance of mind that could be related to the removal to new situations.

A further circumstance could have led to false negative results. Countervailing forces can cancel each other out: The effects of improved living conditions on mental state could have outweighed the effects of the transition of rehousing. Positive benefits might thus accrue from rehousing. For the purpose of evaluating these, a rehousing plan in an American city was designed in the form of an experiment. Poorly housed families were allocated at random to new housing. Those who were rehoused enjoyed greater optimism and smoother family relations than they had before rehousing and than did their controls who were not rehoused (110). In Boston, working-class people who had perforce to move were reported best adjusted after moving if they showed signs of preparedness for upward social mobility. They were less adjusted if they experienced the loss of close-knit social networks. This poorer adjustment was offset to some degree by improvement in their circumstances (111).

We can conclude that evidence for the effects of migration on mental health is quite persuasive and that these effects can be damped down or stepped up by the context of the move.

Vertical *social mobility* between the strata of a single social system often accompanies geographic mobility. The common pattern with industrialization is a spatial movement of individuals from countryside to city. This move is commonly followed by a gradual social rise in the scale of urban occupations, for the offspring of the migrants if not for the migrants themselves (112). In many societies one could well classify this type of transition with the normal upward steps in the unfolding of the life cycle. But it is an item of everyday belief among many educated people to ascribe contemporary ills of body and mind to the strain generated by social mobility and the adaptation to new ways of life. A number of scientific writers have also done so. For example, they have inferred that upwardly mobile persons have high rates of mental disorder (113), more particularly that in petit bourgeois or white-collar families a drive for upward mobility is conducive to schizophrenia (114), and that upwardly mobile persons are at special risk of duodenal ulcer (115) and of ischemic heart disease (116).

These studies and others so far do no more than provide promising hypotheses (117). They focus on the unanticipated consequences of individual striving and achievement. In the common coin of most mobile societies these achievements are approved as due reward for worth. The mundane belief is that the material and social rewards of upward mobility are likely to be accompanied by the psychological rewards of happiness and good mental health. This simple view cannot be rejected as folk fantasy.

To take an extreme case, for example from the Midtown Manhattan survey, mental impairment was less prevalent by far among people who had moved upward into the highest socioeconomic classes than among people who had moved down from these classes. The result does not speak outright for the benefits of upward mobility; it merely poses again the dilemma of the distinction between what is cause, what is concomitant, and what is effect, that is, between selection for mobility, spurious associations, and reaction to mobility.

Mental health probably does predispose to success in an upward social climb, and mental impairment to social decline. An American study lends tentative support to this view. In a national sample of 1,000 adolescent boys, aspirations to upward mobility were positively associated with measures of ego strength and mature personality (118). The result is at most indirect support for the hypothesis: It requires that aspirations to mobility must be taken as predictors of future mobility and that psychological measures designed to test ego strength and personality must be taken as predictors of mental health.

Review shows that knowledge of the part played by social transitions in mental disorders is not conclusive. Everyone exposed does not experience stress with transition, and of those who do, few develop frank mental illness. Knowledge is more secure in some conditions, as in maternity, bereavement, and premature separations of children from disrupted families, than it is in others. In all cases, however, poor adaptation to transition can serve as an early pointer to individuals with problems.

Points of transition can somewhat narrow the focus of case finding among the vast numbers of potential clients. In a survey in New York half the population admitted that they had felt a need for help with personal problems (119); in a national survey of the United States, a quarter reported this felt need (120). Three quarters and more in population studies have reported symptoms regarded by many psychiatrists as pathological (121). Few had had professional help (47). Two thirds and more of people who had "felt impending nervous breakdown" (47) or "worried all the time" (120) had had no psychiatric help.

Preventive work requires less inclusive definitions than these of significant symptoms and of the need for help. Public health screening techniques transferred to the mental health field might be able to define more closely the need for help. In transitions normal to the life arc, those rendered liable, for instance by school entry and school leaving, by maternity, by bereavement, and by retirement, are numerous but readily accessible. Thus the most vulnerable, including those who fail to negotiate transitions, can be identified. Some of their immediately felt need for help might be met by medical practitioners with a concern for personal medicine, by social workers, and by public health nurses (23). That immediate intervention in normal transitions would be preventive in the long-term is conjecture, however. Furthermore, many mental disturbances are transitory. Individual scores on inventories of psychiatric symptoms, for instance, fluctuate with the strain of current social situations (122).

Abnormal transitions are by definition less frequent than normal ones. In the case of migration, while we have found the evidence of its stressfulness quite substantial, the groups truly at risk need to be defined and the means for prevention explored. In the case of long premature separations of children from disrupted homes, the evidence of harmful effects is strong, the event is usually known to social agencies, and palliation is attainable. In the field in general, however, research has still to establish either the long-term significance of the transitions or the therapeutic value of intervention.

References

(1) Lewis N. D. C. and Engle B. eds. 1954 *Wartime Psychiatry: A Compendium of the International Literature* New York, Oxford

(2) Appel J. W. 1946 Incidence of neuropsychiatric disorders in the United States army in World War II (preliminary report) *Amer J Psychiat* 102:433–436

(3) Menninger W. C. 1947 Psychiatric experience in the War 1941–1946 *Amer J Psychiat* 103:577–586

(4) Reid D. D. 1961 Precipitating proximal factors in the occurrence of mental disorders: epidemiological evidence in *Causes of Mental Disorders: A Review of Epidemiological Knowledge 1959* New York, Milbank Memorial Fund pp. 197–216

(5) Reid D. D. 1948 Sickness and stress in operational flying *Brit J Soc Med* 2:123–131

(6) Grinker R. R. and Spiegel J. P. 1963 *Men Under Stress* New York, McGraw-Hill

(7) Fraser R., Bunbury E., Danniel B., Barling M. E., Waldron F. E., Kemp P. M. and Lee I. 1947 *The Incidence of Neurosis Among Factory Workers* Med Res Counc Indust Health Res Bd Rep. 90 London, H. M. Stationery Office

(8) Hemphill R. E. 1941 Importance of first year of war in mental disease *Bristol Med-Chir J* 58:11–18

Dellaert R. 1943 I'influence de la guerre sur le nombre de psychoses *J Belge Neurol et Psychiat* 43:93–106

Abely X. 1944 Diminuation de l'aliénation mentale pendant la guerre *La Presse Médicale* 52:179–180 cited in Murphy H. B. M. 1961 Social change and mental health in *Causes of Mental Disorder: A Review of Epidemiological Knowledge 1959* New York, Milbank Memorial Fund pp. 280–329

Abely X. 1944 Diminuation des psychoses affectives pendant la guerre *La Presse Médicale* 52:227–228 cited in Murphy H. B. M. 1961 Social change and mental health in *Causes of Mental Disorder: A Review of Epidemiological*

Knowledge 1959 New York, Milbank Memorial Fund pp. 280–329

General Register Office 1953 *Statistical Review of England and Wales for the Year 1949—Supplement on General Morbidity: Cancer and Mental Health* London, H. M. Stationery Office

Svendsen B. B. 1953 Fluctuation of Danish psychiatric admission rates in World War II; initial decrease and subsequent increase: trends in psychiatric hospital admission 1939–1948 *Psychiat Quart* 27:19–37

Ødegaard Ø. 1954 The incidence of mental disorders in Norway during World War II *Acta Psychiat Neurol Scand* 29:333–353

(9) Murphy H. B. M. 1961 Social change and mental health in *Causes of Mental Disorders: A Review of Epidemiological Knowledge 1959* New York, Milbank Memorial Fund pp. 280–329

(10) Durkheim E. 1897 *Le Suicide* Paris, Alcan Spaulding J. A. and Simpson G. trans. 1951 *Sucide: A Study in Sociology* New York, Free Press

(11) 1946 *The Effects of Strategic Bombing on German Morale* Vol. II Washington, D.C., Government Printing Office cited by Hyman H. 1955 *Survey Design and Analysis: Principles, Cases, and Procedures* New York, Free Press pp. 114–116

(12) Hyman H. 1955 *Survey Design and Analysis: Principles, Cases, and Procedures* New York, Free Press pp. 184–185

(13) Mandelbaum D. G. 1954 Psychiatry in military society: I *Hum Org* 13:5–15

Mandelbaum D. G. 1955 Psychiatry in military society: II *Hum Org* 13:19–25

(14) Williams A. H. 1950 A psychiatric study of Indian soldiers in the Arakan *Brit J Med Psychol* 23:130–181

(15) Glass A. J. 1954 Psychotherapy in the combat zone *Amer J Psychiat* 110:725–731

(16) Fairweather G. W. ed. 1964 *Social Psychology in Treating Mental Illness: An Experimental Approach* New York, Wiley

(17) Ginzberg E., Ginsburg S. W., Anderson J. K. and Herma J. L. 1959 *The Ineffective Soldier: Lessons for Management and the Nation Vol. 3 Patterns of Performance* New York, Columbia University Press

(18) Eitinger L. 1959 The incidence of mental disease among refugees in Norway *J Ment Sci* 105:326–338

(19) Strom A., Refsum S. B., Eitinger L., Gronvick O., Lonnum A., Engeset A., Osvik K. and Rogan B. 1962 Examination of Norwegian ex-concentration camp prisoners *J Neuropsychiat* 4:43–62

(20) Cohen B. M. and Cooper M. Z. 1954 *A Follow-up Study of World War II Prisoners of War* USVA Medical Monograph Washington, D.C., U.S. Government Printing Office

Leopold R. L. and Dillon H. 1963 Psycho-anatomy of a disaster: a long term study of post-traumatic neuroses in survivors of a marine explosion *Amer J Psychiat* 119:913–921

(21) Wolf S. G. and Wolff H. G. 1947 *Human Gastric Function: An Experimental Study of a Man and His Stomach* London, Oxford

Simmons L. W. and Wolff H. G. 1954 *Social Science in Medicine* New York, Russell Sage Foundation

Wolff H. G. 1956 *The Stress of Life* New York, McGraw-Hill

(22) Lindemann E. 1952 The use of psychoanalytic constructs in preventive psychiatry *Psychoanal Study Child* 7:429–448

Lindemann E. 1960 Psychosocial factors as stressor agents in Tanner J. M. ed. *Stress and Psychiatric Disorder* Oxford, Blackwell

(23) Caplan G. 1961 *An Approach to Community Mental Health* London, Tavistock

(24) Gildea M. C. L. 1959 *Community Mental Health* Springfield, Ill., Thomas

Caplan G. ed. 1961 *Prevention of Mental Disorders in Children* New York, Basic Books

Allinsmith W. and Goethals G. W. 1962 *The Role of Schools in Mental Health* New York, Basic Books

(25) Johnson A. M., Falstein E. I., Szurek S. A. and Svendsen M. 1941 School phobia *Amer J Orthopsychiat* 11:702–711

Hersov L. A. 1960 Persistent non-attendance at school *Child Psychol Psychiat* 1:130–136

Rutovitz E. 1962 Referrals to a child guidance clinic: a statistical analysis Unpublished D.P.H. dissertation Manchester University

(26) Eisenberg L. 1958 School phobia *Pediat Clin N Amer* 5:645–666

Glaser K. 1959 Problems in school attendance—school phobia and related conditions *Pediatrics* 23:371–83

Waldfogel S., Tessman E. and Halin P. B. 1959 Learning problems: III A program for early intervention in school phobia *Amer J Orthopsychiat* 29:324–332

(27) Rodriguez A., Rodriguez M. and Eisenberg L. 1959 The outcome of school phobia: a follow-up study based on 41 cases *Amer J Psychiat* 116:540–544

(28) Coolidge J. C., Willer M. L., Tessman E. and Waldfogel S. 1960 School phobia in adolescence: a manifestation of severe character disturbance *Amer J Orthopsychiat* 30:599–607

(29) Stein Z. A., Susser M. W. and Wilson A. T. 1965 Families of enuretic children *Develop Med Child Neurol* 7:658–676

(30) Lapouse R. and Monk M. A. 1958 An epidemiologic study of behavior characteristics in children *Amer J Pub Health* 48:1134–1144

(31) Miller F. J. W., Court S. D. M., Walton W. S. and Knox E. G. 1960 *Growing up in Newcastle-upon-Tyne* New York, Oxford

(32) Stein Z. A. and Susser M. W. 1965 Socio-medical study of enuresis among delinquent boys *Brit J Prev Soc Med* 19:174–181

(33) Morris H. H. Jr., Escoll P. J. and Wexler R. 1956 Aggressive behavior disorders of childhood: a follow-up study *Amer J Psychiat* 112:991–997

O'Neal P. and Robins L. N. 1958 Childhood patterns predictive of adult schizophrenia *Amer J Psychiat* 115:385–391

O'Neal P. and Robins L. N. 1958 The relation of childhood behavior problems to adult psychiatric status *Amer J Psychiat* 114:961–969

Robins L. N. and O'Neal P. 1958 Mortality, mobility and crime: problem children thirty years later *Amer Sociol Rev* 23:162–171

Robins L. N. and O'Neal P. 1959 Adult prognosis for runaway children *Amer J Orthopsychiat* 29:752–761

(34) Morris D. P., Soroken E. and Burrus G. 1954 Follow-up studies of shy, withdrawn children: I Evaluation of later adjustment *Amer J Orthopsychiat* 24:743–754

(35) Shepherd M., Oppenheim A. N. and Mitchell S. 1966 The definition and outcome of deviant behavior in childhood *Proc Roy Soc Med* 59:379–382

(36) Erikson E. H. 1950 *Childhood and Society* New York, Norton

(37) Susser M. W. and Watson W. 1962 *Sociology in Medicine* London, Oxford

(38) United Nations 1955 *Report of the First United Nations Congress on the Prevention of Crime and Treatment of Offenders* London, H. M. Stationery Office

(39) General Register Office 1960 *The Registrar-General's Statistical Review 1958 Part I Tables* London, H. M. Stationery Office Medical Table 17

(40) Glueck S. and Glueck E. T. 1959 *Predicting Delinquency and Crime* Cambridge, Mass., Harvard University Press

Gregory I. 1965 Anterospective data concerning childhood loss of parent: I Delinquency and high school dropouts *Arch Gen Psychiat* 13:99–109

Gibbens T. C. N. 1966 Psychiatric research in delinquency behavior *Brit Med J* 2:695–698

(41) Cohen Albert K. 1955 *Delinquent Boys: The Culture of the Gang* New York, Free Press

Cloward R. A. and Ohlin L. E. 1960 *Delinquency and Opportunity* New York, Free Press

(42) Rapoport R. N. and Rapoport R. 1965 Work and family in contemporary society *Amer Sociol Rev* 30:381–394

(43) Malzberg B. 1940 *Social and Biological Aspects of Mental Disease* Utica, N. Y., State Hospital Press

Adler L. M. 1953 The relationship of marital status to incidence of, and recovery from, mental illness *Social Forces* 32:185–194

Ødegaard Ø. 1953 Marriage and mental health *Acta Psychiat Neurol Scand Suppl* 80:153–161

Thomas D. S. and Locke B. Z. 1963 Marital status, education and occupational differentials in mental disase *Milbank Mem Fund Quart* 41:145–160

Kramer M. 1965 *Some Implications of Trends in the Usage of Psychiatric Facilities for Community Mental Health Programs and Related Research* Paper read at annual meeting of American College of Neuropsychopharmacology, San Juan

(44) Pugh T. and MacMahon B. 1962 *Epidemiologic Findings in United States Mental Hospital Data* Boston, Little Brown

(45) Adelstein A. M., Downham D., Stein Z. A. and Susser M. W. 1965 *Inceptions and Episodes of Mental Illness in Salford* Paper read at annual scientific meeting Society for Social Medicine, Sheffield, Eng. (incorporated in Appendix A)

(46) Innes G. and Sharpe G. A. 1962 A study of psychiatric patients in Northeast Scotland *J Ment Sci* 108:447–456

(47) Srole L., Langner T. S., Michael S. T., Opler M. K. and Rennie T. A. C. 1962 *Mental Health in the Metropolis: The Midtown Manhattan Study* New York, McGraw-Hill

(48) Miles H. C., Gardner E. A., Bodian C. and Romano J. 1964 A cumulative survey of all psychiatric experience in Monroe County, N. Y. *Psychiat Quart* 38:485–487

(49) Bellin S. S. and Hardt R. H. 1958 Marital status and mental disorders among the aged *Amer Sociol Rev* 23:158–162

(50) Knupfer G., Clark W. and Rower R. 1966 The mental health of the unmarried *Amer J Psychiat* 122:841–851

(51) Essen-Möller E. 1961 A current field study in the mental disorders in Sweden in Hoch P. H. and Zubin J. eds. *Comparative Epidemiology of the Mental Disorders* New York, Grune & Stratton

(52) Sampson H., Messinger S. L., Towne R. D. and Ross D. 1964 *Schizophrenic Women: Studies in Marital Crisis* New York, Atherton

(53) Rogler L. and Hollingshead A. B. 1965 *Trapped: Families and Schizophrenia* New York, Wiley

(54) Kreitman N. 1964 The patient's spouse *Brit J Psychiat* 110:159–173

(55) Penrose L. S. 1944 Mental illness in husband and wife: a contribution to the study of assortative mating in man *Psychiat Quart Suppl* 18:161–166

Gregory I. 1959 Husbands and wives admitted to a mental hospital *J Ment Sci* 105:457–462

Kreitman N. 1962 Mental disorder in married couples *J Ment Sci* 108:438–446

(56) Slater E. and Woodside M. 1951 *Patterns of Marriage* London, Cassel

(57) Marcé L. V. 1858 *Traité de la Folie des Femmes Enceintes, des Nouvelles Accouchées et des Nourrices* Paris, Baillière

(58) Thomas C. L. and Gordon J. E. 1959 Psychosis after childbirth *Amer J Med Sci* 238:363–388

Seager C. P. 1960 A controlled study of postpartum mental illness *J Ment Sci* 106:214–230

Paffenbarger R. S. Jr., Steinmetz C. H., Pooler B. G. and Hyde R. T. 1961 The picture puzzle of the postpartum psychoses *J Chron Dis* 13:161–173

Hamilton J. A. 1962 *Postpartum Psychiatric Problems* St. Louis, Mosby

Tod E. D. M. 1964 Puerperal depression: a prospective epidemiological study *Lancet* 2:1264–1266

(59) Winokur G. and Ruangtrakool S. 1966 Postpartum impact on patients with independently diagnosed affective disorder *JAMA* 197:242–246

(60) Tetlow C. 1955 Psychoses of childbearing *J Ment Sci* 101:629–639

Pugh T. F., Jerath B. K., Schmidt W. M. and Reed R. B. 1963 Rates of mental disease related to childbearing *New Eng J Med* 268:1224–1228

(61) Hummel F. C., Sternberger H. R., Hunscher H. A. and Macy I. G. 1936 Metabolism of women during reproductive cycle; utilization of inorganic elements; continuous case study of multipara *J Nutrit* 2:235–255

(62) Porak C. 1880 *De l'Influence Réciproque de la Grossesse et des Maladies du Coeur* Unpublished thesis, University of Paris

(63) Hull E. and Hafkesbring E. 1937 Toxic postpartal heart disease *New Orleans Med Surg J* 89:550–557

Seftel H. and Susser M. W. 1961 Maternity and myocardial failure in African women *Brit Heart J* 23:43–52

(64) Jansson B. 1963 Psychic insufficiencies associated with childbearing *Acta Psychiat Scand Suppl* 172

(65) Lindemann E. 1944 Symptomology and management of acute grief *Amer J Psychiat* 101:141–148

(66) Marris P. 1958 *Widows and their Families* London, Routledge

(67) Tyhurst J. S. 1957 The role of transition states—including disasters in mental illness *Symposium on Preventive and Social Psychiatry* Washington, D.C., Walter Reed Army Institute for Research pp. 149–169

(68) Parkes C. M. 1964 Recent bereavement as a cause of mental illness *Brit J Psychiat* 110:198–204

(69) Gruenberg E. M. 1961 Mental health survey of older persons in Hoch P. H. and Zubin J. eds. *Comparative Epidemiology of the Mental Disorders* New York, Grune & Stratton pp. 13–23

(70) Sainsbury P. 1955 *Suicide in London* Maudsley Monogr 1 London, Chapman & Hall

(71) MacMahon B. and Pugh T. F. 1965 Suicide in the widowed *Amer J Epidem* 81:23–31

(72) Bowlby J. 1952 *Maternal Care and Mental Health* WHO Monogr 2 Geneva, World Health Organization

(73) Beck A. T., Sethi B. B. and Tuthill R. W. 1963 Childhood bereavement and adult depression *Arch Gen Psychiat* 9:295–302

Gregory I. 1966 Retrospective data concerning childhood loss of parent *Arch Gen Psychiat* 15:354–361

(74) Greer S. and Gunn J. C. 1966 Attempted suicide from intact and broken parental homes *Brit Med J* 2:1355–1357

(75) Spence J. C. 1947 The care of children in hospitals *Brit Med J* 1:125–130

Brazelton T. B., Holder R. and Talbot B. 1953 Emotional aspects of rheumatic fever in children *J Pediat* 43: 339–358

Prugh D. G., Staub E. M., Sands H. H., Kirschbaum R. M. and Lenihan E. A. 1953 A study of the emotional reactions of children and families to hospitalization and illness *Amer J Orthopsychiat* 23:70–106

Blom G. E. 1958 The reaction of hospitalized children to illness *Pediatrics* 22:590–599

Robertson J. 1959 *Young Children in Hospitals* New York, Basic Books

Vernon D. T. A., Foley J. M., Sipowicz R. R. and Schulman J. L. 1965 *The Psychological Responses of Children to Hospitalization and Illness: A Review of the Literature* Springfield, Ill., Thomas

(76) Bowlby J., Ainsworth M., Boston M. and Rosenbluth D. 1956 Effects of mother-child separation: a follow-up study *Brit J Med Psychol* 29:211–247

(77) O'Connor N. 1956 The evidence for the permanently disturbing effects of mother-child separations *Acta Psychol* 19:174–191

Wootton B., Seal V. G. and Chambers R. 1959 *Social Science and Social Pathology* London, Allen & Unwin

Clarke A. D. B. and Clarke A. M. 1960 Some recent advances in the study of early deprivation *Child Psychol Psychiat* 1:26–36

Casler L. 1961 *Maternal Deprivation: A Critical Review of the Literature* Soc Res Child Develop Monogr 26 Chicago, University of Chicago Press

World Health Organization 1962 *Deprivation of Maternal Care: A Reassessment of Its Effects* Public Health Papers 14 Geneva, World Health Organization

(78) Lewis Hilda 1954 *Deprived Children: A Social and Clinical Study* London, Oxford

(79) Goldfarb W. 1943 The effects of early institutional care on adolescent personality *J Exper Educ* 12:106–129

Goldfarb W. 1945 Effects of psychological deprivation in infancy and subsequent stimulation *Amer J Psychiat* 102: 18–37

(80) Provence S. and Lipton R. C. 1962 *Infants in Institutions: A Comparison of Their Development with Family-Reared Infants during First Year of Life* New York, International Universities Press

(81) Birch H. G. and Belmont L. 1961 The problem of comparing home rearing versus foster home rearing in defective children *Pediatrics* 28:956–961

(82) Lorenz K. 1956, 1958, 1960 in Tanner J. M. and Inhelder B. eds. *Discussions on Child Development Vols. I–IV* New York, International Universities Press

Harlow H. F. and Harlow M. K. 1962 The effect of rearing conditions on behavior *Bull Menninger Clin* 26:213–224

Harlow H. F. and Harlow M. K. 1962 Social deprivation in monkeys *Sci Amer* 207:136–146

(83) Scott J. B. 1963 *The Process of Primary Socialization in Canine and Human Infants* Soc Res Child Develop Monogr 28 Chicago, University of Chicago Press

(84) Widdowson E. M. 1951 Mental contentment and physical growth *Lancet* 1:1316–1318

(85) Stein Z. A. and Susser M. W. 1966 Nocturnal enuresis as a phenomenon of institutions *Develop Med Child Neurol* 8:677–685

(86) Illingworth R. S. and Lister J. 1964 The critical or sensitive period with special reference to certain feeding problems in infants and children *J Pediat* 65:Part 1, 839–848

Mackeith R. C. 1964 A new concept in development *Develop Med Child Neurol* 6:111–112

(87) Stein Z. A. and Susser M. W. 1967 Social factors in the development of sphincter control *Develop Med Child Neurol* 9:692–706

(88) Bakwin H. 1942 Loneliness in infants *Amer J Dis Child* 63:30–40

Engel G. L., Reichsman F. and Segal H. L. 1956 A study of an infant with a gastric fistula *Psychosom Med* 18:374–398

Richmond J. B. 1959 The role of the pediatrician in early mother-child relationships *Clin Proc Children's Hosp* 15:101–117

Yarrow L. J. 1961 Maternal deprivation *Psychiat Bull* 58:459–490

(89) Mezey A. G. 1960 Psychiatric aspects of human migration *Int J Soc Psychiat* 5:245–260

(90) Blau P. M. 1956 Social mobility and interpersonal relations *Amer Sociol Rev* 21:290–295

Gordon R. E. and Gordon K. K. 1958 Emotional disorders of children in a rapidly growing suburb *Int J Soc Psychiat* 4:85–97

Kantor M. B. 1965 Some consequences of residential and social mobility for the adjustment of children in Kantor M. B. ed. *Mobility and Mental Health* Springfield, Ill., Thomas pp. 86–122

(91) Abramson J. H. 1966 Emotional disorder, status inconsistency and migration *Milbank Mem Fund Quart* 44: Part 1, 23–48

(92) Ødegaard Ø. 1945 Distribution of mental diseases in Norway: a contribution to the ecology of mental disorder *Acta Psychiat Neurol Scand* 20:247–284

Astrup C. and Ødegaard Ø. 1960 Internal migration and mental disease in Norway *Psychiat Quart Suppl* 34:116–130

(93) Allers R. 1920 Uber psychogene störungen in sprachfremder umgebung *Z Ges Neurol Psychiat* 60:287–289

(94) Ødegaard Ø. 1932 Emigration and insanity: study of mental disease among Norwegian born population of Minnesota *Acta Psychiat Scand Suppl* 4:1–206

(95) Malzberg B and Lee E. S. 1956 *Migration and Mental Disease: A Study of First Admissions to Hospital for Mental Disease 1939–1941* New York, Social Science Research Council

Lee S. E. 1963 Socio-economic and migration differentials in mental disease *Milbank Mem Fund Quart* 41: 249–268

(96) Murphy H. B. M. 1965 Migration and the major mental disorders: a reappraisal in Kantor M. ed. *Mobility and Mental Health* Springfield, Ill., Thomas pp. 5–29

(97) Lazarus J., Locke B. Z. and Thomas O. S. 1963 Migration differentials in mental disease: state patterns in first admissions to mental hospitals for all disorders and for schizophre-

nia in New York, Ohio and California as of 1950 *Milbank Mem Fund Quart* 41:25–42

(98) Ekblad M. 1948 A psychiatric and sociologic study of a series of Swedish Naval conscripts *Acta Psychiat Neurol Scand Suppl* 49:1–201

Sundby P. 1956 Occupation and insanity: frequency distribution of psychoses within different occupational groups, with special reference to psychosis among ordinary seamen *Acta Psychiat Neurol Scand Suppl* 106:276–287

(99) Fried M. 1964 Social problems and psychopathology in *Urban America and the Planning of Mental Health Services* New York, Group for the Advancement of Psychiatry pp. 403–447

(100) Commission on Lunacy 1885 *Report on Insanity and Idiocy in Massachusetts* Boston, Public Document No. 144 pp. 65–85 quoted by Goldhamer H. and Marshall A. 1953 in *Psychosis and Civilization: Two Studies in the Frequency of Mental Disease* New York, Free Press

(101) Buck C., Wanklin J. M. and Hobbs G. E. 1955 Symptom analysis of rural-urban differences in first admission rates *J Nerv Ment Dis* 122:80–82

Buck C., Wanklin J. M. and Hobbs G. E. 1956 Environment change and age of onset of psychosis in elderly patients *AMA Arch Neurol Psychiat* 75:619–623

(102) Dohrenwend B. P. and Dohrenwend B. S. 1965 The problem of validity in field studies of psychological disaster *J Abnorm Psychol* 70:52–69

(103) Dunham H. W. 1961 Social structure and mental disorders: competing hypotheses of explanation in *Causes of Mental Disorders: A Review of Epidemiological Knowledge 1959* New York, Milbank Memorial Fund pp. 227–265

Hoch P. and Zubin J. eds. 1961 *Comparative Epidemiology of the Mental Disorders* New York, Grune & Stratton

Blum R. H. 1962 Case identification in psychiatric epidemiology: methods and problems *Milbank Mem Fund Quart* 40:253–258

(104) Cassel J. and Tyroler H. A. 1961 Epidemiological studies of culture change *Arch Environ Health* 3:25–33

(105) Gampel B., Slome C., Scotch N. and Abramson J. H. 1962 Urbanization and hypertension among Zulu adults *J Chron Dis* 15:67–70

(106) Geiger H. J. and Scotch N. A. 1963 The epidemiology of essential hypertension: I Biologic mechanisms and descriptive epidemiology *J Chron Dis* 16:1151–1182

Scotch N. A. and Geiger H. J. 1963 The epidemiology of essential hypertension: II Psychologic and socio-cultural factors in etiology *J Chron Dis* 16:1183–1213

(107) Jaco E. G. 1960 *The Social Epidemiology of Mental Disorders: A Psychiatric Survey of Texas* New York, Russell Sage Foundation

(108) Taylor Lord and Chave S. 1964 *Mental Health and Environment* London, Longmans

(109) Hare E. H. and Shaw G. K. 1965 *Mental Health on a New Housing Estate* Maudsley Monogr 12 London, Oxford

(110) Wilner D. M., Walkley R. P., Pinkerton T. C., Tayback M., Glasser M. N., Schram J. M., Hopkins C. E., Curtiss C. C., Meyer A. S. and Dallas J. K. 1962 *The Housing Environment and Family Life: A Longitudinal Study of the Effects of Housing on Morbidity and Mental Health* Baltimore, Johns Hopkins Press

(111) Fried M. 1965 Transitional functions of working class communities: implications for forced relocation in Kantor M. ed. *Mobility and Mental Health* Springfield, Ill., Thomas pp. 123–165

(112) Lipset S. M. and Bendix R. 1959 *Social Mobility in Industrial Society* Berkeley, University of California Press

(113) Hollingshead A. B., Ellis R. and Kirby E. 1954 Social mobility and mental illness *Amer Sociol Rev* 19:577–584

(114) Myers J. K. and Roberts B. H. 1959 *Family and Class Dynamics in Mental Illness* New York, Wiley

(115) Ruesch J., Harris R. E., Christiansen C., Loeb M. B., Dewees S. and Jacobsen A. 1948 *Duodenal Ulcer: A Socio-Psychological Study of Naval Enlisted Personnel and Civilians* Berkeley, University of California Press

(116) Friedman M., Rosenman R. H. and Carrol V. 1958 Changes in the serum cholesterol and blood clotting time in

men subjected to cyclic variation of occupational stress *Circulation* 17:852–861

Friedman M. and Rosenman R. H. 1959 Association of specific overt behavior pattern with blood and cardiovascular findings *JAMA* 169:1286–1296

Wardwell W. I., Hyman M. M. and Bahnson C. B. 1964 Stress and coronary heart disease in three field studies *J Chronic Dis* 17:73–84

Syme S. L., Hyman M. M. and Enterline P. E. 1965 Cultural mobility and the occurrence of coronary heart disease *J Health Hum Behav* 6:178–189

(117) Kantor M. ed. 1965 *Mobility and Mental Health* Springfield, Ill., Thomas

(118) Douvan E. and Adelson J. 1958 The psychodynamics of social mobility in adolescent boys *J Abnorm Soc Psychol* 56:31–44

(119) Perkins M. E., Padilla E. and Elinson J. 1965 Public images of psychiatry: challenges in planning community mental health care *Amer J Psychiat* 121:746–751

(120) Gurin G., Veroff S. and Feld S. 1960 *Americans View Their Mental Health* Joint Commission on Mental Illness and Health Monogr Ser 4 New York, Basic Books

(121) Leighton D. C., Harding J. S., Mackler D. B., Macmillan A. M. and Leighton A. H. 1963 *The Character of Danger: Psychiatric Symptoms in Selected Communities* Stirling County Study 3 New York, Basic Books

(122) Dohrenwend B. S. and Dohrenwend B. P. 1966 Stress situations, birth order and psychological symptoms *J Abnorm Psychol* 71:215–223

6

Stressful Situations: Anomie, Social Isolation, and Social Disintegration

In focusing on the cure and prevention of mental disorder, this discussion has so far skirted the question of "positive" mental health, or the desired state that a health program would seek to promote. A first and difficult problem is to define the concept and the relevant criteria. Various subjective reports of happiness and a sense of well-being; various psychological judgments of ego strength, emotional maturity, and the perception of reality; various psychiatric judgments of "normality" and the absence of mental symptoms; and various social judgments of competence, performance, and mastery of the environment may each be used as an index of mental health (1).

These indexes do not measure the same elements, and they may vary independently of each other. Moreover, in a diverse world, criteria of mental health cannot have universal validity. The chosen definitions ultimately depend on which subjective states, which qualities of personality, and which kinds of competence are valued by the users. Values are particular to societies and groups. Kingsley Davis long ago analyzed the middle-class foundations of the mental health movement in the United States (2). Such components of emotional maturity as "self-awareness" and "actualization of self" are cultivated by the middle-class urban cultures of industrial societies and discouraged by many working-class and rural cultures. In societies dominated by urban middle-class cultures these traits are bound to be adaptive and to be associated with a subjective sense of well-being and successful social performance. The few studies of mental health are in accord with this view. One can conceive that in other societies where such traits are less adaptive they would be associated not with well-being but with distress and social failure. D. H. Lawrence grew up in a coal-mining village self-aware but with a mind scored by childhood misery (3).

In the United States intriguing use has been made of "happiness" as an index of mental health (4, 5). It is seemingly naïve as a measure of so complex a phenomenon, but replies to questions about feelings of happiness have been found to relate consistently to the attributes of income, education, sex, and age. The poor, the uneducated, and the old reported themselves less happy than the rich, the educated, and the young (4).[1]

The distribution of some other responses intended to measure mental composure and distress, however, seemed contrary. The categories of people who declared themselves least happy also reported less worry and frustration. This paradox, it was inferred, arose because people in these categories were pessimistic, resigned, and unaspiring. They were less troubled by their own inadequacies, attributed their problems to external circumstances, and tended not to seek help for them from others. The rich, the educated, and the young, while declaring themselves happy, were also more often worried and

1. The variations of the psychological indexes with sex in this study were consistent with the "nurturant" roles of women and the active "instrumental" roles of men in the culture. Women were more self-deprecating than men and emphasized their shortcomings of personality, whereas men emphasized their shortcomings in achievement. Women reported more tension than men, either because they were more subject to strain, or because they were more sensitive to it, or because they were more aware of it. Awareness is probably a factor in the result, as the findings for highly educated men resembled those for women.

frustrated. This second paradox, it was inferred, arose because the people in these categories were fully engaged with the problems of living, optimistic, and aspiring. They were also psychologically oriented toward introception in that they tended to perceive distress introspectively as a personal problem for which they were ready to seek help.

In the United States, then, the socially privileged positions of the rich, the educated, and the young confer a subjective sense of happiness and optimism or a willingness to express these feelings. These positions, whose incumbents most closely express the dominant culture, were also associated with a tendency to frustration and worry and to introception (described as a "mature" psychological orientation). The converse is true for the poor, the uneducated, and the old.

The cutting elge of these data as a basis for preventive programs is blunted by the value judgments already noted, which entangle biological, psychological, and social definitions of mental health in circularity. Nevertheless, the data do point to a relationship of "happiness" with favorable social and material conditions. This observation can cause no surprise to the bulk of mankind with millennia of struggle to improve conditions behind them.

There is a better supply of knowledge about the connection of frank *mental disorder* with the environment. This knowledge has a longer history of testing and cumulation, although it too is not free of uncertainties in definition, diagnosis, and interpretation (6). No direct evidence is available to connect the distribution of mental disorder in the population with that of the indexes of positive mental health discussed above.[2] The published data suggest, as might be expected, that mental disorder and mental health do tend to vary inversely.

The fit is not precise. The discrepancies could be attributed to the methods used to obtain the data. But even within the limits of single surveys, responses to inventories of mental

2. In the national study of American mental health, reports both of happiness and of psychologial symptoms were in fact obtained. Unhappily the report did not present cross-tabulations of the two sets of indexes (4).

symptoms and reports of "nervous breakdowns" showed a degree of autonomy in relation to the distribution of happiness. The indexes are therefore not measuring the same thing. Taken overall, however, mental symptoms and mental disorder are concentrated in the same conditions as reported for unhappiness, that is, among those in less privileged social positions (7, 8, 9, 10). To this general finding there are few noteworthy exceptions. Two are incidence studies of patients entering psychiatric care, one carried out in Aberdeen, northeast Scotland, and another in Texas (11). Two English studies based mainly on symptom questionnaires also failed to find important social class differences (12).

When mental disorder is analyzed by diagnosis, only some types are found to excess in the lower social classes (13, 14). Schizophrenia invariably has been thus distributed in large cities (15, 16, 17, 18); one study of a small town, Hagerstown in Maryland, did not find an excess in the lower social classes (19). Psychoneurosis, in most studies, as well as the psychopathies and the sociopathies, show gradients that rise toward the lower social classes. But depressive psychosis is evenly spread. On repeated study these distributions, particularly of psychoses, are fairly consistent by age, sex, and marital state, as well as by social class. Consistency underpins uncertain methods.

Anomie and Social Isolation

Among the hypotheses advanced to explain the uneven social distribution of mental disorders, a seminal one attributes it to anomie. The concept of anomie was elaborated by Émile Durkheim at the end of the last century to describe the condition of depressed urban groups who had become detached from the mainstream of society (20). Durkheim sought to show by an epidemiologic analysis that such deviant forms of conduct as suicide followed the dissociation of social groups from guiding norms and shared values. A number of studies of suicide have supported and modified Durkheim's findings (21, 22, 23).

R. K. Merton's analytic model developed the notion of anomie in more specific terms (24). He separated the elements of cultural structure from those of social structure. By cultural structure he referred to "that organized set of normative values governing behavior which is common to members of a designated society or group." By social structure he referred to "that organized set of social relationships in which members of the society or group are variously implicated." Anomie is then conceived as a breakdown in the cultural structure.

Anomie can arise from a conflict of values between groups in the same society, as between immigrants and their hosts, or from the deterioration of values in a social group, particularly where the social structure prevents achievement of approved goals by approved means. Anomie is thus generated by disjunction between the goals after which a culture impels people to strive and the social structure that determines their capacity legitimately to attain the goals. Common cultural goals are readily attained from certain social positions and almost impossible to attain from others. Striving for success in an open-class society is a widespread, even a fundamental, value, but the social system does not allow everyone to be equally successful. The outcome of this contradiction between goals and the possibility of fulfilling them, it is postulated, is deviant social behavior, including group delinquency, crime, homicide or suicide, and mental disorder.

Merton himself derived from his model a typology of alternative modes of individual adaptation in the face of disjunction between cultural goals and the structure of opportunities. These types depend on two variables: the individual's acceptance or rejection on the one hand of cultural goals and on the other of the institutionalized means to attain them. *Conformity* involves acceptance of goals and means. *Innovation* requires acceptance of the goals and rejection of the means. In *ritualism* the goals are not sought after but the means are complied with. In *retreatism* neither goals nor means are accepted. *Rebellion* (or, better, *revolt*) is different from all these modes; it seeks to change the cultural and social structure and to substitute new goals and new procedures to attain them. Merton made a distinction, to fit the case of rebellion, between deviant responses that are nonconformist and those that are aberrant. The nonconformist shares the ultimate values of the society if not the nearer goals from which he openly dissents; he challenges the legitimacy of the social norms he rejects and tries disinterestedly to change them. The aberrant has self-centered and antisocial values; he accepts the legitimacy of social norms and hides his violations in order to escape social sanctions. The aberrant response is typified by sociopathic and psychopathic disorders (25).

The discovery by R. E. L. Faris and H. W. Dunham in Chicago that patients admitted to mental hospitals with schizophrenia came predominantly from deteriorated urban areas where a high proportion of people lived alone was consistent with the anomie hypothesis. It seemed that the coincidence of cultural and social isolation "bred" schizophrenia (14, 15, 16, 26).

Elucidation turned out to be a difficult matter because of the complexity of the social process. Even in similar areas of Chicago ten years later, the results of Faris and Dunham could not be exactly replicated (27). For the time being, therefore, we shall put aside the direct questions raised by anomie and cultural isolation in order to clarify the related questions raised by social isolation.

Social Isolation

Social isolation has been indicted by ecological studies as a possible cause of schizophrenia, of the mental disorders of the aged, of suicide, and of attempted suicide (15, 22, 23, 28). It is a condition well suited to test the stability of values and of norms of behavior in individuals, because isolated people are little sustained by interaction and the continual reinforcement of what others expect.

The physical, social, and psychological elements of isolation overlap but are distinct. Surveys of old people in England and the United States show that those living alone and physically isolated may not be socially isolated. Many have close relatives as neighbors (29). Moreover they may be healthier than their age peers who live with others. Among people over eighty in the northern English city of Stockport, for example, those who lived alone were the still independent survivors (30). The dependent sick lived with kin or in institutions. Independent old people often lived in poor circumstances, however, and failed to maintain an adequate diet and to husband their resources.

Psychological isolation, or the subjective sense of loneliness, also may not coincide with physical or social isolation. A number of socially isolated persons do not complain of loneliness and pursue with equanimity the limited social intercourse to which they are accustomed. Conversely some, especially those who have suffered recent bereavement or depressive illness, feel lonely even though they share homes with others (29). We have observed earlier that among old people who were mentally impaired the experience of feelings of loneliness depended not only on the frequency of interaction with others, but on the kin relationships of the interacting parties. When mental illness supervened, old people felt neglect and loneliness according to the frequency of the visits of their relatives only (31). No one has evoked the loneliness of the crowd better than Francis Bacon.

> Little do men perceive what solitude is, and how far it extendeth. For a crowd is not company, and faces are but a gallery of pictures, and talk but a tinkling cymbal, where there is no love. The Latin adage meeteth with it a little—magna civitas, magna solitudo—because in a great town, friends are scattered; so that there is not that fellowship for the most part, which is in less neighborhoods.

P. Sainsbury used this quotation to adorn his study of social isolation in suicide (22).

Social isolation is often the involuntary consequence of a set of related conditions. It affects chiefly the old, and chiefly women among the old, for they survive in greater numbers than men and outlive their spouses. Restricted physical mobility as well as the loss of spouse and peers accompany old age and diminish social contact. Marriage is a factor, for the elderly in the single state will have accrued neither spouses nor children and must usually rely for contacts on the survival of sibs. Finally, retirement from a lifelong occupation enforces withdrawal from a major set of social relations.

On the other hand, social isolation can be a voluntary withdrawal from the responsibilities of reciprocal roles. An extreme form of disengagement from society is found among the derelicts of "Skid Row," as in the Bowery in New York and on the fringes of society in any great city (32). Some whose dereliction has followed heavy drinking still seek face-to-face exchanges. But others have avoided social exchanges outside the dispassionate encounters of their casual occupations. Among such people there may be a pool of latent schizophrenics, for it is from areas of similar social ecology that many schizophrenic patients enter mental hospitals.

Many of the studies on social isolation have been ecological. They seek correlations between environment and population. Such correlations do not necessarily hold for individuals in the population (33). For instance, whereas the Skid Row phenomenon is found in most large cities, in an ecological study its presence can be masked by other factors. Drinking habits are not the same across cultures either in quantity or in type of alcohol consumed or in the social position of the drinkers (34).[3] In England and Wales, for example, the nation's highest rates both of alcoholic psychoses and of cirrhosis of the liver (alcoholism is its common cause) are found not in the poor but in the upper social classes (35).

Social Isolation and Schizophrenia

The complexities of ecology are illustrated by the crabwise advance in unraveling the relationship of schizophrenia to social isolation. Clinicians have long regarded psychological withdrawal and social retreat as signs of schizophrenia, that is,

3. Even within such a restricted social group as British physicians, proportionately more from Ireland and Scotland appear to be disciplined by the general Medical Council for drinking offenses.

as consequences of the disorder. The work of Faris and Dunham brought isolation into prominence as cause rather than consequence (15). Reviewers of their work were quick to observe, however, that other explanations of the findings were tenable. Symptoms are not equally visible and tolerable in all social situations, nor is support equally available. The excess of schizophrenia in deteriorated urban areas could therefore have reflected lack of tolerance and lack of support (36). Alternatively, people afflicted by schizophrenia or predisposed to it might have "drifted" into deprived and isolated social situations as the result of their disability or of their psychological need to retreat from society (37), as in the case of the dwellers on Skid Row.

A number of studies have explored these hypotheses. The descriptive findings, to which we have already referred, have a degree of consistency. Schizophrenic patients at first admission to the hospital are preponderantly young single men engaged in casual occupations low on the social-class scale; they are drawn principally from deteriorated central areas of cities; and they tend to be separated from their families and to live alone (14, 15, 16, 17, 18, 26, 38).

All these circumstances can coincide without the intrusion of schizophrenic illness. The critical problem with etiological studies of schizophrenia is by now familiar to the reader. It is to disentagle the cycle of events in time and to distinguish variables antecedent to the illness from those consequent upon it. The illness could be either cause or consequence of any of its known associations. Healthy individuals might come to be exposed to the circumstances associated with schizophrenia by accidents of birth and rearing, in which case they would be antecedent and causal. Alternatively, susceptible individuals might come to be exposed through behavior determined by a predisposition to schizophrenia. Some of the possible time sequences of the variables are illustrated in Figure 2, a chart of pathways to recognized morbidity. Schizophrenia can be inserted as a plausible antecedent or intervening factor at any point in the sequence. Only if one of the associations of schizophrenia arranged in sequence across the chart precedes the onset of schizophrenic behavior in the cycle of events can it be regarded as a candidate among competing causes. Obvious as this point may appear, the tangle of sequence has confounded more than one generation of research workers.

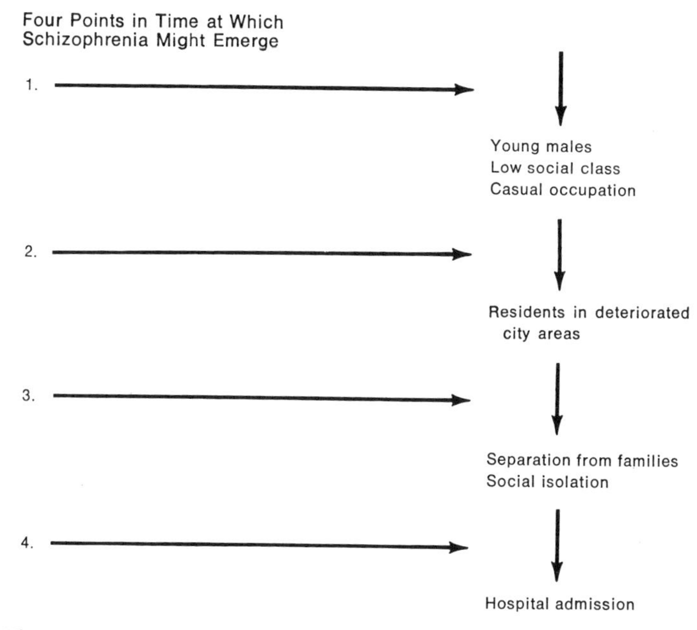

Figure 2. Possible Time Sequences of Social Factors Associated with Schizophrenia

The question raised by these findings cannot be settled by ecological studies alone. The first step in sorting out the complex of ecology is to specify the relationships between the disorder in individuals within a population and the suspected causes. The next step is to specify the time sequence between the onset of the disorder and the suspected causes. This ostensibly simple requirement presents formidable obstacles of research design in a chronic disorder of insidious onset and imprecise definition. If the research is done retrospectively, the historical data may be unreliable and the time of onset uncertain; the population studied is one of survivors and may be biased by the loss of unknown numbers of cases with unknown attributes; and historical changes will have supervened whose impact can only be guessed at. If the research is done prospectively, large populations will have to be observed to obtain a sufficient number of cases; the populations take a long time to mature, and losses occur; and historical changes will supervene to alter the conditions under study.

The disadvantages of each type of study are not inalienable. Economical retrospective studies can be endowed with some of the virtues of longitudinal prospective ones. For instance, one ingenious and inexpensive approach to measuring "drift" down the social-class scale in schizophrenia was to compare patients' occupations with those attributed to their fathers on their birth certificates (39). Downward drift was evident between these generations in a significant number of cases. This comparison did not allow for the historical changes between generations in the content and social prestige of particular occupations that determine their positions on the social-class scale—or for the "dropouts" among the schizophrenics in the population who did not reach the hospital. The historical change would be amenable to control through a comparison with sons and fathers taken from the general population.

The process of drift long precedes diagnosed illness and hospital admission, and hence the downwardly mobile individuals are likely to appear as fresh cases in the lower social classes. Downward mobility has also been observed in the lifetimes of schizophrenic people in London and New Orleans, though not in Buffalo and New Haven (8, 40). Although a healthy naïveté would not rule out real differences in the phenomenon between cities, differences in method most likely underlie these results. For instance, in the Buffalo study the long-term follow-up located only a small proportion of subjects.

In a study in Manhattan, a comparison of the social position of individuals with their social origins indicated that mobility can also complicate the distribution of personality types and of deviant behavior in the population. Upward social movement was associated with obsessive types, downward movement with "character" disorders (41). These characteristics are considered to form early in life, and the results point to the part of social selection in their distribution. The many aspects of social selection thus preclude straightforward assumptions about causes derived from the link between illness and the social class in which its onset is observed.

The occasion for this digression into the tangle of the associations of schizophrenia, I should perhaps remind the reader, was the question of the potency of social isolation as a cause of mental disorder. For the time being we can only conclude that social isolation can be a consequence as much as a cause of schizophrenia, whether the isolation comes about by preference, by extrusion as a result of family friction, or involuntarily. This ambiguous conclusion is supported by studies of the careers of schizophrenic isolates. In one study about one third of schizophrenic patients, and of depressive patients as well, had histories of limited social intercourse in youth for which external factors did not account (42). In another study about half of a sample of isolated schizophrenic patients lived alone by preference or because of family friction, and half did so involuntarily (43).

Anomie

It is time to consider the anomie hypothesis in the light of this review of social isolation. Even firm knowledge of the association of mental disorder with social isolation, or with such other deprived circumstances as poverty and low social class, would not establish anomie as a cause of mental disorder. Anomie is likely but not certain to supervene in such social situations; it describes a cultural condition to be expected in certain positions in the social structure. In the data adduced so far, anomie is an intervening variable whose existence is hypothesized and remains to be demonstrated.

Two major studies have considered anomie in fairly direct terms (9, 10). These were studies of the prevalence of mental disorder in samples of general populations, and both took pains to eliminate the use of services as a source of error. We have several times noted that selective processes determine the dispositions of people into social and geographical locations, and that these dispositions include entry into mental hospitals. The research confirmed once more, in regions as contrasting as "Stirling County" in rural maritime Nova Scotia and the great metropolis of New York, that the lowest social strata carried the heaviest load of mental disorder.

The Nova Scotia study focused on social integration as a group characteristic. This concept is a close relative of anomie and can be equated with it. The degree of social integration and disintegration of each small community selected for the study was inferred from observation. The broad pointers included poverty, admixture of subcultures, and disaffiliation from churches (as well as other items that proved less useful). Confirmation was sought in data on the frequency of broken homes, of hostility, and of crime and in data on the quality of associations and communication, of leadership, and of recreation (44).

The measure of mental disorder was derived from a questionnaire. It put standard questions about the presence and severity of symptoms and about social behavior and performance. Psychiatrists assessed the responses and classified them by predominant symptom complex, by the degree to which they approximated to a workaday psychiatric case, and by the degree of functional impairment.

The Nova Scotia study yielded results congruent with the anomie hypothesis. High frequencies of mental impairment were found in communities rated as disintegrated and low frequencies in those rated as integrated. A subsequent test of the hypothesis used the same method in the dissimilar culture of the Yoruba people of Nigeria (45). The results were consistent with those obtained in Nova Scotia.

The methods of these studies will be further discussed in a later chapter. (See pp. 205 ff.) One difficulty should be noted here, namely, that the studies do not control the factors of mobility and migration in relation to mental disorder.[4]

4. Migration might account, for instance, for the odd finding that in both studies there appear to be more young women than young men. The excess of young women seems greater than can be accounted for by the fact that

Migration of people healthy in mind from disintegrated communities could bring about the association of mental disorder with social disintegration. The departures would weight the remaining population with those impaired in mind. Despite such loopholes, the bulk of evidence and its consistency with other studies incline one to take the results at face value.

When mental disorder is ascribed to such a broad configuration of circumstances as collective anomie, it can be dealt with only by sweeping social action. No one agent in the environment can be identified, isolated, and attacked. Poverty and many other deprivations simultaneously beset people in the lowest social positions. Social reform needs no justification. But if action is to be at all specific, the variables that intervene between collective anomie and mental disorder must be discovered. The Midtown study in New York made a beginning (10).

The measure of anomie used in this study was a questionnaire that probed the attitudes and the perceptions respondents had of the surrounding society. This measure is of the subjective experience of individuals. Srole named their condition anomia. Merton was at pains to point out that anomia, the state of mind of an individual, cannot be equated directly with Durkheim's concept of anomie, a state of organization and interaction of a social group. For the purpose of finding what consequences anomie has for individuals, a personal measure is essential. Subjective states reflect social situations, as Merton's typology of adaptations clearly implies. (See p. 122.) The subjective states of people, treated together, can yield a direct appraisal of the impact of the social condition on populations—but only an indirect appraisal of its impact on individuals. The subjective states of individuals, however, do yield an appraisal of the impact of the social condition on the personal condition.

Unfortunately for the needs of this text, the exact analysis

---

the samples were of married couples, and wives are generally younger than husbands. Among the polygamous Yoruba, where wives can be expected to be much younger than husbands, the sampling method would have had greater effect on the age composition of the two sexes.

of the Midtown data required to test the anomie hypothesis directly was not reported. Scores on the anomia scale were shown to relate to social position as expected; high scores occurred with low positions. But the next step of relating the scores to mental impairment was not taken.

A part of the work that is relevant to the effects of anomie tried to relate social experience to subsequent mental impairment. As if to confirm the multiplicity of hostile forces in anomic situations, mental impairment was found to relate to the quantity and not to the type of strains reported in the histories of respondents. The stressors of childhood and adult life defined and elicited in the study were more common among people with impaired mental function when counted together, but not when counted singly and specifically.[5]

Greater impairment was found among members of the lower social classes than among those of the higher for the same number of defined stressors (41). At first sight these unequal effects of a similar amount of strain might be attributed to variations in the individuals subjected to them. Lower-class people might have less resilience than others. But the environment by itself could be the important factor. The higher-class social environment has many characteristics that cushion strains, the lower-class environment those that exacerbate them (46).

In the Midtown study the link between strain and mental impairment generally remains open to three interpretations. Mental impairment might have been caused by the reported strains. Alternatively the classes of individuals with an excess of mental impairment might have attracted or even created strains. The association could be the result of a third mechanism residing in the method: The questionnaire may have elicited responses with a bias toward indicating impairment.

5. Certain symptom complexes, considered separately from other measures of mental impairment, did show some correlation with past strain. In these studies the fact that reported stress, symptom complexes, impaired mental function, and social performance to some extent varied independently of each other confuses interpretation of the data. The results emphasize that disturbances of mind are not conterminous with disturbances of social function and the assumption of the sick role; circumstances conducive to the one may not always be conducive to the other.

With questionnaires, ostensible differences in the effects of strain on the social classes could be simply an artifact of differences between the classes in what is thought noteworthy, or in what is too undesirable to report to interviewers (47), or in what is recalled, or in what is understood by the questions. A short questionnaire adapted from the Midtown study has shown some differences of this kind between ethnic groups (48). Variations in "response set" (49) were demonstrated between the ethnic groups of whites, Negroes, and Puerto Ricans. In other words, the instrument produced a disposition to give answers in a particular way, and the bias was characteristic for each group. The questionnaire was also overloaded with psychophysiological symptoms, and it tended to neglect the symptoms of severe psychoses, paranoid reactions, and sociopathy. On the other hand, the instrument proved reliable in a number of respects, and the testing need not be taken to invalidate all aspects of the research.

One study has examined the anomie hypothesis in more direct fashion. The authors used their results to test the discrepancy between aspiration and achievement (50). In this research among Negroes in Philadelphia, the standardized rates of admission to mental hospitals and to selected psychiatric facilities were reported to be lower, unexpectedly, for migrants from the South than for natives. Migrants also had lower scores on a symptom inventory (the Cornell Medical Index) that was used as a measure of psychoneurosis. Difference in social standing was first tried as an explanation and dismissed, for the natives were of higher standing by occupation and education. The data were consistent with a second explanation, namely, that high rates of mental impairment arose from discrepancy between individual aspiration and actual achievement. The core of the anomic situation outlined by Merton resides in such discrepancies. By the measures used, the gap between aspiration and actual occupation was significant, and for education it was in the same direction but not significant. More work must be done before such factors as varying use of services can be excluded, and the influence of anomie in mental disorder can be taken as established.

Status Inconsistency

Discrepancy between actual statuses was also tested in this Philadelphia study, and the hypothesis of "status inconsistency" (51) can be given brief consideration here. Inconsistencies in social statuses imply that in terms of one or another status the individual is a marginal figure; he lacks social attributes common to the social position he occupies. These various inconsistencies reflect disjunctions between his social positions and his cultural affiliations and aspirations. In this respect if not in others they resemble the disjunctions of anomie.

In the Philadelphia research, occupation, education, and income were used as indexes of status, and dissonance among them was judged and scaled. An excess of mental problems did not relate to inconsistencies in statuses. Other studies have revealed such relationships. The interrelations of education, occupation, and ethnic origin were thus examined in a national sample of the United States by means of a questionnaire. Reports of psychophysiological symptoms were frequent among women who were of high education but married to men in low-standing occupations. Symptoms were also frequent among men of low education in occupations of high standing (52). In Israel too high scores on a symptom inventory were found among immigrants whose occupation and education were not consonant (53).

Another form of inconsistency between statuses has been characterized as *contextual dissonance*. In this situation the individual has cultural and social statuses and ties different from those of people with whom he must associate. It is the typical position of the member of a minority group. In the United States children who in local context are members of religious and ethnic minorities have higher indexes of anxiety (derived from standard questionnaires) than do children of surrounding majorities (54). In Britain children of the middle classes who attend the secondary modern schools, which are predominantly working class, feel themselves isolated (55).

The significance of inconsistencies varies from one context

to another. Thus in the United States sample, young people with inconsistencies of status had normal symptom scores (52). Since the future is before them, they may be less likely to feel their aspirations limited by their current social positions. Similarly in Israel natives with status inconsistencies as distinct from immigrants had normal symptom scores, perhaps because of their unique system of values.

This review of antecedent factors in mental disorder has shown that the targets on which we might train prophylactic weapons are fuzzy. One conclusion stands clear. Social disadvantage is also a disadvantage to mental well-being. Theories of anomie, alienation, social isolation, status inconsistency, and deprivation are offered to explain what appears to be a causal connection. On this score researchers are still groping. Social disadvantage therefore, not subject to attack by specific therapy, calls for the broad barrage of social policy. Isolation in the concourse of cities is one particular aspect of social disadvantage connected with much disability. By discovering and penetrating isolation, we can alleviate disability, although we do not know if the associated mental disorder can be prevented. Social transitions also serve somewhat as pointers for directing effort. The obscurities that still surround these ills of social circumstance press us toward more precise research and experiment.

References

(1) Jahoda M. 1958 *Current Concepts of Positive Mental Health* Joint Commission on Mental Illness and Health Monogr Ser 1 New York, Basic Books

(2) Davis K. 1938 Mental hygiene and the class structure *Psychiat* 1:55–65

(3) Moore H. 1955 *Intelligent Heart: The Story of D. H. Lawrence* New York, Farrar, Straus

(4) Gurin G., Veroff J. and Feld S. 1960 *Americans View Their Mental Health* Joint Commission on Mental Illness and Health Monogr Ser 4 New York, Basic Books

(5) Bradburn N. and Caplowitz D. L. 1964 *Reports on Happiness* Chicago, Aldine

(6) Pasamanick B. ed. 1959 *Epidemiology of Mental Disorder* Washington, D.C., Amer Assn Advanc Sci Publ 60

Plunkett R. J. and Gordon J. A. 1960 *Epidemiology in Mental Illness* Joint Commission on Mental Illness and Health Monogr Ser 6 New York, Basic Books

Reid D. D. 1960 *Epidemiological Methods in the Study of Mental Disorders* Public Health Papers 2 Geneva, World Health Organization

Hoch P. and Zubin J. eds. 1961 *Comparative Epidemiology of the Mental Disorders* New York, Grune & Stratton

Lin Tsung-Yi and Standley C. C. 1961 *The Scope of Epidemiology in the Study of Mental Disorders* Public Health Papers 16 Geneva, World Health Organization

Milbank Memorial Fund 1961 *Causes of Mental Disorder: A Review of Epidemiological Knowledge 1959* New York, Milbank Memorial Fund

Zubin J. 1961 *Field Studies in the Mental Disorders* New York, Grune & Stratton

(7) Hyde R. W. and Kingsley L. V. 1944 Studies in medical sociology: 1 Relation of mental disorders to community socioeconomic level 2 Relation of mental disorders to population density *New Eng J Med* 231:543–548, 571–577

Norris V. 1959 *Mental Illness in London* Maudsley Monogr 6 London, Oxford

Brooke E. M. 1959 National statistics in the epidemiology of mental illness *J Ment Sci* 105:893–908

Stein Z. A. 1964 Some preliminary results of the survey of mental sickness in Salford in Susser M. W. *Report on the Salford Mental Health Services for 1963* City of Salford, Eng., Health Department pp. 11–23

(8) Hollingshead A. B. and Redlich F. C. 1958 *Social Class and Mental Illness* New York, Wiley

(9) Leighton D. C., Harding J. S., Macklin D. B., Macmillan A. M. and Leighton A. H. 1963 *The Character of Danger: Psychiatric Symptoms in Selected Communities* Stirling County Study 3 New York, Basic Books

(10) Srole L., Langner T. S., Michael S. T., Opler M. K. and Rennie T. A. C. 1962 *Mental Health in the Metropolis: The Midtown Manhattan Study* New York, McGraw-Hill

(11) Jaco E. G. 1960 *The Social Epidemiology of Mental Disorders: A Psychiatric Survey of Texas* New York, Russell Sage Foundation

Innes G. and Sharp G. A. 1962 A study of psychiatric patients in North-east Scotland *J Ment Sci* 108:447–456

(12) Taylor Lord and Chave S. 1964 *Mental Health and Environment* London, Longmans

Hare E. H. and Shaw G. K. 1965 *Mental Health on a New Housing Estate: A Comparative Study of Health in the Two Districts of Croydon* Maudsley Monogr 12 London, Oxford

(13) Tietze C., Lemkau P. V. and Cooper M. M. 1941 Schizophrenia, manic-depressive psychosis and social-economic status *Amer J Sociol* 47:167–175

(14) Hare E. H. 1956 Mental illness and social conditions in Bristol *J Ment Sci* 102:349–357

(15) Faris R. E. L. and Dunham H. W. 1939 *Mental Disorders in Urban Areas: An Ecological Study of Schizophrenia and Other Psychoses* Chicago, University of Chicago Press

(16) Clark R. E. 1948 The relationships of schizophrenia to occupational income and occupational prestige *Amer Sociol Rev* 13:325–330

Clark R. E. 1949 Psychoses, income and occupational prestige: schizophrenia in American cities *Amer J Sociol* 54:433–440

(17) Hare E. H. 1956 Mental illness and social class in Bristol *Brit J. Prev Soc Med* 9:191–195

(18) Stein L. 1957 Social class gradient in schizophrenia *Brit J Prev Soc Med* 11:181–195

(19) Clausen J. A. and Kohn M. L. 1957 Schizophrenia and the social structure of a small city *Public Health Reports* 72: 578–580

(20) Durkheim E. 1897 *Le Suicide* Paris, Alcan Spaulding J. A. and Simpson G. trans. 1951 *Suicide: A Study in Sociology* New York, Free Press

(21) Halbwachs M. 1930 *Les Causes du Suicide* Paris, Alcan

Porterfield A. L. 1952 Suicide and crime in folk and in secular society *Amer J Sociol* 57:331–338

Henry A. F. and Short J. F. Jr. 1954 *Suicide and Homicide: Some Economic Sociological and Psychological Aspects of Aggression* New York, Free Press

Schmid C. F. and Van Arsdal M. D. Jr. 1955 Completed and attempted suicides: a comparative analysis *Amer Sociol Rev* 20:273–283

Breed W. 1966 Suicide, migration and race: a study of cases in New Orleans *J Soc Issues* 22:30–43

(22) Sainsbury P. 1955 *Suicide in London: An Ecological Study* Maudsley Monogr 1 London, Chapman & Hall

(23) Stengel E. and Cooke N. 1958 *Attempted Suicide: Its Social Significance and Effects* Maudsley Monogr 4 London, Chapman & Hall

(24) Merton R. K. 1957 *Social Theory and Social Structure* rev. ed. New York, Free Press

(25) Clinard M. B. ed. 1964 *Anomie and Deviant Behavior: A Discussion and Critique* New York, Free Press

(26) Gerard D. L. and Houston L. G. 1953 Family setting and the social ecology of schizophrenia *Psychiat Quart* 27:90–101

(27) Freedman R. 1950 *Recent Migration to Chicago* Chicago, University of Chicago Press

(28) Gruenberg E. 1961 A mental health survey of older persons in Hoch P. H. and Zubin J. eds. *Comparative Epidemiology of the Mental Disorders* New York, Grune & Stratton pp. 13–23

(29) Townsend P. 1957 *The Family Life of Old People: An Inquiry in East London* London, Routledge

(30) Brockington F. and Lempert S. 1966 *The Social Needs of the Over-80's* Manchester, Manchester University Press

(31) Kay D. W. K., Beamish P. and Roth M. 1964 Old age mental disorders in Newcastle-upon-Tyne: Part I A study of prevalence *Brit J Psychiat* 110:146–158

Kay D. W. K., Beamish P. and Roth M. 1964 The old age mental disorders in Newcastle-upon-Tyne: Part II A study of possible social and medical causes *Brit J Psychiat* 110:668–682

(32) Bahr H. M. and Langfur S. J. 1967 Drinking and social attachment in skid row life histories *Soc Prob* 14:464–472

Edwards G., Hawker A., Williamson V. and Hensman C. 1966 London's skidrow *Lancet* 1:249–252

(33) Morrison S. L. 1959 Principles and methods of epidemiological research and their application to psychiatric illness *J Ment Sci* 105:999–1011

(34) Bales R. F. 1946 Cultural differences in rates of alcoholism *Quart J Stud Alcohol* 6:480–499

Honigman J. J. 1954 *Culture and Personality* New York, Harper

Snyder C. R. 1958 *Alcohol and the Jews: A Cultural Study of Drinking and Sobriety* New York, Free Press

(35) Brooke E. M. 1960 Mental health and the population *Eugen Rev* 51:209–215

(36) Owen M. B. 1941 Alternative hypotheses for the explanation of some of Faris' and Dunham's results *Amer J Sociol* 47:48–52

(37) Meyerson A. 1940 A review of Mental Disorders in Urban Areas *Amer J Psychiat* 96:995–997

(38) Ødegaard Ø. 1956 The incidence of psychoses in various occupations *Int J Soc Psychiat* 2:85–104

Brooke E. M. 1959 National statistics in the epidemiology of mental illness *J Ment Sci* 105:893–908

(39) Goldberg E. M. and Morrison S. L. 1963 Schizophrenia and social class *Brit J Psychiat* 109:785–802

(40) Harris A., Linker I., Norris V. and Shepherd M. 1956 Schizophrenia, a prognostic and social study *Brit J Prev Soc Med* 10:107–114

Lapouse R., Monk M. A. and Terris M. 1956 The drift hypothesis and socioeconomic differentials in schizophrenia *Amer J Pub Health* 46:978–986

Lystad M. H. 1957 Social mobility among selected groups of schizophrenic patients *Amer Sociol Rev* 22:288–292

(41) Langner T. S. and Michael S. T. 1963 *Life Stress and Mental Health* New York, Free Press

(42) Kohn M. and Clausen J. A. 1955 Social isolation and schizophrenia *Amer Sociol Rev* 20:265–273

(43) Hare E. H. 1956 Family setting and the urban distribution of schizophrenia *J Ment Sci* 102:753–757

(44) Hughes C. C., Tremblay M., Rapoport R. N. and Leighton A. H. 1960 *The Stirling County Study of Psychiatric Disorder and Sociocultural Environment Vol 2 People of Cove and Woodlot: Communities from the Viewpoint of Social Psychiatry* New York, Basic Books

(45) Leighton A. H., Lambo T. A., Hughes C. C., Leighton D. C., Murphy J. M. and Macklin D. B. 1963 *Psychiatric Dis-*

order Among the Yoruba Ithaca, N. Y., Cornell University Press

(46) Myers J. K. and Roberts B. H. 1959 *Family and Class Dynamics in Mental Illness* New York, Wiley

(47) Edwards A. L. 1957 *The Social Desirability Variable in Personality Assessment and Research* New York, Dryden

(48) Dohrenwend B. P. 1966 Social status and psychological disorder: an issue of substance and an issue of method *Amer Sociol Rev* 31:14–34

(49) Couch A. and Kenniston K. 1960 Yeasayers and naysayers: agreeing response set as a personality variable *J Abnorm Soc Psychol* 60:151–174

Kassebaum G. G. 1961 Response set: a methodological problem in complaint inventories *Amer J Pub Health* 51: 446–449

(50) Kleiner R. J. and Parker S. 1963 Goal striving and social status, and mental disorder: a research review *Amer Sociol Rev* 28:189–203

Kleiner R. J. and Parker S. 1965 Goal striving and psychosomatic symptoms in a migrant and non-migrant population in Kantor M. B. ed. *Mobility and Mental Health* Springfield, Ill., Thomas pp. 78–85

(51) Lenski G. E. 1954 Status crystallization: non-vertical dimension of social status *Amer Sociol Rev* 19:405–413

Goffman I. W. 1957 Status consistency and preference for change in power distribution *Amer Sociol Rev* 22:275–281

(52) Jackson E. F. 1962 Status consistency and symptoms of stress *Amer Sociol Rev* 27:469–480

(53) Abramson J. H. 1966 Emotional disorder, status inconsistency and migration *Milbank Mem Fund Quart* 44:Part 1, 23–48

(54) Rosenberg M. 1962 The dissonant religious context and emotional disturbance *Amer J Sociol* 68:1–10

(55) Himmelweit H. T., Halsey A. H. and Oppenheim A. N. 1952 The views of adolescents on some aspects of the social class structure *Brit J Sociol* 3:148–172

Oppenheim A. N. 1955 Social status and clique formation among grammar school boys *Brit J Sociol* 6:228–245

part three

The Operation of Services

7

Facilities for Community Care: Problems of Operations

A variety of situations and facilities is required to realize the therapeutic potential of the accumulated knowledge about mental disorder in the community. In England the Mental Health Act faced local health authorities (the public health arm of local government) with the task of developing psychiatric services for patients outside mental hospitals. The inventiveness of hospital psychiatrists in extending their work in the community provided a starting point, and the experience of public health in dealing with tuberculosis as a chronic ambulant sickness provided a model for development (1).

The list of facilities additional to those of hospital inpatient and outpatient services includes day centers, psychotherapeutic clubs, residential arrangements, and social work. This discussion will not attempt a systematic description since there is much room for improvisation. It will attempt to identify some features and problems of operation that are general to facilities of this type.

Day Centers, Social Clubs, and Residential Arrangements

Day centers can be made to provide a range of activities almost as wide as do mental hospitals, depending on the staff and facilities installed. These activities fall into four broad classes. First, day centers can serve as medical treatment centers, or day hospitals, since psychotherapy and even much of the physical treatments for psychiatric patients do not require the concentration of technical staff and equipment to be found in the large modern hospital.

The second class of activities is specific training in such well-defined skills as will help patients to maintain themselves in society. Industrial training, for instance, fits the patient for a particular job ostensibly suited to his needs and abilities and to the labor market. Formal education enables the patient with high-grade subnormality to learn a modicum of reading and reckoning and so to better his mastery of the environment and his chances of employment. The acquisition of domestic skills is encouraged to the same end.

A third activity of day centers is to provide long-term occupations for patients who need special employment because they are too disabled to compete in the open market. The large number of such patients suffer from mental subnormality or from schizophrenia. These occupations may be in fortuitous niches or in units designed especially to provide them, and they may simulate the roles of the outside world more or less closely. Official "sheltered" employment programs in Britain are modeled on the hours and the wage practices in open industry; the regulations of the Ministry of Labour under which units can be set up leave little room to deviate from this model. Together with the permanence of the arrangement, it makes the orientation one of caretaking rather than of therapy; the important product tends to become the material object at the end of the production line rather than the rehabilitated patient. Less formal programs, with free movement between activities to meet the changing needs of patients, are less subject to this deformation of goals.

A fourth class of activities offers vehicles for more diffuse and general aspects of socialization. Although they are the least specific, they are usually the most imaginative of day-center activities, and so far they are also the least evaluated. In this category fall group discussions of personal and social and general topics, group projects, self-government and the assumption of duties and responsibilities by patients, "occupational" therapy, recreation and hobbies, and continual informal exchanges (2).

These activities are designed to facilitate the playing of roles reckoned important to everyday life. Economic production through industrial or craft methods, when its object goes beyond specific training, can also be included under this head. The aim is to transfer to outside situations not the work skill but the work habit and the modes of social interaction. The transfer is not a simple matter. Experiments described in earlier pages show that, in the hospital setting, task groups with patient leadership and group cohesion have a more beneficial influence on social behavior and performance than do individual tasks and workshop activity directed by staff. (See pp. 50, 60.) The same experiments, however, have confirmed that new contexts may override such social effects and prevent their transfer outside the hospital (3).

Therapeutic social clubs belong to this fourth class of activities. They provide a setting in which patients can learn or relearn the proprieties of social intercourse. In this setting patients may break through social isolation, gain support from personal relationships, and develop self-confidence in the exercise of social activities and in helping others.

Patients can also assume responsibilities and learn the middle-class skills of committeemen by running their club. After a period of apathy and decline in a club for patients in Salford, for example, a remarkable efflorescence came about when a physician induced the club members to elect a committee and govern themselves (4).

Social clubs afford opportunities for unobtrusive education and for familiarizing relatives with the ambience of therapy. "Significant others" can be key persons in the management of mental patients. They themselves may be in serious need of education and support, and many studies show that close relatives are frequently disturbed in mind. Through social clubs isolated families can find support, expand their contracted social networks, and enter new social roles (4, 5).

In summary, day centers and clubs through their manifold activities fulfill the functions of the diffuse socialization of patients and of rehabilitation for work and for life in the home. At the same time, they support families by sharing the burden of "minding," by shortening the duration of contact between patient and family, and by breaking into social isolation.

The balance of functions and types of activity shifts according to the composition of the patient group. Activities must naturally differ because of differing capacities between the sexes, between adults and children, and between the mentally ill and the mentally subnormal. Strict segregation between categories such as the mentally ill and mentally subnormal adults need not be maintained, although polarization occurs because of the disparities in their abilities and needs.

Among children day center care provides chiefly for the mentally subnormal. Although young subnormal children and their families can benefit from nurseries for normal children, special centers cater for those whose physique outgrows that of their peers in playing age, for those with marked physical handicaps, and for those with marked behavior disturbances. At some stage most severely subnormal children and psychotic children can benefit from special day centers that substitute for schools. Such categorization into special groups creates the risk that the facets of the child's individuality other than his handicap will be ignored to his detriment. On the other hand, care in these centers, as compared with schools, can usually be ruled more by the individual needs of a child than by the group needs of an age set. Staffing is more generous and standards of performance more flexible than in most schools. This form of care for severely subnormal children is discussed at length in a later chapter.

In Britain the Social Psychiatry Research Unit of the Medical Research Council has made notable contributions in evaluating industrial rehabilitation centers both for mentally subnormal patients and for those with chronic psychoses. These studies leave no doubt that such centers can improve the individual development, the job performance, and the employment records of patients (6).

Hostels, foster homes, small self-sustained households of patients, and prearranged lodgings can all serve patients who are partially dependent because of mental disorder but who do not require hospital treatment. Such patients have often remained in hospitals merely because they required a substitute home and not for any special treatment (7). Some patients need a substitute home because no effective kin are available, some because of a failure of accommodation within the home. Other patients require support when they first resume social relations in the community after discharge from the hospital. Hostel residence enables the patient to maintain some roles within the community while yet being given support. With such support many patients are capable of getting and keeping jobs when they have long been disabled, nonproductive, and socially dependent (8).

Hostels have thus been seen by administrators as a means of reducing the call on mental hospital beds by avoiding unnecessary admissions and unnecessarily long stays; they have been seen by clinicians as a means of preventing the onset of "institution neurosis" and impeding the advance of the syndrome of "social breakdown," or of restoring patients already affected by these conditions. These clinical conditions are widely attributed to the structure and values generated by large isolated institutions with formal bureaucratic organization. The stay of patients in hostels is often short but may have to be long-term or even permanent.[1] It is possible in these circumstances to replace the large isolated institution with a small isolated institution. Staff and patients conditioned by large institutions to the use of authoritarian methods of administration can transfer these forms of relationships to hostels. The alternative methods present many difficulties: We have still much to learn about the organization of therapeutic group living.

1. Data on hostel usage for the period 1962–1964 in Salford are given in Appendix B. Figures include diagnosis, reason for admission, age and sex groups, discharges, and outcome.

Group Relations in Community Care

Our experiences in Salford over the past several years reveal a number of problems that are general to community care programs. Some are problems of external relations and coordination, which will be analyzed in a later chapter. Others to be considered at this juncture are internal, and they are mainly concerned with group living, for instance, with problems of recruitment and exclusion and of leadership.

Each unit among the facilities for care is concerned to form continuing groups, whereas individual members pass more or less rapidly through them. Continuity is essential to building up and transmitting a workable system of norms of behavior and of rules and sanctions to limit deviations from these norms. These definitions of behavior must be appropriate to life in the community and at the same time consistent with the stability of formal relationships of authority within the institution. The two requirements are not readily compatible in every situation; it is peculiarly difficult to approximate the norms of hostel living to those of the home. Much hangs on the form or structure of the organization, on the character of the group, and on the training and personality of staff.

We have noted that the typical structure of large institutions for residential care cannot provide the whole range of roles common to the world outside. This structure therefore cannot socialize directly for community life, perhaps not even with radical reorganization. Intensive studies of groups in closed wards have yielded insight into their structure and dynamics. Some of the sharpest of these reveal the abnormalities of group interaction imposed by the limitations of space and of alternative roles (9, 10).

The ideology of the hospital authorities and the status of the patients allow considerable variation in the forms of social interaction, for instance, between state and private hospitals in the United States. Yet the best of these conditions are far from simulating interaction outside the ward. Biologists have learned that the behavior of caged animals cannot be taken as the norm for those that run free.

For want of information, effective socialization for community life cannot yet be claimed for hostels either, even though roles in the community are accessible to residents. The effects of the many variations in the contexts provided by hostels are now being studied. Dissimilar contexts can be expected to change the values, the forms of relationships, and the nature of the effects of primary groups on their members (11). The initial results of a study in Lancashire initiated by the author indicate that subnormal adults living in homes prefer them to the large traditional institutions and that they do take up family and community relations; but the extent to which these changes occur depends on the staff of each hostel. The theme of social structure as a force that influences context will be taken up in detail later. (See Chapter 13.) Here I shall mention only some observations on group relations.

The character of a group is partly determined by the attributes of its members, their age, sex, type of mental disorder, social class of origin, and social mobility. These attributes make up each patient's persona and delimit his status in the various situations of community care. They give a degree of predictability to behavior in the recurring encounters of particular roles. In weighing the chances of assimilating new recruits to a group, all these attributes must therefore be included. They must be reckoned also in the obverse of assimilation, that is, exclusion and segregation.

Assimilation is a two-way process. In subjective psychological terms it is effected through the congruence of the patient's self-image with that of the group to which he is recruited and with the reciprocal images of those who are already members of the group. For example, in an active club for mental patients in Salford, assimilation failed when the admission of a number of young, severely subnormal adults with physical stigmata retarded the further recruitment of older mentally ill patients. Social class discriminated in an equally powerful way between the new members. Similar difficulty was met in recruiting mentally ill patients to an industrial center in which the majority were severely subnormal people.

The images and perceptions that thus seem to hinder recruitment are shaped by the stereotypes of a culture, but they are probably not fixed (12). Continuing interaction can dissolve the stereotype and replace it with the face behind the mask; long-established members of the club readily accepted subnormal patients as members. Submissiveness, as with some institutionalized and some subnormal patients, or withdrawal, as with some schizophrenic patients, may make the stereotype irrelevant. These traits are commonly found with the "social breakdown" syndrome. They alter the patterns of response on both sides of a social interchange. In the industrial center, submissive patients with prolonged experience of institutions were not difficult to recruit to groups whatever their composition, and withdrawn schizophrenic patients tended to avoid contact with all groups and not only with the obviously subnormal.

The subjective psychological dimensions of assimilation tie in with objective sociological dimensions. Successful recruitment follows when the newcomer finds roles in the group that satisfy him and that are accepted by others. Within larger groups cliques form that offer more or less satisfying roles on the basis of common interests and cultural affinities (13). There is much to learn about reducing the disruptive tendencies of cliques and realizing their therapeutic and supportive potential for members. To some degree this must depend on their obtrusiveness and on the choices open to those excluded. In a social club the mere provision of space in which groups of varying composition can disperse to follow their diverse activities may obviate conflict and enhance both pleasure and personal support.

A group consists of a mesh of reciprocal roles. In "milieu" therapy the roles a group affords its members are the basic instruments of learning. If the statuses and attributes of group members are homogeneous, the variation in roles and the types of exchanges are thereby limited. Everyday observation teaches that homogeneous groups of patients can be expected to cohere and easily to assimilate new members (14). They can also be expected to generate certain of the values that characterize the single-sex groups found in such institutions as the armed forces and boarding schools. These are not the values of the community and must tend to maintain the separateness of patients from the community. Loyalties among peers are built on reciprocal systems of obligations, norms, and sanctions that create a separate and secret culture of subordinates in the institution. This culture provides a defense against the assaults of authority, a cloak for insubordination, and a means of defeating chafing rules and of "working the system" (10).

Heterogeneous groups of patients generate a greater variation in roles, learning situations, and values and reduce the pressure toward exclusiveness and segregation. This proposition, derived in the course of day-to-day work and observation in Salford, has found support in an experiment with small task groups of hospital patients. Heterogeneous groups performed better than homogeneous groups. The heterogenous group with a range of talents and abilities afforded better opportunities for articulating roles within the groups (3).

Heterogeneous groups, however, make much greater demands on the staff. They must learn how to gain acceptance in the group for decisions that discriminate between members precisely because they respect the individuality of each member. The comfortable tradition of uniform nondiscriminating treatment within each group is carried over from traditional mental hospitals by both staff and patients and has to be overcome. In hostels, for instance, conflicts over discrimination can arise because the dependence of some patients is tolerated as inevitable and permanent, while at the same time other patients are pressed toward independence; in day centers, an effective system of incentives might well have to discriminate between subnormal and schizophrenic patients, if the experiments noted earlier are to be taken into account. (See pp. 59, 60.)

When patients come into conflict with authority, therefore, heterogeneity imposes solutions that discriminate between individuals. The nuclear family provides an analogy for socialization in the heterogeneous group. Conflict is an integral accompaniment of the family process, and it is handled in an individual way by means appropriate to the status of the participants in the conflict. The integrity of the family group is maintained by the conditioned acceptance from birth of an asymmetrical relationship of superordination and subordination between the old and the young generations, by the continual reinforcement of affective bonds, and by legal obligations. Cohesion of this order is not available to groups in institutions to protect their continuity; thus staff who are asked to allow for idiosyncratic needs may become anxious about maintaining authority. "If you let one do it, then all want to do it."

The difficulty of making such individual decisions is enhanced because the groups are new and arbitrarily constructed. The staff can draw neither on their own socialization experiences and those of others, as parents do, nor can they appeal to the uniform rulings of the typical institution. At the outset the sanctions available in a hostel with voluntary patients are few, and their range is limited by the quality of domestic life that it affords. They are soon exhausted in those hostels that serve as little more than dormitories, and the ultimate sanction of exclusion is quickly reached. Discipline is better accepted by group members when they themselves feel responsibility for it.

Self-government through elected committees helps to foster a "morality of cooperation" rather than a "morality of constraint." This proposition too has found confirmation in experiments with small groups of mental hospital patients. Groups with minimal supervision fared better on all measures (except the patient's own reports) than did those with "normal" supervision. Staff too fared better. They much preferred the role of professional adviser, who was expected to assume authority only on the appeal of self-activated groups, to that of director of group activities who had immediate authority over patients (3). The task of group supervision is difficult and demanding, the more so since success may require the abrogation of supervision.

Social Work

The social worker guides people through the complexities of social agencies in the modern industrial state to the agency appropriate to their needs. In the course of the exploration, he advises about those personal problems that emerge or for which his help is solicited. In counseling, his field of operation is not so much intrapsychic as interpersonal; he is concerned with the field of social relations. It must be allowed that many psychiatric social workers do in fact subsume the intrapsychic field to that of social work and even see individual psychotherapy as a central activity. In Britain social work outside the hospital is carried out by a variety of workers with appointments in hospitals and other agencies, but chiefly by mental welfare officers. The mental welfare officer is the executive agent of services for the community care of mental disorder. If community care is to be effective, therefore, he must be able to work in collaboration with the psychiatrists and general practitioners responsible for the medical care of the patient, as well as with his colleagues in the public health team.

Evidence for the efficacy of social work in maintaining the social performance of mental patients is not plentiful. Evaluation of the effects of social work is a complex undertaking that seldom has been essayed with scientific thoroughness. The undertaking tends to be expensive. Follow-up is essential and requires measures uncontaminated by the possible bias of the professionals who give the service. Where social work evaluation has been approached with methodical safeguards, unforeseen snags have frequently crippled the endeavor.

The classic research design requires experimental and control groups, and at once it raises the ethical problem of denying available services to controls and the practical problems of sustaining the denial in the face of clinical need. Should this snag be circumvented by comparing service units separated by location, the many uncontrolled accompaniments of specific treatment and the variable quality of personnel in separate service units can complicate the comparability and the interpretation of results.

In psychiatric social work, evaluation cannot avoid the further trial of uncertain compliance. In any medical treatment compliance is a factor that intervenes between prescription and effects. With drug treatments objective measures of urinary excretion reveal that up to 50 per cent of psychiatric patients may fail to take take prescribed drugs (15). Patients may fail to comply even when, as in tuberculosis, the threat of death attends recalcitrance (16).

In the case of psychiatric patients, intrapsychic factors arising from the illness as well as the dictates of personality and culture may interfere with the motivation to comply. In an American study to evaluate the effect of a rehabilitation center, the whole project faltered, if it did not quite founder, on this obstacle (17). In this study, unusual for its uncompromising design, social work was offered as part of a rehabilitation program centered on industrial training. Discharged male patients were first screened for their suitability for training, and a random selection was made from those deemed suitable. The number who then (having been found suitable and allocated at random to treatment) entered the program and ultimately persisted with it was so small as to cast doubt on the final negative result.

Such attrition, not often written about by researchers, is a special snag of controlled trials in which representative sampling of the whole range of cases in a population is attempted. Similar losses were met in a trial of conditioning treatment in enuresis that attempted to include all those eligible from a community sample of enuretic children. Some cases had remitted spontaneously between the discovery of the case and the mounting of the trial, some did not desire treatment, some were judged by the clinician unsuited to treatment, and some entered treatment and failed to execute it properly or to complete it. The starting number of 118 was reduced to 23 who completed the treatment prescribed by the experimental design (18). Controlled trials in medicine are often less simple than the published accounts reveal (19). Trials of social work cannot pretend to be simple.

The sum of results from evaluations of social work is damping. Favorable results have been obtained only from studies defective in design or open to more than one interpretation, and negative results from those executed with rigor. To take an example of a favorable result from a Salford study (admittedly a preliminary one), a retrospective analysis suggested that good immediate prognosis for discharged patients, as measured by their return to hospital, was related to early follow-up by social workers (20). In this study there are two obvious weaknesses. First, a bias in the selection of cases could not be ruled out as a factor in the result. Second, return to the hospital is at best an ambiguous measure of deterioration, since it could reflect the active treatment of hopeful cases. Furthermore, the patient who remains out of the hospital may be far from well, as emerged in the earlier discussion of the accommodation of mentally ill people in community roles.

A second British study, this one properly controlled by random selection of the treatments, gave support to these favorable findings (21). This study of schizophrenic and depressed women discharged from the hospital measured the effects of care given by nurses in a day center and at home against care given entirely in outpatient clinics. The social support, however, was given by nurses and not by social workers, and in this case also the effect of the program was measured by the unsatisfactory criterion of readmission.

More elaborate studies contrast with these results and have demonstrated little benefit from social work. In the ten-year Cambridge-Somerville study, social work services were given to more than 300 boys selected because of a predicted high risk of delinquency. Adjustment was not substantially better than in controls (22). In a four-year study with similar aims, a sample of potential "problem" cases among high school girls was allocated at random to treatment and control groups. The treatment was through an agency, which offered casework and group counseling. A battery of criteria was used to measure effects. Again few statistically significant differences were found between the experimental and control groups (23).

It can be argued that neither of these projects evaluated social work in its usual sense, for both were preventive in intent. Help was not proffered in response to recognized dependence arising out of sickness or out of some similar source of social disability. As with the mass screening programs of personal preventive medicine, there was a reversal of the usual role between professional and client in which the client solicits help. In both studies a further criticism follows in part from their preventive character, because the numbers in treatment and the amount of treatment were limited by the meager response among those who were solicited. A reanalysis of the data of the Cambridge-Somerville study makes the criticism more cogent. While still negative in the overall result, this analysis showed benefit in one small category of cases. These few boys received regular intensive contact with a friendly adult counselor (which it was originally intended all the boys should have). Perhaps all that can legitimately be said about the study as a whole is that routine social work did not deter potential young delinquents from crime.

A closer approximation to the social work role in psychiatry than was tested in these experiments can be found in the evaluation of the New York Chemung County project designed to help "multiproblem" families on the books of the state welfare agency. In this careful experiment, families were given intensive help by caseworkers of superior training who had special access to the facilities of other social agencies. These families fared no better than control families who received the usual social work services (24). From this study we need not conclude that social work is ineffective, for there was a slight degree of improvement on the chosen indexes in families exposed to both types of service. We must conclude that intensive "casework" carried out by persons with high qualifications produced no better results than the routine service. This contradicts the interpretation of the subgroup analysis of the Cambridge-Somerville study noted above. The studies are not strictly comparable, and further work may reconcile their results.

The difficulties of "multiproblem" families are characteristically intractable. So too is the difficulty of demonstrating positive results in the evaluation of social projects. For both technical and more general reasons the results obtained so far should not be taken as entirely discouraging. On technical grounds we should note first that social work itself has not yet been the subject of a carefully controlled trial among psychiatric patients. The results of an evaluation of two community psychiatric services in comparable areas in the South of England suggest in retrospect that social work made an important contribution to the well-being of the families of mental patients (25).

In one service at Chichester 18 per cent of referred patients were admitted to the hospital at their entry to the study, and many more treated at home or in a day hospital. In the second service at Salisbury 52 per cent of referred patients were admitted to the mental hospital. The domiciliary-based service at Chichester was somewhat more successful than the hospital-based service at Salisbury in dealing with old patients, equally successful in dealing with younger patients with severe disorders, but less successful in dealing with younger patients with milder disorders. The measures used to compare results, in a two-year follow-up, included the anxiety and distress of close relatives, the extent of their added household burdens, and the employment of the patients.

The success of Chichester with old people was probably owing to the good liaison between general practitioners and the community psychiatrists; the researchers suggest that the practitioners referred more old people for help because they found they could be helped. The success of Salisbury with younger patients was probably due to social work. Retrospective analysis showed that the hospital-based Salisbury service had an active social work service well coordinated with other social agencies in the area and that the help it gave was far greater in amount than in Chichester. Fifty-nine per cent of the family needs recognized by the researchers had been attended to in Salisbury and only 20 per cent in Chichester. Patients and families had much more regular contact with the social work service in Salisbury, as well as help with employment and other matters.

These results are encouraging, if not conclusive because of the many components of the two programs. They give substance to the technical objection that social work with psychiatric patients has not been subject to direct test. Some other technical reasons for further study can be raised. The sensitivity, the discrimination, and the validity of some of the measures of response can be questioned. The satisfaction felt by clients also tends not to be reflected in measures of their performance. Sensitive measures of effects are needed to include the three dimensions of the intrapsychic processes of patients, their full range of social performance, and the impact of their illness on their families.[2]

Further technical questions can be raised about the input of the treatments being evaluated. "Casework" is no more amenable to simple and agreed definition than is psychotherapy. However this may be, therapeutic input will remain far from optimal as long as social work begins after the patient leaves the mental hospital. Intervention at this point is late in the cycle of interaction between the patient and "significant others," especially in those cycles that escalate from the denial of disorder in an individual to his ultimate extrusion from the household.

On general grounds there is neither more nor less reason to question the utility of social work than there is to question that of the medical and other professions whose function is to absorb some segment of the multiform strains of social deviance. On a pragmatic view social workers in contemporary societies serve a growing need which can hardly be met without the help of a specialized profession.

In this respect social work is a close relative of psychiatry. The resemblance remains close when the empirical results of evaluation are considered. Comparisons of a variety of types of psychotherapy, carried out with a variety of degrees of rigor, have revealed no conclusive superiority for any one type. In some cases comparisons revealed no superiority for active therapy over the healing effects of time alone (27). The analogy remains close when highly trained professional therapists are compared with therapists of little training. One study shows that the results obtained by medical students stand up well to those of psychiatrists (28).

The response to this array of evidence might be despair

2. Systematic efforts to devise and test such indexes have been made and provide useful measures (26).

that expensive training, intense intellectual effort, and subtle skills achieve no more than do cruder approaches. A more creative response is to put the results to use in a reordered framework. They permit us to strive, with few misgivings, for the comprehensive cover of communities at the sacrifice of sophistication. This is already the implicit premise of community psychiatry in Britain. In most countries of the world, health services face a crisis of manpower, however various are the causes, the circumstances, and the needs. The more general and unspecialized the professional role, the more acute the shortage. India has more cardiac surgeons than she can put to work; the United States has a sufficient number of research workers by the standards of any other country; neither country meets the requirements of comprehensive general medical cover of the total population.

The disparities of maldistribution are perhaps most obvious in industrialized countries that can afford psychiatric services. The Midtown Manhattan study contains a striking example. At one level of measurement about a quarter of the sample population could be regarded as psychiatrically impaired (29). Only 5 per cent of this staggering proportion were in treatment. Yet the data show than an equal number who were not regarded as impaired were in psychotherapy.

The sum of the evidence suggests that in social work as in psychiatry the gains from high standards and sophistication do not balance the loss of cover for the population entailed by intensive and expensive individual care. A thorough examination of the functions carried out by the total range of social welfare services in an English county revealed that in specialized agencies such as welfare, qualified social workers were likely to be overtrained in relation to the type of demands made upon them (30). This observation seemed least true for probation officers and mental welfare officers. In making such judgments, demands should not be viewed as static. A homeostatic balance surely exists between the type of services offered and the calls made upon a service, a balance mediated by mutual expectations between agency and clients.

Most of the measures that have been used to assess psychiatric and social services have focused on the direct contact between the individual professional worker and his patient or client. These measures do not reflect the contribution of knowledge, skill, and sophistication at the level of giving direction to the work of an agency. Such direction involves identifying the nature of the needs and planning to meet them and supplying consultation and guidance for the less-sophisticated workers. One can assume the necessity for these activities. Consulting functions are informally allocated among professional colleagues in organizations, even when specifically prohibited (31).

A rational conclusion would be to seek an allocation of function among psychotherapists and social therapists commensurate with the skill and training required to achieve the results within our reach. Such a service would rely on a relatively small number of highly trained persons to identify needs and generate policy, to facilitate effective work by others less highly trained, and to diffuse their skills by consultation and teaching. It would use much larger numbers of people trained less intensively and in a different manner to carry out many of the functions required in the community care of mental disorder. Something not dissimilar is perhaps in the course of evolution in Britain through the generic two-year courses for psychiatric social workers.

The scientific evaluation of social work is a typical contemporary problem raised by the imperatives of the scientific ethos. The newer a field of professional activity is, the more likely that it must incorporate and face up to scientific modes of operation and evaluation. We shall consider this question of evaluation in detail in the next chapter.

References

(1) May A. R. and Gregory E. 1963 An experiment in district psychiatry *Public Health* 78:19–25

Wright S. L. 1963 The adult psychiatric patient in the community *Public Health* 77:218–222

(2) Morgan G. D. and Tylden E. 1957 The "Stepping Stones Club" *Lancet* 1:877–878

(3) Fairweather G. W. ed. 1964 *Social Psychology in Treating Mental Illness: An Experimental Approach* New York, Wiley

(4) Kushlick A. 1962 Report on the "Stepping Stones Club" in Susser M. W. *A Report on the Mental Health Services of the City of Salford for 1961* City of Salford, Eng., Health Department pp. 7–16

(5) Bierer J. 1944 New form of group psychotherapy *Mental Health* 5:23–26

Bierer J. ed. 1949 *Therapeutic Social Clubs* London, Lewis

Lerner R. C. 1960 The therapeutic social club: social rehabilitation for mental patients *Int J Soc Psychiat* 6:101–114

(6) Carstairs G. M., O'Connor N. and Rawnsley K. 1956 Organization of a hospital workshop for chronic psychotic patients *Brit J Prev Soc Med* 10:136–140

O'Connor N. and Tizard J. 1956 *The Social Problem of Mental Deficiency* London, Pergamon

Clarke A. M. and Clarke A. D. B. eds. 1958 *Mental Deficiency: the Changing Outlook* London, Methuen

Wing J. K. and Giddens R. G. T. 1959 Industrial rehabilitation of male chronic schizophrenic patients *Lancet* 2:505–507

(7) Lowe C. R. and McKeown T. 1950 The care of the chronic sick Part 2 Social and demographic data *Brit J Prev Soc Med* 4:61–74

Stein Z. A. and Susser M. W. 1960 Estimating hostel needs for backward citizens *Lancet* 2:486–488

Rawnsley K., Loudon J. B. and Miles H. L. 1962 Attitudes of relatives to patients in mental hospitals *Brit J Prev Soc Med* 16:1–15

(8) Clarke D. H. and Cooper L. W. 1960 Psychiatric half-way hostel *Lancet* 1:588–590

(9) Stanton A. H. and Schwartz M. S. 1954 *The Mental Hospital: A Study of Institutional Participation in Psychiatric Illness and Treatment* New York, Basic Books

Henry J. 1964 Space and power on a psychiatric unit in Wessen A. F. ed. *The Psychiatric Hospital as a Social System* Springfield, Ill., Thomas pp. 20–34

Lebar F. M. 1964 Some implications of ward structure for enculturation of patients in Wessen A. F. ed. *The Psychiatric Hospital as a Social System* Springfield, Ill., Thomas pp. 5–19

(10) Goffman E. 1961 *Asylums: Essays on the Social Situation of Mental Patients and Other Inmates* Chicago, Aldine

(11) Shils E. A.. 1950 Primary groups in the American Army in Merton R. K. and Lazarsfeld P. F. eds. *Continuities in Social Research* New York, Free Press

(12) Richardson S. A., Hastorf A. H., Goodman N. and Dornbusch S. M. 1961 Cultural uniformity in reaction to physical disabilities *Amer Sociol Rev* 26:241–247

Goodman N., Richardson S. A., Dornbusch S. M. and Hastorf A. H. 1963 Variant reactions to physical disabilities *Amer Sociol Rev* 28:429–435

(13) Smith H. L. and Thrasher J. 1963 Roles, cliques and sanctions: dimensions of patient society *Int J Soc Psychiat* 9:184–191

(14) Festinger L. A. 1954 A theory of social comparison process *Hum Rel* 7:117–140

(15) Parkes C. M., Brown G. W. and Monck E. M. 1962 The general practitioner and the schizophrenic patient *Brit Med J* 1:972–976

(16) Benstead N. and Theobald G. W. 1952 Iron and physiological anaemia of pregnancy *Brit Med J* 1:407–410

Haler D. 1952 Therapeutic response of secondary anemias to organic and inorganic iron salts *Brit Med J* 2:1241–1243

Mohler D. N., Wallin D. G. and Dreyfus E. G. 1955 Studies in home treatment of streptococcal disease: failure of patients to take penicillin by mouth as prescribed *New Eng J Med* 252:1116–1118

Simpson J. M. 1956 Simple tests for detection of urinary PAS *Tubercle* 37:333–340

Dixon W. M., Stradling P. and Wootton I. D. P. 1957 Outpatient PAS therapy *Lancet* 2:871–882

Luntz G. R. W. N. and Austin R. 1960 New stick tests for PAS in urine *Brit Med J* 1:1679–1684

Davis M. S. and Eichorn R. L. 1963 Compliance with medical regimens: a panel study *J Health Hum Behav* 4:240–249

Wilcox D. R. C., Gillan R. and Hare E. H. 1965 Do psychiatric outpatients take their drugs? *Brit Med J* 2:790–792

(17) Meyer H. J. and Borgatta E. F. 1959 *An Experiment in Mental Patient Rehabilitation* New York, Russell Sage Foundation

(18) Forrester R. M., Stein Z. A. and Susser M. W. 1964 A trial of conditioning therapy in nocturnal enuresis *Develop Med Child Neurol* 6:158–166

(19) Joyce C. R. B. 1962 Patient cooperation and the sensitivity of clinical trials *J Chron Dis* 15:1025–1036

Reynolds E., Joyce C. R. B., Swift J. L., Tooley R. H. and Weatherall M. 1965 Psychological and clinical investigation of the treatment of anxious outpatients with three barbiturates and placebo *Brit J Psychiat* 3:84–95

Porter A. W. M. 1966 Patients and tablets? *Brit Med J* 1:1301

(20) Susser M. W. 1963 *A Report of the Mental Health Services of the City of Salford for 1962* City of Salford, Eng., Health Department pp. 8–10

(21) Sheldon A. 1964 An evaluation of psychiatric after-care *Brit J Psychiat* 110:662–667

(22) Powers E. and Witmer H. 1951 *An Experiment in the Prevention of Delinquency: The Cambridge-Somerville Youth Study* New York, Columbia University Press

McCord J., McCord W. and Zola I. 1959 *Origins of Crime: A New Evaluation of the Cambridge-Somerville Youth Study* New York, Columbia University Press

(23) Meyer H. J., Borgatta E. F. and Jones W. C. 1965 *Girls at Vocational High: An Experiment in Social Work Intervention* New York, Russell Sage Foundation

(24) Wallace D. 1967 The Chemung County evaluation of casework service to dependent multiproblem families: another problem outcome *Soc Serv Rev* 41:379–389

(25) Grad J. C. 1968 A two year follow-up in Williams R. H. and Ozarin L. D. eds. *Community Mental Health: An International Perspective* San Francisco, Jossey-Bass pp. 429–454

(26) Hunt J. Mc V. and Kogan L. 1950 *Measuring Results in Social Casework: A Manual on Judging Movement* New York, Family Service Association

Geismar L. L. and Ayres B. 1960 *Measuring Family Functioning* St. Paul, Minn., Family Centered Project

(27) Wallace H. E. R. and Whyte M. B. H. 1959 Natural history of the psychoneuroses *Brit Med J* 1:144–148

Berelson B. and Steiner G. A. 1964 *Human Behavior: An Inventory of Scientific Findings* New York, Harcourt

Giel R., Knox R. S. and Carstairs G. M. 1964 A five-year follow-up of 100 neurotic outpatients *Brit Med J* 2:160–163

(28) Heine R. W. ed. 1962 *The Student Physician as a Psychotherapist* Chicago, University of Chicago Press

(29) Srole L., Langner T. S., Michael S. T., Opler M. K. and Rennie T. A. C. 1962 *Mental Health in the Metropolis: The Midtown Manhattan Study* New York, McGraw-Hill

(30) Jefferys M. 1965 *An Anatomy of Social Welfare Services: A Survey of Social Welfare Staff and Their Clients in the County of Buckinghamshire* London, Joseph

(31) Blau P. M. 1964 The research process in the study of the dynamics of bureaucracy in Hammond P. ed. *Sociologists at Work: Essays on the Craft of Social Research* New York, Basic Books pp. 16–49

8

The Tools of Evaluation

Current proposals for the community care of mental disorder, in their naked form, may well have appalled the great reformers of the last century. These men and women devoted themselves to achieving humane care for the mentally ill who crowded the poorhouses and the prisons and to protecting them from the neglect and the hostility of the "community." Such personages as Lord Shaftesbury in Britain and Dorothea Dix in the United States campaigned among an ignorant public, persuaded apathetic legislatures, and fought the self-interest, complacency, and ideological rigidity of their enemies. It is the institutions they helped to build that the movement toward community care now seeks to reform, replace, or abandon.

This is a recurring irony in the history of social reform. One generation of reformers has created the abuses of the next. The means of prediction have been inadequate to envision all the consequences of new forms, just as on the grandest scale the use of the Marxist dialectic failed to predict untoward consequences of the Bolshevik revolution. Contemporary reformers can hope to do better by arming themselves with instruments of prediction more precise if smaller in scale. Even so, rapid historical change outruns the conditions in which prediction holds good. We need to fashion social institutions that are homeostatic in function and sensitive to pressure, with a built-in propensity for change. One mechanism that can help to achieve homeostasis is continuous epidemiological and sociological appraisal. This type of analysis can serve both as a sharpener of prediction and as a prod to maintain momentum.

The focus of this chapter is therefore on evaluation as a need of health organizations and on the mechanisms and methods by which they can put it to use. The question of the meaning to be attached to evaluation is bound to arise. For the purposes of this discussion its meaning must be wide enough to contain the perspectives of the therapist, administrator, and research worker and the gamut of methods from the simplest to the most sophisticated. I shall treat as evaluative all conscious and systematic approaches to the study of the functions and effects of health organizations. These approaches are made through surveys, case studies, and experiments.

Surveys rely on information that can be elicited from existing sources and quantified, provided suitable mechanisms are set up to collect it. One use of surveys is descriptive, that is, to set out norms in numerical terms (1). Surveys of this type set out the attributes of populations, of environments, and of trends in time. A second use of surveys is explanatory, that is, to compare different populations in relation to environments and trends in time and to account for the variation among them. The aim of this type of survey is to establish relationships between phenomena considered as effects (dependent variables) and their causes (or independent variables). In order to do so, specific variables or combinations of them must be conceived and isolated and the effects of their presence or absence compared. Comparison of the differences and similarities in the past or awaited experience of populations is the essence of the survey method.

Case studies rely on observers to collate and select, in one or several cases, their direct observations. They observe process in terms of social structure, function, and interaction. The observations may be quantified and systematic, but a large qualitative element is inherent in them. The good case study collects quantitative data to provide a basis for judging how far it is typical in its setting.

Experiment introduces a new element into an existing situation and measures its effect. The social experiment differs from the survey in that it studies the effects of active and directed intervention. Experiment is prospective only; it aims at a planned comparison, which controls the introduction of the variables to be studied.

The survey is distinct from the social experiment because it is at the mercy of events. A survey exercises no direct control over the variables of central concern; it exploits natural environment and history. But it shares with the experiment the comparative method of analysis and interpretation. A survey, even when retrospective, can approximate the social experiment by the judicious reconstruction of past experience. Such a reconstruction employs the same safeguards as the social experiment and is alert to the same sources of error.

Evaluation can be conducted at varying planes according to need, resources, and opportunity, each level requiring successively deeper probes. Three logical prerequisites must be met before evaluative research can be undertaken. First, the ultimate *objectives* of the project must be conceived in a manner that satisfies its sponsors. Second, the hoped-for *effects* are specified within the framework that the objectives provide. Effects both intended or untoward are specified as far as possible, for instance according to the individuals and groups aimed at by the project, the nature of the functions involved, and the times and places they are expected. Third, the *program* must be outlined in all its detail. The program is the "treatment," or experimental variable; its components must be made explicit, and its application to the experimental situation must be observed or available to measurement.

The design of the evaluative research follows from these prerequisites. Surveys and case studies serve to describe the treatment as it is delivered. A central strut of evaluative research is to check the intention of a program against what is actually done. This has been termed "evaluation of technique"

(2). For testing outcome against ultimate objectives, which has been termed "evaluation of accomplishment," experimental designs serve best. I shall begin with surveys.

Surveys

A convenient classification of evaluation surveys in ongoing organizations is made in terms of the degree to which their execution requires research designs and data collection independent of the activities of the organization. We shall discuss these activities under the four headings of "routine audits," "operations studies," "opportunist surveys," and "tailormade surveys."

Routine Audits. The simplest level of the survey is that of the routine audit. This audit can be likened to the bookkeeping, costing, and accounting essential to any large contemporary organization. In a bureaucracy responsibility is referred upward through a hierarchy, and this structure generates a reciprocal need for the control of functions delegated downward. Systematic records of the "input" of a program, such as the size and type of staff engaged in it and measures of work done, together with records of "output," such as referrals and consultations, have usually satisfied these requirements. These quantitative data are compiled and scrutinized over convenient time periods in forms that permit continuing comparison of selected items and categories of information. In other words, even at this simplest level the data is used to establish norms, and to compare performance over time, between categories of employees and between subsystems of the organization. The elaborations of method in social research can all be treated as sophistications of the themes of norms and comparisons.

Table 1 is an example of routine auditing. This table shows the work load of the social workers (mental-welfare officers) of the mental-health service of the City of Salford in terms of referrals. Salford is a city of about 150,000 people in the southeast conurbation of Lancashire. Table 1C reveals an apparent decline in caseload, measured by referrals, as the num-

Table 1. The Case Load of the Mental-Welfare Officer*

	1959	1960	1961	1962	1963	1964
A. Mental Illness						
Number of new patients referred	233	239	255	260	298	301
Numer of known patients referred	197	259	215	207	210	231
Total patients referred	430	498	470	467	508	532
Second and subsequent referrals during calendar year	73	89	85	122	85	125
Total referrals	503	587	555	589	593	657
Mental Subnormality						
Number of new patients referred	41	38	26	29	32	60
Total new patients referred						
Mental illness and mental subnormality	274	277	281	289	330	361
B. Total number of visits†	8,560	7,427	6,752	7,849	9,992	9,579
Number of officers (units time per annum)	6	5.6	5.06	6.63	9.03	9.13
Average number of visits per officer	1,427	1,326	1,334	1,184	1,106	1,049
C. Average number of new patients referred per officer	46	49	56	44	36	40
Average number of known patients referred per officer	33	46	42	31	23	25
Average number of referrals per officer	91	112	114	93	69	79
D. Average number of visits per new patient referred	31	27	24	27	30	26
Average number of visits per total referrals	16	12	11	13	16	13

* Excludes cases resident outside Salford (24 in 1964).   † Includes office interviews, visits to hospital, and so on.

ber of mental-welfare officers increased. This decline was the intended result of a policy designed to give more attention to each client. Indexes to confirm the intended result were sought in the average number of visits made for each referral (Table 1D), which might have risen, and in the proportion of known patients repeatedly referred (Table 1A), which might have fallen. Both were negative. To be certain that the policy had achieved its result and that the amount of work had not declined, a further datum is wanting, namely the time spent on consultations.

Categories thus gain meaning from specificity. To know the sex and age divisions among patients, as well as their numbers, helps to describe the nature of the services and the location of its effects in the community.

Operations Studies. Data specified to this degree have entered a second level; they are already in the demesne of operations research (3). Operations research seeks to enhance the efficiency with which an organization achieves its avowed aims. It studies the procedures of production and distribution. Large-scale organization generates external as well as internal needs for data. Private organizations want to know how their costs are distributed in order to compete in the market. Public organizations want to justify their costs in order to compete for scarce resources.

Table 2 gives a simple example of an operations study. In Salford in 1957 an analysis was made of the traveling time of

Table 2. Visiting Time of Mental-Welfare Officers

	Awaiting Bus	*Traveling on Bus*	*Walking to Visit and to and from Bus*	*Interview Time*	*Total Visit Time*
Total time in minutes	1,207	1,668	1,556	4,509	8,940
Average time per visit in minutes	6	8	8	22	44

Adapted from M. W. Susser, *A Report on the Mental Health Services of the City of Salford for the Year 1958*, by permission of Health Department, Salford, England.

the six mental-welfare officers during 202 visits in a consecutive two-week period.

On the assumption that traveling time in private cars in Salford (where parking is easy) would be no more than that in public buses, it was shown that the use of private cars could save one third of the total time spent on visits. Further calculation showed that to use private cars would add the equivalent of one and two-thirds officers to the staff of six, or one for two existing officers. On the strength of this a mileage allowance, long resisted in principle by the City Council, was introduced.

The comparison implicit in this small operations study could be made without setting up a control to demonstrate that waiting time was eliminated by private cars. It employed the useful comparative technique of arguing from norms established by previous research or experience. Economy of method was enhanced by collecting data through a slight modification of the officers' working diaries and by taking a short sample of time.

The routine accumulation of data enables trends to be examined. Thus the most frequent comparisons made in the study of operations are segregated by time. In Salford one of the objects of policy was to transform the style of work of mental-welfare officers from that of authorized officials acting by legal criteria (which give priority to the needs of society at large) to that of social workers acting by professional criteria (which give priority to the needs of individual patients). Table 3 sets out one index of the desired change.

Table 3. Mode of Admission to Mental Hospitals

Hospital Admissions	*1957*	*1958*	*1959*	*1960*	*1961*	*1962*
Compulsory	193	172	119	147	132	78
Voluntary	94	100	152	144	133	152
Total	287	272	271	291	265	230

Adapted from M. W. Susser, *A Report on the Mental Health Services of the City of Salford for the Year 1962*, by permission of Health Department, Salford, England.

In 1957 two thirds of admissions were compulsory and involved the exercise of the officers' legal powers. Six years later only one third were compulsory. The alteration in the pattern of work of the mental welfare officers was further illustrated by a steady increase in the number of referred patients given support at home. In 1957 more than two thirds of patients referred by general practitioners to the mental-welfare officers were admitted to the hospital, and in 1962 only one third. From a cross-analysis it could be inferred that the patients not admitted to the hospital were indeed receiving professional help, for in 1957 no action was taken in 20 per cent of all referrals, whereas in 1962 no action was taken in only 4 per cent.

A second object of policy in the Salford mental-health service was to bring the work of mental-welfare officers and general practitioners into closer coordination. The hoped-for change in the referring habits of general practitioners is seen in Table 4.

Table 4. General-Practitioner Referrals to Salford Mental-Health Service in 1958 and 1962

REFERRAL RATE PER DOCTOR PER ANNUM		
Referral Rate	*Number of G.P.s in 1958*	*Number of G.P.s in 1962*
0	24	3
1	3	7
2	10	6
3	8	7
4	5	3
5	10	1
6	5	4
7	1	1
8	2	2
9	–	8
10	–	5
11	–	4
12	–	9
13	1	2
14	–	2
15	–	3
16	–	1
17	–	1
18	–	–
Total	69	69

Adapted from M. W. Susser, *A Report on the Mental Health Services of the City of Salford for the Year 1962*, by permission of Health Department, Salford, England.

Table 5. Duration of Stay

Discharges (Excluding Deaths) of Salford Patients from Springfield Hospital, 1959–1962

LENGTH OF STAY (IN DAYS)	PERCENTAGE OF PATIENTS IN EACH CATEGORY			
	1959	*1960*	*1961*	*1962*
1—29	27.5	26.5	30.3	40.4
30—59	23.7	27.2	19.1	29.0
60—89	12.3	12.9	20.2	8.4
90—119	8.8	6.1	8.6	7.4
120—149	7.3	5.1	5.1	2.0
150—179	2.3	4.4	2.7	2.7
180—209	2.6	3.4	2.3	2.4
210—239	2.3	1.4	1.2	1.0
240+	12.9	12.9	10.5	7.1
	100	100	100	100
Number of Discharges	341	294	257	297

Adapted from M. W. Susser, *A Report on the Mental Health Services of Salford for the Year 1963,* by permission of Health Department, Salford, England.

A third object of policy was to make more use of facilities outside the hospital wards to enable patients in treatment better to maintain their everyday social relationships. The shift of care out of the mental hospital could be demonstrated by an analysis of admissions, discharges, and durations of stay. Seventy per cent of patients discharged left the hospital within two months of admission in 1962, compared with about 50 per cent in each of the preceding three years (see Table 5), without any compensatory rise in the number of admissions nor of patients detained in the hospital. The records of the

*Table 6. Disposal of All Psychiatric Patients Referred to Salford Mental-Health Service 1959–1963**

Agency	*1959*	*1960*	*1961*	*1962*	*1963*
Mental hospital admissions	52%	48%	45%	35%	41%
Outpatient, Family doctor, Home visit, and Other	48%	52%	55%	65%	59%
Total Numbers	430	498	470	467	508

* Disposal at first notification in calendar year.
Adapted from M. W. Susser, *A Report on the Mental Health Services of Salford for the Year 1964,* by permission of Health Department, Salford, England.

other facilities demonstrate the concurrent rise in their use. (See Table 6.)

Certain reservations must be made in interpreting these data about the shift of care from hospital to community. First, the percentage shifts alone could be brought about merely by lowering the threshold for referrals to psychiatric agencies. There need have been no shift in the pattern of care for patients who would have qualified for referral by the higher threshold of previous years. Numbers as well as proportions must be specified to show this shift of care—and also those attributes of patients that could indicate any changes in the populations served. Data of this kind were available from the psychiatric register maintained in Salford.

Second, "before and after" measurements can effectively demonstrate change, but alone they cannot isolate the causes of change. Internal policy might have caused change, but external forces cannot be excluded. The continuity of the trends, however, does exclude single external events such as the initiation of the Mental Health Act (1959) at the end of 1960.

Third, these data have more bearing on the input of a psychiatric service program than on the ultimate effects in the target population that the program is intended to achieve. As noted at the outset, routine audits and operations studies describe the delivery of the "treatment."

Operations studies built into organizations have definite limitations. Compromises have to be made for the sake of economy or for the sake of those refractory professional workers, untrained in the significance of routine records, who have not incorporated record keeping in their concepts of their professional roles. Notwithstanding such obstacles, routine audits and operations studies are mandatory for any organization that pretends to aims other than its own perpetuation.

Opportunist Surveys. We have observed that details of the attributes of patients add meaning to interpretation. With differentiated data, analysis can probe qualitative as well as quantitive questions. These possibilities bring us to a third level, the opportunist survey. This economical form of research exploits existing sources to answer questions that do not have immediate significance for the local operation of services, although they do have on the long view. It uses local opportunities to answer questions of general significance.

The opportunist survey can be descriptive; it can also be explanatory in that it seeks to develop or to test hypotheses or to evaluate a program. Each service can act as an epidemiological checkpoint; it yields a distinctive cut into the strata of morbidity. We can learn from such surveys about the social and individual forces in the selection of patients between services, about the scope and reliability of the material from hospitals and other sectors in relation to the whole, and about historical trends of disease and of sickness.

In Salford a register has been maintained, since 1959, of all patients from the area who come into the care of any psychiatric service. Basic information, the lowest common denominator of that which could be accurately obtained from all the agencies concerned, was recorded on a precoded schedule. In order to produce such data, it was necessary to discover and link up all the ports of entry to psychiatric agencies, to codify in a routine way information already available to the particular agency even if it was not always recorded, and to ensure thereafter that it was recorded. Data are reliable in so far as collection and recording are reliable. A law relevant to keeping registers states that the research worker's confidence in data increases as the square of his distance from their source.

Electronic computers have opened a new potential for morbidity registers and for operations data. The continuous linking and analysis of information assembled on patients through the years is inestimably enhanced by their advent. In order to process the Salford data, we developed in Manchester a program for the Atlas computer of a generality sufficient to analyze data from any survey and to take instructions stated in a "command language" near to that of everyday. A program of this type enables the researcher to remain in command of his own data even with the intervention of a middleman as programmer. Furthermore, time-sharing devices can serve the researcher with instant analysis. Tried programs and the preparation of data in a format suitable to alternate methods of processing them prevent serious breakdown. Toil and anguish accompany the implementation of untested programs on prototype machines.

Figures 3 to 5 are culled from the Salford register. They illustrate a study of the incidence of mental illness. The unit observed is each episode of illness known to the psychiatric agencies, including those outside Salford and private psychiatrists. Two incidence measures, inceptions (or first episodes ever) and total episodes, are used.[1] For the evaluator these are norms against which the effectiveness of specific community programs can be measured.

Tailormade Surveys. The questions that can be answered by the *ad hoc* methods of opportunism are limited in scope. Particular services cover restricted populations and they have limited tolerance for the intrusions of research on service. By means of internal comparisons of registered referrals in Salford, those who were admitted to the hospital and those who were not could be compared in respect of family support, or of social mobility, or of the severity of the social disturbance. The register could not be used, however, to describe the relation of these same factors to people being referred and thus becoming patients, as by definition all had experienced referral. For this purpose, comparisons external to the register had to be made so that the referred population as numerator could be set against that of the general population as denominator. Denominators can sometimes be obtained from existing sources, for instance from the national census, but more often special surveys provide them.[2]

1. See Appendix A for details of the survey method. We have failed so far to devise an economical and reliable marker of duration of episodes, as A. Bahn and others have attempted to do (4). With a measure of duration the amount of treatment being called for could be better stated. We did not have the resources to set up a continuing follow-up study, which would give still better control.

2. As surveys grow in number, it becomes realistic to build up data banks. Another economical approach is the amalgamated survey in which a number of users combine to obtain their information from the same sample (5).

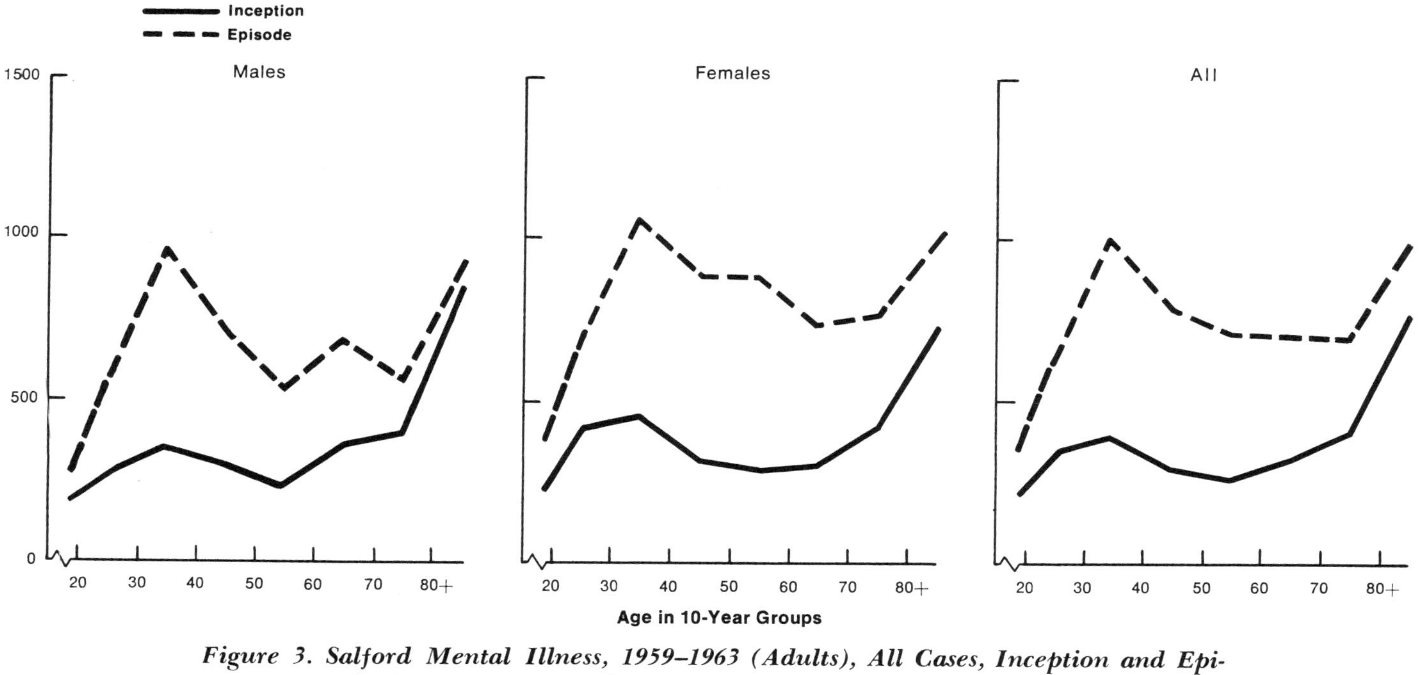

Figure 3. Salford Mental Illness, 1959–1963 (Adults), All Cases, Inception and Episode Rates per 100,000 by Age and Sex

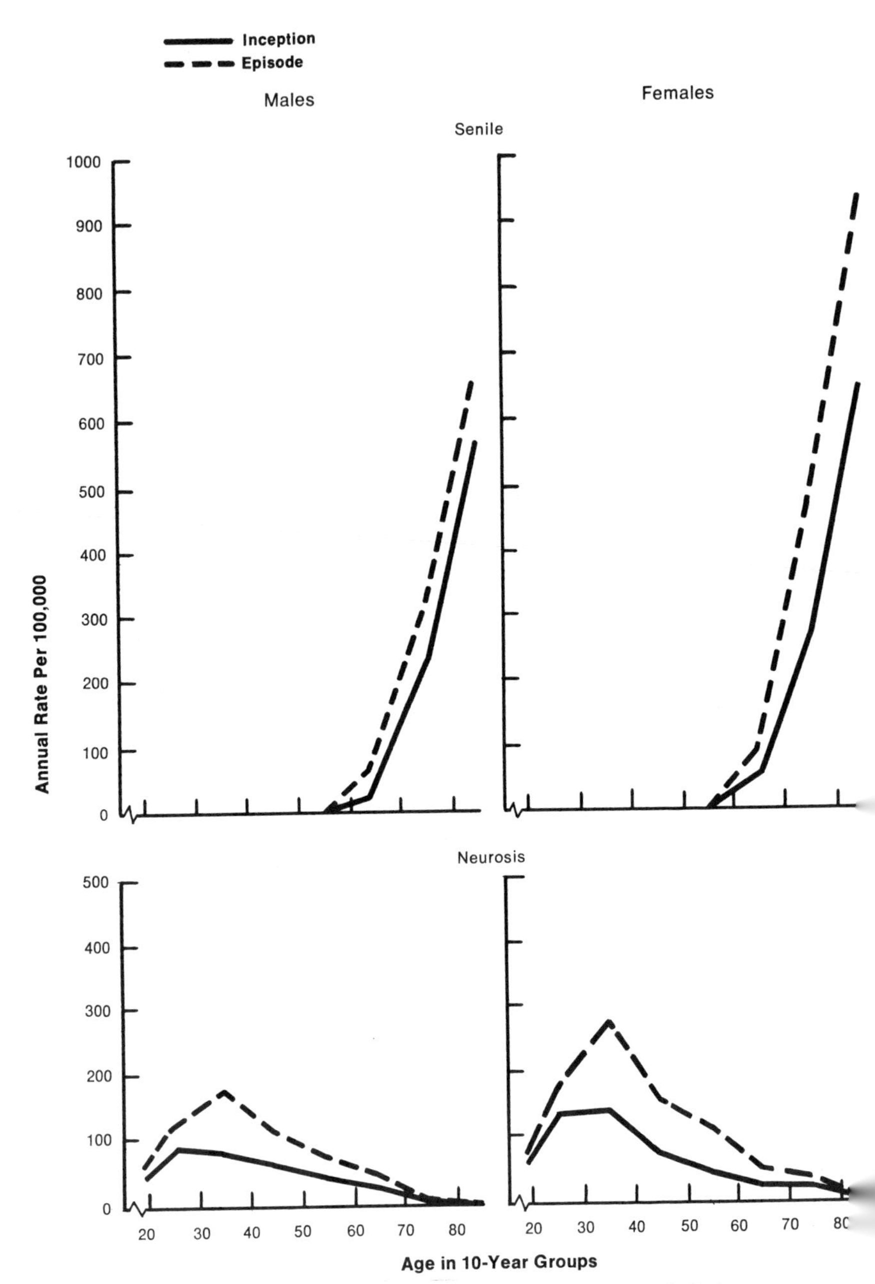

Figure 4. Salford Mental Illness, 1959–1963 (Adults), Inception and Episode Rates by Age, Sex, and Selected Diagnosis

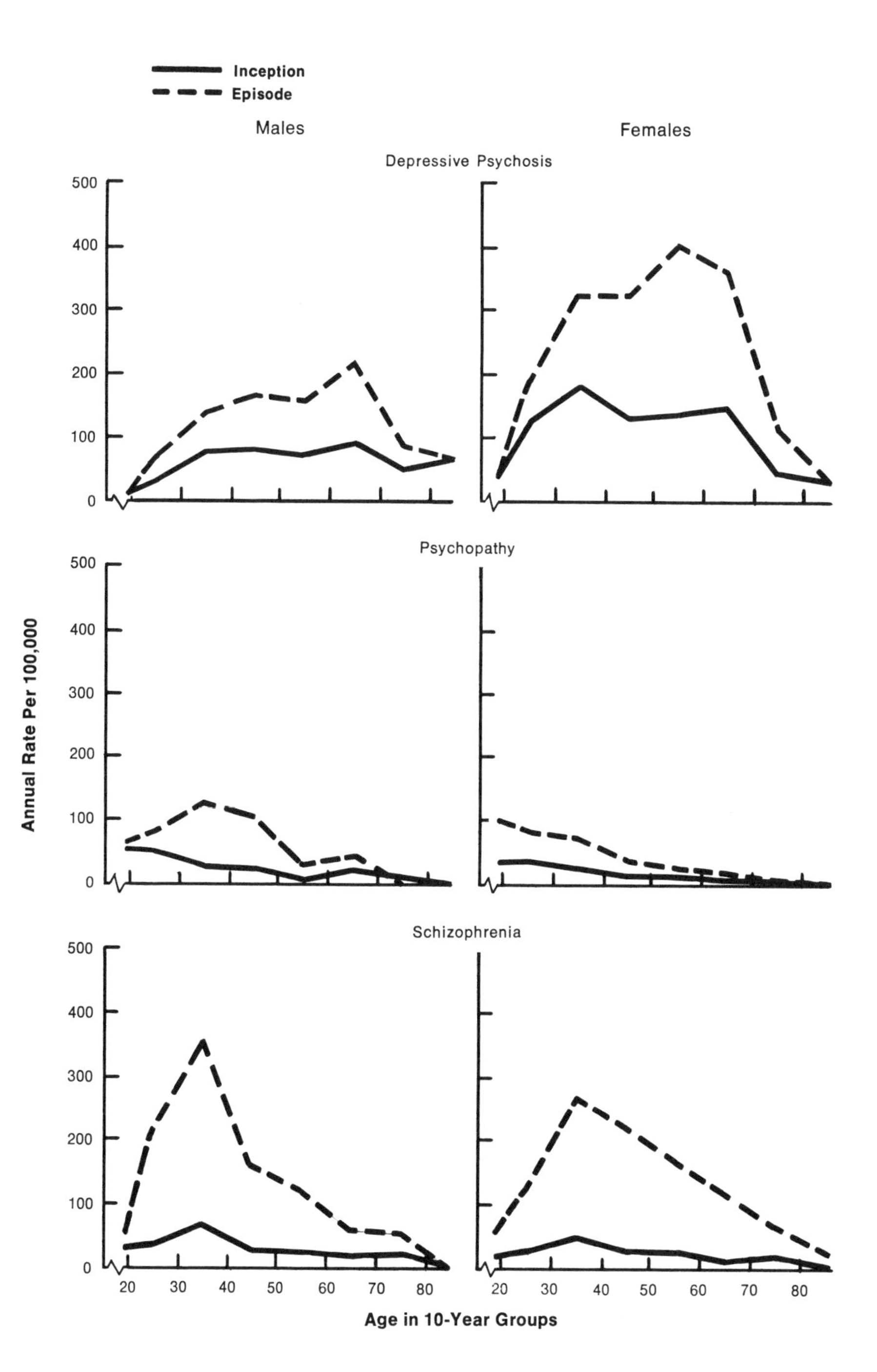

Inception
Episode
Males
Females
Depressive Psychosis
Psychopathy
Schizophrenia
Annual Rate Per 100,000
500
400
300
200
100
0
20
30
40
50
60
70
80
Age in 10-Year Groups

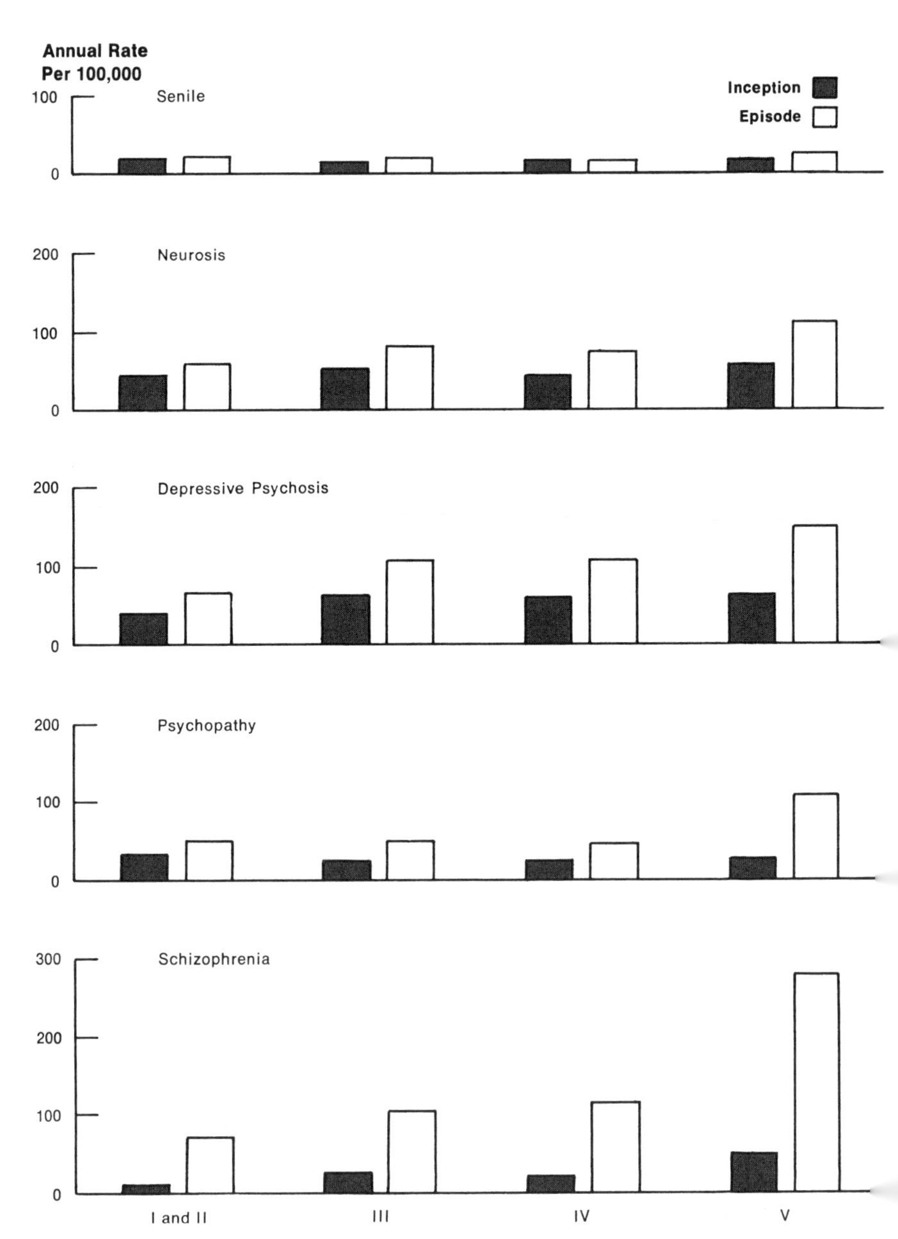

Figure 5. Salford Mental Illness, 1959–1963 (Adults), Inception and Episode Rates by Social Class, and Selected Diagnosis, Males Only

These extensions into the population at large carry survey research onto the plane of tailormade studies. In the tailormade survey the objects of research have priority. Hypotheses can be independent of service operations as with the opportunist approach, but their detachment from service aims is taken a step further. The organization becomes the vehicle for investigations specially mounted and superimposed on its everyday functions. The hypotheses of tailormade surveys, unlike those of opportunist surveys, are not limited to those that can be examined through existing resources.

Contrivance can meet some of the requirements for external comparisons within a single organizational system, for instance by the use of matched controls. The association between smoking and lung cancer was revealed by comparing the smoking habits of lung cancer patients with controls drawn from the same hospitals (6). Such controls are not truly comparable. The factors by which lung cancer patients are selected or self-selected for admission to the hospital may not be the same as those that obtain for other patients. And those unknown factors could have been the determinant of the differences in smoking habits.

Yet virtually all scientific doubts about the link of lung cancer with cigarette smoking have been stilled. The strength of the finding derives in large part from its consistency and specificity on repeated tests. Each survey has examined the same association in differing situations, in differing populations, and by different methods. This is an epidemiological alternative to the exact replication of complete experiments that is the standby of the physical sciences. It was an alternative thoroughly exploited by Émile Durkheim in his studies of suicide (1, 7). In epidemiology, variation in the conditions and subjects of study is the one constant. The epidemiologist has to find ways of making variation work in his favor.

A main safeguard in social and epidemiological research is the considered choice of populations for study and comparison. It requires continual awareness, based on knowledge of the norms of the study populations, of the possibilities of error. In the physical world, duplication of the subjects of experiment is attainable because the limits of variation are so much narrower than in the psychosocial world. The lapse of time between repeated experiments, which does little to alter material conditions, may radically alter psychosocial conditions.

The tailormade survey raises in acute form the question of what are proper relations between researchers and other branches of a health organization. The same question is implicit if less obvious in routine audits and the operations studies, which I have said no organization should be without. It has been many times demonstrated that audits and operations studies can be carried out without setting up independent researchers. In these cases the interests of the administrators coincide with those of the researchers; both try to improve the organization's work. If conflicts arise they usually center on the different interests and values of service personnel. But when the object of research is to test hypotheses not directly linked with service needs, conflicts of interest and values between administrators and researchers may also emerge. Depending on the distribution of power in the organization, the long-term objects of the research may be diverted to the short-term objects of administration. These conflicts of organizational structure need to be considered in setting up programs to carry out evaluations, whether by means of tailormade surveys, case studies, or experiments. They are discussed in detail in a collation of the experiences of forty-nine separate psychiatric rehabilitation projects (8).

Case Studies

Whereas the survey has been the characteristic method of epidemiology and sociology, the case study has been that of clinical medicine and anthropology. Surveys can collect systematic data on large numbers of cases. To do so, they rely on indicators from which a more general meaning is inferred, as for instance social class is inferred from the occupation and education of the subject.

By contrast the observer of the case collects all the data that he suspects have significance for his hypotheses and formulations. He collects them more or less systematically over extended periods of time, as they happen and emerge from his contacts with informants. The element of time gives the observer the special advantage of a sense of process and of contingent careers and events unfolding. The resulting data are more diffuse but can be more penetrating than that of surveys. The case study is an excellent method for the study of organizations.

Few case studies have been given the formal label of evaluation research. Many studies of organizations, however, can be classed as such without unduly stretching the rubric. When E. Goffman, as participant-observer in the guise of staff attendant on the wards of a state mental hospital, describes the patient culture and the typical patterns of adaptation, he is making an implicit evaluation. He has described the input of the treatment as seen by patients; he has described the effects of treatment on them; and from his sense of process he has inferred the causal connection of treatment and effects (9).

Evaluation is implicit in this study. Evaluation requires that the effect of treatment be judged against the objects of the treatment program. Here the objects of treatment were not specified, but from the consensus of norms about the aims of mental treatment in our society we can safely argue that the intended treatment failed. Unsought and undesired effects of the institution were so severe as to outweigh the intended effects of specific treatments. Resigned or rebellious or demoralized patients were caught up in a culture hostile to that of the authorities responsible for their care. The studies of A. H. Stanton and M. S. Schwartz and others can be interpreted in a similar manner (10).

Case studies open an additional avenue to evaluation. They describe directly the input of a treatment program and actual behavior in response to it. Furthermore, the case study may be the only possible means of unraveling the tangles of interacting processes. It is difficult to conceive another method that could have elicited the blocks in communication and their pathological effect on patient behavior in the hospital studied by Stanton and Schwartz or the nature of the obstructions to rational coordination of services in Salford described in a later chapter (11).

The case study need not abjure standardized survey data. The baseline data of routine audits and operations also benefit case studies. In Salford the analysis of the case combined such data with the observations and interpretations of a participant. The combination of survey and case material adds strength to the method. By this means hypotheses derived from initial observations can be tested by systematic interviews. Case studies share the advantages of surveys in another way if a large number of cases is included.

The role of the student of cases in social anthropology, as in medicine, has typically been that of the detached observer, a stranger uninvolved with the alien culture or the pathological state. A second more recent variant of this role is that of participant-observer. The researcher assumes a participating role within the setting he wishes to study, either an informally defined one as with W. F. Whyte and his street-corner gang or a formally defined one as with W. Caudill when he entered a psychiatric hospital as patient (12). (It should be noted that Caudill abandoned this disguise as unethical and unworkable.)

In the field of psychiatry this approach of the detached observer was pioneered by H. Rowland's work in a state mental hospital (13). Free interchange is facilitated for the participant-observer by his assumption of a role understood by others in the setting. Personal experience augments empathy with the role and the validity of interpretation.

A third observer variant is perhaps best described as the "action researcher." In this approach the observer enters the organization as consultant. Such research cannot be divorced from the object of improving the organization that gained him entry (14).

A fourth variant germane to my theme of evaluation within organizations is found in the Salford study, where the writer's office was that of director of mental-health services in the local public health service. The role differs from that of the consultant in action research in that the office was a permanent one. Research from such a position is a fragment of ongoing operations and evaluative studies. In Salford a principal objective of policy was to achieve the coordination of agencies. The position of director of mental-health services was a good vantage point for observing the relevant interaction between psychiatric agencies. It facilitated direct observation, the gathering of operations data to support it, and an exceptionally long observation period. It took five years for the policy of coordination to be given full effect. Few research roles that are not built into an organization offer the opportunity for such extended assessments.

Each observer role has its own problems. The unattached observer has the widest access to all the levels of an organization, for he is not restricted to a particular position in the structure by a defined role. But he is likely to have shallower access to relevant information at each level, and he must work hard to define his role for his informants in order to avoid being perceived as prying or threatening.

The participant-observer has restricted access to levels of the organization other than his own. In some traditional mental hospitals, for instance, demarcations and articulations between roles are found that can cloud a psychiatrist's view of life on the ward. The "good" psychiatrist works in symbiosis with the charge nurse and ward attendants, accepts their reports on patients as a basis for their proper treatment, and avoids interfering with their areas of control. On the other hand, a ward attendant gets a close view of life on the ward but a distant view of the forces that determine high policy. A participant-observer who strongly identifies with some roles, as exemplified by Goffman in relation to patients, may lose empathy with reciprocal roles, in his case with those in authority. Intimate knowledge and realism are gained at the risk of bias.

Like the participant-observer, the action researcher may lose access to certain levels of organization, and he may lose detachment because of commitment to particular policies. Personal identification with a role may also lead to identification with its interests. All these difficulties are intensified for the officer of an organization.

The case-study method is at the polar extreme of the observer bias common to the whole of science. Even in such technical procedures of medicine as reading radiographs and electrocardiograms or listening to heart sounds, error may be as high as 20 per cent. Systematic bias is more dangerous yet. Experiments with experimenters dispel the idea of dispassionate science; an experimenter's hypothesis influences what he observes (15). What the observer expects, what he desires in the results, and what he feels may all play a part. In the case study the control of bias rests in large part on the observer's understanding of value systems and structural forces and on his resulting sensitivity to judgments derived from his own values and position. In the Salford case an added check on bias was the testing of the analysis and interpretation against the criticism of the chief participants.

Social Experiments

The most cogent evaluations of social projects have been quasi-experimental. R. A. Fisher made a fundamental advance when he developed the methods by which agriculture and biology could approximate the certainty of physical experiment (16, 17). Some believe that the technique of random allocation was an advance as great as any in medicine in the past two centuries. Much ingenuity has since gone into contriving the controlled conditions of biological experiment for the psychosocial world of man. Evaluators of health programs must look to adaptations of these designs for crucial tests (18, 19).

A number of experimental evaluations of special facilities for community care have been made. Most have been concerned with rehabilitation and socialization. Examples from Britain are the studies of the Medical Research Council's Social Psychiatry Research Unit in the fields of mental subnormality and chronic mental illness, and from the United States the Altro project (20). Notable among them for this discussion are the experiments of G. W. Fairweather because, as staff psychologist of a veterans' hospital, he conducted them from within his organization.

Few have essayed to evaluate a total program for the community care of mental disorder. One such attempt is to be found in New York State (21) and another in the south of England, to which we referred in discussing the evaluation of social work (22).[3] (See p. 157.) I shall refer to the British experiment as a paradigm, together with incidental examples, around which to examine some questions of design.

This experiment was set up to assess "community care" in the psychiatric service in the largely rural area of Chichester. The service had recently brought about a marked reduction in hospital admissions by the use of outpatient treatment, a day hospital, and domiciliary visits by psychiatrists. The Salisbury service was chosen for comparison because of the similarities of the two areas.

The first step in evaluation research, we remarked at the outset, is to clarify the objectives of the experimental project. These tend to be less specific than with other therapeutic trials commonly met in medicine. Aims are often vaguely conceived and may even be conflicting among several sponsors. A lay administrator might opt for community care for reasons of economy, a superintendent of a mental hospital might do so in the interests of relieving pressure on its beds, and a practicing psychiatrist might do so for therapeutic purposes. The possibilities for conflict inherent in organizations for psychiatric care was a central theme of the Salford case study. (See Chapter 10.) It can therefore be difficult to discover a consensus of clear objectives. Without clarity in conceptualization, the results of evaluation are bound to lack meaning.

Once objectives are clearly conceived, the components of the program and its hoped-for effects can be specified. The more precise are these specifications of input and effects, the more likely is the research to be sharp and comprehensive. Definitively to weigh up the results of the Chichester-Salisbury study, one requirement is that the judge be able to specify in

3. Since this chapter was written, an important account of an experimental home-care program for schizophrenic women has been published. See B. Pasamanick, F. R. Scarpitti and S. Dinitz 1967 *Schizophrenics in the Community: An Experimental Study in the Prevention of Hospitalization* New York, Appleton

what respects the input of the two programs differed. Without this knowledge, the causes of any observed effects in the target group can only be guessed. A program in action is not the same as a program on paper. Studies of effects are wasted if, as not uncommonly happens, the supposed treatment is not delivered.

As is usual with research conducted by an independent agency, in the Chichester evaluation input was outside the control of the researchers. Separation from control is an aid to the detachment called for in making unbiased assessments, but the researcher may find that he is measuring some other variable than the one he selected as crucial for his experiment. Community care in Chichester chiefly comprised the treatment of a high proportion of patients outside the hospital wards by psychiatrists working in close cooperation with general practitioners. In Chichester only 18 per cent of patients were admitted. Salisbury admitted 52 per cent of patients, but we have seen that it maintained high standards of social work. The experiment might therefore be better conceived of as a test of different combinations of services rather than as a test of a unitary community care program.[4] The comparison was thus between psychiatric treatment centered outside the mental hospital with the support of general practitioners and treatment centered in the hospital wards with the support of social workers.

The effects of a program can be specified in terms of person, time, and place, that is, in terms of who is likely to be affected, when, where, and in what manner. In specifying effects, the researcher draws on his scientific imagination and on his own experience and that of others in the attempt to predict unanticipated consequences of programs of treatment. The Chichester-Salisbury studies can be seen in a sense as an exercise in the study of unanticipated consequences. Their main emphasis was not so much on effects on patients, although these

4. Overlaps in the input of programs seem to be a special risk of studies where the experimental group has been contiguous with the control group. Competition between them to attain good results leads to spilling over from the experimental into the control situation (23). (Chichester and Salisbury were not contiguous or in competition.)

were not ignored, as on the effects on the families of patients. The researchers used imagination to conceptualize the program as one that impinged on the patient as a unit in a social system.

The repercussions of a program for the care of mental disorder can be traced beyond the family to the larger social system. They can thus be weighed in economic terms, as they influence productivity and the costs of care. They can be weighed in terms of morbidity in the population, and in terms of community capacity to offer care. Such distant effects can become difficult to measure and difficult to connect with a specific program.

Once objectives, program, and effects are clearly conceived, a further step is to develop the methods and the instruments that enable effects to be measured. The choice of instruments requires a nice balance between the reliability and the validity of information (24). An instrument is reliable when its results are consistent in similar conditions. Reliability is got most easily by strictly defined, systematic procedures, for instance by a structured precoded questionnaire. The Chichester study took pains to test the reliability of questionnaires by which it described the psychiatric state of patients and the condition of their families. In order to calibrate its diagnostic instruments, pairs of psychiatrists interviewed and filled in symptom inventories and diagnoses for the same patients. The degree of their concordance was then examined.

An instrument is valid when its results actually describe what it purports to describe. For all the uncertainties of diagnosis in psychiatry, there is no method that can yet replace the clinician as final court of appeal. In studies that have relied on questionnaires and lay interviewers, psychiatrists have had to set the standards for validity. In respect of psychiatric diagnosis and symptomatology in the Chichester study, there was no logical need to improve validity, for psychiatrists made the clinical assessments.

There was a practical need, however; for the reliability and validity of individual psychiatrists are improved by training and buttressed by system. In contrast with the conditions that promote reliability, validity is best ensured by a many-faceted approach that tries to take into account all aspects of the phenomenon. For example, the response to psychiatric treatment can encompass manifold functions and processes of the mind, including mental symptoms. It can also encompass social performance and the reactions of others to it in a range of situations. Multiple methods of observation are required to comprehend all of this and to detect those unforeseen effects that cannot gain inclusion in the structure of a ready-made questionnaire or a single interview.

Experiment exposes a particular group of subjects to a defined treatment. A major step in experimental evaluation is to construct a practicable research design that controls both the bias of observers and the extraneous influences that might obtrude on the results. Two broad tactics can be used to obtain standards against which the effects of the treatment can be measured. One tactic is to measure the same group or set of circumstances before and after their exposure to treatment. Another is to compare the effects of different treatments in comparable groups of subjects.

Comparison Before and After. In designs that rely on observation before and after exposure to treatment, the same group of subjects is measured on each occasion. Hence no difficulties arise about the equivalence of the groups under comparison. They do arise in relation to the interim between observations. Several factors extraneous to the experiment can obtrude and confuse the results in the intervening lapse of time.

The "Worthing experiment," which preceded and inspired the Chichester evaluation carried out from the same hospital, provides an example of comparisons before and after exposure (25). Its object was to reduce the necessity for admissions to a hard-pressed mental hospital by intensive outpatient work. The Worthing design made use of three hospital catchment areas. In two the "treatment" was introduced, but at successive points in time. The third area was left without treatment. The "before and after" measurements of admission rates confirmed that a sharp halt in hospital admissions had taken place. There was a fall in the number of admissions soon after the introduction of the program in each of the treated areas, but not in the untreated control areas. (See Table 7.)

We have noted that a simple "before and after" design does not rule out historical changes in the world external to the experiment that influence response. Without the third untreated control area, the Worthing results would have been open to this criticism on logical grounds. Logic can be unseated by pragmatism. Even lacking an untreated control the result would gain credence from the rapid and twice-repeated treatment-response cycle. The fall in the number of admissions was immediate in each area.

Table 7. Annual Admissions to Graylingwell Mental Hospital from Each of Three Catchment Areas from 1956 to 1962

Year	*Worthing*	*Chichester*	*Horsham*	*Total*	*Rate per 100,000*
1956	645	444	219	1,308	364
1957	284*	463	246	993	268
1958	247	228*	256	731	191
1959	269	263	227	759	195
1960	295	293	239	827	208
1961	332	329	278	939	227
1962	325	389	311	1,025	245

* New service begun.
Adapted from J. Carse, N. E. Panton, and A. Watt, "A district mental health service: the Worthing experiment," *Lancet*, 1 (1959), 39–41.

Responses over a period of time may also be influenced, and results confused, by changes internal to the experimental group. People alter their responses as they age and develop. They mature without the active intervention of others. Maturation is a special hazard of longitudinal studies that rely on "before and after" measures without other controls. It is most obvious in phases of rapid growth such as in childhood. Contemporary medicine well understands that a treatment, for enuresis or tics, for example, cannot claim efficacy without controls because such conditions remit spontaneously with aging. The problem of maturation can be generalized, however, to the old as well as the young. In essence it is the central concern in the controlled trial of any medical treatment. The assumption that even in a chronic condition the status quo would continue without external intervention is now seen as naïve.

"Before and after" comparison gives rise to a third problem, which resides not so much in the passing of time as in the repetition of measurements. The responses being measured are bound to manifest a degree of random fluctuation. The fluctuation is allowed for by studying groups of adequate size. But the responses of a group that have an abnormal distribution to begin with invariably have a tendency, inherent in their selection, to regress toward a statistical mean. The regression is created by the position of the group at the extreme of the distribution for the total population of which it is a part; movement can take place in one direction only.

In order to recognize regression, the character of the experimental group in relation to an appropriate universe should be known at the outset. In Worthing, hospital admission rates at the outset were high for the country. For this reason they could have been expected to approximate in some degree to the national rate. The result could be posed as questioning why without a special program the Worthing rate had not fallen in concert with those of the rest of the country.

Repetition causes other effects in longitudinal studies. The experience of being tested and measured can influence subsequent responses. In repeated psychometric tests an allowance is commonly made for the boost from repetition. Learning by practice, while important in psychology and education, usually has minor bearing on sociomedical studies of the Chichester type.

Another kind of learning can confuse the results of experiments that require repeated testing. The measures used in social research and the questions raised may alter the set of mind so that the same questions come to be viewed in a new light. To take an experimental example, the attitudes of school children toward mental disorders became less negative merely on retesting and without any other known intervention (26). R. L. Solomon, who demonstrated that preliminary tests could alter subsequent responses, called this phenomenon sensitization (27).

In the Chichester-Salisbury study such an imponderable might have been at work in one of its results discussed in a previous chapter. Families in both services were found to have gained relief soon after the initial referral and before specific treatment of the patients could be expected to have affected the family situation. Because all families included in the samples were interviewed, it is not possible to distinguish the influence of the research interview on family stress from that of professional contact and referral. Sensitization possibly worked against the area with the most active home care program. The investigation was carefully designed to locate and elicit problems in caring for patients at home. Sensitization might thus be expected to produce the greatest shift in a setting where extramural intervention is less active and where, in normal circumstances, families are less likely to make their helpers aware of such problems.

Yet another source of error in longitudinal studies lies in the selective survival of the individuals in an experimental population through the period of study (also described as experimental mortality, or the "dropout" phenomenon). A high rate of follow-up, as in Chichester and Salisbury, reduces the possible error.

For the sake of illustration I shall therefore digress from the Chichester experiment to the Salford survey. Dropouts may act either to exaggerate or to diminish a result. In the case of an increasing prevalence of severe mental subnormality observed from the register kept in Salford, the partial cause could have been selective emigration as the city's population declined. Since mentally subnormal people resident in hospitals were not at risk of emigration, there must have been at least a degree of selective migration of the healthy population, thereby leaving a residuum of affected persons. The converse case of rates lowered by selective survival can be found in the mental illness register in Salford. Total episodes of schizophrenia decline in frequency with age, despite the continued inception of new cases to add to the pool at risk of repeated episodes. A partial cause was the removal of patients for long periods into mental hospitals. They were "dropouts," who were excluded from contributing repeated episodes of schizophrenia.

The Comparison of Groups. A second tactic in quasi-experimental research circumvents timebound obtrusions on validity by using, for controlled comparison, a group unexposed to the experimental treatment or exposed to different treatment. The chief pitfalls with this tactic lie in the selection of subjects in a manner that takes into account the possible differences between the experimental and the comparison groups beside the planned difference in the single respect of treatment.

Random selection from the appropriate population alone is safe. Yet it may not be practicable. It is rarely possible to select at random for a social experiment carried out within a single geographical area. Ethical questions about discrimination and inequities of service soon arise. In the evaluation of the Chichester service, a next best expedient was used by selecting for comparison an area of similar demographic and geographical character. If description of the two areas before an experimental variable is introduced shows areas to be comparable, the differences in subsequent measurements are assumed to reflect exposure to the variable. The skimpier the description of the areas the more vulnerable is the assumption. But description can never be complete. We have noted that unknown bias cannot be excluded even by matching a sample of cases and controls. The matching of two geographical areas is an extreme of this procedure. It has the added danger that there may be unequal exposure of the two areas to extraneous events in the course of the experiment.

The problem goes beyond selection procedure to the decision as to the appropriate universe from which selection should be made. In experiment it is desirable to restrict the universe so that the influence of unwanted variables, which may render results inconclusive, can be eliminated. The population can be broken down according to an unwanted factor, and the controls selected for the cases in each of the resulting strata. If it is known that social class affects the readiness of patients to accept and continue in a particular treatment, the experimenter might stratify his sample of cases and controls by class. In doing so he risks eliminating other unknown and possibly important factors together with social class.

On the other hand, categories like social class are in themselves so imprecise, or the groupings used by the researcher are so broad, that their elimination is far from perfect. In such a case the experiment may be confounded by the concealed effects of a variable that the experimenter falsely believes he has controlled.

An instance arose with regard to age grouping in the comparison of patients on the Salford register by marital status. Although taken from a survey, the same principles hold in experiments. When age was held constant by twenty-year age groups, it appeared that in some age groups marriage was associated among women with unfavorable incidence rates of mental illness. When age was controlled by ten-year age groups, however, these high incidence rates of mental illness associated with marriage disappeared. Within twenty-year age groups, age had been inadequately controlled. In these groupings married women were older than the single women, and the higher incidence of mental illness at older ages thus produced an untoward association of marriage with high incidence. This is a special hazard with dichotomous variables where there is a rapid rate of transit from one status to the other.[5] Social experiment cannot entirely eliminate its jokers from the pack by design; they must be exposed and indirectly controlled by analysis (1).

The Chichester study illustrates both the disparities that can arise between ostensibly comparable groups and some of the indirect means of dealing with them. The psychiatric services in Chichester reached a wider segment of the population than in Salisbury, resulting in the desired inclusion of more patients with illnesses of short duration. This can be counted as in itself a favorable achievement for the Chichester service. But low admission rates and any other benefits to patients and families observed in association

5. Herbert Hyman cites a close analogy taken from Durkheim's analysis of suicide by age and marital state (1).

with the service might flow from the mildness of the illness treated rather than from its detailed provisions for patient care.

The investigators were able to show by subgroup analysis that this lowering of the threshold for seeking service could not account for the whole of the lower admission rate in Chichester. Although the main reduction was effected among patients diagnosed as neurotic, among the employed and among the married, the low rate was apparent in all types of illness.

Analysis also indicated that the advantages of the Chichester service were unlikely to derive from the selection of the patients alone. The initial severity of the illnesses, inferred from symptoms, from the impact of patients on families, and from the distribution of diagnoses, was not less in Chichester than in Salisbury.

Subgroup analysis of some of the results supported this view. A preliminary assessment made four weeks after the patient's referral concentrated on the family at home and on the burden that mental illness imposed on it. The results were contrary to what might have been expected had Chichester obtained advantage from an unduly high intake of patients with mild conditions. In the milder conditions Chichester relatives were at a disadvantage compared with Salisbury. In severe conditions they were at an advantage.

These results based on a short-term follow-up serve for illustration. The final assessments of the two-year follow-up are still to be published. (See pp. 156 ff., Chapter 7.) It may be remarked in passing, however, that the device of taking measures at an intermediate stage is tactically sound. It enables processes of change to be reconstructed and insures against total loss should some disaster intervene. Staff may move away, funds run out, or projects be abandoned.

We can now consider further the complications of comparisons between groups. Given that maldistribution between samples chosen for comparison is controlled, most of the sources of error in longitudinal or repeated observations are either balanced out or insubstantial. Change and maturation internal to the experimental groups, historical events external to them, statistical regression, and selective survival all cancel out. Possible exceptions in the case of sensitization were noted above: Groups may be unequally responsive because of the conditions created by the experiment.

Simultaneous comparisons between experimental groups are beset by a source of error similar to test effects and sensitization in that they are a product of experimentation. In this case, however, the problem is with the treatment and not the preliminary tests. In controlled trials of medications the "placebo" effect is a well-known phenomenon. The placebo, or dummy treatment, given to control nonspecific effects of interaction between patient and doctor, can be accompanied by undeniable improvement (28). In social experiment the "Hawthorne" effect describes a response similar in type (29). A halo of nonspecific social and personal influences inevitably surrounds any medical or psychiatric or social treatment and sets subtle traps for the evaluator of the long-term social experiment.

With community care for mental disorder it is necessary to distinguish the influence of change itself, and of the enthusiasm and interest that so often accompany experiment, from other attributes of the social milieu that can be regarded as part of the treatment. These effects of change and enthusiasm are not to be neglected even with the most precise of material treatments. They take on extra significance when they must be dissociated from less tangible psychological and social treatments (28). In Chichester the new services may well have evoked fresh commitment. Such an orientation could have favored the experimental Chichester service.

Sensitization and test effects can be avoided by reserving a randomly allocated group for testing only after exposure to treament. Distortions interwoven with the experimental treatment are less easily mastered. Nor is it always clear that they should be removed. It can be argued, as I shall do in a later chapter on mental subnormality, that an advantage of "community" services is an organizational structure that induces commitment to therapeutic goals, while that of the traditional mental institution damps it. In other words, maintained commitment is an intrinsic part of the community care program. A similar situation holds for drug treatment in psychiatry, where drugs and social situation interact and mutually enhance their effects. In a long-term trial of drug against milieu treatments, change of milieu alone produced no notable effects, whereas use of drugs produced only short-term effects. The best results came from both milieu and drug treatment together (30).

The test and the control of Hawthorne effects resides partly in the passage of time. Enthusiasm evoked by innovation alone will not remain constant. The excitement of expectancy may mark the entry of the first cohorts; the assurance or the apathy of the known and well-trodden may mark that of later ones. A further maneuver, where resources and scale permit, is to vary treatment programs in degree around the independent variable under test. Change would then operate in both experimental and control groups. These maneuvers could also help, in comparisons between areas, to modify the contribution of the quality of personnel. In most studies this must remain an imponderable. It may be reasonable to count as an intrinsic part of those programs, however, the social selection and the self-selection that bring certain personalities into particular types of project.

The permutations on the two broad tactics of control in social experiments permit of many variations (1, 16, 19). Design is always a compromise between ideal and reality. Tests that should be crucial are hedged about by the demands of practicability. Even the elegant double-bind trial has its snares. In social research, however, logical criticism must be kept in its place. It tells us what could be wrong with an experiment that may yet have empirical validity.

This is a time for experimental research with services and their flexible development. Most agree today that practical models and demonstrations should be evaluated, although not all are aware of the rigors and the labors demanded by scientific procedures. Social research can gain by taking the opportunities of evaluation studies to probe beyond evaluating the effects of operation alone. In good hands the benefits that flow from the intimate combination of research with practical projects are more than the sum of each. The determined and dispassionate worker in a research-oriented organization can hope to rise above the bias produced by the pressures to identify with the organization in which he works. Enlightened administration tries to maintain the independence of research and is ready to face the sharpness of investigation and the harshness of its results.

Research develops new insights from the study of institutions. These insights in turn alter the institutions. The fact of research woven into the fabric of an institution alters its nature and the way it is likely to work and to develop. The same result may not follow when the research activity is an appendage, even a prized one. Constant evaluation within organizations offers one means of converting demonstrations and experiments into stable operations.

This need of health organizations can be promoted by recruiting a new generation of health and medical planners. Such planners would develop the resources for evaluation inherent in their organizations and exploit their opportunities for research oriented to the long term. This is not to say that every organization would carry out experimental evaluations of every innovation, for there is a danger that elaborate evaluation can overshadow the projects being evaluated. Judgment and experience are the guide to what experimental evaluations may prove worthwhile and general in local conditions.

There is no better model for the health planner than Sir John Simon, who more than a century ago was appointed London's first medical officer of health and then England's first chief medical officer (31). Once aware of a possible problem area, Simon's approach was to investigate it by survey. On the basis of his results he then sought the administrative power to take action. With these powers he put social action in train and investigated afresh to evaluate its effectiveness. By means of this recurring cycle of action and research he laid the foundations of modern public health. In the contemporary world it is a reasonable hope that a combination of epidemiology and the social sciences will remedy as many ills.

In Simon's time effective action was often twenty years behind the recognition of a problem. In our rapidly changing world the necessity for experiment and research with services is even greater. No other means can ensure adaptation to the future.

References

(1) Hyman H. 1955 *Survey Design and Analysis: Principles, Cases, and Procedures* New York, Free Press

(2) MacMahon B., Pugh T. F. and Hutchinson G. B. 1961 Principles in the evaluation of community mental health programs *Amer J Pub Health* 51:963–968

(3) Bailey N. T. J. 1962 Operational research in Welford A. T., Argyle M., Glass D. V. and Morris J. N. *Society, Problems and Methods of Study* London, Routledge pp. 111–125

(4) Bahn A. K., Chandler C. A. and Lemkau P. V. 1962 Diagnostic characteristics of adult outpatients of psychiatric clinics as related to type and outcome of services *Milbank Mem Fund Quart* 15:407–442

(5) Elinson J. and Loewenstein R. 1963 *Community Fact Book for Washington Heights, New York City 1960–1961* Unpublished mimeo, Columbia University School of Public Health and Administrative Medicine

(6) Doll R. and Hill A. B. 1952 Study of the etiology of carcinoma of the lung *Brit Med J* 2:1271–1286

(7) Durkheim E. 1897 *Le Suicide* Paris, Alcan Spaulding J. A. and Simpson G. trans. 1951 *Suicide: A Study in Sociology* New York: Free Press

Selvin H. C. 1958 Durkheim's suicide and problems of empirical research *Amer J Sociol* 63:607–619

(8) Kandell D. B. and Williams R. H. 1964 *Psychiatric Rehabilitation: Some Problems of Research* New York, Atherton

(9) Goffman E. 1961 *Asylums: Essays on the Social Situation of Mental Patients and Other Inmates* Chicago, Aldine

(10) Stanton A. H. and Schwartz M. S. 1954 *The Mental Hospital: A Study of Institutional Participation in Psychiatric Illness and Treatment* New York, Basic Books

(11) Susser M. W. 1962 Changing roles and co-ordination in mental health services in Halmos P. ed. *Sociology and Medicine: Studies within the Framework of the British National Health Service* Sociol Rev Monogr 5 pp. 61–90

(12) Caudill W. 1958 *The Psychiatric Hospital as a Small Society* Cambridge, Mass., Harvard University Press

Whyte W. F. 1958 *Street Corner Society: The Social Structure of an Italian Slum* Chicago, University of Chicago Press

(13) Rowland H. 1938 Interaction processes in a state mental hospital *Psychiatry* 1:323–327

Rowland H. 1939 Friendship patterns in a state mental hospital *Psychiatry* 2:363–373

(14) Jaques E. 1952 *The Changing Culture of a Factory* New York, Dryden

Sofer C. 1962 *The Organization from Within: A Comparative Study of Social Units Based on a Socio-Therapeutic Approach* Chicago, Quadrangle

(15) Rosenthal R. 1963 On the social psychology of the psychological experiment: the experimenter's hypothesis as unintended determinant of experimental results *Amer Scientist* 51:268–283

(16) Fisher R. A. 1935 *The Design of Experiments* Edinburgh, Oliver & Boyd

(17) Fisher R. A. 1928 *Statistical Methods for Research Workers* Edinburgh, Oliver & Boyd

(18) Riecken H. 1952 *The Volunteer Work Camp: A Psychological Evaluation* Cambridge, Mass., Addison-Wesley

Klineberg O., Jahoda M., Barnitz E., Selltiz C., Beaglehole E., Smith M. B., Moss L., Wright C. R. and Miller K. M. 1955 Evaluation techniques: Part I Methods and results *Int Soc Sci Bull* 7:346–442

Hayes S. P. 1959 *Measuring the Results of Development Projects: A Manual for the Use of Field Workers* Paris, UNESCO

Hyman H., Wright C. and Hopkins T. 1962 *Applications of Methods of Evaluation: Four Studies of the Encampment for Citizenship* Berkeley, University of California Press

(19) Campbell D. T. and Stanley J. S. 1963 Experimental and quasi-experimental designs for research in teaching in Gage N. L. ed. *Handbook of Research on Teaching* Skokie, Ill., Rand McNally

(20) O'Connor N. and Tizard J. 1956 *The Social Problem of Mental Deficiency* London, Pergamon

Meyer H. J. and Borgatta E. F. 1959 *An Experiment into Mental Patient Rehabilitation* New York, Russell Sage Foundation

Wing J. K. and Giddens R. G. T. 1959 Industrial rehabilitation of male chronic schizophrenic patients *Lancet* 2:505–507

Tizard J. 1964 *Community Services for the Mentally Handicapped* London, Oxford

Fairweather G. W. ed. 1964 *Social Psychology in Treating Mental Illness: An Experimental Approach* New York, Wiley

(21) Brandon S. and Gruenberg E. M. 1966 Measurement of the incidence of chronic severe social breakdown syndrome: evaluation of the Dutchess County services in *Evaluating the Effectiveness of Mental Health Services* *Milbank Mem Fund Quart* 54: Part 2, 129–149

Gruenberg E. M., Brandon S. and Kasius R. V. 1966 Identifying cases of social breakdown syndrome: evaluation of the Dutchess County services in *Evaluating the Effectiveness of Mental Health Services* *Milbank Mem Fund Quart* 54: Part 2, 150–155

(22) Sainsbury P. and Grad J. 1966 Evaluating the Graylingwell Hospital community service in Chichester: aims and methods of research in *Evaluating the Effectiveness of Mental Health Services* *Milbank Mem Fund Quart* 54: Part 2, 231–242

(23) Hammond K. R., Kern F. Jr., Crow W. J., Githens J. H., Groesbeck B., Gyr J. W. and Saunders L. H. 1959 *Teaching Comprehensive Medical Care: A Psychological Study of a Change in Medical Education* Cambridge, Mass., Harvard University Press

(24) MacMillan A. M. 1959 A survey technique for estimating the prevalence of psychoneurotic and related types of disorders in communities in Pasamanick B. ed. *Epidemiology of*

Mental Disorder Washington, D. C., American Association for Advancement of Science pp. 203–208

Cartwright A. 1960 Interview surveys in *A Symposium on the Burden on the Community: The Epidemiology of Mental Illness* London, Oxford pp. 31–47

Selltiz C., Jahoda M., Deutsch M. and Cook S. W. 1966 *Research Methods in Social Relations* New York, Holt, Rinehart & Winston

(25) Carse J., Panton N. E. and Watt A. 1958 A district mental health service: the Worthing experiment *Lancet* 1:39–41

(26) Nunnally J. C. 1961 *Popular Conceptions of Mental Health* New York, Holt, Rinehart & Winston

(27) Solomon R. L. 1949 An extension of control group design *Psychol Bull* 46:137–150

(28) Joyce C. R. B. 1962 Patient cooperation and the sensitivity of clinical trials *J Chron Dis* 15:1025–1036

Liberman R. 1962 An analysis of the placebo phenomenon *J Chron Dis* 15:761–783

Ross S., Krugman A. D., Lyerly S. B. and Clyde D. J. 1962 Drugs and placebos: a model design *Psychol Rep* 10:383–392

Lyerly S. B., Ross S., Krugman A. D. and Clyde D. J. 1964 Drugs and placebos: the effects of instructions upon performance and mood under amphetamine sulphate and chloral hydrate *J Abnorm Soc Psychol* 68:321–327

Klerman G. L. 1966 *The Social Milieu and Drug Response in Psychiatric Patients* Paper read at annual meeting sociobiology session American Sociological Association, Miami Beach

(29) Roethlisberger F. J. and Dickson W. J. 1939 *Management and the Worker: An Account of a Research Project Conducted by the Western Electric Company Hawthorne Works, Chicago* Cambridge, Mass., Harvard University Press

(30) Greenblatt M., Solomon M. H., Evans A. S. and Brooks G. W. eds. 1965 *Drug and Social Therapy in Chronic Schizophrenia* Springfield, Ill., Thomas

(31) Lambert R. 1963 *Sir John Simon 1816–1904, and English Social Administration* London, Macgibbon & Kee

Brockington C. F. 1965 *Public Health in the 19th Century* Edinburgh, Livingstone

9

Measuring the Amount of Mental Illness in the Community

The demand for services is an insistent question that faces the administrator in his capacity as provider. Whether he leads or follows, he takes cues from demands made known by the community through its use of services, its allocation of funds, and its expressions of belief and values. A more basic question that faces the administrator, in his capacity as planner, is the need he must meet. To deal rationally with the shifting forces of demand, he must seek objective measures of need.

The word itself has shifting meanings, but needs once specified are by definition absolute; they are set against some ideal standard. Needs in any one situation can therefore be determined from the specified criteria. Demand, which is relative, settles the priorities between needs. Which needs should be specified and measured depends on the purposes of the planner or researcher. In some communities health and medical services aim to do no more than treat episodes of declared disease among those who can pay for the treatment. In other communities services aim to be more comprehensive and continuous; some espouse the whole spectrum of care, including the systematic prevention of disease and even the promotion of well-being. The conservative planner will measure needs related to the aims of existing services. The reformer will measure needs related to the hiatus in services. The radical will measure needs related to ideal goals.

In psychiatric terms need stems from disturbances of the psyche. These disturbances can be conceived in several ways. Among the criteria mentioned in previous chapters have been the degree of subjective well-being and happiness; the number and type of discomforting symptoms; syndromes, or patterns of symptoms, which psychiatrists recognize as meaningful in relation to the nature of their cause, course, and prognosis; and the quality of social performance. Each of these criteria yields a different estimate of disturbance and of need; further differences may be exacted from the variety of indexes which can be used for any one criterion. The objectives of study determine the appropriate choice of criteria and indexes.

In epidemiological terms estimates of community need vary according to the segment of the population and the duration of time to which these criteria are applied. A primary division is between studies of prevalence and of incidence.

Prevalence

Prevalence rates describe the amount of disorder existing in a defined population at a point in time (point prevalence) or over some defined period of time (period prevalence). They can be used as measures of existing need and of calls for service. Point prevalance is one means of getting a sense of the current load a service does or should provide for. Period prevalence extends the notion to cover the total load of cases that exists through a defined period. The prevalence of a condition that is stable in a population is a product of the rate at which it arises through time (that is, its *incidence*) and its duration. Both components are influential in determining the amount of prevailing illness. Point prevalence and incidence are notions that can be clearly distinguished. Period prevalence links the two and blurs the distinction between them.

In order to answer certain questions, it is helpful to

separate the components of incidence and duration. In seeking out causes, for instance, only the circumstances that precede the inception of disorder are relevant. Prevalence studies take a cross-sectional view of a population's experience and cannot establish with certainty the circumstances in which disorders of long and variable duration arose. We have seen in a previous chapter that with a chronic disorder such as schizophrenia, both illness and circumstances may change and interact with each other between the time of onset and enumeration.

A second instance shows the usefulness of separating incidence and duration. In order to establish recovery rates for a particular condition in a population, at least two of the three quantities of incidence, duration, and prevalence need to be known. By relating the incidence of neurosis to its prevalence in each age group, M. Shepherd and E. M. Gruenberg could infer recovery from the fact that psychoneuroses in overt form must have been of limited duration (1).

Prevalence studies have the advantage that the investigators can go out to discover and enumerate existing illnesses in representative samples of defined populations. Thus they need not wait for what turns up, but a problem of sampling inheres in their cross-sectional view. A sample of illnesses prevalent at any one point in time is not an unbiased sample of all illnesses experienced by the defined population. An influenza epidemic could be missed altogether, and so too could congenital anomalies that cause foetal and perinatal deaths, whereas disorders of long duration have a good chance of appearing in a census.

One approach to giving a fuller picture of the experience of illness in a population is to take "lifetime prevalence" as a measure. This rate is calculated by combining current illnesses with reports of illnesses suffered in the past. The method has been widely used by Scandinavian workers in order to calculate individual risks of particular disorders for their genetic studies. Studies of inheritance require that the histories taken from related individuals show whether or not they were *ever* affected by the disorder in question. The cases are sometimes identified from existing records or from the information obtained in surveys of the general population.

For the purpose of assessing the need for services, lifetime prevalence gives estimates of dubious accuracy. Both records and memory are fallible. The strong feelings that attach to mental disorder interfere further with recall and reporting. About one third (32 per cent) of the subjects in the United States national health survey who were known to have been in a hospital for mental and personality disorders within the previous year failed to report the hospital episode, and the accuracy of reporting declined as the event receded into the past (2). Failure to report these episodes was far more frequent than for other types of illness. Thus personal histories taken in interviews cannot be relied on to correct for the "dropouts" who once were ill but are not ill at the time of the interview. In the Stirling County survey of a sample of a population in Nova Scotia, "total reportable prevalence" (the researchers' modification of lifetime prevalence) did not rise with age in a manner consistent with the cumulation of illnesses through life. The curves flatten out in middle age and above seventy years of age they actually fall (3). Histories of past mental disturbance thus added less than expected to the prevalence at the time of the study, although the use of dissimilar criteria for the inclusion of past and present disturbance may also have contributed to this result.

Reliable prevalence surveys of total populations are large undertakings. They require first that contact be made with a total population or with a randomly selected sample of the population. This population must then be subjected to standard procedures that serve to identify the cases in the population.

When the chosen criterion is a selection of symptoms taken from those that psychiatrists use to diagnose psychopathology, and when these are elicited by a structured interview that covers the ground systematically, few persons are found to be quite free of symptoms. By the most sensitive measures used in the Midtown Manhattan survey, the number of adults aged twenty to fifty-nine years who had always been free of significant symptoms was less than one in five (4) and in Stirling County, Nova Scotia, between one in two and one in three (3).

The fact that the presence of symptoms is the norm in a population does not necessarily rule out their pathological significance. Schistosomiasis is the norm in the fellahin of parts of the Nile delta, malaria among Gambians, and undernutrition among the masses of India and Africa. In the case of psychiatric symptom inventories, however, the risk they entail of future mental illness is unknown. Whatever their true significance, estimates based on the bare presence of symptoms can be put aside for the pragmatic purposes of planning. No resources and methods now available could cope with a problem of the magnitude presented by taking symptoms alone as an indication for providing help.

A less inclusive cutoff point is available for both the Midtown Manhattan and Stirling County surveys. The psychiatrists rated each case by severity. In Midtown at the time of the study about one in four (23 per cent) suffered mental impairment from symptoms classed as marked, severe, or incapacitating on a six-point scale. In Stirling County about one in five (17 per cent) had suffered "significant" mental impairment (in that by prevailing standards psychiatric care was required) at some time in his life. When the same criteria were applied to the greater amount of information collected in a special sample, the proportion was more than one in three (36 per cent). Staggering as these percentages were at their first appearance, the researchers claimed that they made conservative judgments of their case data. Surveys using similar methods have given results that fall within the same high range. About one in five (21 per cent) adults suffered psychiatric symptoms at any one time in a new housing estate in London and in a comparison group (5), and about one in three in the nearby new town of Harlow and in comparison groups (6).

Attempts to care for postulated needs of such a proportion of the population must surely result either in failure or in psychiatric valetudinarianism. People suffering from the common cold rarely need doctors; the condition has no specific treatment and resolves of its own accord. Minor psychiatric symptoms may be analogous; they too can be transient (7). A Swedish survey of point prevalence in two small parishes gave a similar high yield (19 per cent of those over fifteen years of age) of psychiatric conditions of all levels of severity (8). In this study the results were obtained by direct clinical assessment. Four psychiatrists studied a population familiar to them through personal knowledge and access to local records.

Many prevalence surveys, beginning with the pioneer studies of C. Brugger in South Germany (9), have yielded much lower rates of psychiatric disorder than those we have discussed so far (10). This divergence between surveys is too great and haphazard to attribute either to biological, social, or geographic forces. Nor can the imperfect comparability of the populations at risk, with their considerable differences in age, sex, and social groups, account for the greater part of the variations. If comparisons are restricted to urban or rural places, to particular geographic areas, and to particular ethnic groups, they do little to reduce divergence in prevalence rates (26).

The greatest source of variation is in the methods of the surveys. Many small snags with large consequences are encountered in comparing studies. It is wise to be alert for the precise rates used (incidence of new cases, incidence of all cases, point prevalence, period prevalence, lifetime prevalence), for the precise numerators (all cases, hospital cases, all cases excluding mental deficiency, all adult cases, all adult cases under retiring age), and for the precise denominators (an age-specific population, the adult population, the total population). In the following discussion, it is assumed that such snags are ironed out.

Important discrepancies arise from two aspects of methods used to identify cases: first, the decisions about what are to be regarded as cases and, second, the means of finding cases.

The determination that a respondent qualifies for inclusion as a case, we have seen, may derive from types of information as various as systematic symptom inventories and the trained observations of a psychiatrist. In Stirling County a standard set of questions, some closed and some open, was asked by interviewers who were not psychiatrists. The answers were later assessed by psychiatrists. The assessors were trained to consistency with each other in classifying the clinical condition of the respondents, in rating the severity of any mental impairment, and in judging the likelihood that the respondent would qualify for psychiatric care (11). The procedures of the Midtown study were similar (12).

In this method the decision as to what is a case is an arbitrary one made by the survey analysts. They choose the threshold of severity appropriate to their purpose, usually according to the number of symptoms reported or according to their nature. The decisions of the analysts of surveys can therefore create disparities in estimates of prevalence between surveys, even when disparities within surveys are controlled.

The decisions of any psychiatric judge are influenced by his background and by the content of the material put before him. The training and ideology of psychiatrists affect their judgments (13), and they disagree about what constitutes neurosis or personality disorder or schizophrenia (14). In addition social conditions sometimes dictate fashion in diagnosis; in the United States during the economic slump of the 1930s, "personality disorders" are said to have multiplied among the unemployed.

The conflicts of theory are exaggerated by the uncertainties of practice. Uncertainty grows when the clinical content of the material with which the psychiatrist must deal is limited by a routine screening procedure. The contact is unsolicited by the respondent, and the screening psychiatrist is denied clues provided in the normal clinical situation by the history of the events that lead to referral. Psychiatrists required to examine recruits at army induction stations are in a similar situation. In a World War II study of 100,000 men screened at induction stations throughout the United States, the proportion rejected on psychiatric grounds varied from 0.5 per cent at one station to 50.6 per cent at another. The fluctuations in the distribution of diagnosis were equally astonishing (15).

For the purpose of comparing groups, standard inventories of symptoms were shown in these studies to have an advantage in consistency over subjective judgments. Standard questions also promote consistency when used as a basis or a support for psychiatric judgment (16). Reasonable consistency between psychiatrists trained in common procedures has been attained between as well as within studies (17, 18).

Attempts to achieve consistency are now being made between countries, for instance by the World Health Organization. The first step, in psychiatric as with other diseases, is to standardize nomenclatures and classifications and to ensure that the same phenomena are allocated to the same classes. The attempts to standardize disease classifications for statistical purposes already have a history of more than a century on which to draw. Classification can produce considerable disparity even within closely similar circumstances. A general practitioner might count among his psychiatric cases only those patients whose disorders are primarily mental, or add to the count those patients with somatic disorders accompanied by mental disorders or those with somatic disorders thought to be of psychic origin as well (19).

The gains in consistency and economy attained through symptom inventories are offset, as compared with the clinical judgment of psychiatrists, by their lack of penetration. The content of the information obtained from a standard inventory of symptoms is limited by the questions asked. The amount and the type of information influence results. The effect of the amount of information is apparent in the Stirling County analysis. A sample in which maximum information was collected produced prevalence rates almost double those for samples in which less information was collected. The effect of type of information is also apparent in this survey. The questionnaires were not calculated to reveal the more bizarre psychiatric symptoms, and they were heavily loaded with questions about "psychophysiological" reactions. The loading is reflected in the high frequency of psychophysiologic symptom patterns revealed by the surveys. The room for disagreement about psychophysiologic and other mild symptoms is high. Disagreement tends to be less between psychiatrists, and between surveys, when attention is confined to severe symptoms and the psychoses.

The second aspect of case identification that creates disparity between survey results resides in the means of case finding. The cases may be discovered through direct contact with total populations or samples of populations. Cases may be counted from the information obtained, on home visits, from household members about the remaining household members. The records of local agencies may provide the information, on occasion supplemented by key informants in the community. Finally, cases may be collected in treatment agencies, whether from general practitioners, or mental hospitals, or several agencies at once.

The data already quoted show that the direct screening of populations by nonpsychiatrists who put standard questions gives a big yield of symptoms and of "cases." With many of the symptoms thus declared, no other person would have been privy to them before the interview. Divergence is likely to arise from the inclusion of self-reports of such inapparent symptoms. Indirect case finding by screening the records of agencies and interviewing key informants gives a smaller yield of cases and a different spectrum of symptoms and illnesses. More of the symptoms elicited by indirect search will reflect disturbances of behavior visible to others and agreed upon among a number of people. These overt aberrations are characteristic of the severe disorders. In relation to this second aspect of case identification, therefore, analysis confined to severe disorders and the psychoses could again be expected to reduce divergence.

The available data support this view. In an array of population surveys, the prevalence rates of all kinds of mental impairment range from rather more than 300 per 1,000 to less than 10 per 1,000 (3, 4, 5, 6, 9, 20, 21, 22, 23, 24). In these same surveys the prevalence rates for psychoses alone, where they can be derived from given data, range between 16 and 4 per 1,000. Discrepancy is somewhat reduced if lifetime prevalence rates are set aside. (The rates of psychoses reported from Scandinavia tend to be higher than elsewhere; the high rates could be due to their thoroughness, to classification and nomenclature, or to the use of the statistical device of lifetime prevalence.)

Excluding these and very small surveys, the rates of psychoses range from 7 to 4 per 1,000 adults. By these manipulations a proportionate difference between maximum and minimum of thirty to one, in the total rates of mental disorders in population surveys, is diminished to about two to one for psychoses alone. To account for this order of difference, it becomes reasonable to entertain hypotheses that invoke social and biological variation between populations as well as methodological variation between surveys.

The credibility of the results of population surveys has been enhanced by replications and by retrospective analysis of the Midtown Manhattan survey (25, 26). A short, twenty-two item symptom inventory developed from the Midtown Manhattan survey was tested in Kalamazoo County, Michigan (25). Some contrary results were obtained in attempts to validate the questionnaire. But with a cutoff point for severe impairment arbitrarily taken to be a score of ten or higher, 34 per 1,000 aged twenty to fifty-nine years living outside of mental hospitals had severe illness in Kalamazoo, and 37 per 1,000 in Midtown Manhattan.

In the original Midtown data, the category described as "incapacitated" was intended by the psychiatrists to encompass patients who on clinical grounds would be admitted to psychiatric hospitals. It comprised 27 per 1,000 of the sample of people aged twenty to sixty years and 32 per 1,000 if patients in mental hospitals were added. In the Stirling County study the most abnormal category comprised 30 per 1,000 in the sample where maximum information was available and 10 per 1,000 in the sample where the information was less. Severe total impairment, which seems comparable to the social breakdown syndrome, was reported for 7 to 10 per 1,000. In Salford the prevalence among people fifteen years and over of patients in the category of chronic disability, including those in the mental hospital and outside it, was approximately 5 per 1,000. These patients had been unable to perform their roles at work or in the home for at least twelve months.

Prevalence surveys of the general population come up against a special problem when a condition is relatively uncommon. To gather enough cases for refined analysis and the control of relevant factors, field surveys must be large. In Baltimore a stratified sample survey of 1,200 adults yielded 809 who agreed to be examined and uncovered 17 psychotic patients among them (23). This number is insufficient to set out distributions with confidence in more than one dimension, as for instance by age, sex, and diagnosis. With schizophrenia, incidence is of the order of 0.2 (27) to 0.5 (28) per 1,000 adults per year; the lifetime risk is of the order of 10 per 1,000; and, although it is a disease of long duration, prevalence is never likely to exceed 4 or 5 per 1,000. With depressive psychosis, registered incidence may be roughly three times higher, 0.7 (27), but duration is shorter and prevalence is probably less than in schizophrenia.

The prevalence rates of patients in treatment are naturally much affected by the available facilities. The chief variations between urban populations in treatment are found in the rates for outpatients, that is, again in the situation where patients with milder conditions congregate. For instance, the prevalence of inpatients per 1,000 adults calculated from more or less contemporaneous data was in Midtown Manhattan, 5 (4); in Baltimore, 5[1] (29); in Rochester, 6[1] (29); and in New Haven, 6 (24). The respective rates per 1,000 for outpatients were 8,[2] 5,[1] 3,[1] and 2.

To sum up, this review of prevalence studies suggests that, of every 100 adults aged less than sixty years in the cities of industrial countries at any one point in time, more than half will admit to some psychiatric symptom; between 20 and 30

1. Age and sex adjusted to 1960 U. S. Census population.

2. Manhattan is said to be occupied by 20 per cent of all American psychiatrists and has the highest concentration of private psychiatrists in the world.

will have a constellation of symptoms and a degree of impairment that most psychiatrists would regard as pathological; between 1 and 3 will be "most abnormal"; and 1 will be in psychiatric treatment. About 1 in 200 will exhibit the social breakdown syndrome, or frank psychosis, or be an inpatient. Prevalence is higher among the aged, especially for the organic psychoses that follow cerebral deterioration (30).

Incidence

Incidence studies are carried on through time and they have the advantage that they can relate illness to the immediate circumstances in which it arises (31). Incidence studies have another advantage in that they can generate large numbers. They ordinarily use the statistics of service agencies and, if necessary, wait for them to grow. These agencies persist, unlike the field research teams that conduct prevalence surveys. In these times there has been a shift in treatment from mental hospitals to outpatient clinics, and private doctors and many patients are served by more than one agency. To be meaningful, incidence studies must survey all these facilities and devise means of linking their records continuously and routinely.

Because of the clinical context in which they appear, the severe and relatively uncommon mental disorders can usually be given a diagnostic label. They can be sorted into tables of several dimensions by age and sex and occupation and social class and other attributes. By using large numbers of cases in this way, incidence studies can break down the global rubric of mental disorder into discrete groupings without straining their data.

Unfortunately, the clinical context does not banish gross uncertainties of diagnosis. Congruence between independent clinicians is hard to attain. Specialist psychiatrists are more consistent with each other and with standard symptom inventories than are general practitioners (16). But psychiatrists also diverge in diagnosis, even in the same institutions and on the same cases seen together (14). A large series of cases usually involves many psychiatrists, and therefore the risk of inconsistency is high. Psychiatric observers disagree less, however, about the presence of symptoms or of overt behavior than about diagnosis; therefore symptoms have been the index used in some studies (32).

A second uncertainty of incidence studies is the completeness with which they identify the cases to be found in the population (33). They enumerate illness that has been socially recognized and sifted through medical agencies. Although the definition of the case is not the arbitrary decision of the researcher, we have emphasized in previous chapters that an informal referral system regulates the flow of cases into services. This system gears local people's perception of what is psychiatric to the capacity of treatment facilities. In Salford half the patients coming into psychiatric care for the first time had exhibited the presenting symptoms for longer than six months before they were referred for psychiatric care (34). The threshold for the sick role, furthermore, can vary from place to place and from one type of illness to another. This difficulty in determining the point of onset of psychiatric disorder can have serious effects on incidence studies that aim to link illness with circumstances that may cause it. In the interval between onset and the assumption of the sick role, fresh events and changed circumstances may supervene, although with less likelihood than in prevalence studies.

The two difficulties in incidence studies of ensuring reliable diagnoses and of determining onset affect the numerator of the rate. A third difficulty affects the denominator. The numerator in an incidence rate is the number of cases collected over a defined period of time. On the other hand, the denominator must usually be taken as a population at one point in time, for a census can seldom be taken more often than once a year, if as often. Problems of interpretation are created by population changes in the time, which may be a decade or more, that elapses between censuses.

The focus of this chapter is less on causes of mental illness than on its scale in the population. In this regard the delayed declaration of illness weakens incidence studies as a measure of the scale of need. Incidence studies are a more precise measure of the scale of demand. An approximation to a measure of need, however, can be obtained through incidence studies based on the first contact of patients with doctors. The patient's quest for help after he becomes aware that he may be sick enables the doctor to make the diagnosis of mental disorder, should it exist. Incidence studies can provide an ostensive measure of need where medical services are freely available to all and used by almost all, as they are in Britain, the U.S.S.R., and some other countries.

Surveys in general practice can give such measures. Like prevalence surveys, however, their estimates fluctuate wildly. Total mental disorder is reported in the range 15 to 130 per 1,000 per unit population (6, 35). This fluctuation is due in part to differences among practitioners in their sensitivity to the presence of mental disorder and in their concepts of what constitutes mental disorder (36). Some authors suggest that large-scale surveys of general practice appear to obtain consistent results. What is consistent, however, is the distribution of practitioners who make high, average, or low estimates of mental illness in their practices.

Another approach to estimating the amount of mental illness to be found in general practice has been to screen the consulting patient populations through general practitioners and to have psychiatrists validate some of the cases selected by practitioners (37, 38). A survey in one practice obtained a period prevalence for "conspicuous psychiatric morbidity" of 90 per 1,000 adults fifteen years and over (37), and a survey of several practices, a rate of 104 (39). When psychiatric disorder accompanying organic illness was included, the rate rose to about 150 per 1,000 (39). One weakness of the approach through general practice lies in the selection of practitioners. They are usually volunteers and subject to bias on that account. They are likely to have a special interest in psychiatric disorders and to attract patients who seek psychiatric help. Some surveys have been able to overcome the problem of volunteers by enlisting all the practitioners in the study area.

We have observed that the amount of mental disorder referred to psychiatric agencies is a precise measure of the

Table 8. Rates of Inception of Mental Illness in Several Studies*

Area of Study	*Definition of Inception*	*Numerator Age Groups*	*Denominator Age Groups*	*Population at Risk*	*Duration of Study*	*Annual Rate/1,000*	*Adjusted*
New Haven†	All cases entering psychiatric care first time ever	15 and over	15 and over	174,300	6 mos.	2.5	
Salford	All cases entering psychiatric care first time ever	15 and over	15 and over	117,374	5 yrs.	3.3	3.3 (by age and sex to New Haven population 1951: correction factor 1)
Lundby	All cases entering psychiatric care first time ever	15 and over	15 and over	1,944	10 yrs.	5.6	5.6 (by age and sex to New Haven population 1951: correction factor 1)

North East Scotland	All cases entering psychiatric care who had not entered care in preceding 12 mos.	Over 15	Over 15	494,384	1 yr.	5.7	
Monroe County	All cases entering psychiatric care for first time since beginning of study on 1/1/60	All	All	586,000	1 yr.	8.5 (1960)	8.1 (1962–1963) (by age and sex to 1960 U.S. census)
Maryland	All cases entering psychiatric care for first time in calendar year of study	All	All	3,367,000	1 yr.		5.5 (by age and sex to 1960 U.S. census)
Hawaii	All cases entering psychiatric care for first time in calendar year of study	All	All	633,000	1 yr.		3.5 (by age and sex to 1960 U.S. census)

* The denominator for these rates, taken strictly, should be adjusted to remove from it all those not at risk of inception because they have had previous episodes.

† Dr. A. B. Hollingshead kindly supplied information for the calculation of New Haven rates.

scale of demand. Comprehensive registers of psychiatric referrals from defined areas (see also pp. 175 ff.) provide a sound basis for such estimates, and a number have been compiled in Scandinavia, Britain, and the United States (29, 40, 41). Registers cannot be dismissed for the purpose of estimating need. For illnesses with a high probability of being referred for psychiatric care, they can provide a good basis for estimates. In most developed countries mental disorders with high rates of referral for care constitute those of severe degree, in particular schizophrenia and the organic psychoses. Counts of referrals omit many cases of mild depression, psychoneurosis, and psychopathic and sociopathic disorders.

Inceptions of mental illness for the areas that have compiled registers covering all psychiatric services are given in Table 8. Few rates are exactly comparable as given, nor can they all be made comparable with the data available. The reader should not be deceived by the fact that problems of comparability have been glossed over in the preceding pages in the interests of a comprehensible account. Nonetheless, these rates of total incidence of mental illness, obtained from registers, are more congruent with one another than prevalence rates have been. The Salford register is unique in that it gives for *each* diagnosis the first contact ever with psychiatric services (that is, an inception rate). Although the population covered is smaller than those of some registers, the analysis of the data covers five years. (See Figures 3–7; see also Appendix A.)

One set of data permits exact comparison: that from the incidence study by O. Hagnell (42). This study covers the experience of two Swedish parishes (Lundby, population 2,297) over a period of ten years. Compared to Salford, the age- and sex-specific rates for all mental illness in Lundby are much higher, although they reveal a similar pattern. If total cases are counted, rather than only those that made contact with psychiatric agencies, the Swedish rates are, as expected, even higher.

The incidence data of August B. Hollingshead and F. Redlich (1957) for New Haven over a period of six months are based on the same definition of inception as are the data from Lundby and Salford. The rates adjusted for age and sex to the New Haven population of 1951 actually required no correction. The Lundby rate was 5.6 per 1,000 per year, the Salford rate 3.3, and the New Haven rate 2.5.

For estimates of the demand in very large populations only mental hospital statistics are available, and many analyses have been made. National statistics giving details of admissions and residence have been published for Norway, England and Wales, the United States, Israel, France, and other European countries (43). In the United States detailed statistics for hospitals across the country participating in a voluntary reporting scheme have been analyzed, and much useful data have been put out for New York and some other states (44). Extensive use has been made of such data in predicting trends of mental hospital use (45). In the earlier part of this century they showed the rising use and thereby the inferred needs of the elderly. More recently these data have pointed to the rising use of mental hospitals by adolescents and young adults and to their varying use by different groups defined by such attributes as age, sex, occupation, duration of residence, and diagnosis. Lately these data have revealed the declining bed occupancy of mental hospitals and the reduced average length of stay of patients.

These statistics provide a background in each country for more intensive local studies. Local studies establish to what degree and in what manner selection of mental-hospital patients takes place from a more broadly defined psychiatric population. In the United States and Britain outpatient clinics, in comparison with mental hospitals, deal hardly at all with the old, deal more with women and with higher social strata, and treat less severe types of illness (29, 46).

Mental-hospital statistics among countries have been useful so far only for broad comparisons (47). The supportive services of each country impose unique patterns of referral; psychiatrists in each country ascribe diagnoses in unique distributions; and, finally, the populations undoubtedly suffer different rates of certain mental disorders. To take an example of cross-national comparisons, a predominance of male admissions is common to several countries with preindustrial economies. In England and Wales this predominance has changed over half a century to a predominance of females (48). Similar change has not been observed in the United States.

One explanation is that in the United States women use private psychiatrists more than men do. In a study in Texas the addition of statistics from private facilities more than redressed the balance between the sexes (41). In Monroe County and in Maryland the trend was in the same direction, although private care did not contribute enough to reverse the sex ratio among psychiatric referrals.

Another notable Anglo-American divergence is in rates of schizophrenia and depression. The explanation that in the United States the relatively high mental-hospital rates for schizophrenia and low rates for depressive psychosis arise only from different use of inpatient and private facilities for these two conditions is not supported by the data of the complete psychiatric registers. Some investigators have the impression that the Anglo-American difference is a matter of nomenclature and classification among psychiatrists; American psychiatrists are thought to diagnose mental illness as schizophrenia more readily than do the British and the British to diagnose depressive psychosis more readily than do the Americans. Diagnostic nomenclature seems the likely explanation for the high frequency of senile dementia in Britain in contrast with cerebral arteriosclerosis in the United States.

The differences in the rates of functional psychoses could also be a cultural one between the incidence of mental disorder in the two populations. In the case of alcoholism and alcoholic psychosis, cultural differences are one likely cause of the disparity in rates between Britain and the United States. The diagnosis of gross cases presents little difficulty, and the fact that American alcoholics resort to psychiatric treatment or are obliged to do so seems insufficient to account for the disparity. A recent analysis makes a case for attributing the differences to the accessibility of alcohol in the two societies (49). Investigation has still to establish the origin of these differences. In doing so, causal relationships between social phenomena and mental disorder may be elucidated, including the impact of particular forms of care on its course.

At present the best estimates of need and demand derive from registers. In the context of providing care for large populations, the differences between the rates they yield are substantial. Further study will remove some of these differences. As can be seen in Table 8, certain registers have inflated their incidence rates for the first years of study by including cases making their first contacts in the period of study or shortly before, whether or not the patients have had contacts in earlier years. Another possible source of inflation is in the failure to eliminate repeated episodes in the same patient, for he may appear in a different facility, under a different name, and with a different address.

Registers of incidence provide a useful continuing measure of what type of serious illness, and how much, arises in any one community. They can demonstrate shifts in the use of services, changes in methods of disposal, and the impact of new policies. They can also identify groups in the community who are most vulnerable in psychiatric terms and those who make the heaviest demands on services, as well as social circumstances that need to be explored as a possible source of mental disorder.

A register of incidence is a ready measure of demand within a service, for it derives from the calls upon it, and these calls are almost always recorded. To strengthen the results of a register, it should be supplemented by a continuous record of prevalence. Once the apparatus for a register is set up, the effort needed to obtain data on the existing case load for prevalence rates is much reduced. In addition the more complete data that can make evaluation possible is relatively easily generated. The chief additional requirement for evaluation is some means of follow-up. Local resources can often be found for this purpose, for instance among public health nurses and social workers. By these means, too, we can study the natural course of mental illness and keep alive to its fresh manifestations. The study of illness is a foundation for its control.

References

(1) Shepherd M. and Gruenberg E. M. 1957 The age for neuroses *Milbank Mem Fund Quart* 35:258–265

(2) U.S. National Health Survey 1961 *Reporting of Hospitalization in the Health Interview Survey* Washington, D.C., Public Health Service Publ 584-D U

(3) Leighton D. C., Harding J. S., Macklin D. B., Macmillan A. M. and Leighton A. H. 1963 *The Stirling County Study of Psychiatric Disorder and Socio-Cultural Environment Vol. III The Character of Danger: Psychiatric Symptoms in Selected Communities* New York, Basic Books p. 129

(4) Srole L., Langner T. S., Michael S. T., Opler M. K. and Rennie T. A. C. 1962 *Mental Health in the Metropolis: The Midtown Manhattan Study* New York, McGraw-Hill, p. 138 Tables 8–3

(5) Hare E. H. and Shaw G. K. 1965 *Mental Health on a New Housing Estate: A Comparative Study of Health in the Two Districts of Croydon* Maudsley Monogr 12 London, Oxford

(6) Taylor Lord and Chave S. 1964 *Mental Health and Environment* London, Longmans

(7) Dohrenwend B. P. and Dohrenwend B. S. 1965 The problem of validity in field studies of psychological disorder *J Abnorm Psychol* 70:52–69

(8) Essen-Möller E. 1956 Individual traits and morbidity in a Swedish rural population *Acta Psychiat Neurol Scand Suppl* 100:1–160

(9) Brugger C. 1929 Zur Frage einer Belastungsstatistik der Durchschnittsbevölkerung *Z Ges Neurol Psychiat* 118:459

Brugger C. 1931 Versuch einer Geisteskrankenzählung in Thüringen *Z Ges Neurol Psychiat* 133:352–390

Brugger C. 1938 Psychiatrische Bestandesaufnahme im Gebiete eines medizinisch anthropologischen Zensus in der Nähe von Rosenheim *Z Ges Neurol Psychiat* 160:189–201

(10) For reviews see:

Plunkett R. J. and Gordon J. A. 1960 *Epidemiology and Mental Illness* Joint Commission on Mental Illness and Health Monogr Ser 6 New York, Basic Books

Lin T.-Y. and Standley C. C. 1961 *The Scope of Epidemiology in the Study of Mental Disorders* Public Health Papers No 16 Geneva, World Health Organization

(11) Leighton D. C., Harding J. S., Macklin D. B., Macmillan A. M. and Leighton A. H. 1963 *The Stirling County Study of Psychiatric Disorder and Socio-Cultural Environment Vol. III The Character of Danger: Psychiatric Symptoms in Selected Communities* New York, Basic Books

(12) Srole L., Langner T. S., Michael S. T., Opler, M. K. and Rennie T. A. C. 1962 *Mental Health in the Metropolis: The Midtown Manhattan Study* New York, McGraw-Hill

(13) Mason A. S. and Sacks J. M. 1959 Measurement of attitudes toward the tranquilizing drugs *Dis Nerv Syst* 20:457–459

Mowbray R. M., Blair W., Jubb L. G. and Clark A. 1961 The general practitioner's attitude to psychiatry *Scot Med J* 6:314–321

Pearlin L. J. 1962 Treatment values and enthusiasm for drugs in a mental hospital *Psychiat* 25:170–179

Strauss A., Schatzman L., Bucher R., Ehrlich D. and Sabshin M. 1964 *Psychiatric Ideologies and Institutions* New York, Free Press

Klerman G. L. 1966 *The Social Milieu and Drug Response in Psychiatric Patients* Paper read at Annual Meeting American Sociological Association, Miami Beach

(14) Pasamanick B., Dinitz S. and Lefton M. 1959 Psychiatric orientation and its relation to diagnosis and treatment in a mental hospital *Amer J Psychiat* 116:127–132

Kreitman N., Sainsbury P., Morrissey J., Towers J. and Scrivener J. 1961 The reliability of psychiatric assessment: an analysis *J Ment Sci* 107:887–908

(15) Stouffer S. A. 1955 Indices of psychological illness in Lazarsfeld P. and Rosenberg H. eds. *The Language of Social Research* New York, Free Press pp. 63–65

(16) Rawnsley K. 1966 Congruence of independent measures of psychiatric morbidity *J Psychosom Res* 10:84–93

(17) Leighton A. H., Lambo T. A., Hughes C. C., Leighton D. C., Murphy J. M. and Macklin D. B. 1963 *Psychiatric Dis-*

order among the Yoruba Ithaca, N.Y., Cornell University Press

(18) Goldfarb A., Downing J. J. and Moses L. E. 1967 Reliability of psychiatrists' ratings in community case finding *Amer J Pub Health* 57:94–106

(19) Crombie D. L. 1963 The procrustean bed of medical nomenclature *Lancet* 11:1205–1206

(20) Lin T.-Y. 1953 A study of the incidence of mental disorder in Chinese and other cultures *Psychiatry* 16:313–336

(21) Uchimura Y., Akimoto H., Kan O., Abe Y., Takahashi K., Inose T., Shimazaki T. and Ogawa N. 1940 Über die vergleichend psychiatrische und erbpathologische Untersuchung auf einer Japanischen Insel *Psychiat Neurol Jap* 44:745–782

Akimoto A. 1942 Demographische und psychiatrische Untersuchung der abgegrentzen Kleinstadtbevölkerung *Psychiat Neurol Jap* 47:351–375

Kaila M. 1942 Über die Durchschnittshäufigkeit der Geisteskrankheiten und des Schwachsinns in Finnland *Acta Psychiat Neurol* 17:47–67

Tsugawa T., Okada K., Hanasiro S., Asai T., Takuma T., Morimura S. and Rsuboi F. 1942 Über die psychiatrische Zensusuntersuchung in einem Stadtbezirk von Tokyo *Psychiat Neurol Jap* 46:204–218

Roth W. F. and Luton F. B. 1943 The mental health program in Tennessee *Amer J Psychiat* 99:662–675

Fremming K. H. 1947 *Morbid Risk of Mental Disease and Other Mental Abnormalities in an Average Danish Population on the Basis of Catamnestic Study of 5500 Persons Born 1883–87* Copenhagen, Munksgaard

Mayer-Gross W. 1948 Mental health survey in a rural area *Eugen Rev* 40:140–148

Sjögren T. 1948 Genetic-statistical and psychiatric investigations of a west Swedish population *Acta Psychiat Neurol Scand Suppl* 52

Strömgren E. 1950 Statistical and genetic population studies within psychiatry: methods and principal results in *Actualités Scientifiques et Industrielles* Paris, Herman pp. 155–188

Bremer J. 1951 A social psychiatric investigation of a small community in northern Norway *Acta Psychiat Neurol Scand Suppl* 62

Fremming K. H. 1951 *The expectation of Mental Infirmity in a Sample of the Danish Population.* Occasional Papers on Eugenics 7 London, Eugenics Society pp. 4–53

Larsson T. and Sjögren T. 1954 A methodological, psychiatric and statistical study of a large Swedish rural population *Acta Psychiat Neurol Scand Suppl* 89

Eaton J. W. and Weil R. J. 1955 *Culture and Mental Disorders* New York, Free Press

Trussell R. E., Elinson J. and Levin M. L. 1956 Comparisons of various methods of estimating the prevalence of chronic disease in a community: The Hunterdon County study *Amer J Pub Health* 46:173–183

Cole N. J., Branch C. H. H. and Shaw O. M. 1957 Mental illness: a survey assessment of community rates, attitudes and adjustments *Arch Neurol Psychiat* 77:393–398

Llewellyn-Thomas E. 1960 The prevalence of psychiatric symptoms within an island fishing village *Canad Med J* 83:197–204

Cole N. J., Branch C. H. H. and Allison R. 1962 Some relationships between social class and the practice of dynamic psychotherapy *Amer J Psychiat* 118:1004–1012

Primrose E. J. R. 1962 *Psychological Illness: A Community Study* Mind and Medicine Monogr 3 London, Tavistock

Gnat T., Henisz J. and Sarapata A. 1964 *A Psychiatric-Socio-Statistical Study of Two Polish Towns* Paper read at First International Congress of Social Psychiatry, London

(22) Lemkau P., Tietze C. and Cooper M. 1941–1942 Mental hygiene problems in an urban district *Ment Hyg* 25:624–646; 26:100–119; 275–288

(23) Pasamanick B., Roberts D. W., Lemkau P. W. and Krueger D. B. 1959 A survey of mental disease in an urban population: prevalence by race and income in Pasamanick B. ed. *Epidemiology of Mental Disorder* Washington, D. C., American Association for the Advancement of Science Publication 60 pp. 183–201

(24) Hollingshead A. B. and Redlich F. C. 1958 *Social Class and Mental Illness* New York, Wiley pp. 212–216

(25) Manis J. G., Brawer M. J., Hunt C. L. and Kercher L. C. 1964 Validating a mental health scale *Amer Sociol Rev* 28:108–116

(26) Dohrenwend B. P. 1966 Social status and psychological disorder: an issue of substance and an issue of method *Amer Sociol Rev* 31:14–34

(27) Adelstein A. M., Downham D., Stein Z. A. and Susser M. W. 1965 *Inceptions and Episodes of Mental Illness in Salford* Paper read at annual scientific meeting Society for Social Medicine, Sheffield, Eng. (included in Appendix A)

(28) Warthen F. J., Klee G. D., Bahn A. K. and Gorwitz K. 1966 *Diagnosed Schizophrenia in Maryland* Paper read at American Psychiatric Association Regional Research Conference on Psychiatric Epidemiology and Mental Health Planning, Baltimore

(29) Bahn A. K., Gardner E. A., Alltop L., Knatterud G. L. and Solomon M. 1966 Admission and prevalence rates for psychiatric facilities in four register areas *Amer J Pub Health* 56:2033–2051

(30) Parsons P. L. 1965 Mental health of Swansea's old folk *Brit J Prev Soc Med* 19:43–47

Gruenberg E. M. 1961 A mental health survey of older persons in Hoch P. H. and Zubin J. eds. *Comparative Epidemiology of the Mental Disorders* New York, Grune & Stratton pp. 13–23

Pollack E. S., Locke B. Z. and Kramer M. 1961 Trends in hospitalization and patterns of care of the aged mentally ill in Hoch P. H. and Zubin J. eds. *Psychopathology of Aging* New York, Grune & Stratton pp. 21–56

Kay D. W. K., Beamish P. and Roth M. 1964 Old age mental disorders in Newcastle Upon Tyne: Part I A study of prevalence *Brit J Psychiat* 110:146–158

Kay D. W., Beamish P. and Roth M. 1964 Old age mental disorders in Newcastle Upon Tyne: Part 2 A study of possible social and medical causes *Brit J Psychiat* 110:668–682

Williamson J., Stokoe I. H., Gray S., Fischer M., Smith A., McGhee A. and Stephenson E. 1964 Old people at home: their unreported needs *Lancet* 1:1117–1120

(31) Kramer M. 1957 A discussion of the concepts of incidence and prevalence as related to epidemiologic studies of mental disorders *Amer J Pub Health* 47:826–840

Morris J. N. 1957 *Uses of Epidemiology* London, Livingstone

(32) Kreitman N. 1961 The reliability of psychiatric diagnosis *J Ment Sci* 107:876–886

(33) Blum R. H. 1962 Case identification in psychiatric epidemiology: methods and problems *Milbank Mem Fund Quart* 40:253–258

(34) Susser M. W. 1965 Review of services for mental illness in Susser M. W. ed. *Report and Papers of the Salford Mental Health Service for 1964* City of Salford, Eng., Health Department pp. 3–15

(35) Logan W. P. D. and Cushion A. A. 1958 *Morbidity Statistics from General Practice Vol. 1* General Studies on Medical and Population Subjects 14 London, H.M. Stationery Office

Watts, C. A. H. 1962 Psychiatric disorders in *Morbidity Statistics from General Practice Vol. 3* General Studies on Medical and Population Subjects 14 London, H.M. Stationery Office

Watts C. A., Cawte E. C. and Kuenssberg E. V. 1964 Survey of mental illness in general practice *Brit Med J* 2:1351–1359

(36) Rawnsley K. and Loudon J. B. 1962 Factors influencing the referral of patients to psychiatrists by general practitioners *Brit J Prev Soc Med* 16:174–182

(37) Shepherd M., Fischer M., Stein L. and Kessell W. I. N. 1959 Psychiatric morbidity in an urban group practice *Proc Roy Soc Med* 52:269–274

Kessel W. I. N. 1960 Psychiatric morbidity in a London practice *Brit J Prev Soc Med* 14:16–22

(38) Jones A. and Miles H. L. 1964 The Anglesey mental health survey in McLachlan G. ed. *Problems and Progress in Medical Care* London, Oxford pp. 205–263

(39) Shepherd M., Cooper B., Brown A. C. and Kalton G. W. 1964 Minor mental illness in London: some aspects of a general practice survey *Brit Med J* 2:1359–1363

(40) Innes G. and Sharpe G. A. 1962 A study of psychiatric patients in north-east Scotland *J Ment Sci* 108:447–456

Nielsen J., Juel-Nielsen N. and Strömgren E. 1962 Psychiatric diseases in general practice *Ugeskr Laeg* 124:1103–1108

Stein Z. A. 1964 Some preliminary results of the survey of mental sickness in Salford in Susser M. W. *Report on the Salford Mental Health Services for 1963* City of Salford, Eng., Health Department pp. 11–23

Bahn A. K., Gorwitz K., Klee G . D., Kramer M. and Tuerk I. 1965 Services received by Maryland residents in facilities directed by a psychiatrist (first year of a state case register) *Public Health Rep* 80:405–416

Wing J. K. 1965 *The Camberwell Psychiatric Disease Register* Unpublished mimeo, Medical Research Council Social Psychiatry Research Unit, London

Miles H. C., Gardner E. A., Bodian C. and Romano J. 1964 A cumulative survey of all psychiatric experience in Monroe County, New York *Psychiat Quart* 38:458–487

(41) Jaco E. G. 1960 *The Social Epidemiology of Mental Disorders: A Psychiatric Survey of Texas* New York, Russell Sage Foundation

(42) Hagnell O. 1966 *A Prospective Study of the Incidence of Mental Disorder* Stockholm, Svenska

(43) General Register Office 1953 *Statistical Review of England and Wales for the year 1949—Supplement on General Morbidity, Cancer and Mental Health* London, H.M. Stationery Office

Ødegaard Ø. 1960 A statistical study of factors influencing discharge from psychiatric hospitals *J Ment Sci* 106:1124–1133

General Register Office 1961 *Registrar General's Statistical Review of England and Wales 1957–1958—Supplement on Mental Health* London, H.M. Stationery Office

General Register Office 1962 *Registrar General's Statistical Review of England and Wales 1959—Supplement on Mental Health* London, H.M. Stationery Office

Pugh T. and MacMahon B. 1962 *Epidemiologic Findings in United States Mental Hospital Data* Boston, Little Brown

Brooke E. M. 1963 *A Cohort Study of Patients First Admitted to Mental Hospitals in 1954 and 1955*—General Register Office Studies on Medical and Population Subjects 18 London, H. M. Stationery Office

Zdravotnická Stayistika ČSSR *Psychiatrická Péče V Roce 1963, 1964, 1965* Ministerstvo Zdravotnictví

World Health Organization Regional Office for Europe 1966 *Published National Statistics on Mental Illness in Europe* Unpublished mimeo

(44) *The Twelfth Annual Conference of the Model Reporting Area for Mental Hospital Statistics at Madison, Wisconsin, May 1962* Public Health Service Publ 1126 Washington, D. C., U.S. Government Printing Office

Kramer M. 1963 Collection and utilization of statistical data from psychiatric facilities in the United States of America *Bull WHO* 29:491–510

Malzberg B. and Lee E. S. 1956 *Migration and Mental Disease: A Study of First Admissions to Hospitals for Mental Disease New York 1939–1941* New York, Social Science Research Council

Malzberg B. 1958 *Cohort Studies of Mental Disease in New York State 1943–1949* New York, National Association for Mental Health

Bahn A. K. 1961 *Methodological Study of Population of Outpatient Psychiatric Clinics Maryland 1958–59* Public Health Monogr 65 Public Health Service Publ No. 821 Washington, D. C., U.S. Government Printing Office

Moon L. E. and Patton R. E. 1965 First admissions and readmissions to New York State mental hospitals: a statistical evaluation *Psychiat Quart* 39:476–486

(45) Kramer M., Goldstein H., Israel R. H. and Johnson N. A. 1955 *A Historical Study of the Disposition of First Admissions to a State Mental Hospital: Experiences of the Warren State Hospital During the Period 1916–1950* Public Health Monogr 32 Washington, D. C., U.S. Government Printing Office

Pollack E. S., Person P. H., Kramer M. and Goldstein H. 1959 *Patterns of Retention, Release and Death of First Admissions to State Mental Hospitals* Public Health Monogr 58 Washington, D.C., U.S. Government Printing Office

Person P. H. 1964 *Hospitalized Mental Patients and the Outcome of Hospitalization* Washington, D. C., U. S. Government Printing Office

(46) Susser M. W. 1965 Review of services for mental illness in Susser M. W. ed. *Reports and Papers of the Salford Mental Health Service for 1964* City of Salford, Eng., Health Department pp. 3–15

(47) Kramer M. 1963 Some problems for international research suggested by observations on differences in first admission rates to the mental hospitals of England and Wales and of the United States *Proceedings of the Third World Congress of Psychiatry,* III Montreal: McGill University Press pp. 153–160

(48) Lowe C. R. and Garratt F. N. 1959 Sex pattern of admissions to mental hospitals in relation to social circumstances *Brit J Prev Soc Med* 13:88–102

(49) Terris M. 1967 Epidemiology of cirrhosis of the liver: national mortality data *Amer J Pub Health* 57:2076–2088

10

Coordination of Community Care: A Case Study

The proper use of all the facilities for community care, we have argued, requires a comprehensive assessment of the mental patient. This assessment takes into account the demands he makes on his family and others in terms of physical organization, psychological resilience, and social resources. It takes into equal account the demands that families and others make on the patient and considers the patient and his family as an interacting system within a particular culture. In industrial societies assessment cannot ignore the patient's associations outside family and kin. Some persons have no immediate kin, but everyone has some associations outside of kin, whether for work or for leisure, whether to obtain services or to fulfill the obligations of citizenship.

These manifold functional associations are more or less discrete. The ways in which the needs of a patient are perceived by a particular service agency tend to be limited by

This chapter is a revised version of M. W. Susser, "Changing Roles and Coordination in Mental Health Services," in *Sociology and Medicine: Studies within the Framework of the British National Health Service,* Sociological Review Monograph 5 (1962), by permission of Sociological Review Monographs.

this discrete quality of functional associations in our society. This universal predicament of perception, manifest in diverse forms as egocentric, or culturebound or ethnocentric, is exaggerated by the self-sufficiency of large organizations. In the hospital the patient is totally encapsulated and he tends to be seen in terms of the restricted roles of one dependent on the hospital for all his needs; in the public health service he tends to be seen as a person with disordered relations with his family, other supportive institutions, or the law; in industry he is seen as a worker who has observable effects on productivity.

Each of these frames of reference is accurate in itself, but insufficient and biased in relation to the set of references encompassed by the patient's life. The psychiatric observer's conscious effort to attain a frame of reference adequate to the whole range of the patient's interactions through time is eased by free access to each observation point. Incoordination of psychiatric services obstructs free access, and for this reason alone presents a fundamental defect in a system of medical care. The administrative structure of the psychiatric services of the first half of this century evolved around the custodial functions required by the laws concerned with mental disorder; the role of mental patient was almost entirely confined to the mental hospital and the flow between hospital and community was a mere trickle. Continuity of care, insofar as it was recognized as a therapeutic need, was ensured by prolonged stay in the mental hospitals, which for the bulk of people combined the functions of guard and guardian with the only accessible source of treatment.

The old structure cannot sustain the rising flood of patients passing between hospital and community of recent years. In Britain its legal forms have been dismantled, but the inertia of traditional forms of organization enable many of its wasteful features to persist. Hence the current drive toward coordination and continuity of care. Coordination eliminates the unhelpful alternative of hospital or community, expands the range of therapeutic situations, and allows the best use to be made of available facilities. The mental hospital can then be an institution that not only serves the community but also interacts with it.

The need for coordination is all the greater in times of reorganization and rapid change, when there is a general tendency to defend old positions in the face of an uncertain future, thus giving a defensive tenor to relationships among individuals who represent interacting interests and organizations. Ironically, the need is felt more acutely in Britain, where a comprehensive system of medical care exists, than in the United States, where no such system exists and where the actual need is therefore greatest. In the United States the fragmentary organization of highly developed technical resources and multiple services has so far failed to bring about the juxtapositions that stimulate awareness of incoordination and make it visible.

Coordination does not come about, however, simply because the providers of services see the need and desire it. To realize coordination can take years of patient work, except in favorable circumstances as when a vacuum of services exists or where individuals and organizations are already poised for it. Analysis of the social forces that hinder coordination can help to circumvent obstructions and hasten its achievement. In this chapter I shall attempt such an analysis. The method will be to describe a particular case in the hope that it will afford generalizations that can be applied elsewhere.

The nub of the analysis that follows is in the opposition among organizations that resides in their structure and culture and in the effects of social change on this opposition. Main components that determine the structure and culture of organizations for medical care are their service functions and the professional roles organized around them. Service functions have changed with new orientations in the care of mental disorder, and the content of a number of professional roles performed in giving this care has had to be adapted to meet the changes. Relations among professions are affected by past development as well as by present arrangements.

We shall therefore begin with a review of the past developments of professional psychiatric work to guide us to the assumptions underlying the present allocation of duties to each branch of the service. This review may guide us also to sources of conflict between the allocation of duties and their performance. Against this backdrop of changing roles we can proceed to examine the case of the psychiatric services of the city of Salford, first as to the circumstances that existed at the outset, and then as they evolved toward coordination.

Psychiatric Roles in Different Service Settings

Psychiatry in Personal Medical Practice. In several large-scale industrial societies in recent times general practice has not flourished. It did not survive the revolution of 1917 in the U.S.S.R., it is on the decline in the United States, and in Britain there is anxious reappraisal of its place in medical care (1, 2). In general practice in this sense the doctor is the first to be called upon for every type of patient and for any medical condition. In the eyes of many doctors the advance of technology and specialization in medicine has seemed to reduce the proficiency of the general practitioner, although in absolute terms his potential proficiency has been much improved by new techniques and treatments. In Britain, however, general practice is entrenched by the cleavage between general and special services in the National Health Service. In this setting, a main function of the general practitioner is to maintain the traditional professional relationship between doctor and patient, in other words, "to undertake full and continuing responsibility for his patient." The National Health Service makes this possible through its legal and administrative structure, and consistent with this, the capitation fee is based on responsibility for patients and not on services.

With more or less design, the medical-care systems of other countries maintain or redistribute these functions among a variety of health professionals. But wherever doctors have personal responsibility for individual patients, the questions that arise are similar to those in general practice.

The medical profession emphasizes, in its professional ethic, full responsibility, privacy, and continuity of treatment for patients. This ethic is connected with economic realities; for instance, continuity contributes to good practice and at the same time controls competition for patients among doctors. No less important to the medical ethic, however, were the necessities of practice before science and technology had given doctors a range of effective remedies. Doctors had then to rely in large part on an understanding of the natural history of disease and to accommodate diagnosis, prognosis, and treatment to the psychological needs and the social circumstances of the patient. This overall care was made possible by the special qualities of the relationship between doctor and patient. Its essence is the rapport that derives from the patient's voluntary surrender of his person, body and mind, to the doctor and from his acceptance of the doctor's authority and responsibility in return for professional confidence, professional standards, and the knowledge that the patient's needs always have precedence.

The concept of overall responsibility encourages the doctor to extend the boundaries of medical care to whatever concerns the patient's health and places an obligation on him to deal with the psychological and social as well as the physical aspects of illness. The rules of confidence enable the doctor to probe the intimate details of the patient's life in order to obtain a complete history, and in so doing they create special conditions for treating psychological disorders. These conditions are not found in every contact between patient and doctor, nor with all doctors, but they facilitate psychological and social investigation. It is no accident that psychotherapy arose from the practice of medicine and not from other disciplines or professions that have a concern with psychological problems.

Until recently, however, the function of nonspecialists in psychiatry has not had general recognition. Although the content of past medical curricula in Britain had a strong vocational bias and kept the needs of general practice much in mind, little account was taken of this function. Nevertheless, there has been growing awareness of it in recent years. In Britain formal recognition of a psychiatric function for the general practitioner is expressed in the Mental Health Act of 1959. The act gives responsibility to him in the first instance for the care of mentally disordered patients. Previously he could ignore this responsibility and avoid any formal part in the compulsory admission of his patients, whereas he is now asked to participate in the decision by making a recommendation that has legal force. This requirement brings general practitioners explicitly into the field of psychiatric care. The exercise of compulsion by the doctor is in conflict with his traditional mode of behavior toward patients; nevertheless, the role here accorded the general practitioner emphasizes his responsibility.

Psychiatry and the Mental Hospital. Specialization is not compatible with the traditional professional relationship characteristic of general practice except in those specialities defined by the stages of the life cycle and responsible for the whole person, as in pediatrics, geriatrics, and obstetrics. By definition, specialization limits professional competence, and it excludes overall responsibility for the whole person when it is based on organs or systems or on technical services, as for instance clinical pathology and radiology. Despite this fact, the fullest use and the most extensive and minute analysis of the professional relationship between doctor and patient has been made by specialists, namely the psychoanalysts. In this case special elements of the relationship have been adapted as a means of therapy, so much so that some analysts have insisted on the therapeutic value of a fee.

The prescribed role of the doctor, in the eyes of the profession, is one of "affective neutrality" in a benevolent figure of authority (3), also described as "detached concern" (4). In receiving the symptoms and complaints of the patient, the doctor neither judges nor blames nor exculpates; he accepts all, but he responds with calculated restraint and without spontaneous personal involvement. Given the safeguard of professional confidence, the patient can thus reveal himself without fear and in the expectation of tolerance. The emotional catharsis of the patient can be tolerated and encouraged by the doctor without fear for himself, because his own emotional responses are sealed off by the barrier of affective neutrality.

This model has been so much a part of medical thinking that doctors have perceived only with difficulty that they may be emotionally involved with their patients and that these emotions are suppressed. Psychoanalysts had given much thought to the phenomenon of transference, in which the patient's habitual emotional responses are transferred from important childhood figures to the psychiatrist, and they made it a foundation of therapy. But some time passed before they gave much attention to the two-way process that is common to every relationship and went on to study the countertransference of the psychiatrist. From the point of view of the patient and of society, however, these suppressed emotions of the psychiatrist are not recognized or are not permitted to appear, and the psychiatrist may be punished for giving rein to expressions of love or even seeming to do so. Indeed, the analysis of countertransference can be seen as a means of controlling it and strengthening affective neutrality in the therapeutic situation. The form of relationship between doctor and patient has thus become the foundation for a specialized and influential form of psychological treatment.

Western culture has been pervaded by Freudian concepts at many levels. The social norms of a culture define the bounds of mental disorder. In medicine, under the impact of Freud and related cultural movements, the bounds of mental disorder shifted to incorporate the great mass of neuroses. These became conditions for the doctor to treat as well as to diagnose, by methods that generally relied on the professional relationship.

The early promise of psychoanalysis, since reinforced by the successes of physical methods of treatment in mental illness and by the successes of the rediscovered social methods, engendered a mood of therapeutic optimism. In the early part of this century, when most psychiatrists in mental hospitals did not share this mood, they accepted as a chief function the custody of those socially deviant members of society who were regarded as a potential danger because of their acts or their genetic make-up and whose behavior could be attributed to mental disorder. This was not primarily a therapeutic function, as the low rates of discharge show (5), and it was conferred on psychiatrists by the law and not by the medical ethic. The traditional legal code insists on the personal responsibility of individuals, does not view behavior as determined by the dynamics of the psyche, and does not prescribe therapy but punishes to deter. This legal point of view was one reason for the relative stagnation of psychiatry.

The legislation that determined the structure of psychiatric services toward the end of the last century derived in the first instance from the social ethic surrounding private property, individual rights, and individual responsibility. These laws aimed to protect society from mentally disordered persons by confining them in institutions, and to protect the sane from unjustly being confined as insane. To this end the law set up definitions of social incapacity, not immediately related to the clinical criteria of treatment and prognosis, by which to judge the need for hospital admission. The mental hospital was used as the place of custody; the chief concern of the law for the welfare of inmates was with their living conditions rather than with their recovery.

This function has important effects on the organization of mental hospitals. Contemporary custodial and disciplinary institutions have shared a bureaucratic structure, for it produces a high degree of predictable behavior in all the members of the institution, and efficient discipline and control. In the mental hospital the law thus vested final authority and responsibility in the medical superintendent, so that he might carry out the provisions of the Lunacy Acts. The system of authority and the hierarchy of ranks, including doctors, nurses, and patients as well as administrators, tended to produce an authoritarian regime with poor communication between doctors and patients. Orders might be directly transmitted from above downward, but communication from below upward might follow devious routes and encounter many blocks. The process by which patients adapt to these restrictions, and their typical responses, have been well described (6).

The bureaucratic system of authority in its ideal form is in conflict with the professional relationship and with the requirements of psychotherapeutic rapport, and hence there were obvious strains in the system, both between patients and staff and between superintendents and their consultant colleagues. Psychiatrists have often complained that superintendents interfered to ill-effect in the management of patients in their clinical care, as an extensive correspondence in the *Lancet* of 1960 showed. Superintendents have retorted that central authority leads to administrative efficiency and makes possible a controlled therapeutic milieu.

In Britain, recognition of the therapeutic potential of psychiatry had begun the swing back to an ambience of optimism when in 1948 the psychiatric services of the National Health Service were established. During World War II the needs of the armed services for conformity and discipline in millions of men subject to extraordinary stresses had given psychiatrists an opportunity to demonstrate the scope of psychiatry and even to widen it (7).

The distinctions between custody, caretaking, and therapy are not without overlap and continuity. The values placed upon specialized medical occupations by the medical profession have changed during the past century as the possibilities of therapy have changed. High values seem always to have been accorded to therapy. Two generations back surgeons were activists, some of whom were impatient with the impotence of physicians in internal medicine. One generation back the chest physician, who cared for the chronic and often hopeless tuberculosis patient in the sanatorium, ranked low until first thoracic surgery and then effective drugs made his calling respectable. Psychiatrists began their rise to respectability aided by the successive advent of psychotherapy, electroshock, milieu therapy, and drugs.

After the war, in the National Health Service, the newfound standing of psychiatrists was formalized and promoted by giving them consultant status and equality with colleagues in other branches of medicine. The effects of this status on intercourse among colleagues helped many psychiatrists to emerge from the fastnesses of mental hospitals and to join the mainstream of medicine.

We have noted in a previous chapter that the recommendations of the Commission on the Laws Relating to Mental Illness and Mental Deficiency, which preceded the Mental Health Act of 1959, derived from the traditional medical ethic and its optimistic therapeutic approach. In contrast with what had gone before, the report emphasized the medical needs of individual patients, tended to replace legal criteria of social incapacity with medical criteria of sickness, and encouraged conditions in which the traditional professional relationship could be established.

The policies arising from that report favor the development of professional relationships in the mental hospitals by giving consultants full responsibility for their patients in hospitals, although theoretically this type of relationship is still hindered by the fact that patients may be under legal and physical constraint. The trend toward voluntary relationships between doctors and patients in Britain has probably been fostered by the comprehensive cover of the National Health Service, which serves nearly all classes. Before 1930 all who entered mental hospitals under certain legal provisions were categorized as paupers, and this must surely have restricted the use of mental hospitals by those who could afford other treatment. The rising number of manic-depressive patients entering mental hospitals for the first time (8) might be taken to support this inference, for the increment has probably been drawn from the higher social classes. This psychosis is fairly evenly distributed among the social classes; in contrast, the first admissions for a disorder such as schizophrenia, which is concentrated in the lower social classes, have shown little change. Patients from a wider range of social strata might be expected to induce more symmetrical relationships between mental hospital staff and their patients and a greater respect for individuals. Since the introduction of the National Health Service, practice in British mental hospitals has several times been put forward as an example of progress, particularly in the United States, where many psychiatric institutions have lagged behind in these matters (9). This difference between Britain and the United States may be related to the class structure of the patient populations they serve, the importance of which has been emphasized by a number of studies (10).

In Britain the conscious use of the relationship between doctor and patient in psychiatry, the return of therapeutic optimism, and the altered legal framework have conspired to emphasize the therapeutic and medical elements of the role of the mental hospital, and to diminish and even to deny the custodial elements.

Public Health and Psychiatric Care. In Britain the local health authorities are the public-health arm of municipal government. Although stripped of many powers by the National Health Service Act, they were given functions in the psychiatric services through which they too came to participate in the optimistic climate of psychiatry. At that time their officers were given statutory duties in arranging the admission to the hospital of individuals subject to the Lunacy and Mental Treatment Acts and in administering the Mental Deficiency Acts by supervising mental defectives in the community. The provision of community care for mental defectives by local health authorities, and their duty under the National Health Service Act to provide aftercare for all hospital patients, including those discharged from mental hospitals, caused movement in the new direction. The emphasis of all local health authority work had been social and preventive, in accord with the philosophy of public health and medical care that had evolved with industrialization and urbanization during the nineteenth century. Until recently, however, local authorities tended to serve a restricted class of patients, because of their various associations with the administration of welfare and their concentration on the problems of poverty.

The Royal Commission on the Laws Relating to Mental Illness and Mental Deficiency recognized the experience of local health authorities in social problems and turned to them to meet the needs of psychiatric patients for social care. These authorities, it was suggested, should provide support through social workers and through special centers for training, resettlement, and sheltered employment. It was made plain in preceding chapters that community support has become even more important with recent policy, because a positive attempt is being made to shift the weight of care from mental hospitals to outpatient units and general hospitals. This policy is consistent with the intention of treating mental disorder in the same way as other illnesses, for other special branches of medicine have made increasing use of outpatient services. Now that many psychiatric patients are kept outside hospitals, the supportive social agencies are called upon to resettle them in their previous occupations or train them for new ones, to take the daily burden of nursing care off the nuclear family, and to provide conditions in which their social and clinical responses can be observed.

In order to meet these demands of medical care, the Salford local health authority through its health department developed, as have a number of others, new institutions for the support of patients outside the hospital and at the same time tried to acquire and train a staff to administer them and to carry out social work. The facilities included the day centers for the subnormal and for patients with mental illness, therapeutic social clubs, and residential arrangements described in earlier pages.

Mental-welfare officers carry out the social work that is essential to make these institutions effective. Social work is but one part of a system of medical care, although it is not always carried out in conjunction with clinical care. When it is, a third element is added to the two contributions of social work in guiding individuals and families toward appropriate supportive agencies and in giving counsel in personal and family problems, for it can add depth to the medical understanding of the environment and the relationships of patients.

The relations that professional social workers have tried to build up with clients and patients are voluntary and similar, in principle, to those between doctor and patient. Like the physician who is superintendent of a mental hospital, however, the social worker who is also a mental-welfare officer has another frame of reference; he is an official with prescribed legal duties in the compulsory admission of patients to the hospital. This role is in conflict with the voluntary professional relationship between social worker and client. The relative importance of compulsion in the work of the community service has, however, declined since the introduction of the National Health Service, in the same way as have the custodial functions of mental hospitals.

Before the Act of 1959 mental-welfare officers were *duly authorized officers,* that is, they took their official designation from the legal authority given them for precisely this purpose of arranging the compulsory admission of mentally disordered patients. No special qualification was required of duly authorized officers, and they were recruited from such diverse sources as mental-hospital nurses, ambulance men, and clerks. In recent years, at the same time that the nature of the work has changed, qualified social workers have begun to fill the posts of mental-welfare officers (11).

In Salford the change in the relationship between mental-welfare officers and patients was shown by the steady fall in the numbers of compulsory admissions and the rise in voluntary admissions (as can be seen in Table 3, p. 171) and by the rarity with which physical restraint is now used in taking a patient to the hospital. An increasing proportion of patients and families sought help from the mental health service of their own accord and without being referred by other agencies. Violence is seldom done to mental-welfare officers, and tales of escape, pursuit, and assault are no longer heard among them. Two thirds of admissions were compulsory in 1957 and one third six years later in 1962. In the same period the proportion of referrals who were provided social work but not admission doubled. Furthermore, in 1957 no action was taken in 20 per cent of all referrals, and in 1962 only in 4 per cent.

These trends may be connected with a change in the attitudes of patients and families or with a change in the type of patients referred. Patients might be less grossly disturbed, or referred at an earlier stage, and it seems probable that a larger proportion are drawn from higher social classes than before the introduction of the National Health Service. During the years 1959–1963, however, little change could be detected in the sex, age, diagnosis, and social class of referred patients (12). Whatever the cause, the trends cannot but represent a real change in the quality of the relationships and in the work done by mental-welfare officers.

Coordination of Services

We can now turn to the topic of the coordination of psychiatric services for the mentally ill. The illustrative case is the single locale of Salford. As medical director of the mental-health services of the local health authority, the writer's role in these developments was that of active participant and instigator of policy. We noted in our discussion of evaluation methods that an observer so much involved may well be suspect or partisan, for he is faced with a considerable task of self-analysis. The analysis that follows has been scrutinized and reworked many times to reduce bias. In addition the active participants in the case have had the opportunity to read and comment on this account of it. Psychiatrists, medical officers, hospital social workers, and mental-welfare officers have all reviewed it and accepted the emendations of points with which they expressed disagreement.

The Setting. The organization of the psychiatric services is set out in Figure 6, which also shows the flow of patients between the various agencies. The numbers are based on a count, over a calendar year, of all patients from the administrative area who were referred for special psychiatric care in the National Health Service. This period immediately preceded the actual introduction of the Mental Health Act in 1960.

General practitioners were the main source from which patients came to the psychiatric services. The majority of patients referred by them were directed to the community mental-health service of the local health authority, although another large group were referred to psychiatric outpatient clinics in general hospitals. The general practitioner who considered that his patient either should be admitted to the mental hospital, or required the help of a social worker, referred to the community service through which these services could be obtained. At that time more than 60 per cent of such referrals

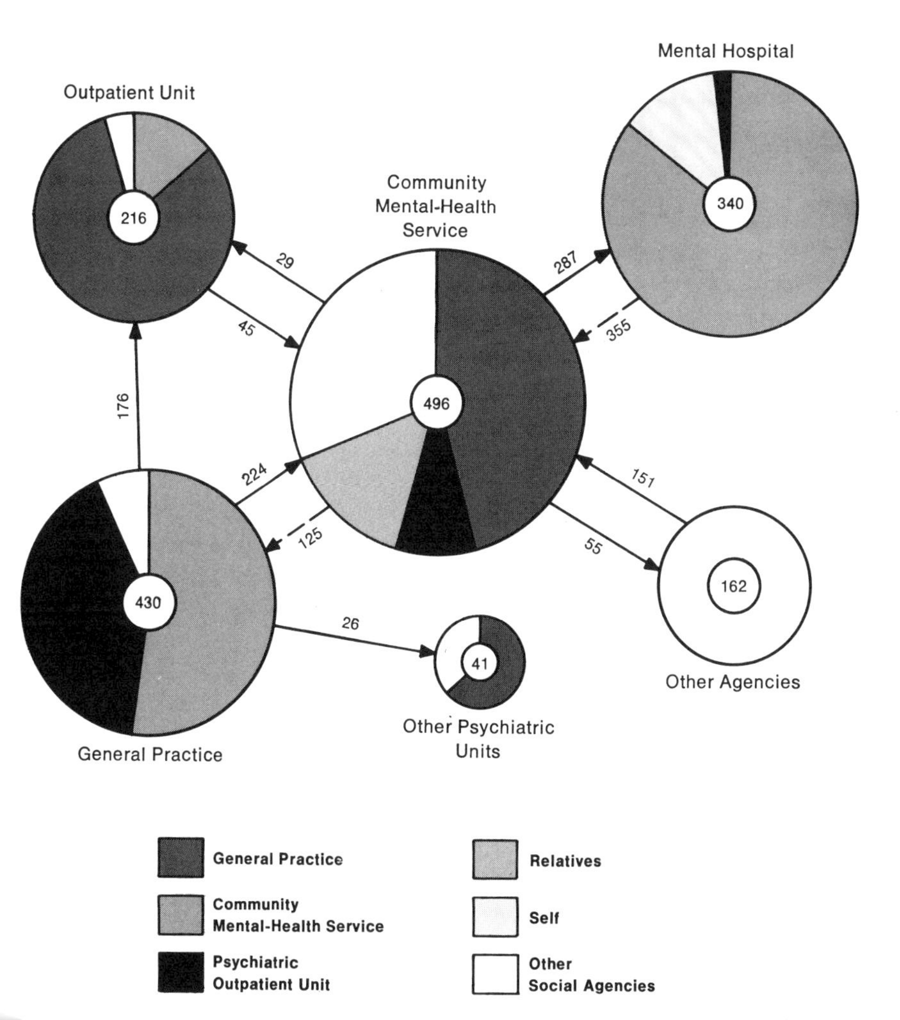

Circle for general practice shows the proportion distributed *to* the different psychiatric services; all other circles show the proportions of referrals received *from* different services. Actual numbers of referrals are shown by the figures with arrows.

Figure 6. Flow of Referrals Between Agencies

Adapted from M. W. Susser, "Changing Roles and Co-ordination in Mental Health Services" in *Sociology and Medicine: Studies within the Framework of the British National Health Service,* Sociological Review Monograph 5 (1962), by permission of Sociological Review Monographs.

ended in admission; many were emergencies. Fourteen per cent were subsequently seen by a psychiatrist as outpatients, and 17 per cent were supported only by the social worker in collaboration with the general practitioner. On the other hand, if the general practitioner considered that his patient might benefit from treatment as an outpatient, he could refer directly to the outpatient unit, which operated independently of the mental hospital. The length of the outpatient waiting list imposed a wait of many weeks, however, and this must have affected the doctor's choice.

The outpatient psychiatrists, like the general practitioners, referred to the community service in order to obtain the help of social workers or in order to have a patient admitted to a mental hospital where treatment could be undertaken, under legal constraint if necessary, by other psychiatrists.

The community service received the majority of its patients from general practitioners. But 20 per cent of practitioners made no referrals to the service (although only 5 per cent did not have patients notified to the service from any source), another 30 per cent made single annual referrals, and 20 per cent referred more than four times each. (See Table 4, p. 172.) The remainder of the patients received by the community service came from other agencies, such as the police and probation officers, health visitors, the Welfare Department, the outpatient clinics, and direct from relatives.

Nearly all admissions were to a single mental hospital, and whether compulsory or voluntary, were made through the community services. The number of routine notifications made to the community service after the patient's discharge from the mental hospital is shown in the broken arrow and is not included in the total number shown for referrals to the mental-health service.

It can be seen that the continuity of patient care was interrupted at a number of points. The general practitioner may have wanted his patient to have outpatient treatment, or hospital admission, or the support of a social worker, but he could not readily obtain a combination of all three services. There was no direct link between the outpatient unit and the main mental hospital. The mental-welfare officer, once he had arranged admission, lost contact with his patient until notified of his discharge after the patient had left the hospital, and in "aftercare" he acted virtually as an independent agent, if he could act at all.

The continuity of relationships, it is generally assumed, provides the foundation for the methods of social work as well as for psychotherapy and for family doctoring. The disruptive effects of discontinuity were often apparent. The mental-welfare officer's central position in the referral system forced on him responsibilities that were more properly those of a psychiatrist. He often had to decide that the case was a psychiatric one, to select the appropriate form of treatment, and to obtain it. Because of the difficulties of gaining access to the mental hospital outside the jural apparatus, the mental-welfare officer acted as supplicant to obtain it on behalf of his clients.

The specialization of each agency and the discontinuity between them led to fragmented treatment. No psychiatrist had access to all institutions. As a result some patients were not admitted soon enough, some stayed in the hospital longer than necessary, and others were discharged into unsuitable circumstances.

Discontinuities in patient care are not found everywhere. In some places they appear to have been overcome by bringing all services together under the guidance of a single psychiatrist who acts for the local health authority as well as for the hospital board (13). In others, often where the local health authority has made rudimentary provision, the community service has been bypassed by services based primarily on mental hospitals (14). In still others the discontinuities have not yet been recognized, or have been passively accepted as in the nature of things. In many, however, they present a difficult problem in coordination. A study of similar innovations attempted in California suggests that the difficulties can be more than problematic, and may become explosive (15).

Impediments to coordination are fostered by the structure of the National Health Service itself. The service was built on the tripod of general practice, hospitals, and public health authorities. Although these services all strive to meet the medical and health needs of patient and community, their apparent unity of purpose conceals many divergencies. Divergence stemmed from the different and separate functions developed by the three medical services over the years and carried out independently of each other. It was perpetuated in the National Health Service by giving each service a distinctive form of organization and method of control. Their present-day functions have been linked and made complementary, and therefore many individual patients are served by all three. Active coordination is needed to insure continuity of care for the patient as he passes from one organization to another, to avoid duplication of services, and to prevent a conflict of interests when organizations provide care for the same patients concurrently.

As the form or organization of each branch of the National Health Service is special and discrete, except at the highest level in the Ministry of Health, efforts toward coordination must be made separately with each organization. We shall discuss in turn, therefore, the efforts of this single local health authority to achieve coordination with each of the organizations complementary to it.

General Practitioners and the Community Service. The areas of jurisdiction of Executive Councils that contract with general practitioners coincide with those of local health authorities. As guardians of the traditional professional ethic, general practitioners are subject to the least degree of formal organization that exists within the National Health Service. The Executive Councils have exercised virtually no control over professional activities except to see that practitioners fulfill their contracts of service to patients and that prescribing is within reasonable limits. Relationships of practitioners with the community mental-health service are thus individual and show little uniformity, as is clearly shown by the disparities among practices in the annual number of referrals to the community service, which have ranged from 0 to 18. (See Table 4, p. 172.)

Because the function of the general practitioner is to assume overall responsibility for his patient, the critical decision in his work with the mental-welfare officer is how much responsibility he delegates. This is a question of real difficulty, for the general practitioner is not accustomed to sharing his responsibility with nonmedical workers. There are no rules to guide him, and the limitations of his medical training leave him to discover empirically how a social worker might help him or his patient. In Salford some doctors delegated all their responsibility and handed over the case to the mental-welfare officer entirely. Others gave over only a part of their responsibility, worked out the problems of care together with the mental-welfare officer, and shared decisions with him. Yet others called upon the mental-welfare officer to carry out some strictly defined and limited duty that they could not do themselves, usually admission to the hospital.

Mental-welfare officers, for their part, responded according to the doctor's mode of delegating responsibility. Some welcomed full responsibility, although others were made anxious by it; most were gratified by taking over partial responsibility and sharing decisions; and most resented strictly limited duties such as escorting patients to the hospital. These reactions are a consequence of the position of social work as a profession, which in Britain is in many respects equivocal. The giving over of a case by the doctor tended to be seen by the mental-welfare officers as an escape from the doctor's professional responsibility and a failure of medical competence; the sharing of responsibility indicated recognition for social workers by a powerful, long-established group of high social prestige; and depreciation and rejection of their professional status was implicit in strictly limited duties and responsibilities.

The community service took steps to promote coordination. First, care was taken to keep practitioners informed. At intervals letters from the director of the mental-health service were sent to doctors in the area to explain the work and facilities of the community service, and case summaries were made for all referrals and copies sent to the referring practitioner. Second, the work of mental-welfare officers was based on the doctors' practices and not on administrative areas, so that each doctor had a particular officer to call upon, and the mental-welfare officers were encouraged to consult the general practitioner in all cases.

A third measure independent of community service policy assisted relations with practitioners. When in November 1960, the Mental Health Act was given full effect, a change occurred in relations between general practitioners and mental-welfare officers. Previously the decision to arrange admission of a patient to the hospital had often rested with the social worker as duly authorized officer, or devolved upon him. This now became the responsibility of doctors, one of whom was to be by preference the general practitioner. Doctors continued to work with mental-welfare officers. The new arrangements entailed that most practitioners observed the mode of work of a social worker and had the chance to work with him, as both had to join in making applications for hospital beds. The mental-welfare officers for their part appreciated meeting face to face with doctors to agree on a course of action.

Continuity of care between the community service and general practitioners seemed to have been more easily achieved than between the community service and other organizations. A clear trend toward increased cooperation in this sphere of community mental-health work could be inferred from the referral pattern of practitioners. (See Table 4, p. 172.) It developed despite the heritage of antagonism between practitioners and local authorities, which had its origin, before the days of the National Health Service, in competition for patients. The overriding modern problem of general practice is to find the means to bring new and special scientific knowledge to bear in the exercise of overall responsibility for patients. This problem holds in the social and psychological as well as in more technical fields, and cooperation with the social worker is one means of meeting it.

Hospitals and Community Service. A first and obvious proposal made by the local health authority to bring together services was to link the mental hospital with the local out-patient unit of the general hospital. This could not be achieved, because both general-hospital and mental-hospital psychiatrists resisted the proposal. For psychiatrists from the outpatient unit of the hospital the proposal meant doing part of their work in the mental hospital, a type of psychiatry to which they were unaccustomed and even found distasteful. The outpatient psychiatrists would have had to work within the administrative jurisdiction of a medical superintendent, and this involved some surrender of independence. The mental hospital, on the other hand, had commitments far beyond the Salford local authority area and would have had to give special treatment to the particular local authority concerned. The proposal was made before the introduction of the Mental Health Act, and at the time the mental hospital would also have had to devise new forms of organizations so that each consultant psychiatrist could have his own beds and juniors.

A second proposal was for the hospital psychiatrists to undertake the clinical psychiatry on the community service, for instance the surveillance of patients in day centers and hostels, and consultations with mental-welfare officers. In this way the psychiatrists would have replaced the medical officers of the local authority. This proposal also was not possible, for the area was understaffed and the available psychiatrists heavily engaged, and none found himself able to give the necessary time. Both these proposals had therefore to wait upon the future appointment of new consultant psychiatrists. Such appointments are the responsibility of Regional Hospital Boards. This course was readily agreed to by the Regional Hospital Board, which, by its composition, had few special local interests to oppose the plan and some to favor it.

Coordinated day-to-day working relationships between the community service and the mental hospital and between the community service and the outpatient units were no less difficult to achieve. For this purpose direct negotiation was required, and it continued over a period of five years. The relations of the community service with the mental hospital and with the outpatient units will be considered in turn.

The Mental Hospital. The main proposals of the local health authority for coordination with the mental hospital were concerned to obtain continuous relationships between social workers and patients and to make full use of the service that social workers can provide for psychiatrists and for patients under their care. Information collected by the social workers before the patient's admission can be useful to the psychiatrist who knows how to evaluate it; the uncertainties of this evaluation can be reduced by making the information objective, by trying to standardize subjective judgments of the social worker, and by knowledge of his quality and personality. During the course of the patient's stay in the hospital, the social worker can keep the psychiatrist posted on the situation in the patient's home and deal with social problems that might otherwise go unrecognized. After the patient leaves the hospital, the social worker can ensure a low default rate in follow-up clinics, report on conditions in the home, and assist in the patient's resettlement. In order to make use of these services, however, the hospital staff must first recognize that the social worker has a place in the work with patients who are admitted, allow him entry to the ward so that he can continue his relations with the patient, and guide him in the management of the family and of the patient who has left the hospital.

The simplicity of this program was deceptive, and years passed before it became effective. On the patient's admission the hospital desired no more than a brief note of the grounds for admission from the mental-welfare officer; during admission he could not keep contact with the patient, apart from indirect reports he might obtain at a monthly meeting held with the hospital psychiatric social worker; finally, more than 90 per cent of discharges were made without reference to the mental-welfare officer.

Some advance followed when the medical superintendent of the mental hospital began to attend the weekly meeting held by the writer, as director of the community mental-health service, with the mental-welfare officers. The medical director had been appointed to a paid post by the local health authority at about the same time as the medical superintendent of the mental hospital was appointed its honorary psychiatric adviser. The weekly meeting was a means of training in casework, and a channel of communication through which policy could be transmitted from above or modified from below. The attendance of the superintendent of the mental hospital tended to turn this meeting into a dialogue in which the two doctors stated their views, often opposed, on the proper use of services. This helped to clarify the difficulties in the way of coordination. Some of these difficulties related to the way each institution saw its place in providing a service, some to overlapping interests, and some to the complexity of the organizations themselves.

The community service, like others throughout the country, was struggling to take up the more favored position recently allotted it by national policy, but many factors impeded it. At the outset doctors, social workers, and other staff of local health authorities lacked training and experience in what was required of them. Not unnaturally, therefore, many psychiatrists and general practitioners, who themselves lack training in the social aspects of medical care, did not recognize that mental-welfare officers and the local health authority might have something to contribute to medicine and psychiatry; some were frankly hostile to work that seemed to obtrude on their own province. These attitudes were also related to the fact that mental-welfare officers inherit, from the duly authorized officers, a stereotype that is at variance with their present-day work. The evolution of the mental-welfare officer, from an official acting most often through laws of constraint to the social worker who relies on voluntary relationships, is a recent phenomenon. Many had had no formal training, and the change has not yet impinged on all.

The Younghusband Report was a herald of a professional charter for social work in Britain, and the new laws were consistent with its approach, but in some ways these laws added to the insecurities of the mental-welfare officers, who felt that they were losing a well-established position. Previously they had had a statutory part to fulfill in nearly all admissions. There was now little to define their role, which depended on the recognition they could wrest from doctors, who would often resist the tendency for social work to claim an independent function in medical care. For instance, the admission of patients to mental hospitals could now be arranged directly between practitioners and mental hospitals. Although this procedure promoted cooperation and contact between general practitioners and psychiatrists, it could bypass the mental-welfare officers.

A similar result followed a ruling of the Ministry of Health about aftercare. The ruling abolished routine requests from hospitals to local health authorities for aftercare for discharged patients. Notification and requests could now be made only with the patient's consent. The rule was intended to protect the confidence of the patient and reflected the respect for the traditional professional ethic shown in recent policy. This improvement in attitudes toward mental patients, however, set up a potential administrative obstacle to coordination in the form of an additional rule. In this case it proved an obstacle, for mental-welfare officers were asked to provide aftercare for less than 10 per cent of discharged patients. The multiplicity of rules in large work organizations is such that some must be circumvented in order to obtain rational and efficient function. Conversely, rules can provide a convenient defense, as both trade unions and employers with whom they clash well understand.

The mental-welfare officers were unlikely to feel themselves secure in their new roles until they achieved acceptance by the longer-established branches of the National Health Service. Their position was not altered by the fact that work carried out independently of the other branches of the service was sufficient to occupy them. Furthermore, within their own department new methods and new staff positions tended to create anxiety and resistance, which detracted still further from their security. New methods were viewed as implied criticism of old ones and additional staff positions as competitive with existing ones or as taking from established functions and responsibilities.

The community service therefore strove to gain the cooperation of the mental hospitals and the general practitioners for its own purposes of survival and development, as well as for the sake of its patients. (Hence the likelihood that in most areas the initiative toward coordination will come from local health authorities more often than from other branches of the service, except where mental-hospital psychiatrists have expanded their spheres of interest to fill a vacuum.) In these circumstances reluctance on the part of the mental hospital to enter into joint schemes was usually interpreted by members of the community service in terms of hostility toward their work rather than in terms of the internal problems and therapeutic aims of the hospital.

The hospital was viewed as a monolithic organization, and its internal divisions and disorders were not recognized nor its necessities conceded. Exclusion from the hospital was taken as a rebuff made more acute when the hospital staff did not comprehend the problems of work outside the hospitals.

Rebuffs were common. The criteria of urgency applied by a social worker confronted with a domestic situation are quite unlike those applied by a mental nurse confronted with an assembly of patients on the ward. Only with difficulty can the nurse perceive the domestic pressures toward admission that face the social worker. The mental-hospital nurse is concerned with group discipline and with the control of agression and withdrawal. Her situation puts the strains of domestic interaction suffered by patients and families outside her ken.

The divergence of judgment between nurses and social workers at the time of the patient's discharge is no less great. From a view restricted to the patient in the hospital, community services did not appear to meet needs that were obvious or predictable. Community workers were equally skeptical of the therapeutic activity of the hospital; they saw it as a last resort for the patient who could be managed in no other way.

The mental hospital, in its relationship with the outside world, had also to contend with a stereotyped image of its past, as well as with some skeuomorphs, functionless survivals of the past. This image was of a place for the long-term custody and restraint of dangerous people, a place therefore to be feared, stigmatized, and isolated, a closed organization with an alien culture.

The Mental Health Act, although based on developments worked out in mental hospitals, was an implicit criticism of this past, and its effect on the hospital was to accelerate changes toward a therapeutic approach to mental illness. Notwithstanding internal changes, the mental hospital had to deal with criticism founded on this stereotyped image, as well as with that founded on real events, which came from potential patients and their kin, from the public, and from other organizations. Within the mental hospital, a closing of the ranks in the face of such external criticism affected policies and in some cases diverted attention from the real needs of the patient. It became difficult to accept and to remedy complaints, for instance about hostile behavior of admitting staff to the patient and to his official escort or about an ill-judged discharge.

We have mentioned the belief of many medical superintendents that the dispersal of their responsibility would diminish control of the milieu. The intervention of local health authority doctors, social workers, and resettlement units made a similar threat. It brought about additional relationships for the patient, and these could interfere with the control exercised by the psychiatrist and, as he saw it, with therapeutic rapport.

The new laws and policies cut across the self-sufficiency and isolation of the mental hospital and somewhat shifted the balance of authority and responsibility in psychiatric services. Where local authorities have anticipated the requirement to provide facilities for the care of psychiatric patients, they may have a medical officer for mental health, mental-welfare officers, day centers, and therapeutic clubs. Parallel institutions may exist or develop in the mental hospital, and an active local authority may thus appear to duplicate or even usurp functions of the hospital. In the case under discussion, both the superintendent and the medical officer of mental health administered psychiatric services in the same locality; psychiatric social workers in the hospital carried out duties similar to those of mental-welfare officers and on the same patients; day centers and therapeutic clubs in the hospital shared methods and aims and even patients with those outside. At every level the overlap of interest had to be reconciled. The hospital had a large catchment area and had to deal with a number of local authorities, and the number of reconciliations had to be multipled by the number of authorities because each had to be dealt with separately.

Furthermore, the avowed policy of the Ministry of Health was to "wind up" old mental hospitals and transfer their work to smaller units based on general hospitals. This policy created anxiety in the mental hospital that it might be forced to revert solely to keeping chronic patients in custody. This anxiety was a stimulus to the mental hospital to protect its future by developing a self-sufficiency of services. All this diverted the mental hospital and the community service from achieving a uniformity of aim.

The Outpatient Unit. The psychiatric outpatient unit in this local authority area was located at the general hospital. Only a part-time psychiatric social worker was available, and the psychiatrists had to call on hospital medical social workers (almoners) and on the community service to help with social work. In order to relieve the shortage of social workers, it was arranged that a mental-welfare officer would take up regular duties at an outpatient clinic, thus unifying some of the work on the two services. Within a few weeks, however, the mental-welfare officer had to withdraw, for objections had been raised by the almoners and the psychiatric social worker. The objections were based on the fact that the mental-welfare officer possessed no formal professional qualifications apart from a nursing certificate, that he was assuming duties that the professional workers normally carried out, and that in some cases he seemed to be usurping their authority.

All recognized professions have tried to establish a monopoly in their work in return for a guarantee of high standards of service ensured by qualifications and professional rules. The entry of an unqualified worker into the field was thus a provocation to professional interests, and by rejecting him the qualified workers were guarding their ranks against dilution by the nonprofessional. The role of each social worker had not been clearly defined before the mental-welfare officer took up his duties, and this had left room for uncertainty and invited misinterpretations. Much work followed with the social workers concerned and with their professional associations to repair the damage. The generality of these observations is supported in that much the same pattern evolved in the relations of mental-welfare officers with psychiatric social workers in the different setting of the mental hospital.

The community service felt the lack of coordination with the outpatient unit less acutely than with the mental-hospital patients. The situation resembled that between the community service and general practitioners, which gave the impression of good coordination, whereas examination showed that in one year as many as 20 per cent had made no referrals at all to the community service. The populations served by the community service and the outpatient unit are distinguished by social class, diagnosis, and degree of mental disturbance. The outpatients were of high social class, neurotic rather than psychotic and mild rather than severe cases (12). In these circumstances and from the vantage point of the community service, the lack of integrated work was not obtrusive; it could only be observed if the data were consciously sought. Furthermore, from their vantage point outside the community service, the psychiatrists and general practitioners concerned probably recognized little need for social work in these particular cases and might not have seen how to use it had it been pressed upon them.

Interpretations

The case material described and analyzed in the preceding pages can be conveniently interpreted in two dimensions. The first dimension is spatial and cross-sectional; it deals with relations among organizations and their members. Coordination in this dimension is a matter of external relations, and these relations are determined by the structure and the culture of the participating organizations. The second dimension is temporal and longitudinal; it deals with social change through time. Coordination in this second dimension is a process of articulating roles and organizations; process, by definition, imposes change.

Structure and Culture in Organizations. The coordination of external relations among institutions must deal with the conflicts underlying the outlook of the members of each institution. Conflicts may arise from their views of what are appropriate roles in relation to patients and of what are appropriate roles for each institution. Although separate institutions might agree on broad ends, they work toward these ends by different means, and they tend to see their own objectives and functions as primary and self-sufficient. Each specialized staff, with its own type of training and internal structure, imposes a special pattern of relations within the organization, with patients, and with other organizations.

This invisible structure can distort relationships no less than the unconscious mind can distort individual behavior; to extend the analogy, it is easier to apprehend the sources of irrational behavior in other organizations than in one's own. The organization of mental hospitals and of local health authorities has been bureaucratic in form, and the many advantages of this form are balanced by disadvantages (16, 17). We have discussed the conflict between professional and bureaucratic relationships in mental hospitals and its effects on treatment. Many subtle pressures act to detach behavior from its original purpose of serving the patient. The official, whatever his place in the hierarchy, is a representative of the power and prestige of the entire organization, and in dealing with outsiders he behaves as such. Loyalty to the organization may come before the purpose for which it exists. The purpose of the health service as a whole can thus be lost sight of and the needs of patients overlooked.

The perception of the rights and obligations of the patient's role and of his needs by those to whom he turns for care varies from one social position to another. The most pressing frame of reference of the mental-hospital staff is likely to be the professional code and the values held by colleagues and the chain of command within the hospital. Pressures from the lay community are lightly felt. In the restricted framework of the institution, perception and decision are likely to make perfunctory reference to the roles the patient has relinquished in the world outside. In any effective hospital setting the patient must be considered as a case and as an object of scientific study. In hospital psychiatry the focus of observation has thus been on the symptoms, behavior, and psychodynamics of the individual rather than on his relationships.

By contrast, general practitioners and mental-welfare officers are subject to continual pressure from the lay community. Their professional decisions in a particular case must refer to the wishes and circumstances of the people who stand in close relation to the patient. Their work, if it is to be successful, must be acceptable to those among whom they work. Repute is founded on the exchanges of each consultation, each visit, and each decision (18).[1] Situations also determine the nature of the work and the type of problems dealt with by social workers. In British mental hospitals the activity of social workers centers on history taking and on individual patient needs for employment and resettlement; in community services their activities include concern with families and with household arrangements as well as with pressing individual needs (20).

The culture of institutions is as distinctive as their structure and may distinguish organizations even when their structure is similar. Each organization has a tradition and a set of attitudes that are shared by members of the staff. There is a built-in tendency to perpetuate this culture through selection and self-selection of staff, through indoctrination, and through the conformity of individuals dependent on the organization. In New Haven, for instance, a striking contrast was shown

1. The validity of this model of perceptions molded by reference groups developed by E. Freidson is supported by an analysis of a series of failures in medical care. It appeared that mistakes of hospital doctors polarized around failures of communication, and those of general practitioners around technical failures (19).

between analytic psychiatrists and so-called directive-organic psychiatrists, not only in their social background and circumstances, but also in their distribution among the types of organizations that gave psychiatric care (10).

The culture of a medical organization influences the terms in which a patient is assessed and what his needs are deemed to be. Often what is good for the organization and what is deemed good for the patients turn out to coincide. Consequently, ideological as well as structural opposition is likely to be found between services, even when staff have a common training, as for example between psychiatrists and public-health doctors, or psychiatric social workers in the hospital and in the public-health authority, or mental nurses and mental-welfare officers drawn from the ranks of nurses.

In psychiatry ideological divergence cuts deep into scientific attitudes and concepts of professional responsibility. Wide disparities exist in the bounds each school sets to psychiatric disorder and to its special competence. Cases that directive-organic psychiatrists might reject as trivial or untreatable are bread and butter to analytic psychiatrists, and cases that are rejected by analytic psychiatrists as noncooperative and beyond help may be accepted by sociologically oriented psychiatrists. Across such divisions rapprochement for the practical business of coordination can be difficult to achieve. Each of these attitudes is likely to influence the place that the psychiatrist accords the social worker and community institutions in the scheme of treatment. His views are related to his underlying values, and dissimilar values may lead to policies and actions that are in direct opposition, despite agreement on motives and aims (17). In the relatively closed systems of separate organizations, even the unifying aim of putting the needs of the patient first may not result in harmonious policy and action. Staff may not perceive the special needs of patients that can be served by those institutions. Consequently the work of other branches of the service in fields of common interest is sometimes duplicated or seen as competitive.

Because of the structural and cultural isolation and opposition of the participating organizations in Salford, the benefits of coordination and the ill effects of incoordination could not readily be made apparent to members inside them, excepting by the public-health service that served as messenger between them. Nor were they likely to become apparent until better coordination was achieved.

Changing Roles. Our second dimension of interpretation in this case is that of social change. When a social system is in equilibrium, the people in it can satisfy their own needs and those of the system at the same time. Equilibrium depends on two conditions: First, the norms that define social roles and the attendant obligations must be held in common; second, social and psychological forces must induce people to act in accordance with these norms (21). Social change disturbs the equilibrium of an established system of norms and expectations. People who are satisfied by an established social system tend to have a vested interest in it; they resist change that threatens their interest.

In his theoretical analysis Talcott Parsons indicated what types of strain may be predicted from social change at the personal, the social, and the cultural levels. This theoretical approach has proved to be a heuristic one. D. Kandell and R. H. Williams (22) used Parson's categories to analyze experiences reported from forty-nine separate projects concerned with psychiatric rehabilitation. Almost every response they describe and classify can be replicated from the Salford case.

Strain at the personal level is classed in four main types: fantasy, anxiety, hostility, and defensiveness. Fantasy is manifested as distorted perception of the real situation and of the motives of others; in Salford examples appear in the mutual perceptions of mental-welfare officers and general practitioners and of mental-welfare officers and hospital workers. Anxiety, hostility, and defensiveness are documented in many places in the preceding text. The psychological forces that underlay these reactions in the forty-nine projects, the authors suggest, were to be found in the threats to self-esteem implied by the need for change and in the loss of established modes of reward. These forces weaken one condition for a stable system, for they reduce the motivation to meet the expectations of new roles.

Strain in the social structure is caused by the breakdown of the established organization of roles. A new organization of roles violates Parson's other condition for a stable system, as shared norms for the reorganized roles cannot exist at the outset; they have to be developed. The strain is felt in several ways. Uncertainty and conflict surround the performance of altered roles. New roles lack definition, and in a new situation existing roles lose definition. The incumbents are frequently exposed to role conflict in that they face incompatible obligations simultaneously, as, for instance, when mental-welfare officers assumed a professional role in addition to their accustomed legal role. (See pp. 251 ff.) Misperception of the roles of others is common when staff are unaware of the changed functions that another institution or profession has assumed.

Strain at the cultural level is also an outcome of confused norms in a changing situation. Conflicts of values, ideologies, and goals that already exist are exaggerated, and new ones arise. Another manifestation of cultural strain appears when change promoted by professional agencies clashes with the values and interests of the community (23). Efforts to set up psychiatric facilities thus sometimes meet hostility from local property owners and the following they can mobilize.

Remedies

From the point of view of the community services in Salford, a main problem in the complex task of achieving coordination was to gain recognition by hospitals and practitioners for the professional work of mental-welfare officers and for the facilities designed to support mental patients outside the hospital. We have pointed out the obstacles to be overcome across barriers of structure and culture in bringing organizations to work together and in reconciling the ideologies of the officials and professionals who guide policy. We have pointed too to other obstacles to be overcome that are thrown up by social change: Individuals and professionals must be persuaded to redesign roles and share authority and responsibility, and the resistance that arises from the reallocation of roles must be dispersed.

In reducing structural and cultural opposition, a first requirement is effective *communication*. At the least communication can lead to more accurate perception of the objectives and roles of others if not to congruence in values. In the Salford case the deliberate opening of communications had a noticeable effect on the relations of the mental-health service. With general practitioners, contact was made through mental-welfare officers and bulletins; with the mental hospital, contact was made through the regular meetings with the medical superintendent.

A second requirement is to establish *interdependence* among the members of the organizations involved. When people feel dependent on others, they are likely to try and win their support. In the United States a systematic survey of professionals in psychiatric services confirmed this winning behavior toward others (as reported in a mailed questionnaire) for those who stood in equal or subordinate positions. When the professionals stood in superior positions and felt independent, they more often sought to reduce the power and influence of peers and superiors and avoided contact with them. They did not feel impelled to cultivate good relations and seek cooperation (24).

The situation observed in the National Health Service in England is consistent with these findings. There have been few formal ties and low levels of interdependence among its branches and only a small head of pressure toward compromise and coordination. The bargaining power of an organization is small when the need for the services it provides is not recognized or is rejected by another organization that might use them. All the more so when the services are new and experimental, personal and intangible, yet competitive insofar as they obtrude on an established professional function. More rapid progress might ensue if new services and new roles, when regarded at the national level as desirable, were entrenched by the statutes and regulations that establish the interdependence of organizations.

A third mode of reducing opposition is to *articulate the related roles* in the separate organizations. A device to this end is jointly to confront problems chosen for their common interest. A more durable device is to unite in a single person those offices in the opposed organizations that are amenable to combination. In the Salford case this device, when eventually achieved, facilitated radical change.

A new post was created for a psychiatrist who held combined appointments in the mental hospital, in the outpatient unit, and in the community mental-health service. Almost at once patient care was rationalized. The psychiatrist's access to services at all levels enabled him to provide continuity in their long-term management. He now participated in the domiciliary screening carried out by mental-welfare officers on referred patients and retained the final decision on disposition. Through his participation and cooperation other changes gradually followed to rationalize the whole system. Partial reorganization in the mental hospital permitted Salford patients to be dealt with by one "firm," headed by the newly appointed psychiatrist (25).

Mental-welfare officers gained effective continuity in their work, from the time of the patient's first referral to his restoration to normal social function, by means of joint appointments with the mental hospital and the general hospital. To complete the process it remained for junior medical, nursing, and ward staff in the mental hospital to extend their work into the community service. This final step was precluded by an acute shortage of personnel and not by the external difficulties of coordination.

These arrangements achieved continuity in therapeutic practice. Further gains might follow from continuity in administration between psychiatric services by linking them through administrators who have a place in each official hierarchy. The link in administration could be through practitioners either in psychiatry or in public health. Ideally they should have training in both fields. The province of orthodox psychiatry is the care of individual patients, but many psychiatrists have also had to be administrators in mental hospitals, and some have had the administration of community services thrust upon them. In this they may be handicapped by a training and outlook usually centered on the individual, only sometimes on the small group, and seldom on the community outside the hospital. The province of public health is the health of the community, and incumbent on the health officer is the administration of services. His training and outlook aim to equip him to see problems overall, in terms of groups and not of individuals. He learns how to measure the extent of disease and sickness and the need for services and how to evaluate medical care. But he has no special knowledge of psychiatry.

Some of the obstacles to coordination created by the second dimension of social change also yield to the treatments for the first dimension of structural and cultural opposition. The need is to reduce strain by promoting the conditions for a stable structure, namely a system of norms to define roles and regulate interaction, and the motivation to adhere to them. Effective communication, the interdependence of organizations, and articulation of roles can all help to induce shared norms and enlist adherence to them.

In addition, foresight can minimize the disruption of the existing system and prevent unwanted repercussions. Reactions of psychiatrists, psychologists, and social workers to each other vary according to profession and according to their actual positions within organizations, and these can be anticipated. For example, in the American study of relations between mental-health professions quoted, psychiatrists in superior positions felt secure and perceived the related professions as supportive, stimulated their cooperation, and encouraged their professional growth. Psychiatrists in positions of uncertain authority felt threatened, perceived the related professions as obstructive, and tried to keep them subordinate (24).

Solutions to the many problems of coordination are difficult to achieve. Most will require continuous and painstaking negotiation. The outlook may be more promising than appears from the analysis presented here; this analysis has focused on the points of strain in a system of psychiatric care. It takes little account of the activity and enthusiasm of individuals, which can transcend the constraints of social structure. The problems of coordination call for a mood of administrative optimism to match the therapeutic optimism of the present time. As with individual treatment, it needs to be informed and open-eyed.

References

(1) Field M. G. 1957 *Doctor and Patient in Soviet Russia* Cambridge, Harvard University Press

(2) Silver G. A. 1958 Beyond general practice: the health team *Yale J Biolog Med* 31:29–39

Fox T. F. 1960 The personal doctor and his relation to the hospital *Lancet* 1:743–760

(3) Parsons T. 1949 *Essays in Sociological Theory: Pure and Applied* New York, Free Press

(4) Fox R. C. 1957 Training for uncertainty in Merton R. K., Reader G. G. and Kendall P. L. eds. *The Student Physician* Cambridge, Mass., Harvard University Press pp. 207–241

(5) Shepherd M. 1957 *A Study of the Major Psychoses in an English County* Maudsley Monogr 3 London, Chapman & Hall

(6) Stanton A. H. and Schwartz M. S. 1954 *The Mental Hospital: A Study of Institutional Participation in Psychiatric Illness and Treatment* New York, Basic Books

Martin D. V. 1955 Institutionalism *Lancet* 2:1188–1190

Goffman E. 1958 Characteristics of total institutions in *Symposium on Preventive and Social Psychiatry* Washington, D. C., Walter Reed Army Institute of Research pp. 43–84

Barton R. W. A. G. 1959 *Institutional Neurosis* Bristol, Wright

Martin D. V. 1959 Problems in developing a community approach to mental hospital treatments *Brit J Psych Soc Work* 5:56–63

(7) Rees J. R. 1945 *The Shaping of Psychiatry by War* New York, Norton

Menninger W. C. 1947 Psychiatric experience in the war 1941–1946 *Amer J Psychiat* 103:577–586

Mandelbaum D. G. 1954 Psychiatry in military society: Part I *Hum Org* 13:5–15

Mandelbaum D. G. 1955 Psychiatry in military society: Part II *Hum Org* 13:19–25

Ahrenfeldt R. H. 1958 *Psychiatry in the British Army in the Second World War* New York, Columbia University Press

(8) Brown G. W., Parkes C. M. and Wing J. K. 1961 Admissions and readmissions at three London hospitals *J Ment Sci* 107:1070–1077

(9) Metcalf G. R. 1961 The English open mental hospital: implications for American psychiatric services *Milbank Mem Fund Quart* 39:579–593

(10) Hollingshead A. B. and Redlich F. C. 1958 *Social Class and Mental Illness: A Community Study* New York, Wiley

(11) Miles H. L., Loudon J. B. and Rawnsley K. 1961 Attitudes and practice of mental welfare officers *Public Health* 76:32–47

(12) Stein Z. A. 1964 Some preliminary results of the survey of mental sickness in Salford in Susser M. W. ed. *Report on the Mental Health Services of the City of Salford for 1963* City of Salford, Eng., Health Department pp. 11–23

(13) Macmillan D. 1956 An integrated mental health service: Nottingham's experience *Lancet* 2:1094–1095

Macmillan D. 1963 Recent developments in community mental health *Lancet* 1:567–571

(14) Carse J., Panton N. E. and Watt A. 1958 A district mental health service: the Worthing experiment *Lancet* 1:39–41

(15) Blum R. H. and Downing J. J. 1964 Staff response to innovation in a mental health service *Amer J Pub Health* 54:1230–1240

(16) Weber M. *Wirtschaft und Gesellschaft* A. R. Henderson and T. Parsons trans. 1947 *The Theory of Social and Economic Organization* London, Hodge pp. 151–187

Gouldner A. W. ed. 1950 *Studies in Leadership: Leadership and Democratic Action* New York, Harper

Susser M. W. and Watson W. 1962 *Sociology in Medicine* London, Oxford

(17) Merton R. K. 1957 *Social Theory and Social Structure* rev. ed. New York, Free Press pp. 131–194

(18) Freidson E. 1960 Client control in medical practice *Amer J Sociol* 65:374–382

(19) Stein Z. A. and Susser M. W. 1964 Hypothesis: failures in medical care as a function of the doctor's situation *Medical Care* 2:162–166

(20) Rehin G. F., Houghton H. and Martin F. M. 1964 Mental health social work in hospitals and local authorities: a comparison of two work situations in McLachlan G. *Problems and Progress in Medical Care* London, Oxford pp. 319–354

(21) Parsons T. 1951 *The Social System* New York, Free Press

(22) Kandel D. and Williams R. H. 1964 *Psychiatric Rehabilitation: Some Problems of Research* New York, Atherton

(23) Cumming J. and Cumming E. 1955 Mental health education in a Canadian community in Paul B. ed. *Health, Culture and Community: Case Studies of Public Reactions to Health Programs* New York, Russell Sage Foundation pp. 43–70

(24) Zander A., Cohen A. R., Stotland E., Hymovitch B. and Riedl O. 1957 *Role Relations in the Mental Health Professions* Ann Arbor, University of Michigan Press

(25) Freeman H. L. 1964 The psychiatrist in a community mental health service in Susser M. W. *Reports and Papers for the Year 1963* City of Salford, Eng., Health Department pp. 31–32

part four

Mental Subnormality in the Community: *A Medical-Care Paradigm*

11

The Mentally Subnormal: Population and Natural History

The vast changes in population of the past two centuries are familiar knowledge. Among the industrialized nations these changes have reached a stage more advanced than elsewhere. The focus of concern in India or China or Indonesia is that the rise in numbers will outpace economic production and local supplies. The focus of concern in the industrialized nations is with the characteristics and density of the surviving population. The balance between working people and dependents who are too young, or too old, or too disabled to work has altered. Fewer dependents are young and soon to develop into producers, and many more are too old or too disabled to produce.

Because of their great productivity, there is no danger that the smaller proportion of workers in the industrialized nations will not produce enough for the whole people. The danger is that the aged, the disabled, the chronic sick, and the mentally disordered will remain neglected in the midst of affluence, as did the slum dwellers of nineteenth-century England until investigators like John Simon and Charles Booth began the accounting and their findings were forced to attention by the restiveness of the slum dwellers themselves. In a world replete with goods, action, and diversion, the disabilities of the dependent may easily pass the rest by. Dependents of industrial societies are dispersed and without political weapons. Others must act for them if they are to have a just share of benefits. People dependent because of mental subnormality are more defenseless than most, although in recent years their parents have learned to band together.

The condition of mental subnormality has been studied sufficiently to build on it a paradigm of rational community care. Mental subnormality has an advantage over mental illness as a paradigm because diagnosis is more assured and less controversial. The object of study, the dependent variable, can be better defined. Within an order of magnitude, therefore, it is possible to describe the present size of the problem, to predict its development, and to prepare for the future. It is possible to analyze its causes and act to prevent some of them. Finally, it is possible to choose forms of care that take account of its effects on the whole individual and his family as well as on his specific condition. Succeeding chapters will deal with these questions.

The first step in taking the measure of the problem is to discover the size of the subnormal population and to reckon its likely trends. Mentally subnormal people can be treated as a special population. A number of population surveys of the prevalence of subnormality have been made, beginning with E. O. Lewis' classic work in the 1920s (1, 2, 3, 4). In Britain numerical data about this population can be obtained from the registers of mentally deficient persons kept by local health authorities. These registers are a by-product of the Mental Deficiency Act of 1913, a piece of law that was effective during half a century. Drawn in the light of the theories of racial degeneracy and the eugenic remedies of that time, it was probably to control breeding among mentally defective persons as well as to provide care for them that local health authorities were required to keep registers. Any data they yield are a secondary gain for the epidemiologist.

Given proper precautions in checking data, the register can provide a measure of the prevalence and distribution of recog-

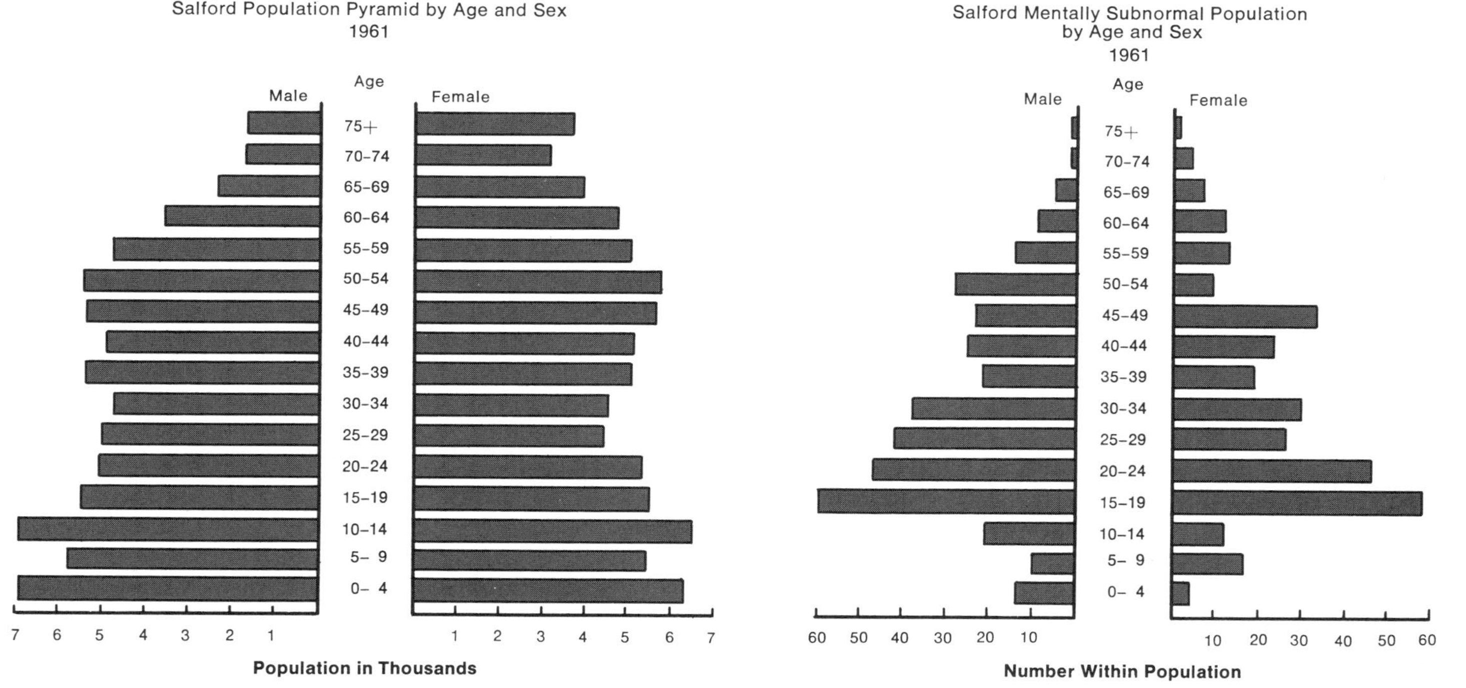

Figure 7. Prevalence and Distribution of Recognized Mental Subnormality

nized mental subnormality in a community. Figure 7 represents this graphically. It compares the age and sex of the registered mentally subnormal population of the city of Salford in 1961 with the total population. The object of the figures is to illustrate the extreme contrast in the age distribution of the two populations. Each bar of these two population pyramids represents a five-year age group. The diamond shape of the subnormal population pyramid is produced by three features: a deficit among the young, a deficit among the old, and a marked excess among adolescents and young adults. This pattern recurs regularly in surveys of populations through several countries (5).

These pyramids represent ascertained prevalence, a cross-section of the population at one point in time, but they are the outcome of a dynamic process continuing through time. In any normal population there is continual increment through births and immigration and continual decrement through deaths and emigration; the survivors of each age group or birth cohort represent the balance.

In the subnormal population there is a sharp increment in prevalence at each successive age group into young adulthood and a sharp decrement thereafter. (See Appendix C.) Neither births nor immigration can account for the rapid increase in numbers during childhood. In the older age groups too, numbers decline more sharply than can be accounted for by deaths among them (even though these are more frequent than in the normal population) or by emigration.

No permanent biological attribute present at birth could produce this picture. Recognized mental subnormality is a social attribute. Recognition is determined by the social roles demanded of individuals at each stage of life. The capacity of individuals to fulfill these roles depends chiefly (although by no means entirely) on biological attributes, but the order of society determines how taxing these roles shall be. The laws of England recognized mental subnormality as early as the fourteenth century (6), but the conditions by which it was then defined were legal matters of property inheritance. In the twentieth century the defining conditions stem from matters of education and training. Only in industrial societies does the need for education and training become universal and so specialized that the family alone cannot undertake it. The compulsory school system by means of standardization socializes large numbers for many new types of roles, but at the same time it creates a new class of subnormality.

What is expected in particular social roles also varies with time, and among societies, and among the classes of a single society. Expectations describe the behavior regarded as appropriate and acceptable or as deviant and beyond the limits of tolerance. These limits and the mechanisms of society to handle deviant behavior depend on the structure and the culture of society; as they have changed, so have the laws and the institutions concerned with mental subnormality.

In modern Britain, with its uniform system of health care and education, diversity in culture and in the expectations governing mental subnormality is still evident. In industrial Salford in 1961 the rate of known subnormality was 4.4 per 1,000 (7). In rural Anglesey a recent survey discovered the same rate of 4.4 per 1,000 (8). In Salford all the cases that comprise the numerator of the rate were known to the local health authority and registered, and almost half were in institutional care. In Anglesey only half the cases were known to the local health authority and registered, and less than a quarter of the total were in institutional care. It was only by an inclusive special survey, which relied on the definitions of the local general practitioners, that the rates could be made to approximate those in Salford.

These two areas lie within 100 miles of each other. Population surveys have usually found higher rural than urban rates, and in this instance different methods could have produced false concord in total prevalence. To explain the disparities between the two services in the recognition of mental subnormality and in the care they provide for it, however, one is obliged to invoke the perceptions and expectations that reside in the culture of each community. Their cultural idiosyncrasies are transmitted from the past, but they must be derived in part from the dissimilar demands of roles in rural and urban communities and from the variable resources and obligations of supportive kin networks. In rural communities there is land to pass on between kin and to bind them.

To sum up, organic factors lay the foundation for the primary deviance of mental subnormality, but the ways in which it becomes manifest depend on social processes. Later we shall see that society not only sets the type and level of the demands made by social roles, but also molds individual capacity to fulfill them. All capacities are not fixed from the outset.

Differentiation of the Subnormal Population

The timetable of individual development is set by the play between biological development and social expectations. The more severe the individual's physical limitations, the sooner and more surely his failure to meet social expectations is likely to be recognized and registered. This point becomes immediately evident when the population is examined by degree of mental handicap. Figure 8 breaks up the mentally subnormal population into three grades of intellectual deficit. The low-grade or idiot category includes those who score less than 20 on standard intelligence tests; the medium-grade or imbecile, those who score 20 to 50; and the high-grade or feebleminded, those who score more than 50, with no defined upper limit. Many individuals classed as subnormal have scores higher than the ceiling of 70 that sometimes is proposed. In a rough approximation each category contributes respectively 10 per cent, 40 per cent, and 50 per cent of the total. Inspection of the diagrams reveals at once that the large high-grade category is responsible for the diamond shape of the mentally subnormal population pyramid in Figure 7. In view of the previous argument that the diamond shape must reflect a social phenomenon, its source can be looked for in this category of subnormality.

The shapes of the pyramids for low- and medium-grade patients (who fit the British legal class of *severe* subnormality) bear a closer resemblance to that of the normal population. The age structure is compatible with the usual view of a

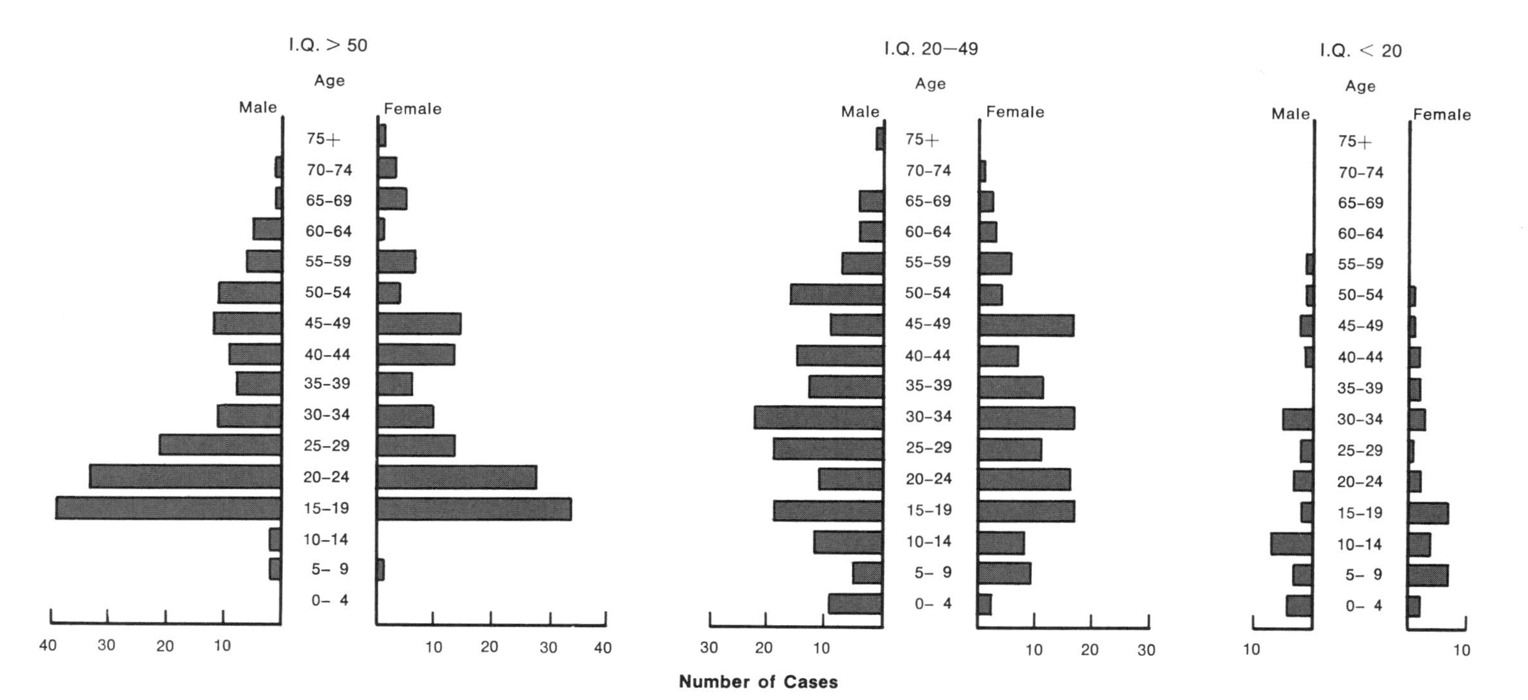

Figure 8. Salford Mentally Subnormal Population by Age, Sex, and Grade, 1961

Adapted from M. W. Susser and A. Kushlick, *A Report on the Mental Health Services of Salford for the Year 1960,* by permission of Health Department, Salford, England.

mentally subnormal population biologically determined at birth and persisting through life with a rate of attrition from deaths that is somewhat higher than in the general population.

Failure in social roles, however, retains its salience in the registration of the *severely* subnormal. Registration is the outcome of a process of perception and action on the part of parents and of perception and reaction on the part of the social and medical agencies that keep the registers. Patients in the lowest grade thus tend to be registered as they fail to develop beyond egocentric infancy, and those in the medium grade as they fail to cope with schooling shortly after school entry. Of cases accumulated over the years and on the Salford register on January 1, 1959, about half the low-grade patients had been registered by the age of five years and more than nine out of ten by ten years.

In the middle grade, only one in twenty patients had been notified by five years and seven out of ten by the age of fifteen. The fact that 30 per cent may escape the register up to the age at which they leave school is surprising. It may reflect withdrawal by teachers, in the abject conditions of some schools, from the task of formal teaching. Almost all are registered by the age of twenty years, in the period when they meet difficulties on entering employment.

In the high grade, that is those with *mild* subnormality, three of four patients were notified after the age of fifteen years, but the great majority (two out of three) were notified before the age of twenty years. Their peak prevalence of 8.7 per 1,000 is reached in the age group fifteen to twenty years.

High-grade and low-grade populations are dissimilar in more than degree, for they are distinct in their age and sex distribution. To be rewarding, analysis must treat them as distinct classes. From such analysis we learn that their mental deficits do not have the same causes, that their lifetime prognosis is not alike, and that as popualtions they have different dynamics.

In the remainder of this chapter, therefore, *mild* and *severe* subnormality will be discussed separately. In each condition an attempt will be made to map the course and prognosis, and also the vulnerable groups and the special problems, within each affected population.

Mild Subnormality: Natural History

Mild subnormality furnishes a dramatic example of a temporary disjunction between the fluctuating demands of social roles at successive stages of the life cycle and the fluctuating ability of individuals to meet these demands. Obvious disjunction arises at adolescence and usually does not endure beyond young adulthood. Within ten years of being notified, two thirds of high-grade patients in Salford had been deleted from the register. In social terms they had recovered from their condition.

In Britain the entry of high-grade subjects to the register has been in part an artifact of the notification system. These notifications reflected the social phenomenon of a vulnerable group and did not determine it. The law served only to narrow down the scatter of age at notification. The adolescent age peak of mild subnormality is not a local Salford phenomenon. Elsewhere in Britain, in the United States, and in Scandinavia the age pattern is similar (1, 9, 10). Furthermore, the many follow-up studies of mild subnormality show a relatively consistent prognosis (11). Two thirds to three quarters of all subjects who are followed up make adequate social adjustments. They hold steady jobs, and they may marry and rear families.

The one quarter to one third that does not make adequate social adjustment, however, is not a negligible number. Adolescence is a time of transition and of discontinuities between statuses. (See p. 87.) In industrial societies no *rites de passage* affirm the transitions of individuals and ratify their new statuses as they become ready for them. Much depends on individual adaptations. At adolescence children draw to the end of their status as pupils; they assume new roles in the adult world of work, in the world of their peers, and with the opposite sex. Although mildly subnormal persons have been relative failures in the school system, their failures are not so gross that schools cannot cope with them by making special provisions or merely by overlooking their special needs. Soon thereafter these deficiencies in education become crucial to adaptation, for the child moves into the world of work. The problems of transition are aggravated if he is illiterate and innumerate, as many are who need not be (12).

Mildly subnormal people tend to come to notice when they repeatedly fail to hold jobs, are apprehended for delinquent acts, or overtly transgress the sexual codes of society at large. A few boys who fail in normal heterosexual relationships may be driven to the deviant course of sexual exhibitionism, a few girls to promiscuity. The most striking characteristic of patients with a poor prognosis has been their family history.

In the Salford study about one third of high-grade patients on the register at any one time were in residential institutions. (See Appendix D.) Virtually all those committed to institutions have displayed some deviant behavior. They have also come from "dysmorphic families" (13, 14). These are families that were disrupted early in the individual's childhood and thus deprived him of the set of enduring family relationships that are the foundation of kin support, of normal affective ties, and of normal socializing experience. For adolescents of low-measured intelligence reared from dysmorphic families, long-term custody in institutions following deviant behavior is a specific hazard.

Also highly represented among the families of delinquent subnormal persons are some which have remained intact. These are *deviant* families that fail to meet minimal standards of child care, so-called "multiproblem" families that get involved with multiple agencies (13). Usually they give their children enough support to keep them out of institutions. These families suffer from anomia; dislocated from the surrounding culture, they display a typical deterioration of norms.

Individuals in the same range of measured intelligence as those from dysmorphic and deviant families, but who are raised in families that are intact in structure and that function within the norms of their local culture, have a much more favorable prognosis. They have low rates of delinquency and they are rarely committed to institutions.

The dynamics of the mildly subnormal population are intimately linked with the causes of the condition. Further discussion of this aspect is therefore deferred to a later chapter that deals with the causes of mild subnormality. We shall see that the outlook is optimistic in population terms as well as in individual terms. (See Chapter 12.) A decline in prevalence can reasonably be expected.

Severe Subnormality: Natural History

We now turn to the problems special to severe subnormality. Delayed social recognition, we have observed, leads to incomplete registration. Registered prevalence therefore understates actual prevalence.

A special case-finding survey in metropolitan London used the population aged ten to fourteen years to arrive at a better estimate (4). It was assumed that in this age group most cases of severe subnormality had become manifest. The age-specific rate was 3.6 per 1,000. This London rate showed remarkable if unexpected consistency with that for known cases in the age group fifteen to nineteen years in the rural counties and marketing towns of Wessex (2, 3). In these areas, and in industrial Salford as well, the age-specific rate of registered cases of severe subnormality was between 3.6 and 3.8 per 1,000.

This rate is not the maximum possible at any age, for an unknown number of cases will not have survived infancy and childhood. Nor is it a rate that is sustained at later ages. Inspection of Figures 7 and 8 shows that the decline in numbers of the severely subnormal among the older age groups is sharper than that for the general Salford population. The age-specific rates confirm this finding; they show that the decline is most evident after the third decade. (See Appendix C.)

The only factor that can explain the deficiency at older ages in the severely subnormal population is a death rate in excess of the general rate. This explanation can be accepted on common-sense grounds despite the lack of direct evidence. In the category of severe mental subnormality, outflow from the registered population cannot be attributed to intellectual or social recovery. It also cannot be attributed to migration. In Salford, migration could only have acted to inflate and not reduce the prevalence at later ages. The total Salford population has been declining for at least a generation; emigrating Salford families lower the denominator of the rate while their mentally subnormal kin in the hospital remain to inflate the numerator. This effect is likely to be exaggerated at older ages, when a higher proportion of the severely mentally subnormal population is in the hospital than at younger ages. Analysis of migration of the subnormal and their families, however, showed that the effect was not important.

Like most other populations, the mentally subnormal population is both dynamic and unstable. It is dynamic in that it has a continual recruitment of new individuals and a loss of old ones (15). It is unstable in that the balance between losses and recruitment is changing.

Losses are occurring at a slower rate than before because the death rate is declining and survival is improving. For evidence we may turn first to studies of mongols. Mongols provide an excellent epidemiologic index. The diagnosis is one of the least equivocal in medicine, and the population is one of the most complete and representative within the whole class of mental subnormality. Life tables constructed for mongols show an undoubted increase in longevity over the past generation. Prevalence at the age of ten years appears to have risen from 1 in 4,000 in 1929 to 1 in 2,000 in 1949 to 1 in 1,000 in 1958 (4, 16). J. Tizard in his surveys of 1961 found a threefold increase in the prevalence of mongolism over that found by E. O. Lewis thirty-five years earlier, and his supporting arguments suggest that the comparison he made with the earlier survey is a valid one (4).

These findings pointing to a longer span of life for mongols can be supplemented by similar findings from Salford for the whole of the severely subnormal population. A. Kushlick reconstructed the 1948 register for subnormality (7). Comparison with the register for 1963 shows that in the fifteen-year interval there was an increase in the registered population of 4.75 per

100,000 per year. Table 9 shows that this increase in the population has been accompanied by aging. The most notable rise occurred in the older age groups, and in 1963 there were more elderly persons than in 1948 in absolute numbers and in proportion.

Table 9. Registered Severely Subnormal Population in Salford in 1948 and 1963 Compared

A. Percentage of Total on Register by 10-Year Age Groups

		AGE GROUPS								
	Total N	*0–9*	*10–19*	*20–29*	*30–39*	*40–49*	*50–59*	*60–69*	*Unknown*	
Jan. 1, 1948	147	8.0	25.2	27.5	22.9	9.5	3.8	2.3	0.8	100
Jan. 1, 1963	238	15.5	21.4	15.1	16.4	16.0	10.1	3.8	0.9	100

B. Age-Specific Rates per 100,000 by 10-Year Age Groups*

	AGE GROUPS						
	0–9	*10–19*	*20–29*	*30–39*	*40–49*	*50–59*	*60–69*
Jan. 1, 1948	70	290	270	221	96	49	39
Jan. 1, 1963	152	209	182	198	180	113	61

* Much of the increased rate in the 0–9 year age group is the result of an active case-finding program instituted about five years before 1963. Improved registration had small effect on the older age groups (7).

Migration and registration occurring unevenly among the age groups distort these patterns. With due caution therefore we conclude that within a fifteen-year time span there has been a true rise in numbers and perceptible aging in the severely subnormal population due to their better chances of survival.

In the general population the falling death rate during the past two centuries improved the life chances of successively less hardy categories. The improvement affected first young adults and adolescents, then young children, then infants. Now, after some lag, the process has reached the mentally subnormal population, including the most handicapped among them.

Despite the rise in the number of cases of severe subnormality in the community, which here has been attributed to survival, there is evidence for a contrasting trend in recruitment to this population. Fresh cases are probably occurring less frequently than before in countries with high standards of living. Although in his survey Tizard obtained a much higher prevalence of mongolism than did Lewis thirty-five years previously, the prevalence of other kinds of subnormality was only about two thirds as high (4). In the face of improved survival in severe subnormality of all kinds, a true decline in prevalence of kinds other than mongolism could come about only through a decline in incidence and recruitment.

Although due allowance must be made for the lack of comparability between the studies of Lewis and of Tizard, a fall in incidence can be the consequence of several factors connected with the technical advance and improved living standards of developed economies. Some favorable trends are autonomous; they are built into economic development. Others can be manipulated in programs of prevention (9, 17, 18).

Maternity services diminish the risk of brain damage *at birth* by many general measures and by some specific ones. For example, jaundice of the newborn occurs either with incompatibility of Rh blood groups between mother and infant or with immature infants. The excess of bile products that gives rise to the jaundice injures the pyramidal nuclei of the brain to cause kernicterus. These ill effects have been much reduced in the past decade by the combination of public health screening methods to pick up mothers at risk of Rh incompatibility with the clinical intervention of obstetricians and pediatricians in treatment (19). Brain damage also has a strong link with low birth weight (20), which in turn has a link with poor living conditions. Thus, in one sequence leading to prematurity, poor social conditions depress height, and small women have smaller babies and greater reproductive losses than tall women (21).

It must be conceded that a decline in the frequency of low birth weight in concert with the secular trends toward better living conditions has still to be satisfactorily demonstrated. It is also not clear how often low birth weight in poor social conditions is a sign of premature birth and how often of an immature or "dysmature" foetus after full gestation.

Low birth weight and other disorders present at birth lead to a consideration of their possible antecedents *in the period of gestation.* Controlled experiments, although beset by problems of execution, suggest that protein and vitamin supplements for pregnant mothers can raise the birth weights of their children (22). Infective and toxic agents acting on and through the mother during pregnancy also affect the foetal environment and the foetus. The disorganizing effects on embryonic growth of infections like the spirochete of syphilis, toxoplasma, and rubella virus, and of chemical agents like thalidomide are well known. The existence of unknown agents that harm the embryonic brain has been inferred by analogy, and recently cytomegalic-inclusion body virus has been incriminated. In pursuit of similar hypotheses, surveys have related complications of pregnancy to mental deficiency (17, 23).

Diverse complications, including toxemia and bleeding in late pregnancy, have been linked with such diverse consequences as behavior disorders, tics, speech and reading disorders, epilepsy, and childhood schizophrenia (24). These important studies, chiefly of B. Pasamanick, H. Knobloch and their coworkers, suggest that prenatal factors are active in mental deficiency. These factors will repay further study. Past studies were retrospective, and mainly for this reason the comparison groups could not be always satisfactory as controls. The connections between the multiple complications of pregnancy and a multiple array of disorders are somewhat tangled. A further pointer to the influence of both the uterine environment of the foetus and the external environment of the mother, however, is the variation of measured intelligence and of mental subnormality with season of birth, and with the environmental temperature during the first three months of gestation (25).

A further suggestion of Knobloch and Pasamanick important to the theme of a declining incidence of severe mental subnormality is that the risk of brain damage during gestation and at birth is greater the harsher the environment (23). They postulate a continuum of reproductive casualty. In this continuum, damage to the foetus ranges from behavior and reading disorders to death at the extreme, according to the severity of insults suffered during gestation and birth.[1] Affluence can be presumed to lessen the frequency of some of these unspecified factors in pregnancy or to cushion their impact.

After birth the risk of brain damage has been lessened by the treatment and prevention made available by advances in medical science. Such causes as bacterial and tuberculous meningitis, syphilis, whooping cough, and lead poisoning have all been brought under better control (26). In preindustrial societies the protein malnutrition of kwashiorkor is followed by depressed intelligence scores and is their probable cause (27). This condition disappears in populations with good diets and good living conditions. In societies with developed medical serviccs, phenylketonuria (28) can be discovered in infants by screening tests of blood, and the mental deterioration it causes can probably be checked by special diets (29). Unforfortunately, the execution of the therapeutic trials leaves the results open to a degree of doubt. Similarly, the thyroid deficiency of the various types of congenital cretinism can be discovered and treated, although again it is not always reversed or checked by early intervention (30). Even if the treatment of phenylketonuria and cretinism were fully effective, however, they are rare and could account for little change in incidence.

Demographic change in the general population is a force interacting with others to influence the incidence of mental subnormality. It can be predicted that the continuing trend

1. The impact of these studies is diluted when mental deficiency is considered under a global rubric. Some results of the initial studies suggest that sharper results could be expected from future resarch that takes fuller account of the clinical dissimilarity of mild and severe subnormality and of their dissimilar social and ethnic distributions. As we shall see in a later chapter (pp. 299 ff.), by far the greater part of mild subnormality that occurs in the lowest social classes is not due to evident brain damage and is responsive to postnatal experience. Natal factors that can damage the brain, therefore, would not be expected to have a strong causal association with this type of subnormality, although they might still be part of a complex of prenatal and postnatal factors in mild subnormality.

toward early marriage and a restricted span of fertility will bring a fall in the incidence of mongolism, because of the association of this condition with high maternal age. In Western societies of the present time, about half of all mongol babies are born to women aged over thirty-five years; the risks increase from 1 in 2,000 at the age of twenty years to 1 in 50 at the age of forty-five years (9, 31).[2]

Some other chromosome anomalies, namely XYY and XXY sex chromosome patterns, are associated with late childbearing but their effect on total incidence of subnormality is small (34). An extra loading of the female X chromosome in males gives rise to Klinefelter's syndrome. Mental subnormality is said to be infrequent with the XXY pattern in this syndrome, but frequent when there are more than two Xs. The total incidence of Klinefelter's syndrome is between 1 and 1.6 per 1,000 live births (34). Childbearing in youth is in general more efficient than at later ages, for the incidence of brain damage as well as that of chromosomal anomalies is lower. In Aberdeen, Scotland, obstetric results were much improved in part by controlling the fertility of elderly women (35).

Genetics also holds some future promise of prevention. The presence of recessive genes that cause phenylketonuria can be inferred from blood levels of phenylalanine (36), if imperfectly as yet, and possibly also the presence of genes that cause the even rarer condition of amaurotic family idiocy (37). Although the actual or potential contribution of many individual factors is small, the contribution of some is more considerable, and their cumulative effects could be enough to cause a noticeable fall in the incidence of severe mental subnormality.

The process of population change among the mentally subnormal resembles in some respects that common to the development of industrial societies during the past century. In these populations increment caused by improved survival was followed by decrement caused by declining birth rates; eventually

2. The frequency of mongolism may differ among races or ethnic groups; it appears to be uncommon among indigenous Southern African peoples. The clustering of cases reported by some observers (32) has raised the possibility of environmental and particularly of infective agents, but so far subsequent studies have failed to support the hypothesis (33).

relative if short-lived stability was reached. There was a much higher proportion of adults and old people because of the deferred age at death and the smaller proportion of births. Among the mentally subnormal, however, we need not anticipate the population "explosion" that has burst upon countries with developing economies. Explosive increase is caused by the fertility of the greater numbers who survive into reproductive age in successive generations. Among the severely subnormal fertility is minimal. For this reason the accumulation of cases in the older age groups can be expected to continue only until the rising death rate in this older segment comes into balance with falling incidence. A decline in prevalence could follow.

References

(1) Lewis E. O. 1929 Report on an investigation into the incidence of mental deficiency in six areas, 1925–1927 in *Report of the Mental Deficiency Committee Part IV* London, H.M. Stationery Office

Bremer J. 1951 A social psychiatric investigation of a small community in northern Norway *Acta Psychiat Neurol Scand Suppl* 62:1–166

Fremming K. H. 1951 *The Expectation of Mental Infirmity in a Sample of the Danish Population* Occasional Papers on Eugenics 7 London, Cassell

Böök J. A. 1953 A genetic and neuropsychiatric investigation of a North-Swedish population with special regard to schizophrenia and mental deficiency: Part I *Acta Genet* 4:1–100

Böök J. A. 1953 A genetic and neuropsychiatric investigation of a North-Swedish population with special regard to schizophrenia and mental deficiency: Part II *Acta Genet* 4:345–414

Lin T.-Y. 1953 A study of the incidence of mental disorder in Chinese and other cultures *Psychiat* 16:313–336

New York State Department of Mental Hygiene Mental Health Research Unit 1955 A special census of suspected referred mental retardation Onondaga County, New York in *Tech-*

nical Report of the Mental Health Research Unit Syracuse, Syracuse University Press

Essen-Möller E. 1956 Individual traits and morbidity in a Swedish rural population *Acta Psychiat Neurol Scand Suppl* 100:1–160

(2) Kushlick A. 1964 The prevalence of recognised mental subnormality of I. Q. under 50 among children in the south of England with reference to the demand for places for residential care *Proceedings of the International Copenhagen Congress on the Scientific Study of Mental Retardation* 2:550–556

(3) Kushlick A. 1965 Community care for the subnormal: the size of the problem *Proc Roy Soc Med* 58:374–380

(4) Tizard J. 1964 *Community Services for the Mentally Handicapped* London, Oxford

(5) Gruenberg E. M. 1966 Epidemiology of mental retardation *Int J Psychiat* 2:78–134

(6) *Report of the Royal Commission on the Laws Relating to Mental Illness and Mental Deficiency: An Inquiry into the Operation of the Total Service for Mental Health 1954–1957* London, H. M. Stationery Office

(7) Kushlick A. 1961 Subnormality in Salford in Susser M. W. and Kushlick A. *A Report on the Mental Health Services of the City of Salford for the Year 1960* City of Salford, Eng., Health Department pp. 18–48

(8) Jones A. and Miles H. L. 1964 The Anglesey mental health survey in McLachlan G. ed. *Problems and Progress in Medical Care* London, Oxford pp. 205–263

(9) Penrose L. S. 1963 *The Biology of Mental Defect* 3d ed. London, Sidgwick & Jackson

(10) Åkesson H. O. 1961 *Epidemiology and Genetics of Mental Deficiency in a Southern Swedish Population* Uppsala, University of Uppsala Institute of Medical Genetics

(11) O'Connor N. and Tizard J. 1956 *The Social Problem of Mental Deficiency* London, Pergamon

(12) Stein Z. A., Susser M. W. and Lunzer E. A. 1960 Reading, reckoning and special schooling among the mentally handicapped *Lancet* 2:305–307

(13) Stein Z. A. and Susser M. W. 1960 The families of dull children: classification for predicting careers *Brit J Prev Soc Med* 14:83–88

(14) Saenger G. 1960 *Factors Influencing the Institutionalization of Mentally Retarded Individuals in New York City* Albany, N. Y. State Interdepartmental Health Resources Board

(15) Kramer M. 1959 Measurement of patient flow in institutions for the mentally retarded *Amer J Ment Defic* 64:278–290

Dingman H. F., Eyman R. K. and Tarjan G. 1964 A statistical model for an institution for the mentally retarded *Amer J Ment Defic* 68:580–585

Tarjan G., Eyman R. K. and Dingman H. F. 1966 Changes in the patient population of a hospital for the mentally retarded *Amer J Ment Defic* 70:529–541

(16) Carter C. O. 1958 A life-table for mongols with the causes of death *J Ment Defic Res* 2:64–74

Collmann R. D. and Stoller A. 1963 A life-table for mongols in Victoria, Australia *J Ment Defici Res* 7:53–59

(17) MacMahon B. and Sowa J. M. 1961 Physical damage to the fetus *Milbank Mem Fund Quart* 39:14–73

(18) Masland R. L., Sarason S. B. and Gladwin T. 1958 *Mental Subnormality: Biological, Psychological, and Cultural Factors* New York, Basic Books

Lin T.-Y. and Standley C. C. 1961 *The Scope of Epidemiology in the Study of Mental Disorders* Public Health Papers 16 Geneva, World Health Organization

Kushlick A. 1967 Social aspects of mental subnormality in Miller E. ed. *Textbook of Child Psychiatry* in press

(19) Armitage P. and Mollison P. L. 1953 Further analysis of controlled trials of treatment of hemolytic disease of newborn *J Obstet Gynaec Brit Emp* 60:605–620

Kelsall G. A. and Vos G. H. 1955 Premature induction of labor in treatment of hemolytic disease of newborn *Lancet* 2:161–164

Forfar J. O., Keay A. J., Elliot W. D. and Cumming R. A. 1958 Exchange transfusion in neonatal hyperbilirubinemia *Lancet* 2:1131–1137

Gorman J. G., Freda V. J. and Pollack W. 1962 Intramuscular injection of new experimental gammaglobulin preparation containing high levels of anti-Rh antibody as means of preventing sensitization to Rh *Proc IXth Congr Int Soc Hemat* 2:545–549

Woodrow J. C., Clarke C. A., Donohoe W. T. A., Finn R., McConnell R. B., Sheppard P. M., Lehane D., Russell S. H., Kulke W. and Durkin C. M. 1965 Prevention of RH hemolytic disease: third report *Brit Med J* 1:279–283

(20) Knobloch H., Pasamanick B., Harper P. and Rider R. 1959 The effect of prematurity on health and growth *Amer J Pub Health* 49:1164–1173

Drillien C. M. 1964 *The Growth and Development of the Prematurely Born Infant* Edinburgh, Livingstone

Macdonald A. D. 1964 Intelligence in children of very low birth weight *Brit J Prev Soc Med* 18:59–74

(21) Illsley R. 1955 Social class selection and class differences in relation to stillbirths and infant deaths *Brit Med J* 2:1520–1524

(22) Wiehl D. G. and Tompkins W. T. 1955 Method of study and description of sample: Part I Maternal nutrition studies at Philadelphia Lying-in Hospital in *The Promotion of Maternal and Newborn Health* New York, Milbank Memorial Fund pp. 11–24

Tompkins W. T., Mitchell R. M. and Wiehl D. G. 1955 Prematurity and maternal nutrition: Part II Maternal nutrition studies at Philadelphia Lying-in Hospital in *The Promotion of Maternal and Newborn Health* New York, Milbank Memorial Fund pp. 25–50

Tompkins W. T., Wiehl D. G. and Douglas R. G. 1955 Toxemia and maternal nutrition: Part III Maternal nutrition studies at Philadelphia Lying-in Hospital in *The Promotion of Maternal and Newborn Health* New York, Milbank Memorial Fund pp. 62–79

(23) Knobloch H. and Pasamanick B. 1962 Mental subnormality: medical progress *New Eng J Med* 266:1045–1051, 1092–1096, 1155–1161

(24) Lilienfeld A. M. and Pasamanick B. 1954 Association of maternal and fetal factors with development of epilepsy: abnormalities in prenatal and paranatal periods *JAMA* 155: 719–724

Lilienfeld A. M. and Pasamanick B. 1955 Association of maternal and fetal factors with the development of cerebral palsy and epilepsy *Amer J Obstet Gynec* 70:93–101

Rogers M. E., Lilienfeld A. M. and Pasamanick B. 1955 Prenatal and paranatal factors in development of childhood behavior disorders *Acta Psychiat Neurol Scand Suppl* 102: 1–157

Pasamanick B., Constantinou F. K. and Lilienfeld A. M. 1956 Pregnancy experience and development of childhood speech disorders: epidemiologic study of association with maternal and fetal factors *J Dis Child* 91:113–118

Pasamanick B. and Kawi A. 1956 Study of association of prenatal and paranatal factors with development of tics in children: preliminary investigation *J Pediat* 48:596–601

Pasamanick B., Rogers M. E. and Lilienfeld A. M. 1956 Pregnancy experience and the development of behavior disorder in children *Amer J Psychiat* 112:613–618

Kawi A. and Pasamanick B. 1958 The association of factors of pregnancy with the development of reading disorders in childhood *JAMA* 166:1420–1423

Vorster D. 1960 An investigation into the part played by organic factors in childhood schizophrenia *J Ment Sci* 106: 494–522

Zitrin A., Ferber P. and Cohen D. 1964 Pre- and paranatal factors in mental disorders of children *J Nerv Ment Dis* 139: 357–361

Pasamanick B. and Knobloch H. 1966 Retrospective studies on the epidemiology of reproductive casualty: old and new *Merrill-Palmer Quart* 12:7–26

(25) Pintner R. and Forlano G. 1943 Season of birth and mental differences *Psychol Bull* 40:25–35

Roberts J. A. F. 1944 Intelligence and season of conception *Brit Med J* 1:320–322

Knobloch H. and Pasamanick B. 1958 Seasonal variation in the births of the mentally deficient *Amer J Pub Health* 48:1201–1208

(26) Berg J. M. 1958 Neurological complications of pertussis immunization *Brit Med J* 2:24–27

Berg J. M. and Kirman B. H. 1959 Syphilis as a cause of mental deficiency *Brit Med J* 2:400–404

(27) Cravioto J. 1964 *Malnutrition and Behavioral Development in the Pre-school Child* Paper read at Pan-American Health Organization Conference on the Prevention of Malnutrition in the Pre-school Child, Washington, D.C.

(28) Fölling A. 1934 Ulskillelse av fenylpyrodruesyre i urinen som stoffskifte anomali i forbendelse med imbecelletet *Nord Med T* 8:1054–1059

(29) Wolff L. I., Griffiths R., Moncrieff A., Coates S. and Dillistone F. 1958 The dietary treatment of phenylketonuria *Arch Dis Child* 33:31–45

Moncrieff A. and Wilkinson R. H. 1961 Further experiences in the treatment of phenylketonuria *Brit Med J* 1:763–769

(30) Smith D. W., Blizzard R. M. and Wilkins L. 1957 The mental prognosis in hypothyroidism of infancy and childhood: a review of 128 cases *Pediatrics* 19:1011–1022

(31) Smith A. and Record R. G. 1955 Maternal age and birth rank in the etiology of mongolism *Brit J Prev Soc Med* 9:51–55

Penrose L. S. and Smith G. F. 1966 *Down's Anomaly* Boston, Little, Brown

(32) Pleydell M. J. 1957 Mongolism and other congenital abnormalities: an epidemiological study in Northamptonshire *Lancet* 1:1314–1319

Stoller A. and Collman R. D. 1965 Incidence of infective hepatitis followed by Down's syndrome 9 months later *Lancet* 2:1221–1223

(33) Fraumeni J. F. Jr. and Lunden F. E. Jr. 1966 Infective hepatitis and Down's syndrome *Lancet* 1:712–713

Leck I. 1966 Incidence and epidemicity of Down's syndrome *Lancet* 2:457–460

(34) Penrose L. S. 1961 Mongolism *Brit Med Bull* 17:184–189

Polani P. E. 1965 Sex chromosome anomalies: recent developments *Sci Basis Med Ann Rev* pp. 141–163

(35) Baird D. 1965 A fifth freedom *Brit Med J* 2:1141–1148

(36) Hsia D. Y.-Y. 1956 Detection by phenylalanine tolerance tests of heterozygous carriers of phenylketonuria *Nature* 178: 1239–1240

(37) Rayner S. and Böök J. A. 1958 Genetics and blood morphology in amaurotic family idiocy *Lancet* 1:1077–1078

12

The Causes and the Care of Mild Subnormality

The outstanding epidemiological characteristic of mild mental subnormality is its social distribution. It occurs much more frequently in those social strata found at the bottom of any scale of social class than it does in those found at the top of the scale. This distribution has been known for a long time. Since Binet devised the first intelligence tests at the beginning of this century, many studies, such as those of Sir Cyril Burt, have confirmed it (1, 2).

One early explanation of this social distribution of mild subnormality attributed it to differing heredity between the social classes. The explanation was reinforced by the investigation of twins. These ingenious studies showed the greater concordance of measured intelligence in monozygotic twins (each pair of which possesses genes derived from a single ovum) than in dizygotic twins (each pair of which derives from two ova). The results of early studies must be qualified by problems of method, for error could not be excluded from the labeling of twin types, and by problems of inference, for identical monozygotic twins share a special life experience different from that of fraternal dizygotic twins (3). Another problem of method that can beset twin studies is that of biased sampling. Cases are selected for study because of the interest aroused by the known similarity of a pair. Within such limits, these studies demonstrated the existence of a genetic component in the intelligence of *individuals* (4).

Genetic explanations of the distribution of intelligence in *social groups* assumed that intelligence tests measured a quality that was inherited and relatively fixed. The distribution of intelligence between the higher social classes and the lower was thought to reflect the genetic composition of the social classes (5). The superiority of the higher classes in intelligence, it was presumed, was maintained by continuous recruitment of persons of high intelligence from the lower social classes; the inferiority of the lower social classes was maintained by recruitment of persons of low intelligence from the higher social classes. Thus mild subnormality appeared as merely the tail end of normal intelligence in the population, the genetic tail coinciding with the social.

There was, however, a parallel line of thought and explanation. Twin studies provide equally good evidence for an environmental component of intelligence. The special environment of twin life presumably accounts for the greater concordance in intelligence test scores found between dizygotic twins than between ordinary sibs. On genetic grounds their concordances should not differ. Environmental factors can also account for the fact that the scores of monozygotic twins are not identical. But this lack of identity could also arise by chance if genes set the limits of development but do not determine it precisely.

The difference in measured intelligence between social classes and other social collectivities was attributed by this line of argument to the different environments to which they were exposed. Environment in this sense includes not only its material and biological content but also its social and cultural content. The levels of intelligence among such social categories as the American Negroes, who share a more or less common pool of genes, were thus shown to vary according to whether their geographical location was in the northern or southern states, according to the length of their exposure to city environments in the North, and according to their relative positions on the scale of social class (6). These findings provided a potent antithesis to the genetic hypotheses, which sought to explain the distribution of high grade subnormality between the social classes. Synthesis must reconcile these genetic facts with the social facts.

An important insight into the effect of adverse environment was provided by the work of H. M. Skeels and coworkers in the 1930s (7, 8). They showed that, when orphanage infants, supposedly retarded, were transferred to situations making possible one-to-one relationships with affectionate even if mentally subnormal adults, the orphans were able to make progress both socially and educationally, whereas control children left undisturbed in the orphanage remained retarded. Now, thirty years later, Skeels (9) has reported on the same study group in adulthood, contrasting the social, economic, and educational advantages that have accrued to those who were transferred with the impoverished limited careers of the controls. Few today will quarrel with Skeels' conclusion that environments that deny a young child the chance of forming adequate human attachments will in some cases lead to retardation.

In Skeels' experimental series, substantial changes in early life apparently led to recovery. A. D. B. Clarke and Anne Clarke have provided evidence that even in later life, recovery from subnormal intelligence can take place (10). They reported that mentally subnormal persons in a mental-deficiency hospital, unlike those of higher intelligence outside, could continue to gain in measured intelligence until their late twenties. Those who had experienced the most severe family deprivations gained most. The Clarkes suggested that such deprivations retarded intellectual growth just as poor nutrition retarded physical growth. This retardation, in the light of their findings and those of Skeels, was not irreversible.

An earlier step forward had been made with the recognition that individuals with mental subnormality could be classified in two distinct categories. In one category fairly obvious abnormalities were apparent in the structure of the body, in the shape of the skull, in the brain, or in metabolism. In the second category there were no abnormalities that could be detected by clinical investigation. This second category, without apparent clinical damage, was found predominantly among those individuals with lesser deficits of intelligence. Furthermore, those people with lesser deficits in intelligence, who fall into the category of mild subnormality, came chiefly from the lowest social classes (11, 12). These findings were supported by the findings of later surveys. In severe subnormality the father's occupation, the mother's fertility, and the home conditions seemed to mirror those of the general population. In mild subnormality these attributes mirrored those of the lowest social classes (13).

The family of origin of an individual of low measured intelligence, we have noted in the previous chapter, has a profound influence on his future career. The family may be an equally potent factor in determining his level of measured intelligence. In our own study of so-called educationally subnormal individuals in Lancashire, England, we investigated the influences on their handicap of social and family background (14). They had been recognized as needing special education within the school system because of mental handicap. The definition is administrative and not clinical, but it covers the range of mild mental subnormality. The study was a follow-up of a random selection of 106 young adults and their families, some ten to twelve years after it had been *ascertained* in school that they were educationally subnormal.

They were classified by their clinical condition into the two groupings mentioned above, that is, according to the presence of detectable physical abnormalities in the form of neurological lesions presumptive of brain damage, or deafness, or any defect that might have proved a serious handicap to learning. Those individuals who were classed as imbeciles on clinical grounds, all of whom had independently measured I.Q.s of less than 55, were presumed to suffer from brain syndromes, because at autopsy brain lesions can be demonstrated in 90 per cent of the cases (15).

The families of the subjects of the study were then classified independently of the clinical classification in a way that was intended to distinguish them by subculture, that is, by the way of life, the systems of value, and the attitudes common to particular sections of our society.

It was possible to define two broad cultural categories among the families by using objective criteria of education and occupation to judge social position and social mobility. One category comprised families that showed no signs of affiliation with the middle class, in particular with its values of achievement through education and occupation; we described them as *demotic*. A second category comprised the families that did show signs of affiliation with the middle class or at least that showed signs of aspirations toward their values; we described them as *aspirant*. In the idiom of the English working class, the two categories comprised "roughs" and "respectables."

A clear distribution of clinical types emerged between the two cultural categories. The clinical type that had in common only a variety of detectable handicaps to learning was drawn from the families of both cultures. Each of the individuals from aspirant families had a clear-cut lesion that could interfere with learning. The clinical type without detectable handicaps was drawn entirely from the ninety-seven families that showed no signs of middle-class affiliation or of aspirations to such affiliation. A second contrast was found when childhood and adult intelligence test scores were compared. Individuals with presumed brain disorders made no significant gains in measured intelligence (mean change: 1.0 I.Q. point); whereas those without any signs of brain disorder made significant gains (mean change: 8.3 I.Q. points).

Regression to the mean, it was noted in an earlier chapter (p. 192) is a statistical bugbear of longitudinal studies of maturation and development. Regression must be taken into account if the starting population falls toward one extreme of the distribution of an attribute under study. In this case the scores of those with brain syndromes were even further polarized than the scores of those without; regression to the mean would therefore act in a direction opposite to the result obtained. Regression could operate within the category without signs of brain disorder if the two groups were different populations with different norms. This would not detract from the results; rather it would provide an indirect confirmation of the thesis that follows, namely, that there were two types of cases.

Their features, classified as heterogeneous and homogeneous, are set out here:

Heterogeneous	Homogeneous
Learning handicaps detectable	Learning handicaps not detectable
All social classes	Demotic subculture only
Static I.Q. in brain syndromes with aging	Gains in I.Q. with aging

These findings suggested that the homogeneous "clinically normal" group suffered from mental retardation that was to some extent reversible and that this condition was specific to the demotic subculture.

A far-reaching conclusion derived from a relatively small study could not carry conviction until many sources of bias had been ruled out. It seemed certain that some social selection must be operating in our sample, and it was necessary to discover it and assess its influence on the validity of the results.

We learned a good deal in the attempt to find sources of bias. The original sample examined in our study had been chosen by standard sampling methods from a population formally ascertained by school doctors as "educationally subnormal." In the process of ascertainment, as they passed through the teachers who referred them to the school doctors who in turn decided on their clinical classification, many forms of selection could operate. The criteria used by the doctors included measured intelligence but also others less well-defined, such as social and family background and behavior. The absence of children from aspirant families in the sample without learning handicaps might have been due to these medical judgments or to their not having been referred by the teachers to the doctors at all. It was necessary therefore to study the processes by which the children came under medical surveillance.

Several forms of selection among children of different categories, it could be inferred from the results, were indeed at work. Local administrative practice, for example, led to large differences in the numbers ascertained educationally subnormal in similar urban communities. Boys were ascertained educationally subnormal more often and over a higher range of intelligence-test scores than girls. Children from broken homes were ascertained to be educationally subnormal more often than those from intact homes. The very backward children who came from families at the bottom of the social class scale were more often treated as *ineducable* and excluded from the school system; children of the same intelligence level but of higher social class were more often kept within the educational system and placed in special schools for the educationally subnormal.

In order to study social selection throughout the school system we classed the schools in Salford, which was a main source of the original sample, according to their social standing. This step revealed still other selective processes. To our initial surprise schools of high standing had not referred fewer children than they should have, although many schools of low standing had (16). On the contrary, there was a surplus of referrals from schools of high standing; they were children in the normal intelligence range who had handicaps of language, chronic illnesses, or emotional difficulties.

None of these forms of special selection and bias, however, detracted from the original result that was under test. Virtually all children retarded in intellect without detectable cause (in the I.Q. range 50–80) came from schools of low social standing. In these schools 3.8 per 1,000 had been recognized as backward and referred. Very few children retarded in intellect without detectable cause came from schools of high social standing. In these schools the referral rate was 0.26 per 1,000, only one fifteenth of the rate in schools of low standing. (See Table 10.)

The disparity that emerged when these referrals were compared with the I.Q. scores of the total school population was even more striking. In the schools of low standing less than one in ten of the children in the eligible I.Q. range was recognized as backward and referred. Schools of high standing over-referred, for many children whose scores were higher than the eligible range appeared as backward among their fellows.

The rarity of I.Q.s in the range 50–80 among children from the higher classes was in concord with data that we drew from previous surveys in Britain and the United States (17, 18). It

Table 10. Referral by I.Q., Clinical State, and Social Standing of Salford Schools (1955–1959), Average Annual Rates Per 1,000 Schoolchildren 7–10 Years of Age

	SOCIAL STANDING OF SCHOOLS				
	Low	*Low Average*	*High Average*	*High*	*All Schools*
Average *N* at Risk	5,501	11,261	1,974	750	19,488
All referrals for backwardness	10	10	7	4	9
All I.Q. 50–79	4.3	3.0	2.8	0.5	3.3
I.Q. 50–79 clinically normal only	3.8	2.7	2.5	0.26	2.9
I.Q. 50–79 with lesions	0.5	0.3	0.3	0.26	0.4

From Z. Stein and M. Susser, *Mild Mental Subnormality: Social and Epidemiological Studies.* Paper read at Annual Meeting, Association for Research in Nervous and Mental Diseases, New York, 1967.

is not too much to say that within the local working class two culturally defined populations exist, namely the aspirant and the demotic, each with a distinctive curve of measured intelligence and educational performance. For children of the aspirant subculture as well as of the higher social classes the curve for "normal" intelligence seemed to tail off at an intelligence quotient of 80–90. For children of the demotic subculture and the lowest social classes it tailed off at scores of 50–60.

So clear-cut a segregation of cases among subcultures conformed with our starting hypothesis that this form of mental subnormality must have a cultural component. A simple genetic explanation appeared improbable, especially if it had also to account for the allied finding of intellectual improvement in those cases from the demotic culture without brain syndromes.

In order to explain the distribution of cases, a genetic hypothesis such as that of J. Conway would require that genes for low intelligence be virtually confined to certain subcultural categories and absent from others (5). For if genes were not so confined, some dull children without detectable learning handicaps should be found in all social classes. Genes for low intelligence could be confined to particular social groups by two processes: endogamy, by which marriage is restricted to particular social groups, and selection for social mobility, by which individuals carrying genes for high or low intelligence transfer to a social class appropriate to their innate intellectual level. In this view I.Q. scores in the range 50–80 would be seen as a biological norm of the demotic subculture.

The degree of endogamy in contemporary British society is in itself insufficient to confine genes for low intelligence to particular social groups. Individuals most often find spouses in the same social class as themselves, but there is frequent intermarriage between classes. This fact is evident both in the sample from our initial study and in national samples (19). The relevant data is set out in tables in Appendix E.

Selection for social mobility by intelligence also fails to provide an adequate mechanism for the strict segregation of intelligence. The three main channels of social mobility are through marriage, occupation, and education. The effectiveness of social mobility as an agent of genetic selection has been argued elsewhere (20). The Aberdeen data on marriage of E. M. Scott and others provide direct evidence of the commingling of various levels of intelligence among social classes (21). Other studies show that any correspondence that exists between measured intelligence and social mobility through occupation can be no more than partial (22). The correspondence between measured intelligence and social mobility through education, which in an "ideal" open society might be expected to be close, is also far from perfect (23, 24).

Hence the correspondence of genes for intelligence and social mobility must be partial. On the available evidence, the correspondence is too small to account for the distribution of intelligence found in Salford. The observation holds even should there be, as some authorities believe, a high correlation between genotypic and measured intelligence (1). A further difficulty for the theory of the genetic segregation of people through social mobility arises from the fact that the distributions of intelligence under consideration derive from school children. The social positions of the individuals concerned could not have been affected by their own social mobility. The theory must therefore find its main support in parental transmission and endogamy.

The social mechanisms of marriage and mobility, which might segregate people according to their genes for intelligence, clearly do not have the force to separate the intellectual heritage of the social classes to the degree required to explain the existing distribution. While genetic models alone might conceivably account for much individual variation in intelligence, they cannot be made to account for the gross disparities between social classes.

On the basis of this analysis, one may remain firm in the conviction that most children with mild mental subnormality and with no detectable handicaps to learning suffer from the effects of the environment in which they were reared. The social class gradient of low intelligence is similar to the gradient for those other disorders and attributes that are closely related to social conditions, such as bronchitis, tuberculosis, heights and weights, infant deaths, and fertility. A generally accepted interpretation of these social class differences, strongly supported by secular trends, is that they are chiefly the result of social conditions. The improvement in intelligence through time shown in the two Scottish National Education Surveys of 1932 and 1947 leads to the same interpretation (17). These studies showed a decline in the percentage of low scorers from 18.7 per cent to 15.4 per cent in a period of fifteen years. A similar trend appears in the prevalence of mild mental subnormality in England at periods separated by thirty years. Estimates suggest that in the 1950s there were little more than half as many recognized cases as in the 1920s. (See Appendix G.)

Such rapid change must certainly have been the result of changing environment.

A number of pointers incriminate the nonmaterial rather than the material aspects of culture as the factor favoring low scoring on intelligence tests. From a close examination of the Scottish data it can be inferred that the secular change was localized to verbal and scholastic ability and did not affect other abilities. Moreover, the improvements were found on group tests rather than on individual tests, which again points to verbal abilities. Such discrete improvements in learning are likely to have originated in the nonmaterial environment. A similar conclusion might be drawn from a recent investigation in New York City (25) that compared various abilities of children from different ethnic origins but from comparable socioeconomic strata. From study of the results of their subjects on four different types of psychological tests, the research workers concluded that while social class regularly influenced the *level* of intellectual performance, ethnicity fostered the development of distinctive *patterns* of abilities regardless of social class.

Better nutrition, the decline of infectious diseases, and similar factors, however, cannot easily be dissociated from the nonmaterial aspects of culture. Such factors also vary in accord with the secular changes in low scoring on intelligence tests and with the social-class gradient on these tests. For example, children from large families score lower on I.Q. tests than do children from small families (17), and even in the 1960s in Britain children from large families eat less well (26). Nutrition may be connected directly with prematurity (30), and in turn prematurity has been connected with mental subnormality, as noted in the preceding chapters. But premature births are also associated with poor living conditions and services (27, 28, 29), so that high rates of prematurity and high prevalence of mild subnormality tend to coexist. Malnutrition might thus be related to subnormality directly, through a connection with prematurity, or through a coincidental relationship with poverty.

Some possible sequences follow:

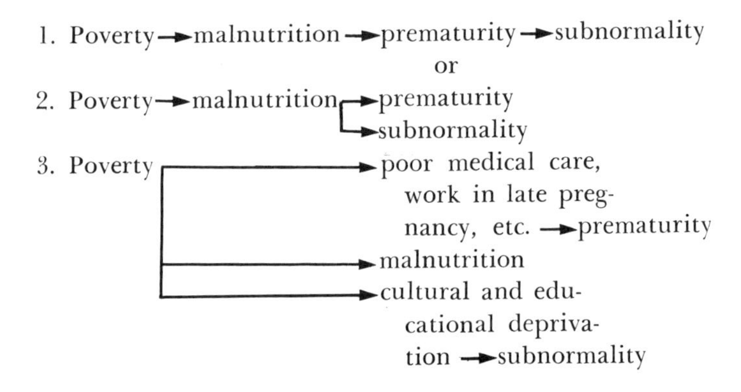

The network of factors could be further extended and may turn out to be extremely complex. Only some of the variables can be controlled in surveys and observation studies. Such studies will not control the confounding variables intimately tied to the dependent variable under examination; experiment and intervention will be necessary to clarify their effects.

Aside from prematurity, an impressive body of evidence also relates toxemia, bleeding of late pregnancy, and high environmental temperature during gestation to subnormality on the one hand and to poor social conditions on the other (31). These associations are more striking for severe than for mild degrees of subnormality. Another factor to be considered is the rate of developmental maturation. Between the two Scottish surveys the percentage of low-scoring girls fell by 26 per cent and the percentage of low-scoring boys by only 9 per cent. Maturation occurring progressively earlier over time might have given girls an advantage at the tests for eleven-year-olds because girls are more mature at this age and advanced maturation at a particular age favors intellectual performance (24, 32). In this case too, however, one might expect maturity to have had a general effect that should have appeared in individual as well as in group tests. Time has brought about change for girls in social as well as in physical conditions.

Much other evidence fully reviewed elsewhere suggests that poor cultural environment can depress intelligence test scores (33). Conversely, a stimulating cultural environment is likely to produce better intelligence test scores than one that lacks intellectual stimuli. Special training of retarded children can lead to spurts in their intellectual development. Although the gains may be short lived, they have been most marked in children without detectable clinical lesions, that is, in the type of case whose handicaps would be thought remediable from our results. The spurts did not occur in control groups from the same poor environment but with no special stimulus from training (34).

If an adverse environment lowers the intelligence scores of a population, then as the environment improves, intelligence scores can be expected to rise and the proportion of subnormals to fall. We have already noted the improvements shown in the scores of Scottish children through time. In the future, therefore, the proportion of the population defined by psychometric means as mildly subnormal might be expected to decline. On this view, I.Q. scores in the range of approximately 50–80 would be seen as the pathological outcome of adverse environment.

This inference contrasts with that from the genetic hypothesis that scores in this range reflect the tail end of a normal curve of intelligence. On this hypothesis, mean intelligence should have declined and the proportion of subnormal should have risen because of the association of low I.Q. with large families. Indeed, the Scottish study was designed to test precisely this prediction, and failed to confirm it.

Individual variation in genetic make-up must nevertheless play its part. For example, boys seem to be more sensitive than girls to environment in this as in other attributes. It is at this point that the environmental and genetic hypotheses attain a comfortable synthesis. The retardation attributed to the demotic culture presumably occurs in individuals endowed with low innate intelligence or with high sensitivity to the environment. Some depression of measured intelligence probably occurs at all levels of intelligence in the lowest social classes, however, for the proportion of high scorers among them is relatively small (although their numbers are not).

The Cultural Syndrome

The features of the condition of cultural mental retardation can be summarized by drawing on the previous data of others together with those outlined in these chapters (2, 10, 13, 35).

Although cultural retardation is characterized as much by the absence as by the presence of certain signs, a positive diagnosis usually can be ventured. Commonly the condition will be found in school children referred for backwardness who have Stanford Binet I.Q.s in the range 50–80 or even 50–90. All known causes of mental subnormality must of course be excluded. When careful examination reveals no positive neurological sign or history suggestive of brain damage and no obvious physical incongruity or metabolic disturbance; when investigation shows no chemical abnormality in the urine, a normal electroencephalograph, the expected sex chromatin on oral smear, and no abnormality of chromosomes; and when there is no other psychiatric disorder, then the diagnosis can be inferred from the the social background.

On the one hand, a child with a father in a nonmanual occupation, or with siblings in grammar school, probably has cryptic brain disorder, unless he suffers from serious maladjustment or chronic illness. This presumption awaits the test of more refined clinical methods. On the other hand, a "clinically normal" child who has a father in manual work, particularly unskilled work, and no siblings in higher, technical, or similar secondary schools is more likely to be suffering from cultural retardation than from cryptic brain disorder. Cases of this type comprised 70 per cent of the subjects with an adult intelligence quotient above 55 in our follow-up of the educationally subnormal. The syndrome is more common in males and in children from large families, especially from those with more than one member who is educationally subnormal.

The eventual mental and social prognosis is good given an intact family of origin; subjects in their mid-twenties and over are then usually indistinguishable from their peers in the same social groups (36). If they have been denied an enduring set of family relations in early childhood, however, they tend to have poor work records, to offend against the law, and to transgress other social norms, as a result of which they have had in the past a high risk of long-term confinement in mental deficiency institutions. More intelligent individuals with similar experiences may show the same behavior, but the consequences are different.

Remedies for Retardation

Sociological and psychological research into the use of language and cognition and into cultural values and motivations has provided us with some clues about how mental retardation might come about in a social collectivity. Language is an important instrument for learning, for intellectual development, and for the direction of behavior (37). The character of a language might therefore influence mental development. B. Bernstein has contrasted middle-class and working-class language; he has demonstrated the poverty of formal construction and syntax in working-class language and its lack of generalization and abstract concepts (38).

Sociological studies have described the cohesion and the shared values of some local working-class cultures and their lack of comprehension of the values of schools and teachers (39). Every social system produces its casualties. Mildly subnormal children can be seen as casualties of such local cultures.

This is a serious diagnosis, because a culture is not changed by exhortation and advice; without tenacity and persistence a culture does not exist. A child learns the values of his culture and its modes of response, and he incorporates them into his personality. In our society the three major agencies of this process of socialization are the family, the peer group, and the school. Together they inculcate the standards of society and its appropriate modes of behavior. Among people hostile or indifferent to educational values, however, schools face a great challenge as agents of culture change. Few have overcome the blocks in communication between purveyors and consumers of education. A number of approaches suggest themselves for the future.

First, we found that among subnormal children the special conditions of special schools produced better results than did the conditions of ordinary schools; the subnormal children who attended special schools had learned more of the basic skills of reading and numbers than those who had not (40). These skills are part of the foundation for independent life (41). We do not know what it is about these schools that promotes learning. It could have to do with an environment that is sheltered and cut off from the more insistent demands of the more able children. It is perhaps more likely to have to do with the smaller number of children within the charge of each specially trained teacher (42). It is necessary to discover what are the important factors and to make use of them in the education of subnormal children. By no means all who are illiterate, innumerate, and of low measured intelligence receive special schooling; in many places the proportion is probably less than one in ten. In England 140,000 children of school age probably have intelligence-test scores of 50–70. Only 40,000 children are in special schools for the educationally subnormal, many with scores both above and below this range (43).

Second, the delay in the intellectual maturation of subnormal individuals without brain disorders and their continued improvement into adulthood suggest that they could benefit from prolonged schooling no less than do children being prepared for higher education. To make continued schooling possible, their families will need persuading of its benefits. The low value that many such families tend to place on education and their view of schools as the agents of an alien culture do not lead them to remark school failure as anything exceptional. Such attitudes receive apparent confirmation when in adulthood their children become indistinguishable from those around them; they provide an example of the self-fulfilling prophecy.

Less formal educational methods in play centers outside school hours might enrich the social experience of the child, extend the range of informal learning provided by the home, and help to penetrate cultural barriers. A New York project suggested that an enriched school program that aimed at getting families as well as children involved could produce a rise in school results (44). Better results might come from an input that took note of the expressive modes of working-class life and of the types of incentive to which working-class children respond. Both normal and retarded boys of the working class have been shown to perform better in response to a tangible reward and middle-class boys to an intangible reward (45).

Third, schools can provide the conditions for exercising a tried technique of preventive medicine, namely, the screening of defined populations to discover symptoms that are early pointers to disorder. Screening and early detection may provide the occasion for preventing the progress of a disorder. Backwardness is an admirable symptom for use in screening school populations. It is often a pointer to emotional disorder, to chronic disease in children, and to family disorder. As long as the school population was treated as an undifferentiated mass, such associations were perforce diluted or concealed by the large body of backward children generated by the demotic culture. The association of backwardness with treatable underlying conditions begins to emerge only when the school population is divided into social classes that are analyzed separately (16).

Fourth, we must consider what help disordered families may need when they are discovered. Our means of helping such vulnerable families are crude and intuitive, and our resources to do so inadequate. Public authorities will surely have to provide more support through public health nursing and social work. They will also have to devise new methods and to experiment with new facilities. We have noted previously that those demographic and social changes that have followed on industrialization have diminished the internal resources of the nuclear family. As a consequence the modern family is poorly adapted to bear the extra strains of dependence created by chronic disorders or of social or mental deviance in any one of its members. Families will increasingly require help to do so.

Among badly needed facilities is a variety of forms of residential care for those without adequate homes. In Britain there has been a move toward using hostels placed in local communities to provide such care rather than the large hospitals, far removed from local communities, that were typical of the past half-century. The values and norms of behavior developed in typical large institutions may unfit those who share them for successful community adaptation. On the other hand, for hostel residents normal work and leisure in the community are accessible. But we do not yet know whether hostels will automatically generate values compatible with normal social life. Nor can they be expected to cope with extreme behavior problems such as repeated physical aggression. We shall therefore need a cool appraisal of the successes and failures of hostels and a variety of approaches to residential care for the subnormal. We need to know if small group homes or foster homes will yield better results, or if some individuals might not do best in semi-independent supervised lodgings. The next chapter moves on to a related issue, which can provide a paradigm for such analysis.

References

(1) Burt C. 1955 The evidence for the concept of intelligence *Brit J Educ Psychol* 25:158–177

(2) Burt C. 1937 *The Backward Child* London, University of London Press

(3) Jackson D. D. 1960 A critique of the literature on the genetics of schizophrenia in Jackson D. D. ed. *The Etiology of Schizophrenia* New York, Basic Books pp. 37–90

(4) Newman H. H., Freeman F. N. and Holzinger K. J. 1937 *Twins: A Study of Heredity and Environment* Chicago, University of Chicago Press

(5) Conway J. 1958 The inheritance of intelligence and its social implications *Brit J Stat Psychol* 11:171–190

(6) Klineberg O. 1935 *Negro Intelligence and Selective Migration* New York, Columbia University Press

(7) Skeels H. M. 1938 Mental development of children in foster homes *J Consult Psychol* 2:33–43

(8) Skeels H. M. and Dye H. R. 1941 A study of the effects of differential stimulation on mentally retarded children *Proc.*

and Addresses at the American Association of Mental Deficiency 44:114–136

(9) Skeels H. M. 1966 *Adult Status of Children with Contrasting Early Life Experiences* Monogr Soc Res Child Developm 105

(10) Clarke A. D. B. and Clarke A. M. 1953 How constant is the I. Q.? *Lancet* 2:877–880

Clarke A. M. and Clarke A. D. B. eds. 1958 *Mental Deficiency: The Changing Outlook* London, Methuen

(11) Paterson D. G. and Rundquist E. A. 1933 The occupational background of feeble-mindedness *Amer J Psychol* 45:118–124

(12) Lewis E. O. 1933 Types of mental deficiency and their social significance *J Ment Sci* 79:298–304

(13) Roberts J. A. F. 1952 The genetics of mental deficiency *Eugen Rev* 44:71–83

(14) Stein Z. and Susser M. W. 1960 Estimating hostel needs for backward citizens *Lancet* 2:486–488

Stein Z. and Susser M. W. 1960 The families of dull children: a classification for predicting careers *Brit J Prev Soc Med* 14:83–88

Stein Z. and Susser M. W. 1960 Families of dull children *J Ment Sci* 106:1296–1319

(15) Crome L. 1965 Causes of mental defect—natal and postnatal in Hilliard L. T. and Kirman B. H. eds. *Mental Deficiency* Boston, Little Brown pp. 142–169

(16) Stein Z. and Susser M. W. 1963 The social distribution of mental retardation *Amer J Ment Defic* 67:811–821

(17) Scottish Council for Research in Education 1953 *Social Implications of the 1947 Scottish Mental Survey* Publ 35 London, University of London Press

(18) Eells K., Davis A., Havighurst R. J., Herrick V. E. and Cronbach L. 1951 *Intelligence and Cultural Difference: A Study of Cultural Learning and Problem-Solving* Chicago, University of Chicago Press p. 338

(19) Berent J. 1954 Social mobility and marriage: a study of trends in England and Wales in Glass D. V. ed. *Social Mobility in Britain* London, Routledge pp. 321–338

(20) Susser M. W. and Watson W. 1962 *Sociology in Medicine* London, Oxford pp. 115–123

(21) Scott E. M., Illsley R. and Thomson A. M. 1956 Psychological investigation of primigravidae: maternal social class, age, physique and intelligence *J Obstet Gynaec Brit Emp* 63:338–343

(22) Anderson C. A., Brown J. C. and Bowman M. J. 1952 Intelligence and occupational mobility *J Polit Econ* 40:218–239

Boalt G. 1954 Social mobility in Stockholm: a pilot investigation *Transactions of the Second World Congress of Sociology* 2:67

(23) Floud J., Halsey A. H. and Martin F. M. 1956 *Social Class and Educational Opportunity* London, Heinemann

(24) Douglas J. W. B. 1963 *The Home and the School* London, Macgibbon & Kee

(25) Lesser G., Fifer G. and Clark D. H. 1965 *Mental Abilities of Children from Different Social-Class and Cultural Groups* Monogr Soc Res in Child Dev 102

(26) Lambert R., 1964 *Diet and Family Size* London, Political & Economic Planning

(27) World Health Organization 1961 *Public Health Aspects of Low Birth Weight* Technical Report Series 217 Geneva, World Health Organization

(28) President of the United States 1962 *National Action to Combat Mental Retardation (Statement on Need)* Washington, D.C., Government Printing Office

Clifford S. H. 1964 High-risk pregnancy *New Eng J Med* 271:243–249

Jacobson H. N. and Reid D. E. 1964 High-risk pregnancy *New Eng J Med* 271:302–307

(29) Shapiro S., Jacobziner H., Densen P. M. and Weiner L. 1960 Further observations on prematurity and perinatal mortality in a general population and in the population of a prepaid group practice medical care plan *Amer J Pub Health* 50: 1304–1317

Butler N. R. and Bonham D. G. 1963 *Perinatal Mortality Vol 1* Edinburgh, Livingstone

(30) Tompkins W. T., Mitchell R. M. and Wiehl D. G. 1955 Prematurity and maternal nutrition: Part II Maternal nutrition studies at Philadelphia Lying-in Hospital in *The Promotion of Maternal and Newborn Health* New York, Milbank Memorial Fund pp. 25–50

Tompkins W. T., Wiehl D. G. and Douglas R. G. 1955 Toxemia and maternal nutrition: Part III Maternal nutrition studies at Philadelphia Lying-in Hospital in *The Promotion of Maternal and Newborn Health* New York, Milbank Memorial Fund pp. 62–79

(31) Knobloch H. and Pasamanick B. 1959 Effect of prematurity on health and growth *Amer J Pub Health* 49:1164–1173

Knobloch H. and Pasamanick B. 1962 Medical progress: mental subnormality *New Eng J Med* 266:1045–1051, 1092–1097

Jones R. E. and Schendel H. E. 1966 Nutritional status of selected negro infants in Greenville County, S. C. *Amer J Clin Nutrition* 18:407–412

(32) Stone C. P. and Barker R. G. 1937 Aspects of personality and intelligence in postmenarcheal and premenarcheal girls of the same chronological ages *J Comp Physiol Psychol* 23:439–455

Boyne A. W. 1960 Secular changes in the stature of adults and the growth of children, with special reference to changes in intelligence of 11 year olds in Tanner J. M. ed. *Human Growth* Oxford, Pergamon pp. 97–120

(33) Sarason S. B. and Gladwin T. 1958 *Psychological and Cultural Problems in Mental Subnormality: A Review of Research* Genet Psychol Monogr 57 pp. 3–290

(34) Kirk S. A. 1958 *Early Education of the Mentally Retarded: An Experimental Study* Urbana, University of Illinois Press

(35) Lewis E. O. 1933 Types of mental deficiency and their social significance *J Ment Sci* 79:298–304

Doll E. A. 1947 Is mental deficiency curable? *Amer J Ment Defic* 51:420–428

Tredgold A. F. 1947 *A Textbook of Mental Deficiency* Baltimore, Williams & Wilkens

O'Connor N. and Tizard J. 1956 *The Social Problem of Mental Deficiency* London, Pergamon

Penrose L. S., Berg J. M. and Lang-Brown H. 1963 *The Biology of Mental Defect* New York, Grune & Stratton

Hilliard L. T. and Kirman B. H. 1965 *Mental Deficiency* Boston, Little Brown

(36) Baller W. B. 1936 A study of the present social status of a group of adults who, when they were in elementary schools, were classified as mentally deficient Genet Psychol Monogr 18 pp. 165–244

Kennedy R. J. R. 1948 *The Social Adjustments of Morons in a Connecticut City* Hartford, Conn.: Mansfield-Southbury Training Schools Social Service Department

Charles D. C. 1953 Ability and accomplishment of persons earlier judged mentally deficient Genet Psychol Monogr 47 pp. 3–71

(37) Luria A. R. and Yudovich F. I. 1959 in Simon J. ed. *Speech and the Development of Mental Processes in the Child: An Experimental Investigation* London, Staples

O'Connor N. and Hermelin B. 1963 *Speech and Thought in Severe Subnormality: An Experimental Study* Oxford, Pergamon

(38) Bernstein B. 1958 Some sociological determinants of perception: an inquiry into sub-cultural differences *Brit J Sociol* 9:159–174

(39) Warner W. L. and Lunt P. S. 1944 *Who Shall be Educated?* New York, Harper

Mays J. B. 1954 *Growing Up in the City: A Study of Juvenile Delinquency in an Urban Neighborhood* Liverpool, University of Liverpool Press

Cohen A. K. 1955 *Delinquent Boys: The Culture of the Gang* New York, Free Press

Kerr M. 1958 *The People of Ship Street* London, Routledge

Riessman F. 1962 *The Culturally Deprived Child* New York, Harper

(40) Stein Z., Susser M. W. and Lunzer E. A. 1960 Reading, reckoning and special schooling among the mentally handicapped *Lancet* 2:305–307

(41) Gunzburg H. C. 1960 *Social Rehabilitation of the Subnormal* New York, Williams & Wilkens

(42) Goldstein H. 1964 The effects of special class vs. regular class placement on educable mentally retarded children *Proceedings of the International Copenhagen Congress on the Scientific Study of Mental Retardation* 1:279–283

(43) Kushlick A. 1965 Community care for the subnormal: the size of the problem *Proc Roy Soc Med* 58:374–380

(44) Wrightson J. W. *et al.* 1964 *Evaluation of the Higher Horizons Program for Under-privileged Children* New York, Board of Education Bureau of Educational Research

(45) Zigler E. and de Labry J. 1962 Concept-switching in middle-class, lower-class and retarded children *J Abnorm Soc Psychol* 65:267–273

13

The Care of Severe Subnormality

This chapter compares the impact of local and of large-scale residential care on the severely subnormal. From this clinically extreme group, analyzed in the context of two extreme situations, generalizations that may hold for less extreme groups are derived.

The meaningful demographic feature of the severely subnormal population is the rise through time in numbers and in age. This rise confronts us with the question of future arrangements for care. The family has always been the institution that provided the bulk of this care. During the past century, when families failed to cope with severely subnormal offspring, industrial societies turned chiefly to large institutions that served large regions. This arrangement remains common even in Britain, where health authorities have made increasing local provision for mentally subnormal people.

The greater the strain put upon families, the more often is the hospital resorted to. The proportion in the hospital is thus higher with mental handicaps that are severe and difficult to care for. The proportion in the hospital also grows with the aging of patients and the concurrent decline in the physical resources of parents or their death (1). (See Appendix D.)

Because of their foreshortened lives, the most severely handicapped patients are to be found in the younger age groups. In what follows we shall examine the special problems of care at these ages. The care and socialization during childhood of this emergent and growing class of patients can be expected to determine much of what can be done for them in later life. As a class, the limited range of their responses, their narrow contact with the wider environment, and their domestication and apparent passivity all aid the observer who analyzes the impact of the environment that they experience.

There can be no doubt about the severity and multiplicity of their handicaps. In London two thirds of severely subnormal children in institutions and one third of those at home had major physical or behavior problems (2). Physical handicap is an important concomitant of severe mental handicap. Among the 83 severely subnormal children under the age of fifteen notified in Salford in the five-year period 1959–1963, 37 per cent in all had physical handicaps; 25 per cent in all had severe handicaps; and 15 per cent in all were almost totally incapacitated and needed as much care as any infant. For the survivors among such cases, hospital care has been the frequent outcome.

One can examine the system of medical care from the viewpoint of individual patient, of family, and of community. Here I begin with community. In the community's terms mental subnormality is a form of deviance (3). Societies manage deviance in many ways. The alternatives include punishment, removal from the community and custody, medical treatment, and attempts to continue and conclude the process of socialization from which deviance is a departure. The agencies, institutions, and professional groups that deal with mental subnormality are a specialized part of the community system for absorbing this deviance.

Objective information about hospitals for the severe categories of mentally subnormal patients is available in the Manchester Hospital Region from a study of the flow of patients through mental-deficiency hospitals and particularly of their waiting lists (4, 5). The hospitals were least able to provide for the class of patients here being considered. The longest waiting time was experienced by patients in the lowest grade of subnormality. Children aged five to nine years formed the largest single age group on the waiting list. Thirty-seven per cent of all those waiting were in need of so-called "cot and chair" accommodation; that is, they were bedfast or too young to be admitted to the wards used for mobile children. The list grew larger as the years passed.

This inability to provide adequate care is not merely a local phenomenon, and it goes beyond national boundaries.

Alienation in Medical Care

Failure of these institutions to meet the rising demand for care did not arise from a lack of ward space and buildings. Nurses and their ward assistants are the essential front line in care, and wards were closed for lack of nurses. This acute lack of ward staff is general, excepting special communities where local conditions have ensured supply. The lack of staff is not only a reflection of the shortage of professional nurses common to all hospitals, as by all accounts the shortage in mental-deficiency hospitals is more acute; nor can it be attributed only to the decreasing number of medium and high-grade subnormal patients who can stand in for staff. In recent years many such patients have been discharged, but their use on the wards masked existing shortages. Rural isolation is not a sufficient explanation of the shortage of staff, because these shortages seem to be more severe than in other types of hospitals similarly situated.

Alienation in Traditional Institutions. In the absence of detailed research, one must conclude that potential recruits place a low value on the professional employment offered by hospitals for mental subnormality. One source of this low value is to be found in their alienation. Alienation is a close relative of anomie; it implies a separation from society and a lack of goals shared with society. In a time of full employment alienated institutions hold few attractions as places of work. A central feature of traditional mental-deficiency hospitals is their caretaking and custodial duties in relation to one of the rejected elements of society. Their isolated sites, although often in pleasant countryside, can be seen as a symptom of their alienation and may reinforce it. During the past several centuries the state has been obliged to participate increasingly in the care of permanently dependent persons. At the same time, the culture of open-class societies has emphasized the value of individual responsibility, which contradicts that of state and community responsibility for the welfare of dependent persons. Dependent people who could not fulfill their social obligations have been at a focal point of ambivalence in the social structure.

This ambivalence is mirrored in culture. Rejection of the socially dependent can be inferred from studies of atttitudes toward people dependent because of specific handicaps. One study of blind people, for instance, suggests that they have the position of a minority group within society. Negative sentiments toward the blind correlate with sentiments that are hostile to minorities and to Negroes (6).[1] At least one study shows that among a wide range of handicapped people, the mentally deficient were the most strongly rejected (8).

Psychological reasons can be advanced for the power of the emotions of "normal" people toward handicapped ones. But the definitions of what are proper objects for obloquy and what for kindness or pity are social. Their source is to be found in group values. Beggars with physical deformities are objects of sanctity among Hindus, and of horror in the West. The stereotypes of physical handicaps held by children are remarkably uniform within social groups, but they vary with their assorted cultural origins. In a vacation camp that mixed normal and

1. The attitudes of others can affect a child's development. Children in situations of "contextual dissonance" (that is, in which their characteristics of race, culture, or class differ from those of the surrounding population) are likely to have low self-esteem, to report symptoms associated with anxiety, and to feel depressed (7).

disabled children, particular handicaps were more or less preferred according to the ethnic origin of the child who was asked to make the judgment (9).

Alienation and the associated bearing of stigma need not be an inescapable condition. Beliefs, attitudes, and values in societies change. The caretaking and custodial function of the hospital for mentally subnormal persons and its partly punitive function for delinquents with high-grade subnormality has been much the same as that of hospitals for the mentally ill of the recent past. Yet in Britain the function of hospitals for the mentally ill has changed; they are less alienated than in the past and more integrated with the communities they serve. Hospitals for the mentally ill are becoming ostensive socializing agents. They have been made visible to the surrounding communities and connected with them by the movement of patients into the hospitals and out again.

The question therefore is to what degree services for mental subnormality might be relieved of their alienation. One alternative to established forms of care in large hospitals is the provision of local services. These can reduce the size of the hospital task. An extensive search for factors that could explain the large variations in demand for hospital places among local areas in the Manchester region turned up only one significant result: The demand for hospital places was inversely related to the provision of day centers by the local health authority (5). This result is significant for the planner of services in more than a statistical sense. The discussion that follows will be concerned to compare traditional institutions with local forms of care.

Alienation and Commitment. Direct studies of alienation in mental-deficiency hospitals are not available. Studies of other kinds of hospitals must serve to draw analogies and generalizations. One such study has been made in the United States by Dr. Rose Laub Coser (10). She contrasted two hospital units sharing the same grounds. One was a large "caretaking" unit; its 650 beds were given over to patients with chronic disabilities classed as incapable of improvement. The second was a smaller unit; its 100 beds were devoted to rehabilitation. Many of the patients in the rehabilitation unit were reported to suffer from chronic disorders no more reversible than those in the larger, caretaking unit.[2]

The focus of the study was the relation between the ideology of the nurses and the manner in which they performed their tasks. The nurses on the caretaking unit described a good ward as one that was clean, neat, and quiet; those on the rehabilitation unit as one in which the patients were active and lively. The complaints of the nurses on the caretaking unit were about conditions and the nature of particular tasks, and they showed little concern with their functions in relation to patients; the complaints of the nurses on the rehabilitation unit were about social and personal relationships that frustrated effective patient care, and they were very much concerned with their work with patients. Nurses on the caretaking unit disliked frequent discharges from the unit, because of the paper work entailed; those on the rehabilitation unit were anxious to see patients discharged.

On the caretaking unit, nurses had infrequent interactions with patients, and these interactions cast patients in passive roles. Indeed, the smaller the staff-patient ratio, the less the nurses interacted with patients and the more among themselves, if only in a quiet social way. They withdrew from the task of care and used a number of devices, such as disconnecting emergency bells, which damped down or silenced the demands patients could make. The interaction of nurses on the rehabilitation unit was frequent with patients and intensive with other staff. Similar patterns could be discerned among doctors as well as among nurses, particularly in their interaction with patients, but the number of observations of doctors were too few to permit of generalization.

In summary, the staff on the caretaking unit regarded work as the routine accomplishment of a series of tasks. These tasks had the quality of ritual in the sense of Merton's model of

2. Rather few data are given to confirm this point, although a number of illustrations support it. A medical critic might well regard diagnosis as an influential variable in nursing performance.

anomie. (See p. 122.) They were tasks quite divorced from the personal goals and aspirations of the staff and were performed because they were prescribed. The staff of the rehabilitation unit identified with the work of their unit, incorporated its goals as personal ones, and strove to effect them. Evidently, custodial and caretaking goals do not tend to arouse spontaneous interest in the individual needs of patients on the part of nurses; therapeutic goals do.

Nothing illuminates better the primacy in medicine of therapeutic over caretaking values than the history of mental deficiency care itself (11). In the aftermath of revolutionary humanism in early nineteenth-century France, pioneering figures such as J. M. G. Itard and E. Seguin provoked attention for the subnormal as they explored the therapeutic possibilities of special training. A surge of interest followed when J. Guggenbühl set out in the spirit of an evangelist to cure "cretins," as others were then essaying to do for mental illness (12). At Abendberg in the Swiss Alps he created the first institution for mental deficiency; this was to be his one lasting innovation. Within a short time, on the wings of 1848, he became internationally renowned. He was made honorary or corresponding member of many societies of scientific prestige: the Swiss Society of Natural Science, the Medico-Chirurgical Society of Zurich, the Imperial-Royal Society of Physicians in Vienna, the Academy of Medicine in Turin, the Imperial Russian Society of Physicians in St. Petersburg, the Medical Society of Erlangen, the Rhenish Association for Governmental Medicine in Baden, the National Society of Medicine in Marseilles, and the Medical Society of Strassburg.

The promise of cure failed, the excitement quieted, the Abendberg ran down in neglect. The next half-century was a phase of caretaking and of expansion of institutions. In the "eugenic panic" of the early twentieth century, all trace of the curative goal was lost. The standing of the physicians in mental deficiency was never lower than in the period that followed.

Goals are defined within the framework of values, and they serve to canalize activity. Goals for which there is little approbation in a particular value system lead to alienation of their protagonists. Depreciated goals do not easily attract the commitments of those who must serve them.

The Social Structure of Traditional Institutions and Day Centers

Some of the characteristics of the caretaking unit described by Coser may be recognized by those who are familiar with large institutions that care for subnormal patients. The children are usually grouped homogeneously according to sex, age, and degree of handicap. In a ward for children with physical handicaps, four or five nurses and assistants among as many as 60 or 80 patients may be engaged in a ceaseless twenty-four hour round of routines: feeding children and changing their diapers, getting them into chairs in the morning, and getting them back into bed in the evening. The patients lie still in bed, except for the moments when they are being tended; the ones who have been got out of bed sit still in their chairs. They may be roused at 4 A.M. to begin the day's rounds.

The ritual has a compulsive quality. In one hospital, where mentally subnormal children share a section of a general pediatric ward, they are roused at 4 A.M. and the pediatric patients some hours later (13). J. Tizard's description of the Fountain Hospital, which was a large London institution under progressive medical direction, supports many of these observations (14).

By contrast, several of the features of the rehabilitation unit described by Coser can be recognized in day centers with a therapeutic ideology that care for mentally subnormal children who are living at home. An example of such a unit has existed in Salford. It has catered to children so retarded that they require the care and assistance ordinarily given to infants. Their incapacity is in some cases a result of the severity of their physical and mental handicaps, in some a result of emotional disorders, and in others of the early age at which they are admitted. The staff are as constantly active as in the hospital ward, but it is activity centered in the interests of the children; it aims at creating the conditions for the children's play and activities. They are preoccupied with finding fresh means of stimulating the children and communicating with them.

In relation to thorough sociological study, these observations are the equivalent of clinical diagnosis without the support of laboratory investigation. Work has been done to provide measuring instruments, but they wait to be applied (15, 16). With confidence thus qualified, one may assert that alienation from therapeutic goals is often found in large hospital units for mentally subnormal children and that commitment to therapeutic goals is often found in day centers.

This divergence in goals and values is not the result merely of differences in knowledge and ability available to hospitals and day centers. The same technical resources can be brought to bear in both settings. Furthermore, some physicians in charge of mental-deficiency hospitals profess therapeutic aims. Their policies, however, do not easily permeate lower levels in the social structure of the hospital. Similarly in mental hospitals the ideology of the staff at various levels, though showing a degree of congruence with prevailing policy, also varies independently of that policy (15). By contrast, in the few day-care centers of which I have knowledge the educational and therapeutic policies of the administration seem to be adopted by a majority of the staff at all levels, although not without conflict. Even the domestic staff sometimes shares in educational tasks.

The execution of a therapeutic policy hangs on a long chain of transmission. The goals of those in authority must reach nurses and their assistants on the wards and teachers in classes and be espoused by them, for it is they who minister to patients. To convert policy into reality, the staff must have accurate knowledge of the policy, as often it does not; if it is to accept the aims of the policy, it must come to share the ideas and values on which they are based; if finally it is to act on the policy, it must have the competence to carry it out and the facilities to make it possible. The sequence leading to action may be interrupted at any or all of these points. The result is the gap so often discovered between averred and actual performance.

Patient Care and Social Structure. The main source of the traditional mental-deficiency hospitals' impermeability to the therapeutic values of the day centers, in my view, is to be found in their *social structure,* that is, in the forms of their persisting relationships. Coser's study demonstrated that within similar social structures different medical objectives based on contrary values could be given effect.[3] This room for variation and maneuver within social structures is not unlimited. Some goals and the value systems that underlie them may be incompatible with particular forms of organization; they are unlikely to be implemented without revolutionary change in social structure.

Structure delimits the roles in which caretakers and patients participate, and it influences their quality. A critical distinction in formal organization is that mental-deficiency hospitals belong to the class of institutions described by E. Goffman as "total," whereas day-care centers do not (17). Goffman took the large mental hospital as a working model of a total institution: Inmates reside there involuntarily, subordinate to a bureaucratic hierarchy of office and centralized authority, and all their active roles are encapsulated within the institution. In this situation patients develop what can be described as a culture of subordination, by means of which they "work the system." Within this patient culture, efforts at therapy tend to be interpreted as a moral and psychological assault upon the self, despite the often good intentions of authority.

This description must be modified in the case of severe mental and physical handicap. The institution encompasses not only all the effective roles of the patient but his whole remaining life. Passive dependence then becomes the natural state of patients already dependent because of physical and mental handicaps. The socialization of inmates of an institution can be only toward assimilating the subcultures to be

3. Not much detail is provided about the social structure of the two units, but, as they were part of the same hospital, one takes them to be similar.

found within it. In the case of severe subnormality, the extreme dependence of patients gives overriding importance to the subculture of the caretakers.

Day centers do not labor under the same structural handicaps as do total institutions. Patients are only partially committed to them, usually with all parties to the placement willing. We need to review how day centers might differ from total institutions in their effects. Two aspects of structure will be considered: one, the complexity of the total set of roles of the caretakers, as determined by the number and types of their roles at any one point in time; two, the content of the roles of caretakers in relation to patients, as determined by the rate of flow of patients into care through a period of time.

The Complexity of Role Sets. In her findings on nurses, Coser put forward the proposition that their contrasting behavior could be ascribed to the complexity of the set of roles in which they were engaged by their work. The proposition applies well to services for the mentally subnormal. Where a staff member has a *complex set of roles* (as he does in the small scope of the day center in relating with children, with colleagues, with superiors, with an array of visiting specialists, and with parents), he is subject to a continuous process of articulating each of these roles with others. He must adjust to the children, colleagues, and superiors, who are the reciprocal role players, and he must reconcile his several roles each with the other. In addition to the process of articulation, a complex set of roles brings about wide and frequent interaction in a single setting. This range of interaction tends to make each role visible and accountable.

Continual revisions of what can properly be expected in each role follow from the process of articulation and from the constraints of visibility. Revisions create congruence of aims between participants. Kushlick described the potential conflicts of day-center staff with doctors, social workers, psychologists, remedial teachers, and other staff, which arose out of the different requirements of their roles (18). Potential conflict was painful to the staff, but suffering was rewarded. In the attempts to resolve conflict, staff members articulated their roles and moved toward congruence in their aims.

Where staff has a *simple set of roles* (as it does in most mental-deficiency hospitals with their long, narrow chains of authority), the diminished range of interaction reduces the stimulus to revise expectations, as well as reducing visibility, accountability, and social control. A lesser congruence and commitment to goals are likely to be achieved than with a complex set of roles.

An expression of the role set is its influence in shaping and modifying the *reference groups* by which the staff sets its standards. These reference groups, in a local community setting and in a segregated total institution, may overlap in some respects but are likely to diverge in many (19).

Day centers are thus embedded in a network of relationships with the local community. Local ties act in subtle ways to maintain staff commitment to therapeutic and educational goals, that is, to the aim of socializing children to the larger culture. One way is through the exchange of information. Parents learn from staff, and staff from parents, about the progress and the problems of the child. Staff becomes aware of the contributions it can sometimes make to the child's maintenance and better integration within the family.

A second way in which local ties maintain staff commitment is by communicating community expectations. In the day center, staff can be isolated with difficulty from the influence of the surrounding community. In the hospital, staff can be isolated with ease by its totality as an institution, by its distant site, and by the jural procedures that may remove parental rights and the patient's civil status. The most pressing frame of reference for hospital staff is likely to be colleagues and superiors and not any local community (19).

At a day center, parents need not be in face-to-face contact with staff for their presence to be felt. Pressures can be brought to bear directly, through elected municipal councilmen, or through "consumer" associations of parents. In one instance the young working-class mother of a hemiplegic child observed a staff member administer a slap to her child. The result of the subsequent confrontation between mother and agency was an upheaval that led to the transfer of the staff member to a center for adults. In this case the mother acted through elected councilmen, through the health officer as nominal head of the agency, and through the threat of publicity. In a far-off mental-deficiency hospital the observation and the confrontation would usually not be possible.

The explicit role of the child in relation to the staff of the day center is that of a dependent recipient of care, as it is in the hospital. At the same time, however, he has roles in relation to his family and to the surrounding community. While the child attends the day center, these roles remain latent. The significant difference from the hospital is that in the day center such latent roles are given implicit recognition by the staff, for family and community are included in its frame of reference. In the day center even those children who live in residential nurseries and have no latent family roles participate in relations influenced by other children who do have families.

Subsidiary factors affect the complexity of role sets and hence commitment to goals. One is the ratio of staff to patients. Day centers have not had difficulty in recruiting personnel from their local areas and can maintain ratios as high as one to five. Hospitals for mental subnormality do have difficulty in recruiting and have low ratios of staff to patients.

An advantage in numbers need not be crucial, as many generals have learned and as Lenin well understood in devising his Bolshevik party. Coser's study shows the overriding influence of commitment to goals on performance. But her study also suggests that there is a critical level beyond which the staff finds the effort to cope with numbers hopeless and withdraws from the task. The lack of staff in the mental-deficiency hospitals is self-perpetuating, for it arises from the alienation to which in turn it contributes.

A second subsidiary factor that influences commitment to goals may be *size* alone. Large-scale organization is often taken to be both economic and efficient. The good general hospital of modern times, it is said, is the big hospital; only in large units is it possible to concentrate the range of facilities, equipment, and technical skill sufficient for all needs. Yet all the advantages are not with giants. In one study of hospitals, communication in the hierarchy of nurses and between nurses and doctors seemed to be less effective the larger the hospital (20). A national study of institutions for old people in Britain found a consistent inverse relationship between size and the quality of amenities, of care, and of living (21). In another national British study the catering in large hospitals was found inferior to that in small ones (22). Increase in the size of state mental hospitals in New England after 1850 against the recommendation of the leading psychiatrists is given as a cause for the decline of "moral treatment" (23). In total institutions, however, the factor of size has rarely been distinct from that of staff-patient ratio. The factors that intervene between the size of the hospital and its effects must be more closely specified.

In the hospitals for mental subnormality, large size and parsimony contribute to poor care. These subsidiary problems could be overcome by reform without a revolution in the social structure of the hospital.

Caretaker Roles and the Flow of Patients. The flow of patients through institutions puts an important imprint on the roles of the staff who take care of them. Constant replacement of patients aids in maintaining commitment to therapeutic and educational goals, for it can give the staff both a sense of continuing development and responsiveness in their patients and a link with the surrounding community. In New England at the height of the "moral treatment" era, when, as the vivid accounts of Charles Dickens and others tell us, some mental hospitals were not alienated institutions (24), the mobility of mental patients was considerable. It is reported that at the Worcester State Hospital in Massachusetts in the 1830s, 70 per cent of patients admitted for illness of less than one year's duration were discharged. In the 1880s, after the decline of moral treatment, the discharge rate was reported as about 5 per cent (25).

Although other forces joined to erode moral treatment (for instance, the altered social status of mental hospital patients of the late nineteenth century, many of whom were indigent), the point of the contrast need not be waived. Inside the hospital the passage of patients provides feedback and reinforcement for a therapeutic ideology. Good results are the preservative of therapeutic goals. Movement and changing populations of patients give grounds (if not justification) for inferring good results.

Several statistical reports of the nineteenth-century mental hospitals in New England seemed calculated to meet the need for feedback. In a follow-up of 1,173 patients admitted to the Worcester State Hospital from 1833 to 1846 and taken to 1881, it is claimed that 50 per cent had no recurrences. The data drew criticism for confusing episodes of admission with patients, for using discharges instead of admissions as the denominator of the rates, and for excluding chronic cases from the numerator (26). Whatever the defects of these statistics, they served to bolster belief in rates of cure.

Entries and exits are more than a matter of movement. The physical transits of an individual through a hospital are accompanied by social transitions. The procedures surrounding admission and discharge can be likened to *rites de passage*. Each entry is accompanied by the transition to the status of patient, each exit by the transition to some other social status. Each of these social statuses carries with it clinical connotations of sickness or well-being. The discharged patient may not be regarded as entirely well by his doctor, but at worst he has exchanged the role of mental hospital patient for the chronic ambulant sick role with its attendant social obligations and the stigma of ex-patient.

The career in the hospital of the patient with severe mental and physical handicap involves few physical and social transitions. Thus the flow of severely subnormal children through the hospitals serving the Salford area was barely perceptible (although the data do not reflect movement between wards). Thirty-three (87 per cent) of thirty-eight children admitted to the hospital in the fifteen-year period 1949–1963 were still in the hospital at the end of a five-year stay, and the remaining five had died (27).

In the day center the movement of patients, although slow, was clearly perceptible. The variety of cases was greater in type and grade than in the hospital, and so too was the variety of possible outcomes. Data for the day center cover only the five years 1959–1963, for the center did not exist before 1959. Of sixty-six entrants, twenty-seven had moved into other educational groups as they qualified for higher levels through individual development. Eighteen were removed for a miscellany of reasons (five of the eighteen went into the hospital, and six died). Only twenty-one of the sixty-six remained, that is, 32 per cent, compared with 87 per cent in the hospital group. This geographical and social mobility gives social expression to the development and socialization of individuals, in analogy with the social roles accorded normal children as they move through schools.

The contrast between the flow of patients in the mental-deficiency hospital and the day centers is not explained by the severity of handicap. In institutions in Southern England about 25 per cent are incontinent and bedfast (28). In the day center about 15 per cent were similarly handicapped. No handicap or combination of handicaps, neither autism, blindness, spasticity, deafness, nor incontinence, was a bar to entry. The rates of patient flow can be expected to deflect therapeutic goals in the mental-deficiency hospital and to reinforce them in the day-care unit.

Analysis of the conflict of therapeutic values and social structure in total institutions leads one to ask whether or not the conflict can be resolved. In attempts to do so in mental hospitals, revolutionary reorderings of organizational structure have been tried (29). Success has not been complete (30). In mental-deficiency hospitals few revolutions as radical have been attempted. The outlook for success is poorer because of the irreversible physical dependence of the patients.

One must raise questions about the future of day care as well. Will mobility through the day-care center be maintained, say, two decades from now? Will cases silt up as their numbers increase and the therapeutic impetus run down? In the discussion on experimental evaluation, we noted the impact that enthusiasm could have on cohorts who enter early cycles of treatment. (See p. 198.) In the day-care units, we may be observing such a periodic phenomenon as R. Frankenberg described in a Welsh village (31). Communal activity flourished in cycles, with brass bands, and football teams, and Eisteddfod choirs. Activity died out as irresoluble conflicts emerged among individuals representing opposed social interests. In the case of centers for day care, the irresoluble conflicts of the future, in the dimension relating to individuals, could be between therapeutic goals and the failure of patients to respond and progress. In another dimension relating to families, the conflict could be between the lifelong dependency of patients and the capacity of families to support them. At this point, therefore, it may be appropriate to examine the issues of care, first as they affect individuals and then as they affect families.

The Impact of Care on Individual Development

A doctrine of therapeutic optimism could not be supported in the face of manifest failure. Purposeless activity cannot be afforded while there remains a scarcity of services. From the point of view of the individual patient, this challenge poses two questions: One, are severely subnormal children capable of intellectual, emotional, and social development? Two, given such development, how far can it be promoted?

Ordinary observation as well as formal testing leave no doubt that severely subnormal children, while much retarded in their timetables, are capable of development (32). This capacity is quite obvious in Salford, where children progress through a series of educational day centers (33). According to the child's level of ability, these centers provide successively free play and nursery school activity, the basic elements of formal education, social and occupational training, and, finally, in some cases even productive roles. One consequence of this grading is a rough sorting out by chronological age in the various classrooms, although in any one class the range is wide and the standard deviation high.

In some texts the statement is still to be found that on reaching adulthood mentally subnormal persons soon begin to deteriorate. The legend of deterioration may have a basis in observation. For the cause of the phenomenon, however, one should look not to the subnormal person, but to the institutions in which he has been confined and observed.

The intellectual, emotional, and social capacities of severely subnormal children can be promoted or hindered. S. A. Kirk showed how development could be promoted by a special setting (34). He exposed an experimental group of young mentally subnormal children at preschool ages to intensive educational stimulus, and he gave detailed care to correcting physical handicaps to learning. On a battery of tests including measures of intelligence and verbal skills, the experimental group made greater progress than a matched control group. The physically handicapped and the brain damaged made progress as well as the remainder, although more slowly.

J. G. Lyle and J. Tizard showed indirectly how development could be hampered by a setting (34). They provided evidence of recovery from the retarding effects of life in the mental deficiency hospital. Lyle showed that subnormal children living in the hospital were at a disadvantage in verbal mental age compared with others living at home; disadvantage accrued with age. Tizard tested an experimental group of subnormal children, drawn from the Fountain Hospital and placed in the experimental Brooklands Home, against a matched comparison group that remained in the hospital. The experimental residential unit aimed at a family atmosphere and at an educational program that emphasized nursery school methods. In a relatively short time the experimental children had achieved an advantage in verbal intelligence and had made manifest gains in social behavior.

Similar negative effects due to institutions are revealed by the work of D. J. Stedman and D. H. Eichorn (36). They compared mongols admitted to an institution within four months of birth with a group that remained in their families.

Those in the institution made slower progress in both verbal and motor skills than those at home.

Two points from this study are of special interest. First, the children in the institution appeared to learn from each other. When some had learned to talk, or to walk, others followed suit rapidly. At the same time, the children appeared to be limited in learning by the limitations of the peers they learned from, so that speech even retrogressed after its acquisition. This result emphasizes the importance of the quality of stimulus as well as of its quantity. It also emphasizes the influence of peer groups on patterns of behavior in very young children.[4]

The second noteworthy point is that the institution with which the family environment was being compared was not a typical institution for mental subnormality. The experimental unit, the authors report, resembled the Brooklands Home set up by Tizard as a demonstration.

These results affirm that in the task of socializing the subnormal child, the institutions so far devised cannot compete with the intact family. Several other studies support these conclusions about families and institutions, although one or two conflict with them. On either side, most have flaws in design. By no means does every family provide an ideal milieu for socializing children, and some are harmful; but on the average, families, with the support of schools and peers, do the work better than residential institutions do.

An analysis of the advantages families have in socializing their members may help in the devising of better residential institutions. One advantage of the family lies with its high commitment to attaining for the child social roles as near normal as possible. A second advantage is its high staff-patient ratio. On these counts the superiority of the family over the institution is self-evident. A third advantage of the family is in the content of the set of roles it makes available to the patient, in terms of the balance of formal authority and informal feeling. This count needs exposition. It involves the extent to

4. In normal children too the social milieu and the behavior of peers appears to influence the acquisition of developmental skills, such as control of excretory sphincters (37).

which social relations between adults and children are ordered, on the one hand by diffuse affective ties and on the other by a formal hierarchy with defined functions. One polar extreme in the balance of authority and feeling is seen in the nuclear family and another in the typical large residential institution.

In the nuclear family, authority is vested in parents. The inevitable conflict between adults and children that results from the exercise of authority is contained by cross-cutting bonds of affection, by loyalty to a corporate notion of the family, and by the values and sanctions of the culture. They maintain the family as an institution in society and also assure the continuity of relations in individual families. The relationships between parents and children are diffuse and multiple. They revolve around manifold functions and are not limited to any specific ones (38).

A consequence of relationships of the family in industrial societies seems to be that there is no marked cultural differentiation into "we" and "they" between the adults in authority and the children who must obey. Such a cultural differentiation is widespread in large institutions and probably characteristic of mental-deficiency hospitals. In typical large institutions the relations of children with adults tend to be limited by specific functions. The functions include nursing care, feeding, and dressing but are often dominated by those in which the adults represent authority and discipline. This authority stems from an office and not from the culturally approved ties of kinship. Under these conditions the children can be expected to form diffuse affective relationships with their peers more readily than with adults. Loyalty is primarily to peers, even if a corporate notion of the institution exists among them; children may band together against adults, and they may see cooperation with authority as treachery to peers.

Authority, however, is not without powerful effects on relations between peers. One study found that social position in a group of boys was altered by their experience of an institution (39). On entry, sociometric measures showed that the most preferred members of the group were also the most intelligent. After some time these more intelligent leaders had moved to peripheral positions in the group. They were also the boys who had been most frequently disciplined. It appeared that their enterprise and activity had earned them, first, the disapprobation of the institution authorities as troublemakers and, later, that of their peers as "dangerous" associates.

Less extreme variants of total institutions than are depicted here can be found. Allowing that there is a play of forces between staff and children in institutions, we can be sure, however, that the standards held by children and staff diverge more than in most families and that the feeling between them is less intense, less positive, and more often hostile. In other words, there is a degree of alienation of the child from the adult world. This cultural divergence between generations is likely to be exaggerated when children are many and adults are few and when the institution and its officers do not share the culture from which the children come. In such circumstances socialization for everyday life must be impeded as compared with the family.

The family is not a perfect socializing agent; it too imposes limitations on socialization. Mentally subnormal children in families probably suffer deprivation of stimuli and experience relative to their siblings. There are places to which they will not be taken, games to which they will not be admitted, explorations they will not be permitted to make, talk into which they cannot enter. The child of school age with the mental age of an infant may not be allowed the same latitude for experiment and learning as his infant sibling of the same mental age (40).

Such relative deprivation may be remediable. Despite the severe limitations of the abilities of the children, their defects are not global. One study in Salford compared severely subnormal children with a group of nursery school children matched for mental age (40). Although the subnormal children showed less verbal facility and fewer associations in response to pictorial themes, they were not less creative and imaginative in play. Some avenues of approach may thus be more rewarding than others.

It is on the assumption that appropriately varied stimuli

can compensate for stimulus deprivation and promote development that the Salford day center bases its activities. Throughout the day these children are engaged in individual play, or in group play during which the mobile ones act as messengers to connect the most immobile or sense-deprived with the others. Parallel with these activities the staff seek contact with the children through tactile, kinetic, visual, auditory, and social stimuli. Some children introduced to this regime made visible progress.

One must make the reservation that the end point of their development is uncertain. Without a comparison group, the degree to which development may exceed what the children might reach unaided must remain unknown. At the least, development will be beyond what could be reached in the traditional mental-deficiency institution because whatever the end point may be, there is no such thing as a social vacuum. The effect of any milieu, whether or not it is deliberately manipulated, must be taken into account.

Impact of Community Care on the Family

It emerges from the preceding discussion that ordinarily the family will be beneficial for a mentally subnormal child. The converse does not hold. It cannot be said that ordinarily the mentally subnormal child is beneficial for a family. The ability of the nuclear family to cope with the permanent dependence and sometimes the total incapacity of one of its members is the unknown in the community care equation.

In the child's family of origin, parents alone and not sibs or other close relatives would wish or might be able to undertake continuing care. In most industrial societies this is a given fact and not a matter for moralizing. A lavish investment has to be made for small return. Parental support itself must be limited in duration. The inexorable stages of the family cycle disperse the children and leave aging parental couples who themselves must decline into dependence and death. Alternative forms of residential care must of necessity be devised for mentally subnormal persons without families and for exceptional cases. Not all families are competent socializing agents, and some may be more damaging than even large institutions can be.

For the rest, the question remains of the cost to the nuclear family of supporting a permanently dependent member in the context of an open-class society. How is this cost to be weighed against the manifest gains of the mentally subnormal child who can remain with his family? The account is a complicated one.

The risk of social and psychological disorders among the parents of mentally subnormal children seems high (41). For the most part this view depends on clinical impression and studies without controls. Little is known about the effects on the family of removing a mentally subnormal child to an institution. Certainly ambivalence and vacillation are a common response to admission. Tizard and J. Grad found in the 1950s that London families with mentally subnormal children at home were burdened with many more problems in such matters as housing, finance, health, and social interaction than those families where the patients had been admitted to institutions (2). Sixty-six per cent had three or more problems of concern when the child was at home and 45 per cent when the child was in an institution. Nevertheless only 17 per cent of families with a subnormal child at home said they had considered admission to an institution, and 29 per cent of families whose children had been admitted claimed that they would not have done so had supportive services or better housing been available. These families were handicapped by physical and material burdens. Yet mothers whose children remained in the family seemed in better mental state than those whose children were in a hospital, and there was no significant difference between the families in their closeness and harmony.

The concept of the subnormal child as a family "burden" is too restrictive to describe the complex relationships of child and family. A family's choices are limited by its material, social, intellectual, and emotional resources. Their decisions may be forced by extreme physical circumstances, especially if there is no adequate structure of supporting services. But many family choices will depend on the psychological balance of social forces and conflicting values. For instance, in some families any loss of outside social contact due to the child's need for care is weighed lightly against the obligations and the satisfactions of providing the needed care.

B. Farber devised a parsimonious set of instruments to compare the responses of families whose mentally subnormal children were at home with those whose children were in institutions (42). In the great majority of families he could demonstrate no significant effects by his measures of marital integration and of communication between parent and child. Unfortunately, the weight of this finding is diminished by the unrepresentative method of sampling, for it relied on volunteers from parents' associations and took parents living together at the time of the survey instead of the parents of all children at risk. Data concerning the clinical and other attributes of the subnormal children themselves are not given. The omission is important; the child, whether in the home or elsewhere, is a party to family interaction.

Certain effects could be demonstrated in closely defined circumstances that concerned a small proportion of families. In these families, although the premarital predictions for marital stability were unfavorable, the parents nonetheless attained a common orientation. In such families "marital integration" was poorer with the mentally subnormal child at home than in an institution (43). This result can be taken to mean that the added strain of a child at home disturbed an already delicate balance. A somewhat similar result was obtained for families in delicate balance in an intensive study of fourteen families whose children were left with permanent disabilities from severe paralytic poliomyelitis (44).

With regard to sibs, in Farber's study communication between parents and children appeared to be somewhat distorted when the retarded child was at home, although in curiously different ways for boys and girls. Boys overestimated their parents' dissatisfaction with them; girls underestimated it (45). The results presumably refer to families in the raw state, without support from services; no mention is made of their intervention.

These are meager differences. Families do not get unequivocal advantages from admitting a mentally subnormal child to an institution. Even when a substantial difference exists, as in practical matters that can be resolved by adequate resources, many problems persist after admission (2). While the child lives, he has a social position through which he continues to influence the relationships of his family even if he is displaced from it. Detailed knowledge of the results of various dispositions is sparse. Agencies may therefore do well to assist families in their preferences rather than to limit their choices by dogmatic advice and by keeping them dependent on a narrow range of services in short supply.

In Salford it has been possible to alleviate at least the material and social problems for many such families. To give this relief, the services must be comprehensive. A comprehensive service meets the whole range of needs of both the subnormal child and his family throughout his life cycle. To do so, the multiple agencies that participate in the care of subnormal persons or impinge on it must be coordinated.

First, local day care is provided for *all* severely subnormal children in the community, whatever the type and degree of handicap. Day care is a relief for the family as well as an educational advantage to the child.

Second, the services have tried to make real the assurance to families that residential care would be made available should the demands of care exceed their capacity for it. The preferred form of care is in small local hostels, residential homes, and foster homes. Few circumstances cannot be coped with by this range of services. It is a rare case that requires continuous skilled nursing and technology such as a hospital is expected to provide, and in contemporary conditions to use hospital facilities merely as substitute homes is wasteful. At the very least, the one third of children (and possibly a larger proportion of adults) who reside in institutions and have no major handicaps could be better placed elsewhere (14).

Third, every effort has been made to bring to bear coordinated medical and social casework as soon as potential severe subnormality is recognized in a child. Effective case finding by the techniques of public health is a precondition for such coordinated work. It should begin from birth and even before. Normality at birth cannot be assumed if cases are to be found early and to be given the full benefit of intervention and support (46).

The administrative framework for coordinated clinical work has been achieved by giving the local consultant pediatrician access to patients in all facilities. Through the public health department he reaches patients and their families in the maternity and child welfare services and in the mental-health service, and he enjoys access through the hospitals as of right. The nature of the problems of coordination can be derived from the previous chapter on the coordination of services for mental illness. The points of resistance are differently distributed, but their sources are the same.

Affirmation of good results may stand the test of faith, but they need to be submitted to the more rigorous tests of science. The discovery in Britain of the virtues of local care for mentally subnormal persons is accident as much as design. The day centers were set up in part because of the failure of the hospitals to meet the demand for care. The responsibility for planned experiment, for evaluation, and for the culling of exact knowledge lies before us.

References

(1) Kushlick A. 1961 Subnormality in Salford in Susser M. W. and Kushlick A. *A Report on the Mental Health Services of the City of Salford for the Year 1960* City of Salford, Eng., Health Department pp. 18–48

(2) Tizard J. and Grad J. 1961 *The Mentally Handicapped and Their Families: a Social Survey* Maudsley Monogr 7, London, Oxford

(3) Mercer J. 1965 Social system perspective and clinical perspective: frames of reference for understanding career patterns of persons labelled as mentally retarded *Soc Prob* 13:19–34

(4) Leeson J. E. 1963 Place of the hospital in the care of the mentally subnormal *Brit Med J* 1:713–717

(5) Leeson J. E. 1964 *Demand for Care in Hospitals for the Mentally Subnormal* Manchester, Manchester Regional Hospital Board

(6) Cowen E. L., Underberg R. P. and Verillo T. 1961 *Adjustment to Visual Disability in Adolescence* New York, American Foundation for the Blind

(7) Rosenberg M. 1962 The dissonant religious context and emotional disturbance *Amer J Sociol* 68:1–10

(8) Semmel M. I. and Dickson S. 1966 Connotative reactions of college students to disability labels *Exceptional Children* 32:443–450

(9) Richardson S. A., Hastorf A. H., Goodman N. and Dornbusch S. M. 1961 Cultural uniformity in reaction to physical disabilities *Amer Sociol Rev* 26:241–247

Goodman N., Richardson S. A., Dornbusch S. M. and Hastorf A. H. 1963 Variant reactions to physical disabilities *Amer Sociol Rev* 28:429–435

(10) Coser R. L. 1963 Alienation and the social structure: case analysis of a hospital in Freidson E. ed. *The Hospital in Modern Society* New York, Free Press pp. 231–265

(11) Kanner L. 1964 *A History of the Care and Study of the Mentally Retarded* Springfield, Ill., Thomas

(12) Deutsch A. 1949 *The Mentally Ill in America: A History of Their Care and Treatment from Colonial Times* New York, Columbia University Press

(13) Raines N. Personal communication

(14) Tizard J. 1964 *Community Services for the Mentally Handicapped* London, Oxford

(15) Gilbert D. C. and Levinson D. J. 1957 Custodialism and humanism in staff ideology in Greenblatt M., Levinson D. J. and Williams R. H. eds. *The Patient and the Mental Hospital* New York, Free Press pp. 20–35

(16) Carstairs G. M. and Heron A. 1957 The social environment of mental hospital patients: a measure of staff attitudes in Greenblatt M., Levinson D. J. and Williams R. H. eds. *The Patient and the Mental Hospital* New York, Free Press pp. 219–226

Gilbert D. C. and Levinson D. J. 1957 Role performance, ideology, and personality in mental hospital aides in Greenblatt M., Levinson D. J. and Williams R. H. eds. *The Patient and the Mental Hospital* New York, Free Press

Pine F. and Levinson D. J. 1957 Two patterns of ideology, role conception and personality among hospital aides in Greenblatt M., Levinson D. J. and Williams R. H. eds. *The Patient and the Mental Hospital* New York, Free Press pp. 209–218

Jackson J. 1964 Towards the comparative study of mental hospitals: characteristics of the treatment environment in Wessen A. F. ed. *The Psychiatric Hospital as a Social System* Springfield, Ill., Thomas pp. 35–87

(17) Goffman E. 1958 Characteristics of total institutions in *Symposium on Preventive and Social Psychiatry* Washington, D.C., U.S. Government Printing Office pp. 43–84

(18) Kushlick A. 1962 Problems of co-ordination in the centers for the subnormal in Susser M. W. and Kushlick A. *A Report on the Mental Health Services in the City of Salford for the Year 1961* City of Salford, Eng., Health Department pp. 7–11

(19) Freidson E. 1960 Client control in medical practice *Amer J Sociol* 65:374–382

(20) Revans R. W. 1964 *Standards for Morale: Cause and Effect in Hospitals* London, Oxford

(21) Townsend P. 1964 *The Last Refuge: A Survey of Residential Institutions and Homes for the Aged in England and Wales* London, Routledge

(22) Platt B. S., Eddy T. P. and Pellet P. L. 1963 *Food in Hospitals* London, Oxford

(23) Bockoven J. S. 1957 Some relationships between cultural attitudes toward individuality and care of the mentally ill: an historical study in Greenblatt M., Levinson D. J. and Williams R. H. eds. *The Patient and the Mental Hospital* New York, Free Press pp. 517–526

(24) Dickens C. 1842 *American Notes for General Circulation* cited in Greenblatt M. and Bockoven J. S. Social treatment in Greenblatt M., York R. H., Brown E. L. and Hyde R. W. eds. *From Custodial to Therapeutic Patient Care in Mental Hospitals* New York, Russell Sage Foundation

(25) Greenblatt M. and Bockoven J. S. 1955 Social treatment in Greenblatt M., York R. H., Brown E. L. and Hyde R. W. eds. *From Custodial to Therapeutic Patient Care in Mental Hospitals* New York, Russell Sage Foundation pp. 407–427

(26) Earle P. 1892 The curability of insanity in Tuke D. H. ed. *Dictionary of Psychological Medicine* London, Churchill pp. 321–324

(27) Susser M. W. ed. 1965 *Reports and Papers on the Mental Health Service of Salford for the year 1964* City of Salford, Eng., Health Department

(28) Kushlick A. 1965 Community care for the subnormal: the size of the problem *Proc Roy Soc Med* 58:374–380

(29) Jones M., Baker A., Freeman T., Merry J., Pomryn B. A., Sandler J. and Tuxford J. 1953 *The Therapeutic Community: A New Treatment Method in Psychiatry* New York, Basic Books

Greenblatt M., York R. H., Brown E. L. and Hyde R. W. 1955 *From Custodial to Therapeutic Patient Care in Mental Hospitals* New York, Russell Sage Foundation

Von Mering O. and King S. H. 1957 *Remotivating The Mental Patient* New York, Russell Sage Foundation

(30) Rapoport R. N., Rapoport R. and Rosow I. 1960 *Community as Doctor: New Perspectives on a Therapeutic Community* Springfield, Ill., Thomas

(31) Frankenberg R. 1957 *Village on the Border: A Social Study of Religion, Politics and Football in a North Wales Community* London, Cohen & West

(32) Woodward M. 1959 The behavior of idiots, interpreted by Piaget's theory of sensorimotor development *Brit J Ed Psychol* 39:60–71

Share J., Koch R. and Webb A. 1964 The longitudinal development of infants and young children with Down's syndrome (mongolism) *Amer J Ment Defic* 68:685–692

(33) Cashdan A. and Lunzer E. A. 1963 Teaching the mentally handicapped in Susser M. W. *Report on the Mental Health Service for the City of Salford for 1962* City of Salford, Eng., Health Department pp. 33–36

Cashdan A. and Lunzer E. A. 1964 Teaching the mentally handicapped in Susser M W. ed. *Reports and Papers on the Mental Health Service of the City of Salford for 1963* City of Salford, Eng., Health Department

(34) Kirk S. A., Karnes M. B., Graham R. and Sloan W. 1958 *Early Education of the Mentally Retarded: An Experimental Study* Urbana, University of Illinois Press

(35) Lyle J. G. 1959 The effect of an institution environment upon the verbal development of institutional children: 1 Verbal intelligence *J Ment Defic Res* 3:122–128

Lyle J. G. 1960 The effect of an institution environment upon the verbal development of institutional children: 2 Speech and language 3 The Brooklands residential family unit *J Ment Defic Res* 4:1–13, 14–23

Tizard J. 1960 Residential care of mentally handicapped children *Brit Med J* 1:1041–1046

(36) Stedman D. J. and Eichorn D. H. 1964 A comparison of the growth and development of institutionalized and home-reared mongoloids during infancy and early childhood *Amer J Ment Defic* 69:391–401

(37) Stein Z. A. and Susser M. W. 1967 Social factors in the development of sphincter control *Develop Med Child Neurol* 9:52–61

(38) Gluckman M. 1959 *Custom and Conflict in Africa* Oxford, Blackwell

Parsons T. 1951 *The Social System* New York, Free Press

(39) Dentler R. A. and Mackler B. 1962 Mental ability and sociometric status among retarded children *Psychol Bull* 59:273–283

Dentler R. A. and Mackler B. 1964 Effects on sociometric status of institutional pressure to adjust among retarded children *Brit J Soc Clin Psychol* 3:81–89

(40) Hulme I. 1965 A comparative study of the play, language and reasoning of severely subnormal children and children of similar mental age. Unpublished M.Ed. thesis, Manchester University

Hulme I. and Lunzer E. A. 1966 Play, language and reasoning in subnormal children *J of Child Psychology and Psychiatry* 7:107–123

(41) Adams M. 1956 Social work with mental defectives: Part 1 *Case Conf* 3:100–107

Adams M. 1957 Social work with mental defectives: Part 2 *Case Conf* 4:2–9

Holt K. S. 1958 The home care of the severely mentally retarded *Pediatrics* 22:746–755

(42) Farber B. 1959 *Effects of a Severely Mentally Retarded Child on Family Integration* Monogr Soc Res Child Developm 24

(43) Farber B. 1960 *Family Organization and Crisis: Maintenance of Integration in Families with a Severely Mentally Retarded Child* Monogr Soc Res Child Develop 25

(44) Davis F. 1963 *Passage Through Crisis* New York, Bobbs-Merrill

(45) Farber B. and Jenné C. 1963 *Family Organization and Parent-Child Communication: Parents and Siblings of a Retarded Child* Monogr Soc Res Child Develop 28:7

(46) Mackay R. I. 1964 The pediatrician and the problem of subnormality in Susser M. W. ed. *Report on the Mental Health Services of the City of Salford for 1963* City of Salford, Eng., Health Department pp. 36–38

14

Epilogue

In these pages the facts of experience and research in the community care of mental disorder have been subjected to the interpretations of social medicine. Relevant knowledge has been turned about and explored, and the degree to which this knowledge is secure or speculative has been weighed. The touchstone of relevance has been the relation of knowledge to real problems encountered in the working field.

The practitioner is bound to ask certain questions as he does his work: what course of action is most needed? what is the likelihood that a particular action will succeed? how shall success be judged? The practitioner who poses these questions has been urged to dig out the assumptions wrapped up in particular programs, to make them explicit, and to confront them. He who does this diligently may often appear to have an opposing magic to that of Midas. What he touches, even gently, turns not to gold but to dust. Yet this course should be pursued with resolution. It may deflate some claims and inhibit some ventures, but it is essential to sustained programs for the care of mental disorder.

The direction of social and economic development ensures that community programs will persist and grow. A critical view will prevent the disillusion that is likely to follow the dispersal of energy in irrelevant action. Action is irrelevant when elaborate evaluations are made of minimal programs, when research tests unformulated hypotheses, and when great medical institutions deal intensively with labyrinthine complexities of minor psychic disorders while major disorders pass them by.

Community programs will help to overcome a lag in concepts about the functioning of health and medical services. This backwardness is exemplified by institutions that conceive of their role in terms of the individual care of episodes of illness at the point of delivery. The lag is more evident in the United States, where social change is also more rapid and the needs it generates more acute, than in many other countries.

Lags and shifts in concepts of health and disease are a symptom of change and of attempts to accommodate to it. Since the Renaissance, medicine has made powerful use of the concept of disease as a specific entity; it became the dominant concept of nineteenth-century medicine. Today's physician, who much of the time must deal with chronic noninfectious disease, is forced to think less of entities and more of systems. Often he does not cure or wait for recovery. In chronic metabolic, heart, and kidney disorders, the physician's main effort is to maintain the physiologic system, and he comes to think of the patient's condition in these terms.

In similar fashion, at the epidemiologic level, thinking about specific agents has been modified. The certainty of the germ theory has been abandoned for theories of multiple causation and interacting systems. The social and economic system encompasses many different levels of organization, from the social through the individual down to the cellular and the molecular. Each level of organization has a multiplicity of factors, which can be conceived of as an interacting system. These factors interact with each other, and each level of organization interacts with the next.

As concepts and scientific techniques have advanced, so can analyses of the social and economic system and of the physical environment advance. Health patterns and health organizations can be analyzed as part of that system. It should be noted, however, that the difficulties faced in the analysis of systems are not merely a function of outmoded concepts and methods. The social systems of present-day large-scale societies involve more interactions and more levels of organization than before. The concentration and growth of populations, their tremendous mobility, and the specialization of labor and other functions multiply interaction and organization. Hence, considerable effort is required to attain an understanding of the links between the large-scale social systems that encompass human populations and the small biological and molecular systems encompassed within individuals.

The foundations for such thought have been laid, but in the health and medical field we are far from using the approach with either theoretical sophistication or practical effect. Conceptual lag has played its part in our tardiness to recognize and deal with the side effects of urban life and to attack them in a systematic way. The weakness is especially evident with those disorders that persist despite our known ability to prevent them.

This conceptual lag contributes to the poor record of the great cities of the United States in dealing with such residual disorders. Their failures are made visible even by so gross a measure as mortality. During the past decade there has been a halt in the long-continued decline of the mortality rates of every age group. The halt has occurred at a level well above that of many countries that do not have the wealth and expertise in medicine and social science available in the United States. For instance, in New York City rates of perinatal, infant, and maternal mortality that mortify conscientious health officials exist side by side with enormous medical virtuosity.

The virtuoso performance of medicine is at the nub of the problem. In the great medical centers the effectiveness of care is likely to be measured, as we have noted, by its quality in an episode of illness at the point of delivery. This is a measure appropriate only to the one-to-one relationships and responsibilities of nineteenth-century physicians and patients. In the twentieth century a more appropriate measure of accomplishment is the impact of a system of medical care on the health of a defined population. Until the frame of reference of the proliferating medical centers includes target populations and areas, and not merely those individual and selective users who happen to knock on the door, the residue of preventable disorders will remain.

The power of the system of medical care, because of an inappropriate frame of reference, is directed at inappropriate targets. Even when there are excellent models of community care, these have usually remained no more than models. There is little capacity to translate demonstrations into working systems that reach total populations. To correct these weaknesses the frame of reference in terms of populations and communities must be made central. Facts must be collected and juxtaposed in a manner that points up changing needs, and institutions must be designed to permit their sensitive response to these needs.

Appendixes

Appendix A. *Episodes of Mental Illness in an English City*

TABLE A.1. All Mental Illness: Inceptions and Episodes in Salford by Sex, Age, and Marital State
TABLE A.2. Men: Inceptions of Specified Diagnoses in Salford
TABLE A.3. Women: Inceptions of Specified Diagnoses in Salford
TABLE A.4. Men: Episodes of Specified Diagnoses in Salford
TABLE A.5. Women: Episodes of Specified Diagnoses in Salford
TABLE A.6. Men: All Mental Illness and Specific Diagnoses in Salford
TABLE A.7. All Mental Illness: Inceptions and Episodes in Salford by Sex and Marital State (age standardized)
TABLE A.8. Inceptions and Episodes of Selected Diagnoses in Salford

Appendix B. *Movements in and out of Hostels*

TABLE B.1. Residence, Admissions, and Discharges at Salford

Appendix C. *Registered Prevalence of Ascertained Subnormality*

TABLE C.1. Males, Salford, January 1, 1961
TABLE C.2. Females, Salford, January 1, 1961

Appendix D. *Location of the Subnormal*

TABLE D.1. The Location of Mentally Subnormal Persons on the Salford Register of 1960

Appendix E. *Marriage Between Social Classes*

TABLE E.1. Families of Origin of Parents
TABLE E.2. Social-Class Origins of Spouses

Appendix F. *The Inception of Mental Illness Related to Widowhood*

TABLE F.1. Duration of Widowhood

Appendix G. *Secular Change in Backwardness in England*

TABLE G.1. Ascertainment 1925–1927 and 1955–1959 Compared

Appendix A *Episodes of Mental Illness in an English City*

A. M. Adelstein, D. Y. Downham,
Zena Stein, and M. W. Susser

The data presented in this appendix (as well as Figure 1 in Chapter 5 and Figures 3–5 in Chapter 8) are derived from the psychiatric register maintained since 1958 in Salford, a city of about 150,000 people in the Southeast Lancashire conurbation and contiguous with Manchester. The study was designed to exploit information that could be culled in a service setting over a continuous period. Systematic data were therefore collected about all adult patients as they came into psychiatric care.

Unit of Observation

The unit observed was the episode of mental illness, identified by the appearance of the patient in the psychiatric agency.

If chronic illness is to be related to the circumstances in which it originates, it is important to differentiate inception from recurrence. In our study, the term "inception" was defined as an episode of illness in which a person entered the care of a psychiatric agency for the first time in his life. The term "episode" includes all episodes, whether first or recurrent.

Recurrent episodes give a measure that relates to the circumstances of relapse, and to chronicity insofar as recurrences reflect chronic illness. A recurrent episode was recorded if a patient was referred after he had been out of treatment or active surveillance for one continuous month prior to the referral.

For further analysis, interpretation, and discussion, see A. M. Adelstein, *et al.*, "The Epidemiology of Mental Illness in an English City," *Social Psychiatry*, Vol. 3, No. 2 (1968).

A count of inceptions or of episodes does not measure, but is affected by, the prevalence and the incidence of chronicity. During the surveillance a number of patients resided for long periods in mental hospitals. Others chronically disabled by mental disorder remained in their homes. The effect of such chronic disablement from mental disorder on the rate of inceptions and episodes should be kept in mind in interpreting these results.

Sources of Data

The results presented differentiate the inceptions from the total number of episodes of mental illness referred to one of the registering agencies through the period 1959–1963. All patients giving Salford addresses were included.

Episodes were enumerated as they were brought to notice in any psychiatric agency in the neighboring regions. These agencies included residential institutions for mental patients, both inpatient and outpatient psychiatric units in general hospitals and in mental hospitals, psychiatrists in private practice, and the Salford local authority mental health service. (See Chapter 9.)

The residential institutions that provided data were located by a preliminary search for Salford patients. In 1958, from a survey made available to us by Miss E. M. Brooke at the Ministry of Health, we made a check throughout England and Wales of those private and public institutions designated by law for the care of mental patients. In this way we discovered the location of patients who at the time of the check had Salford addresses. Arrangements were then made to obtain returns over the ensuing years from all residential institutions that had been shown to have Salford patients.

Virtually all Salford patients in institutions were within the Northwest Hospital Region. Since National Health Service mental hospitals have defined catchment areas, new patients were unlikely to enter institutions outside the region, and a prospective register of patients who used public institutions could be confined to the region with a negligible chance of missing cases. Private institutions do not have defined catchment areas; periodic checks for Salford patients were therefore made of the main private psychiatric hospitals, whether or not they had Salford patients at the time of the check.

In addition, data were obtained in the same form from all psychiatric units in the Northwest Hospital Region that conducted work in general hospitals and among outpatients and from consulting psychiatrists in private practice in the region. The register did not seek returns from private psychiatrists in other areas (for example, from London 200 miles away) and this produced a possible if small source of omissions.

The register of the Salford local authority mental health service can be taken as almost complete for referrals to this type of agency. Because of long-established criteria for eligibility, local health authorities routinely refer patients back to their home services.

Form of Data

Returns were in the form of precoded schedules, completed for every patient from Salford coming into the care of a registering institution. These schedules gave information on age, sex, marital status, address, occupation, sources of referral, family doctor, diagnosis, previous referrals, and whether inpatient or outpatient care was provided. On every patient coming into the care of the Salford mental health service (which was under the direction of this writer) more detailed returns were made by mental-welfare officers. These more detailed returns were made at some point in the registration period for about two thirds of patients. Throughout the period of the study, any problems of coding and interpretation were discussed at a weekly conference.

From these returns the register of all patients from Salford was established. A record of every return dealing with the same person was entered on a single card. Records were matched manually at the same time as the precoded schedules were checked for completeness and consistency. The identification of an episode as an inception was made by collating the historical information, obtained from records and from patients and households, from all the returns in the participating agencies.

Analysis

Inception and episode rates were calculated for the Salford population classified by age, sex, marital state, and social class categories. The population at risk was considered as stationary in the central year of the study, which coincided with the 1961 census. The average annual rates were obtained by dividing the rates for the whole of the five years by five. Adults were defined as people over fifteen years. All the rates are given per 100,000 of the population at risk.

The use of these rates raised a number of problems. Three are problems of the numerator and one of the denominator. First, those persons who gave rise to inceptions necessarily contributed to total episodes. All persons who gave rise to episodes may not have contributed to inceptions, however, for in some recurrent cases the initial episode occurred prior to the establishment of the register on 1/1/59 although with declining frequency as surveillance continued. In a few other cases the inception occurred in another vicinity. About one third of patients gave rise to episodes but not to inceptions.

Second, a cohort study of inceptions and recurrent episodes in individual patients requires individual follow-up in order to take account of migration and deaths. The tables presented in this prospective study follow a different solution: They show community experience, not individual experience, and the effects of immigration and emigration are treated as if in balance.

Third, there is arbitrary assignment of inceptions to the diagnostic category recorded in the inception episode. At the time of analysis, the technical means to relate the several diagnoses made serially in individual patients was not in effect in our general computer program for processing survey data. The diagnosis on each episode had therefore to be treated independently of any other episode. Some anomalies reside in this device. In particular, an episode was not classified as an inception if there had been a previous referral, whatever the diagnosis. For instance, a recent onset of senile psychosis would not be classed as an inception in a patient who was known many years before to have had some other mental illness. In schizophrenia initial episodes can be misdiagnosed as psychoneurosis, but the inception episode will still appear as psychoneurosis. We leave aside the question of the relationship between attacks of a particular mental disorder in the same individual at different stages of life.

Fourth, the inception rates given here gloss over an inflating factor in the size of the denominator population. Thus, the population has not been corrected by subtracting those no longer at risk of inceptions because of previous episodes or deaths, either as they occurred during the five years of study, or by an estimate for the years preceding the study of the numbers who might have had previous episodes.

Social Class

In this paper the social-class categories are derived from the Classification of Occupations, Registrar General, 1951 revision. The occupations used as a criterion in this study varied by age and sex as follows:

Men under 65	Present occupation
Men 65 and over	Peak occupation
Ever married women under 60	Present occupation of spouse
Ever married women 60 and over	Peak occupation of spouse
Single women under 60	Present occupation
Single women 60 and over	Peak occupation

The population with which the social-class distributions of mental illness are compared was derived from a special sample survey of 1,000 households carried out in 1963. Owing to the revision of the Registrar General's Classification of Occupations for the 1961 Census and to the coding of occupations for episodes of mental illness in the 1951 revision of the present study, a contemporaneous population coded by the same occupational classifications as those for people with mental illness was not available. Fortunately, a special sample survey of 1,000 households was carried out by us in 1963, and it provided information about the occupations of men and women. The social-class distributions of mental illness are therefore derived from that survey.

Diagnosis. The diagnostic rubrics were chosen to accord both with local usage and with such standard classifications as that of the *Diagnostic Handbook* of the American Psychiatric Association. Unlike other precoded information, the coding of a final diagnosis was deferred until the collation at the end of each operating year of the register. When more than one diagnosis had been allocated in the course of an episode, a hierarchy of preferences was applied to the diagnosticians; the highest preference was given to the diagnosis by the psychiatrist most intimately concerned with all the Salford services; the next to those by other psychiatrists; the third to diagnoses reviewed and designated by the research team; and the fourth and uncommon preference was given to those of other medical practitioners.

Table A. 1. All Mental Illness: Inceptions and Episodes in Salford by Sex, Age, and Marital State Numbers Observed (1959–1963) and Average Annual Rates Per 100,000 Population

Age	Marital State	Population		MEN				WOMEN				BOTH SEXES			
				Inceptions		*Episodes*		*Inceptions*		*Episodes*		*Inceptions*		*Episodes*	
		Males	*Females*	*N*	*Rates*	*N*	*Rates*	*N*	*Rates*	*N*	*Rates*	*N*	*Rates*	*N*	*Rates*
All	All	55,282	62,092	818	296	1,782	645	1,119	360	2,510	809	1,937	330	4,292	731
All	S	15,356	14,021	283	369	720	938	282	402	684	976	565	385	1,404	956
Ages	M	37,168	37,360	435	234	864	465	593	318	1,319	706	1,028	276	1,833	492
	W	2,360	10,108	76	644	143	1,212	220	435	456	902	296	475	599	961
	D	398	603	9	452	55	2,764	19	630	51	1,692	28	559	106	2,118
15–19	All	5,483	5,522	53	193	74	270	66	239	101	366	119	216	175	318
	S	5,376	5,058	53	197	74	275	58	229	92	364	111	213	166	318
	M	107	463	0	0	0	0	8	346	9	389	8	281	9	316
	W	0	1	0	0	0	0	0	0	0	0	0	0	0	0
	D	0	0	0	0	0	0	0	0	0	0	0	0	0	0
20–29	All	10,021	9,698	142	283	292	583	203	419	341	703	345	350	633	642
	S	4,742	2,849	80	337	200	844	54	379	106	744	134	353	306	806
	M	5,248	6,798	56	213	89	339	139	409	221	650	195	324	310	515
	W	11	14	2	636	3	5,455	4	714	8	11,429	6	800	11	8.800
	D	20	37	0	0	0	0	4	162	6	3,243	4	404	6	2,105
30–39	All	10,071	9,579	176	350	482	957	218	455	507	1,059	394	401	989	1,007
	S	1,964	1,196	60	611	221	2,251	47	786	131	2,191	107	677	352	2,228
	M	7,986	8,115	108	270	232	581	159	392	350	863	267	332	583	723
	W	33	121	1	606	14	8,485	7	1,157	16	2,645	8	1,039	30	3,896
	D	88	147	2	455	15	3,409	5	680	10	1,361	7	596	25	2,128

40–49	All	10,276	10,766	147	286	357	695	169	314	472	877	316	300	829	788
	S	1,358	1,190	34	501	109	1,605	35	588	119	2,000	69	542	228	1,790
	M	8,600	8,770	98	228	207	481	115	262	302	689	213	245	509	586
	W	179	592	9	1,006	13	1,453	13	439	36	1,216	22	571	49	1,271
	D	139	214	4	576	28	4,029	5	467	15	1,402	9	510	43	2,436
50–59	All	10,205	10,946	114	223	275	539	160	292	480	877	274	259	755	714
	S	1,079	1,546	28	519	75	1,390	33	427	96	1,242	61	465	171	1,303
	M	8,620	7,653	76	176	172	399	94	246	285	745	170	209	457	562
	W	394	1,601	7	355	21	1,066	32	400	86	1,074	39	391	107	1,073
	D	112	146	0	0	7	1,250	1	137	13	1,718	1	78	20	1,550
60–69	All	5,875	8,708	105	357	197	671	133	306	321	738	238	327	518	711
	S	546	1,274	16	586	24	879	29	455	82	1,287	45	495	106	1,165
	M	4,638	4,150	64	276	121	522	52	251	110	531	116	264	231	526
	W	658	3,237	23	699	48	1,459	50	309	126	778	73	375	174	893
	D	33	47	2	1,212	4	2,424	1	426	3	1,277	3	750	7	1,750
70–79	All	2,711	5,270	54	398	75	553	112	425	204	774	166	416	279	699
	S	236	726	11	932	16	1,356	16	441	36	992	27	561	52	1,081
	M	1,738	1,273	26	299	36	414	23	361	39	613	49	325	75	498
	W	732	3,260	16	437	23	628	69	423	125	767	85	426	148	741
	D	5	11	0	0	0	0	3	5,455	4	7,273	3	3,750	4	5,000
80+	All	640	1,603	27	844	30	937	58	724	84	1,048	85	758	114	1,016
	S	55	182	1	377	1	377	10	1,099	22	2,418	11	936	23	1,957
	M	231	138	7	606	7	606	3	435	3	435	10	542	10	542
	W	353	1,282	18	1,020	21	1,190	45	702	59	920	63	771	80	979
	D	1	1	1	20,000	1	20,000	0	0	0	0	1	10,000	1	10,000

Table A. 2. Men: Inceptions of Specified Diagnoses in Salford by Sex, Age, and Marital State Numbers Observed (1959–1963) and Average Annual Rates Per 100,000 Population

Age	Marital State	Population	Schizophrenia		Depressive Psychosis		Psychoneurosis		Addiction, Alcoholic Psychosis		Psychopathy		Organic Disorders		Senile Dementia	
			N	Rates	N	Rates	N	Rates	N	Rates	N	Rates	N	Rates	N	Rates (60+)
All	All	55,282	97	35	179	65	162	59	22	8	79	29	54	19	57	124
All	S	15,356	60	78	44	57	57	74	3	4	42	55	19	25	8	192
Ages	M	37,168	31	17	118	63	101	54	14	8	35	19	24	13	26	79
	W	2,360	3	25	16	136	4	34	4	34	2	17	10	85	23	264
	D	398	3	151	1	50	0	0	1	50	0	0	1	50	0	0
15–19	All	5,483	7	26	2	7	12	44	0	0	15	55	2	7	0	0
	S	5,376	7	26	2	7	12	45	0	0	15	56	2	7		
	M	107	0	0	0	0	0	0	0	0	0	0	0	0		
	W	0	0	0	0	0	0	0	0	0	0	0	0	0		
	D	0	0	0	0	0	0	0	0	0	0	0	0	0		
20–29	All	10,021	18	36	19	38	46	92	4	8	26	52	2	4	0	0
	S	4,742	16	67	9	38	26	110	1	4	17	72	1	4		
	M	5,248	2	8	10	38	19	72	3	11	9	34	1	4		
	W	11	0	0	0	0	1	1,818	0	0	0	0	0	0		
	D	20	0	0	0	0	0	0	0	0	0	0	0	0		
30–39	All	10,071	35	70	40	79	41	81	2	4	14	28	6	12	0	0
	S	1,964	23	234	10	102	11	112	1	10	3	31	3	31		
	M	7,986	11	28	30	75	29	73	1	3	11	28	2	5		
	W	33	0	0	0	0	1	606	0	0	0	0	0	0		
	D	88	1	227	0	0	0	0	0	0	0	0	1	227		

40–49	All	10,276	15	29	44	86	33	64	9	18	13	25	5	10	0	0
	S	1,358	9	133	12	177	1	15	1	15	5	74	2	29		
	M	8,600	4	9	30	70	32	74	6	14	7	16	3	7		
	W	179	1	112	2	223	0	0	1	112	1	112	0	0		
	D	139	1	144	0	0	0	0	1	144	0	0	0	0		
50–59	All	10,205	14	27	38	74	21	41	5	10	3	6	13	25	0	0
	S	1,079	3	56	8	148	5	93	0	0	0	0	6	111		
	M	8,620	10	23	29	67	16	37	2	5	3	7	6	14		
	W	394	1	51	1	51	0	0	3	152	0	0	1	51		
	D	112	0	0	0	0	0	0	0	0	0	0	0	0		
60–69	All	5,875	5	17	27	92	8	27	2	7	7	24	19	88	9	21
	S	546	0	0	3	110	1	37	0	0	1	37	4	147	1	37
	M	4,638	4	17	14	60	5	22	2	9	5	22	11	47	6	26
	W	658	0	0	9	274	2	61	0	0	1	30	4	122	2	61
	D	33	1	606	1	606	0	0	0	0	0	0	0	0	0	0
70–79	All	2,711	3	22	7	52	1	7	0	0	1	7	3	22	30	221
	S	236	2	169	0	0	1	85	0	0	1	85	1	85	6	508
	M	1,738	0	0	4	46	0	0	0	0	0	0	0	0	15	173
	W	732	1	27	3	82	0	0	0	0	0	0	2	55	9	246
	D	5	0	0	0	0	0	0	0	0	0	0	0	0	0	0
80+	All	640	0	0	2	62	0	0	0	0	0	0	4	125	18	562
	S	55	0	0	0	0	0	0	0	0	0	0	0	0	1	377
	M	231	0	0	1	87	0	0	0	0	0	0	1	87	5	433
	W	353	0	0	1	57	0	0	0	0	0	0	3	170	12	680
	D	1	0	0	0	0	0	0	0	0	0	0	0	0	0	0

Table A. 3. Women: Inceptions of Specified Diagnoses in Salford by Sex, Age, and Marital State Numbers Observed (1959–1963) and Average Annual Rates Per 100,000 Population

Age	Marital State	Population	Schizophrenia		Depressive Psychosis		Psychoneurosis		Addiction, Alcoholic Psychosis		Psychopathy		Organic Disorders		Senile Dementia	
			N	*Rates*	*N*	*Rates*	*N*	*Rates*	*N*	*Rates*	*N*	*Rates*	*N*	*Rates*	*N*	*Rates (60+)*
All	All	62,092	80	26	382	123	220	71	9	3	62	20	52	17	146	188
All	S	14,021	30	43	80	114	51	73	2	3	30	43	9	13	23	211
Ages	M	37,360	39	21	246	132	152	81	6	3	24	13	29	16	24	86
	W	10,108	9	18	54	107	14	28	1	2	7	14	14	28	96	247
	D	603	2	66	2	66	3	100	0	0	1	33	0	0	3	1,017
15–19	All	5,522	5	18	11	40	15	54	0	0	11	40	1	4	0	0
	S	5,058	3	12	10	40	12	47	0	0	11	43	1	4		
	M	463	2	86	1	43	3	130	0	0	0	0	0	0		
	W	1	0	0	0	0	0	0	0	0	0	0	0	0		
	D	0	0	0	0	0	0	0	0	0	0	0	0	0		
20–29	All	9,698	14	29	60	124	63	130	2	4	20	41	8	16	0	0
	S	2,849	6	42	19	133	10	70	0	0	8	56	2	14		
	M	6,798	7	21	41	121	49	144	2	6	11	32	6	18		
	W	14	1	1,429	0	0	1	1,429	0	0	1	1,429	0	0		
	D	37	0	0	0	0	3	1,622	0	0	0	0	0	0		
30–39	All	9,579	24	50	87	182	64	134	1	2	13	27	5	10	0	0
	S	1,196	10	167	17	284	9	151	0	0	4	67	0	0		
	M	8,115	13	32	64	158	54	133	1	2	7	17	5	12		
	W	121	0	0	5	826	1	165	0	0	1	165	0	0		
	D	147	1	136	1	136	0	0	0	0	1	136	0	0		

40–49	All	10,766	13	24	71	132	38	71	1	2	7	13	8	15	0	0
	S	1,190	2	34	10	168	11	185	0	0	3	50	1	17		
	M	8,770	10	23	55	125	26	59	0	0	2	5	5	11		
	W	592	0	0	5	169	1	34	1	34	2	68	2	68		
	D	214	1	93	1	93	0	0	0	0	0	0	0	0		
50–59	All	10,946	13	24	75	137	24	44	4	7	7	13	14	26	0	0
	S	1,546	5	65	12	155	6	78	1	13	0	0	3	39		
	M	7,653	7	18	50	131	13	34	3	8	4	10	8	21		
	W	1,601	1	12	13	162	5	62	0	0	3	37	3	37		
	D	146	0	0	0	0	0	0	0	0	0	0	0	0		
60–69	All	8,708	6	14	64	147	10	23	1	2	3	7	9	21	25	57
	S	1,274	3	47	8	126	2	31	1	16	3	47	2	31	7	110
	M	4,150	0	0	31	150	5	24	0	0	0	0	3	14	8	39
	W	3,237	3	19	25	154	3	19	0	0	0	0	4	25	10	62
	D	47	0	0	0	0	0	0	0	0	0	0	0	0	0	0
70–79	All	5,270	5	19	12	46	6	22	0	0	1	4	5	19	69	262
	S	726	1	28	3	83	1	28	0	0	1	28	0	0	8	220
	M	1,273	0	0	4	63	2	31	0	0	0	0	2	31	13	204
	W	3,260	4	25	5	31	3	18	0	0	0	0	3	18	45	276
	D	11	0	0	0	0	0	0	0	0	0	0	0	0	3	5,455
80–89	All	1,603	0	0	2	25	0	0	0	0	0	0	2	25	52	649
	S	182	0	0	1	110	0	0	0	0	0	0	0	0	8	879
	M	138	0	0	0	0	0	0	0	0	0	0	0	0	3	435
	W	1,282	0	0	1	16	0	0	0	0	0	0	2	31	41	640
	D	1	0	0	0	0	0	0	0	0	0	0	0	0	0	0

Table A. 4. Men: Episodes of Specified Diagnoses in Salford by Sex, Age, and Marital State Numbers Observed (1959–1963) and Average Annual Rates Per 100,000 Population

Age	Marital State	Population	Schizophrenia		Depressive Psychosis		Psychoneurosis		Addiction, Alcoholic Psychosis		Psychopathy		Organic Disorders		Senile Dementia	
			N	Rates	N	Rates	N	Rates	N	Rates	N	Rates	N	Rates	N	Rates (60+)
All		55,282	469	170	349	126	269	97	67	24	203	73	79	29	84	182
All	S	15,356	287	374	92	120	84	109	19	25	101	132	23	30	11	263
Ages	M	37,168	133	72	231	124	166	88	32	17	87	47	41	22	40	121
	W	2,360	23	195	23	195	15	127	9	76	6	51	13	110	33	379
	D	398	26	1,307	3	151	4	201	7	352	9	452	2	101	0	0
15–19	All	5,483	15	55	2	7	16	58	0	0	18	66	2	7	0	0
	S	5,376	15	56	2	7	16	60	0	0	18	67	2	7		
	M	107	0	0	0	0	0	0	0	0	0	0	0	0		
	W	0	0	0	0	0	0	0	0	0	0	0	0	0		
	D	0	0	0	0	0	0	0	0	0	0	0	0	0		
20–29	All	10,021	108	216	36	72	60	120	5	10	41	82	3	6	0	0
	S	4,742	91	384	23	97	31	131	1	4	28	118	2	8		
	M	5,248	17	65	13	50	27	103	4	15	13	50	1	4		
	W	11	0	0	0	0	2	3,636	0	0	0	0	0	0		
	D	20	0	0	0	0	0	0	0	0	0	0	0	0		
30–39	All	10,071	180	357	70	139	88	175	14	28	63	125	9	18	0	0
	S	1,964	117	1,191	20	204	26	265	4	41	28	285	4	41		
	M	7,986	50	125	50	125	54	135	10	25	30	75	4	10		
	W	33	4	2,424	0	0	7	4,242	0	0	1	606	0	0		
	D	88	9	2,045	0	0	1	227	0	0	4	909	1	227		

40–49	All	10,276	81	158	85	165	55	107	26	51	54	105	9	18	0	0
	S	1,358	35	515	22	324	2	29	10	147	25	368	4	59		
	M	8,600	31	72	60	140	51	119	8	19	24	56	4	9		
	W	179	3	335	3	335	0	0	2	223	1	112	0	0		
	D	139	12	1,727	0	0	2	288	6	863	4	576	1	144		
50–59	All	10,205	61	120	80	157	36	71	19	37	15	29	20	39	0	0
	S	1,079	26	482	15	278	7	130	4	74	1	19	6	111		
	M	8,620	26	60	61	142	28	65	7	16	11	26	13	30		
	W	394	6	305	3	152	0	0	7	355	2	102	1	51		
	D	112	3	536	1	179	1	179	1	179	1	179	0	0		
60–69	All	5,875	17	58	62	211	13	44	3	10	12	41	29	99	20	68
	S	546	0	0	9	330	1	37	0	0	1	37	4	147	1	37
	M	4,638	8	34	39	168	6	26	3	13	9	39	18	78	14	60
	W	658	7	213	12	365	6	182	0	0	2	61	7	213	5	152
	D	33	2	1,212	2	1,212	0	0	0	0	0	0	0	0	0	0
70–79	All	2,711	7	52	12	89	1	7	0	0	0	0	3	22	43	317
	S	236	3	254	1	85	1	85	0	0	0	0	1	85	9	763
	M	1,738	1	12	7	81	0	0	0	0	0	0	0	0	21	242
	W	732	3	82	4	109	0	0	0	0	0	0	2	55	13	355
	D	5	0	0	0	0	0	0	0	0	0	0	0	0	0	0
80+	All	640	0	0	2	62	0	0	0	0	0	0	4	125	21	656
	S	55	0	0	0	0	0	0	0	0	0	0	0	0	1	377
	M	231	0	0	1	87	0	0	0	0	0	0	1	87	5	433
	W	353	0	0	1	57	0	0	0	0	0	0	3	170	15	850
	D	1	0	0	0	0	0	0	0	0	0	0	0	0	0	0

Table A. 5. Women: Episodes of Specified Diagnoses in Salford by Sex, Age, and Marital State Numbers Observed (1959–1963) and Average Annual Rates Per 100,000 Population

Age	Marital State	Population	Schizophrenia		Depressive Psychosis		Psychoneurosis		Addiction, Alcoholic Psychosis		Psychopathy		Organic Disorders		Senile Dementia	
			N	Rates	N	Rates	N	Rates	N	Rates	N	Rates	N	Rates	N	Rates (60+)
All		62,092	480	155	843	272	404	130	26	8	145	47	97	31	239	307
All	S	14,021	169	241	183	261	93	133	5	7	76	108	20	29	49	449
Ages	M	37,360	232	124	519	278	276	148	16	9	51	27	55	29	32	115
	W	10,108	58	115	127	251	31	61	5	10	17	34	21	42	154	396
	D	603	21	697	14	464	4	133	0	0	1	33	1	33	4	1,356
15–19	All	5,522	14	51	11	40	19	69	0	0	28	101	1	4	0	0
	S	5,058	12	47	10	40	15	59	0	0	28	111	1	4		
	M	463	2	86	1	43	4	173	0	0	0	0	0	0		
	W	1	0	0	0	0	0	0	0	0	0	0	0	0		
	D	0	0	0	0	0	0	0	0	0	0	0	0	0		
20–29	All	9,698	60	124	91	188	85	175	5	10	40	82	9	19	0	0
	S	2,849	23	161	29	204	17	119	0	0	19	133	3	21		
	M	6,798	34	100	60	177	64	188	5	15	18	53	6	18		
	W	14	1	1,429	1	1,429	1	1,429	0	0	3	4,286	0	0		
	D	37	2	1,081	1	541	3	1,622	0	0	0	0	0	0		
30–39	All	9,579	127	265	155	324	131	274	4	8	34	71	14	29	0	0
	S	1,196	53	886	33	552	18	301	0	0	10	167	3	50		
	M	8,115	68	168	112	276	109	269	3	7	22	54	11	27		
	W	121	2	331	8	1,322	4	661	1	165	1	165	0	0		
	D	147	4	544	2	272	0	0	0	0	1	136	0	0		

40–49	All	10,766	118	219	175	325	81	150	8	15	21	39	17	32	0	0
	S	1,190	33	555	36	605	17	286	3	50	14	235	3	50		
	M	8,770	72	164	122	278	58	132	4	9	3	68	9	21		
	W	592	7	236	11	372	5	169	1	34	4	135	5	169		
	D	214	6	561	6	561	1	93	0	0	0	0	0	0		
50–59	All	10,946	91	166	221	404	59	108	7	13	13	24	32	58	0	0
	S	1,546	21	272	37	479	21	272	1	13	0	0	6	78		
	M	7,653	50	131	144	376	30	78	4	10	7	18	20	52		
	W	1,601	13	162	36	450	8	100	2	25	6	75	5	62		
	D	146	7	959	4	548	0	0	0	0	0	0	1	137		
60–69	All	8,708	50	115	158	363	20	46	2	5	8	18	16	37	40	92
	S	1,274	21	330	28	440	4	63	1	16	4	63	4	63	12	188
	M	4,150	5	24	70	338	7	34	0	0	1	5	7	34	11	53
	W	3,237	22	136	59	365	9	56	1	6	3	19	5	31	17	105
	D	47	2	851	1	426	0	0	0	0	0	0	0	0	0	0
70–79	All	5,270	18	68	30	114	9	34	0	0	1	4	6	23	124	471
	S	726	4	110	9	248	1	28	0	0	1	28	0	0	19	523
	M	1,273	1	16	10	157	4	63	0	0	0	0	2	31	18	283
	W	3,260	13	80	11	67	4	25	0	0	0	0	4	25	83	509
	D	11	0	0	0	0	0	0	0	0	0	0	0	0	4	7,273
80+	All	1,603	2	25	2	25	0	0	0	0	0	0	2	25	75	936
	S	182	2	220	1	110	0	0	0	0	0	0	0	0	18	1,978
	M	138	0	0	0	0	0	0	0	0	0	0	0	0	3	435
	W	1,282	0	0	1	16	0	0	0	0	0	0	2	31	54	842
	D	1	0	0	0	0	0	0	0	0	0	0	0	0	0	0

Table A. 6. Men: All Mental Illness and Specific Diagnoses in Salford by Social Class; Numbers Observed (1959–1963) and Average Annual Rates Calculated from the 1961 Census of England and Wales

		All Mental Illness			
		INCEPTIONS		EPISODES	
Class	*At Risk*	*Nos.*	*Rates*	*Nos.*	*Rates*
I	768	4	103	6	156
II	5,445	44	162	77	283
III	28,817	341	236	689	478
IV	8,704	101	233	205	471
V	11,548	177	306	490	849
Not known		79		143	
Not applicable		72		172	

	Schizophrenia				Depressive Psychosis			
	INCEPTIONS		EPISODES		INCEPTIONS		EPISODES	
Class	*Nos.*	*Rates*	*Nos.*	*Rates*	*Nos.*	*Rates*	*Nos.*	*Rates*
I	0	0	1	26	0	0	0	0
II	3	11	13	48	12	44	18	66
III	37	26	153	106	90	63	160	111
IV	9	21	51	117	26	60	47	108
V	29	50	161	279	36	62	88	152
Not known	9		41		11		23	
Not applicable	10		49		4		13	
	Psychoneurosis				Addiction, Alcoholism			
I	0	0	0	0	0	0	0	0
II	13	48	17	62	3	11	5	18
III	77	53	124	86	5	3	32	22
IV	21	48	34	78	2	5	3	7
V	35	61	64	111	8	14	17	29
Not known	10		19		3		7	
Not applicable	6		11		1		3	

Table A. 6. (Continued)

	Psychopathy				Organic Psychosis			
I	1	26	1	26	1	26	1	26
II	3	11	7	26	1	4	2	7
III	35	24	77	53	25	17	29	20
IV	10	23	21	48	7	16	10	23
V	15	26	61	106	9	16	20	35
Not known	11		24		2		2	
Not applicable	4		20		9		16	

	Senile			
I	0	0	0	0
II	5	18	6	22
III	19	13	28	19
IV	7	16	7	16
V	9	16	14	24
Not known	6		12	
Not applicable	11		17	

Table A. 7. All Mental Illness: Inceptions and Episodes in Salford by Sex and Marital State (1959–1963); Average Annual Rate Per 100,000 At 1961 Census*

	SINGLE	MARRIED	WIDOWED	DIVORCED
		Inceptions		
Men	493	214	586	550
Women	505	321	534	758
		Episodes		
Men	1,310	412	3,202	2,090
Women	1,380	657	2,791	2,058

* Age standardized against the total Salford population for men and women respectively.

Table A. 8. Inceptions and Episodes of Selected Diagnoses in Salford by Sex and Marital State (1959–1963) Average Annual Rate Per 100,000 at 1961 Census*

		SINGLE		MARRIED		WIDOWED	
		Inceptions	*Episodes*	*Inceptions*	*Episodes*	*Inceptions*	*Episodes*
Schizophrenia	Men	101	488	14	63	32	586
	Women	60	372	23	105	23	369
Depressive Psychosis	Men	98	206	56	107	85	136
	Women	152	396	118	250	210	628
Psychoneurosis	Men	73	116	49	80	45	1,451
	Women	91	179	77	134	27	381
Addiction	Men	5	49	7	14	49	107
	Women	5	13	3	6	1	37
Psychopathy	Men	46	156	18	42	24	157
	Women	41	108	11	32	27	734
Organic	Men	53	62	12	20	27	36
	Women	17	42	15	27	39	47
Senile	Men	33	45	16	24	26	43
	Women	57	122	34	43	49	79

* Age standardized against the total Salford population for men and women respectively.

Appendix B *Movements in and out of Hostels*

Table B. 1. Residence, Admissions, and Discharges at Salford (Average Annual Nos., 1962–1964)

	Men	*Women*	*Both*
Admissions			
One admission only	24	22	46
More than one admission	3	6	9
Reasons for Admission			
No home	4	13	17
Lack of economic resources	3	1	4
Half-way house from hospital	13	6	19
Need for protected environment	6	5	11
Short-term care	5	5	10
Domestic tension	3	9	12
Leave from hospital	1	3	4
En route to hospital	0	0	0

	Men	*Women*	*Both*
Discharges			
One discharge only	20	21	41
More than one discharge	3	7	10
Duration of stay			
<1 month	12	21	33
1 month	7	6	13
3 months	3	4	7
6 months	2	1	3
9 months	1	0	1
12 months	2	4	6

Diagnosis			
Psychosis	12	11	23
High-grade subnormality	6	10	16
Medium-grade subnormality	10	12	22
Neurosis	2	5	7
Psychopath	4	2	6
Not determined	0	3	3
Age Groups			
15–	11	12	23
25–	5	7	12
35–	10	12	22
45–	6	8	14
55–	3	4	7
65+	0	0	0
Number obtained employment after admission	8	8	16

Outcome			
Satisfactory	17	28	45
Left by agreement	3	3	6
Placement (Home, Lodging, Foster-care)	8	16	24
Return home after short-term care	5	5	10
Following leave from hospital	1	3	4
En route to hospital	0	1	1
Unsatisfactory	11	8	19
Deterioration and Admission to hospital	4	3	7
Delinquency and Court action	1	0	1
Left without consultation	5	5	10
Expelled	0.3	0.3	1

Adapted from M. W. Susser, *A Report on the Mental Health Services of Salford for the Year 1964*, by permission of Health Department, Salford, England.

Appendix C *Registered Prevalence of Ascertained Subnormality*

Table C. 1. Males, Salford, January 1, 1961

		I.Q. 50+		I.Q. 20–49		I.Q. UNDER 20		TOTAL	
Males Age Group	*Population*	*No.*	*Per 1000*	*No.*	*Per 1000*	*No.*	*Per 1000*	*No.*	*Per 1000*
0—	6,852	0	0	9	1.32	4	0.58	13	1.90
5—	5,704	2	0.35	5	0.88	3	0.52	10	1.75
10—	6,892	2	0.29	12	1.74	7	1.02	21	3.05
15—	5,483	39	7.11	19	3.47	2	0.36	60	10.94
20—	5,026	33	6.56	11	2.19	3	0.60	47	9.35
25—	4,995	21	4.21	19	3.80	2	0.40	42	8.41
30—	4,729	11	2.33	22	4.65	5	1.06	38	8.04
35—	5,342	8	1.50	13	2.43	0	—	21	3.93

40–	4,899	9	1.84	15	3.06	1	0.20	25	5.10
45–	5,377	12	2.24	9	1.67	2	0.37	23	4.28
50–	5,429	11	2.03	16	2.95	1	0.18	28	5.16
55–	4,776	6	1.26	7	1.46	1	0.21	14	2.93
60–	3,557	5	1.41	4	1.12	0	—	9	2.53
65–	2,318	1		4		0	—		
70–	1,694	1	0.35	0	0.88	0	—	7	1.23
75+	1,657	0		1		0	—		
Unknown	—	1		3		0	—	4	
Total	74,730	162	2.17	169	2.26	31	0.41	362	4.84

Adapted from M. W. Susser and A. Kushlick, *A Report on the Mental Health Services of Salford for the Year 1960*, by permission of Health Department, Salford, England.

Table C. 2. Females, Salford, January 1, 1961

Females Age Group	Population	I.Q. 50+ No.	I.Q. 50+ Per 1000	I.Q. 20–49 No.	I.Q. 20–49 Per 1000	I.Q. UNDER 20 No.	I.Q. UNDER 20 Per 1000	TOTAL No.	TOTAL Per 1000
0–	6,368	0	0	2	0.32	2	0.31	4	0.63
5–	5,417	1	0.19	9	1.66	7	1.29	17	3.14
10–	6,483	0	0	8	1.23	4	0.62	12	1.85
15–	5,522	34	6.15	17	3.08	7	1.27	58	10.5
20–	5,298	28	5.28	16	3.02	2	0.38	46	8.68
25–	4,400	14	3.18	11	2.50	1	0.23	26	5.91
30–	4,506	10	2.22	17	3.77	3	0.67	30	6.66
35–	5,073	6	1.18	11	2.17	2	0.39	19	3.74
40–	5,126	14	2.73	7	1.37	2	0.39	23	4.49
45–	5,640	15	2.66	17	3.01	1	0.18	33	5.85
50–	5,795	4	0.69	4	0.69	1	0.17	9	1.55
55–	5,151	7	1.36	6	1.16	0	0	13	2.52
60–	4,755	1	0.21	3	0.63	0	0	4	0.84
65–	3,953	5 }	0.83	2 }	0.28	0	0	12 }	1.11
70–	3,135	3 }		1 }		0	0		
75+	3,738	1 }		0 }		0	0		
Unknown	0	3		0				3	
Total	80,360	146	1.82	131	1.63	32	0.4	309	3.85

Adapted from M. W. Susser and A. Kushlick, *A Report on the Mental Health Services of Salford for the Year 1960*, by permission of Health Department, Salford, England.

Appendix D *Location of the Subnormal*

Table D. 1. The Location of Mentally Subnormal Persons on the Salford Register of 1960, by Age and Grade, Numbers and Row Percentages

AGE GROUPS	I.Q. 50+				I.Q. 20–49				I.Q. UNDER 20				TOTAL			
	Institution		*Community*		*Institution*		*Community*		*Institution*		*Community*		*Institution*		*Community*	
0–	–		2		–		5		–		7		–		15	
5–	–	10%	4	90%	–	16%	11	84%	1	41%	6	59%	1	17%	21	83%
10–	1		3		2		20		5		7		8		30	
15–	10		85		9		23		8		–		27		108	
20–	8		42		10		20		4		1		22		63	
25–	4	24%	28	76%	15	48%	15	52%	3	90%	–	10%	22	40%	44	60%
30–	8		8		11		18		6		–		25		26	
35–	8		12		23		10		5		1		36		23	

40–	14	11	17	5	1	1	32	17
45–	14	15	18	5	5 }88%	– }12%	37	20
50–	9	4	15 }80%	4 }20%	–	–	24	9
55–	8	1	13	3	1	–	13	4
60–	4 }60%	– }40%	11	2			15 }73%	2 }27%
65–	7	1					7	1
70–	2	–					2	–
75+	1	–					1	–
Age unknown	4	1					13	1
Total	102 (32%)	217 (68%)	144 (51%)	141 (49%)	39 (62%)	23 (38%)	285 (43%)	384* (57%)

* Includes 13 persons of unknown grade.
Adapted from M. W. Susser and A. Kushlick, *A Report on the Mental Health Services of Salford for the Year 1960*, by permission of Health Department, Salford, England.

Appendix E *Marriage Between Social Classes*

Table E. 1. Families of Origin of Parents, of a Cohort of 106 Educationally Subnormal Subjects Born between 1930 and 1934, Who Were Spouses in 102 Marriages in Lancashire, England

ORIGIN OF HUSBANDS	ORIGIN OF WIVES			
	Aspirant	*Demotic*	*Uncertain**	*Total*
Aspirant	3	7	2	12
Demotic	5	46	7	58
Uncertain*	2	20	10	32
Total	10	73	19	102

* The "uncertain" category was in large part owing to the lack of information about parents available to the subjects from dysmorphic families and in some part to the cultural amnesia of mothers of subjects when acting as informants about the families of their husbands.

Table E. 2. Social-Class Origins of Spouses in a National Sample of Cohorts of Marriages 1875–1945

ORIGIN OF HUSBANDS	ORIGIN OF WIVES				
	I	*II*	*III*	*IV*	*All*
I	136	131	75	22	364
II	81	434	524	228	1,267
III	60	451	1,225	540	2,276
IV	10	182	508	493	1,193
All	287	1,198	2,332	1,283	5,100

Adapted from J. Berent, "Social Mobility and Marriage" in D. V. Glass, ed., *Social Mobility in Britain* (1954), p. 331, by permission of Humanities Press Inc. and Routledge & Kegan Paul Ltd., London.

Appendix F *The Inception of Mental Illness Related to Widowhood*

In 1963 the number of widowed men and women in each age group in Salford and the duration of bereavement in each case were determined for 1,989 adults included in a survey of households, selected at random. The same data had been obtained for all patients from Salford seeking psychiatric care during the year 1962.

Among 289 consecutive psychiatric patients, fifteen years old and over, eleven men and thirty-four women were widowed. The expected numbers, applying the age-specific rates of the surveyed population to the patient population, were seven men and twenty-nine women. The number of the widowed was thus higher than expected among those seeking psychiatric care. The excess of the widowed patients was concentrated in early widowhood.

Although the numbers are small, data for much larger numbers from the three year period 1961–1963 show the same tendency for an excess of widows to appear in early widowhood. These data are less representative because information was not obtained on duration of widowhood for patients who obtained care from outpatient units and from centers outside the city.

Table F. 1. Duration of Widowhood: Patients Compared to Survey Population (Percentages in brackets)

DURATION OF WIDOWHOOD	ALL PATIENTS 1962			PATIENTS 1961–1963 EXCLUDING OUTPATIENTS			HOUSEHOLD SURVEY		
	Men	*Women*	*All**	*Men*	*Women*	*All†*	*Men*	*Women*	*All*
1–12 months	2(18)	4(12)	6(13)	5(21)	11(12)	16(14)	2(6)	7(4)	9(4)
1–5 years	3(27)	13(38)	16(36)	8(33)	20(23)	28(25)	10(28)	28(15)	38(17)
5 or more years	6(55)	17(50)	23(51)	11(46)	57(65)	68(61)	24(67)	148(81)	172(79)
Total Number	11(100)	34(100)	45(100)	24(100)	88(100)	112(100)	36(100)	183(100)	219(100)

* Comparing distribution of duration of widowhood among All Patients 1962 (all) and Household Survey (all), $x^2 = 15.43$, $df = 2$. The null hypothesis that duration of widowhood is not associated with inceptions of mental illness is rejected $P < 0.005$.

† Comparing distribution of duration of widowhood among Patients 1961–1963 (all) and Household Survey (all), $x^2 = 15.58$, $df = 2$. The null hypothesis that duration of widowhood is not associated with inceptions of mental illness is rejected $P < 0.005$.

Appendix G *Secular Change in Backwardness in England*

Table G. 1. Ascertainment 1925–1927 and 1955–1959 Compared

	Locale	*Age*	*I.Q.**	*No. of cases*	*No. at risk*	*Rate Per 1,000*	*Sources†*
1920s Prevalence in 6 sample areas	Urban Area B	7–14	>70	181	10,687	16.9	Lewis, Table 13C. p. 185
various ages	All 6 Areas	7–10	>70	761	36,692	20.7	Lewis, Table 17 p. 191
	All 6 Areas	7–14	>70	1,608	66,380	24.2	Lewis, Table 14 p. 186
	3 Urban Areas	7–14	>70	647	37,743	17.1	Lewis, Table 14 p. 186
	3 Rural Areas	7–14	>70	961	28,637	33.6	Lewis, Table 14 p. 186
1950s Prevalence in Salford, Lancashire, at age 10§	All Primary Schools (1955–1959)	7–10	>80	320	19,500	13.3	Stein and Susser

* Note ceiling is I.Q. 70 in E. O. Lewis, *Report of the Mental Deficiency Committee* (London: H. M. Stationery Office, 1929), I.Q. 80 in Salford.

† Lewis, *ibid.* Zena Stein and M. Susser, *Mild Mental Subnormality: Social and Epidemiological Studies.* Paper read at Annual Meeting, Association for Research into Nervous and Mental Diseases, New York, 1967.

§ Lewis reported that prevalence was highest at 10 years of age but does not give data by single year of age.

Index

Abendberg, mental institution at, 328
absenteeism, 81, 100
accommodation (to mental disorder)
  and expectations, 48–51
  and hostility, 51–3
  and kin support, 56–7
  primary, 41–6
  secondary, 46–8
addiction, 73
adolescence, 86, 87, 283
"affective neutrality" as medical role, 238–9
aggression, 316
alcoholic psychoses, 125
alcoholism, 45–6, 73, 125, 222
alienation, 135
  and commitment, 326–9
  in medical care, 324
  in traditional institutions, 324–6
amaurotic family idiocy, 291
anomia, 131, 284
anomie
  and alienation, 324–5
  and social isolation, 121–3, 129–33, 135
anxiety, 75, 98
aspirant subculture, 303, 304, 306
authority, 341
autism, 337

Bacon, Francis, 124
Bateson, Gregory, 19, 35
"before and after" comparisons, 190–4
Bennett, Douglas, 52*n*.
bereavement, 92–4
Bernstein, B., 313
Binet, Alfred, 299
birth rates, 291
birth weight, 288, 289
Bleuler, E., 5
blindness, 337
body shape, 301

Booth, Charles, 275
brain damage, 288–9, 291, 302, 312
brain syndromes, chronic, 71, 72, 73, 98
bronchitis, 308
Brugger, C., 209
bureaucratic hierarchy, 331
Burt, Cyril, 299

caretaker roles, 335–8
caretaking units, attitudes in, 327
case studies, 182–6
"casework," 156, 158
Caudill, W., 184
Chadwick, Edwin, 74
Chiarugi, Vincenzo, 6
child-guidance clinics, 86
children, 84, 85–6
  in broken homes, 305
  mentally subnormal, 55–6, 146, 278, 287, 304–16, 324, 326
  separation of, 94–5
chromosomal anomalies, 291
Clarke, A. D. B., 301
Clarke, Anne, 301
"cognitive map," 44
communication, 266
"community," definitions of, 7–8
community care (of mental disorder)
  concept of, 3–10
  coordination of, 233–69
  facilities for, 143–60
  group relations in, 148–52
  versus hospitalization, 30
  and mental subnormality, 275–347 *passim*
  rationale for, 3–20
Community Mental Health Services Act, 4
concentration camps, 83
conformity, 122
contextual dissonance, 134, 325*n.*
Conway, J., 307
Coser, Rose Laub, 326, 329, 331, 334
countertransference, 239
cretinism, 290
crime, 10, 87
cultural anthropology, 5–6
cultural mental retardation, 312–3
culture and behavior, 82
cytomegalic-inclusion body virus, 289

Davis, Kingsley, 118
day centers, 143–4
  social structure of, 329–38 *passim*
deafness, 302, 337
death rate, 287
demotic subculture, 303, 304, 306, 307, 311
depression, psychotic, 54, 121, 222
depressive reactions and states, 83, 89, 90
"detached concern" as medical role, 238–9
determinism, 10
"deutero-learning," 19
deviance, 11
  Lemert's theory of, 15–6
  and mental subnormality, 284
  and rehabilitation, 47
diagnosis, 363
Dickens, Charles, 335
Dinitz, 187*n.*
"disease model," 10–1
divorce, 30, 88
Dix, Dorothea, 165
dizygotic twins, 299, 300
"double-bind," 35, 198
drugs, 13–4, 17, 241
  and addiction, 73
  and socialization of patients, 19
  and social situation, 197–8
Dunham, H. W., 6, 123, 126
Durkheim, Émile, 82, 121, 131, 181

education
  about mental health, 43–5

education (*continued*)
and mental subnormality, 56, 85, 304–16 *passim*
ego strength, 102
Eichorn, D. H., 339
electroconvulsive therapy, 17, 242
employment, 50
after hospitalization, 57–61
of subnormal people, 60, 284
endogamy, 307
enuresis, 86, 154
environment and intelligence, 300–316 *passim*
epilepsy, 289
eugenicism, 276, 328
evaluation, 165–99

Fairweather, G., 60, 186
families
aspirant, 303, 304, 306
chronic sickness and, 29–38
conflict in, 151
demotic, 303, 304, 306, 307
"dysmorphic," 284
hostility in, 51–3
impact of community care on, 343–7
as microculture, 36–8, 41
Farber, B., 345
Faris, R. E. L., 6, 123, 126
feebleminded, 280
fertility, 308
Fisher, R. A., 186
foetus, 289
folie à deux, 42
foster homes, 147, 346
Frankenberg, R., 338
Freidson, E., 262
Freud, Sigmund, 5, 239

Galen, 32
general practitioners, 246, 248
and community service, 250–2
genes, 299, 307
genetics
and retardation, 291, 299–300, 307–8
and social mobility, 307–8
Goffman, E., 18, 183, 185, 331
Grad, J., 344
group relations, 148–52
groups, comparison of, 194–200
group support, 50–1
Gruenberg, E. M., 206
Guggenbühl, J., 328

Hagnell, O., 220
"happiness" as criterion, 88, 119
"Hawthorne" effect, 197–8
heart failure, peripartum, 92
Heidelberg Clinic, 14
Hippocrates, 10, 98
Hofer, Johannes, 98
Hollingshead, August B., 219, 220
hospitals, hospitalization, 7–8, 13, 89
alienation in, 324–6
and community care, 30–2
custodial function of, 240
discharge from, 46–61
and kin support, 56–8, 90
and migration, 97, 98
and "open door" policy, 9
outpatient treatment in, 45, 246, 259–60
patient roles in, 16–7
and psychiatric roles, 238–43
social structure of, 328–38
treatment in, 17
visits to, family, 57
hostels, 147, 149, 347
hostility and accommodation of patients, 51–3
husbands, schizophrenic, 42
Hyman, H. Herbert, 195*n*.
hypercapnia, 72
hysteria, 83

identity, crisis of, 87

ideology, *see* therapeutic ideologies
imbeciles, 60, 280
incidence studies, 215–23
incontinence, 337
industrialization, 275–6
industrial societies, 233, 278, 283, 322
industrial training, 144
infant deaths, 308
innovation, 122
"institutional neurosis," 16, 147
intelligence, 299–316 *passim; see also* mental subnormality
intelligence tests, 280, 299–311 *passim*
Itard, J. M. G., 328

Jarvis, Edward, 99
juvenile delinquency, 73, 87, 93

Kandell, D., 264
kernicterus, 288
kin support, 56–8, 90, 284; *see also* families
Kirk, S. A., 339
Klinefelter's syndrome, 291
Knobloch, H., 289
Kushlick, A., 286, 332
kwashiorkor, 72, 290

language handicaps, 305
  and working class, 313
Lawrence, D. H., 119
learning
  and socialization, 17–9
  and mental subnormality, 60
legislation, 240
Lemert, E. M., 15
Lewis, E. O., 276, 286, 288
Lidz, T., 35
Lunacy Acts, 240, 243
Lundby study, 220–1
Lyle, J. G., 339

malnutrition, 309, 310
manic-depressive cases, 242
marriage, 125
  discord in, 10
  and social class, 307, 308
  as transition, 88–90
maternity, 90–2
maturation, 310
medical practice, personal, 236–8
melancholia, 98
Mendez, Christobel, 32–3
meningitis, 290
mental deficiency, 4; *see also* mental subnormality
Mental Deficiency Act of 1913, British, 276
mental disorder
  accommodation to, 41–61 *passim*
  antecedent factors in, 71–135
  community care of, 3–20
  defined, 4
  disease model of, 10–1
  and family roles, 41–61 *passim*
  medical model of, 10–20
Mental Health Act of 1959, 4, 13, 143, 237, 252, 253
mental illness
  defined, 4
  measurement of, 204–23
mental subnormality, 4
  in adults, 149, 278
  attitudes toward, 325–6
  in children, 55–6, 146, 278, 287, 304–16 *passim*
  in community, 275–356 *passim*
  and day centers, 146
  detection of, 290–1, 301
  employment of, 60, 284
  mild, 282, 283–5, 299–316
  population of, 275–92
  prevention of, 73
  remedies for, 313–6
  residential care of, 322–47
  severe, 282, 285–90, 322–47
  training of, 144
  see also retardation
Mental Treatment Act of 1930, 14

Merton, R. K, 122, 123, 132, 133
metabolism, 301, 312
middle class, 303, 315
Midtown Manhattan survey, 102, 131, 132, 159, 207–8, 213, 214
migration, 103, 130–1, 133, 193
  and mental subnormality, 286–7
milieu therapy, 150, 242
minority groups, 325
mongolism, 286–7, 288, 291, 339
monozygotic twins, 299, 300
moral treatment, 335

National Health Service, British, 236, 241, 245, 250, 252, 257
National Health Service Act, 243
National Institute of Mental Health, 4
Negroes, 133, 300, 325
"nervous breakdowns," 121
nostalgia, 98
Nova Scotia, 130
nurses, 155, 257
  ideologies of, 327

occupational therapy, 145
occupations after hospitalization, 57–61
Ødegaard, Ø., 98
open-class societies, 325
opiate addiction, 73
organic psychoses, 220
organizations, structure and culture in, 261–4
outpatient units, 259–60

paranoia, 83, 133
parents
  authority of, 341
  loss of, 93–4
Parsons, Talcott, 264
Pasamanick, B., 187*n.*, 289
passive dependence, 331
patients, mental
  and caretaker roles, 335–8
patients, mental (*continued*)
  chronic sickness of, and family, 29–38, 41–61 *passim*
  flow of, 335–8
  and group relations, 148–52
  and impact of care, 338–43
  performance of, factors in, 29–38
  and public opinion, 8–9
  return of, 46–8
  roles of, 16–7
  socialization of, 17–8
peer groups, 313
pellagra, 72–3
personality, 6
"personality disorders," 210
phenylketonuria, 290, 291
physical handicaps, 323
physiological disturbances, 92
Pinel, Philippe, 6
"placebo effect," 197
Plato, 12
"pluralistic ignorance," 43–4
police, 248
poliomyelitis, 345
population of mentally subnormal, 275–92
poverty, 131
pregnancy
  in adolescents, 87–8
  and mental subnormality, 288–9
premature births, 309, 310
prevalence
  period, 205
  point, 205
  rates of mental illness, 205–15
primary groups, 82
"primary socialization," 96; *see also* socialization
psychiatric roles (and services)
  and community service, 252–3
  coordination of, 246–68
  and mental hospitals, 238–43, 252–61
  in personal medical practice, 236–238

psychiatric roles (*continued*)
  and public health, 243–6
  setting of, 246–52
psychoanalysis, 5, 19
  and mental-hospital psychiatry, 239–240
psychoneuroses, 73, 89, 121, 133
psychophysiological symptoms, 134, 211–2
psychoses, 133, 242; *see also specific psychoses*
psychotherapy, 237, 241
  in day centers, 144
  in hospitals, 17
public health and psychiatric care, 243–6
public opinion and mental patients, 8–9
puerperal psychosis, 92

racial degeneracy, theories of, 276
"reactive psychosis," 83
rebellion, 122
Redlich, F., 220
reference groups, 333
referral sources, 45, 246–7
regression, statistical, 303
rehabilitation
  and employment, 57–61
  family roles in, 41–61 *passim*
  and social work, 154
  and war, 83–4
rehabilitation units, 327
research, 165–99
residential arrangements, 147
retardation
  and cultural syndrome, 312–3
  educational, 56, 85, 304–16 *passim*
  remedies for, 313–6
  see also mental subnormality
retirement, 92
retreatism, 122
Rh factor, 288
ritualism, 122
role sets, complexity of, 332–5
Rowland, H., 6, 184
rubella virus, 289

Sainsbury, P., 124
Salford studies, 88, 90, 93, 149, 154, 168–81, 184, 187, 195, 220, 244, 245, 246, 264, 279, 286, 305, 358–363
Scarpitti, F. R., 187*n*.
schistosomiasis, 208
schizophrenia, 5, 14, 35, 98, 144, 150, 155, 194, 222
  in domestic setting, 42, 47, 48, 49, 51, 54
  and kin support, 57
  and marital state, 88–9
  and social class, 242
  and social isolation, 123, 125–9
  tests for, 71
school phobia, 86
schools
  and mental subnormality, 282, 283–4, 302, 304–16
  and social class, 304–7
  as transition, 84, 85–8, 103
Schwartz, M. S., 183
Scott, E. M., 307
Seguin, E., 328
self-awareness, 119
Selye, Hans, 74
senile dementia, 54–5, 93
sensitization, 192–4, 197
sexual behavior, 284
sexual exhibitionism, 284
Shaftesbury, Lord, 165
Shepherd, M., 206
siblings (of mentally subnormal children), 342
"sick role," 11–3
  threshold of, 32–8
"significant others," 145
Simon, John, 199–200, 275
Skeels, H. M., 301
skeuomorphs, 257
"Skid Row," 125

skull shape, 301
slums, 275
"social-breakdown syndrome," 50
social change, 264
social classes, 30, 31, 34–5, 46, 118–119, 125, 126, 128, 215, 362
  and anomie, 131, 132
  and genetic models, 307–8
  and mental subnormality, 299–3
  and psychoses, distribution of, 242
social clubs, 145–6
social conflict, 18
Social Darwinism, 3
social disintegration, 130, 131
social groups and intelligence, 300
social isolation, 48, 94, 123–5
  and anomie, 121–3, 129–33
  and schizophrenia, 125–9
socialization, 17–9
  in day centers, 143–7
  in families, 340–1
  after hospitalization, 46–61 *passim*
  of mentally subnormal patients, 323
  primary, 96
  and social structure of institutions, 331–2
social mobility, 31
  and intelligence, 307–8
  vertical, 101–2, 128
social norms, 239, 264; *see also* social values
social roles, 282, 283
  changes in, 264–8
social structure
  and patient care, 331–2
  strain in, 265
  of traditional institutions, and day centers, 329–38
social support
  as institutional function, 17
  and marriage, 88
social transitions, 84–103
social values, 12, 18, 118-9, 265
social work, 152–60, 245, 251, 254
sociopathy, 133
Solomon, R. L., 193
spasticity, 337
specialization, 238
speech disorders, 289
Spiegel, J. P., 36
spirochetes, 289
Srole, L., 131
Stanton, A. H., 183
status, changes in, 84–5
status inconsistency, hypothesis of, 134–5
Stedman, D. J., 339
"Stirling County" study, 130, 207, 208
stress
  concept of, 74
  and somatic reactions, 74–5
stressful situations, 118–35
stressors, preventable, 71–5
submissiveness, 149, 150
subnormality, *see* mental subnormality; retardation
suicide, 73, 81, 82, 87, 93, 121, 181
Sullivan, H. S., 5–6
supernaturalism, 12
surveys
  operations studies, 170–4
  opportunist, 174–6
  and routine audits, 168–70
  tailormade, 176–82
Susser, M. W., 174*n.*, 233*n.*, 247*n.*
symptom inventories, 133, 134, 135, 211–2
syphilis, 71, 72, 289

tests, 290, 309
  biochemical, 71
  intelligence, 280, 299–311 *passim*
"therapeutic community," 5, 6–7
therapeutic ideologies, 18, 19, 336
Thoreau, Henry David, 18
Tizard, J., 286, 288, 329, 339, 340

toxemia, 289
toxoplasma, 289
tranquilizers, 13
transference, 239
transitions, social, 84–103
tuberculosis, 308
twins, 299, 300

urban culture, 89

verbal ability, 305, 309
violence, 245
vitamins, 72

war and stress, 80–4
Welfare Department, 248
Whyte, W. F., 184
Widdowson, E. M., 95
widowhood, 93
Williams, R. H., 264
witchcraft, 12
wives, schizophrenic, 42
women, household tasks of, 59
working class, 119, 303, 306, 313
World Health Organization, 211
World War I, 83
World War II, studies of stress in, 81–2
"Worthing experiment," 190, 191, 192
Wynne, L. C., 35

Yoruba, 130